BALANCING RISKS

A volume in the series

CORNELL STUDIES IN SECURITY AFFAIRS

EDITED BY Robert J. Art, Robert Jervis, AND Stephen M. Walt

A full list of titles in the series appears at the end of the book.

Balancing Risks

*Great Power Intervention
in the Periphery*

Jeffrey W. Taliaferro

Cornell University Press
Ithaca and London

First published 2004 by Cornell University Press

Printed in the United States of America

Library of Congress Cataloging-in-Publication Data

Taliaferro, Jeffrey W.
    Balancing risks : great power intervention in the periphery / Jeffrey W. Taliaferro.
        p. cm. — (Cornell studies in security affairs)
Includes bibliographical references and index.
    ISBN 0-8014-4221-4 (alk. paper)
    1. World politics—20th century. 2. Great Britain—Foreign relations—1901–1910. 3. Japan—Foreign relations—1912–1945. 4. United States—Foreign relations—1945–1953. 5. Imperialism—History—20th century. I. Title. II. Series.
    D511.T32 2004
    327.1'09'04—dc22

                                                              2003021660

Cornell University Press strives to use environmentally responsible suppliers and materials to the fullest extent possible in the publishing of its books. Such materials include vegetable-based, low-VOC inks and acid-free papers that are recycled, totally chlorine-free, or partly composed of nonwood fibers. For further information, visit our website at www.cornellpress.cornell.edu.

Cloth printing   10 9 8 7 6 5 4 3 2 1

CONTENTS

TABLES AND FIGURES

Acknowledgments

The development of this book required me to take several professional and intellectual risks. Along the way, I have incurred many debts to teachers, colleagues, and institutions. I am particularly indebted to two scholars at Harvard University. Stanley Hoffmann encouraged me to ask important questions, while giving me the freedom to pursue my interests and never trying to steer me in a different direction. Stephen Peter Rosen agreed to serve as an adviser when institutional and intellectual hurdles seemed insurmountable. During my first two years in graduate school Yuen Foong Khong encouraged me to investigate the link between leaders' perceptions and foreign policy. I owe a tremendous intellectual debt to Jack S. Levy, who inspired me not only to apply prospect theory to the study of foreign policy but to go beyond the extant literature. He has been exceedingly generous in providing trenchant criticisms and suggestions at various stages.

Robert Jervis of Columbia University, coeditor of Cornell Studies in Security Affairs, is everything that one could want in a reviewer and scholarly editor. His detailed and thoughtful comments have had a significant impact on the final project. (As it happens, his 1993 *Political Psychology* article, "The Political Implications of Loss Aversion," first aroused my interest in the phenomena of great power intervention in the periphery.) He will always be my model of what a scholar should be. I also thank the outside reviewer for Cornell University Press for his detailed and useful comments. That reviewer, who recently revealed himself as Michael C. Desch, helped me refine my treatment of offensive realism and suggested a possible avenue for a future project. Finally, I join a long line of authors indebted to Roger Haydon at Cornell University Press. His wit, comments, and encouragement made the entire publication process immeasurably easier.

Several scholars were kind enough to provide detailed comments on some or all of the manuscript: Mia Bloom, Thomas J. Christensen, Dale Copeland, James W. Davis, Jr., Jonathan DiCicco, Mark Haas, Colin Elman, Bernard I. Finel, Benjamin Frankel, Alastair Iain Johnston, Paul Kowert, Eric J. Labs, Jeffrey W. Legro, Sean M. Lynn-Jones, Patrick Thaddeus Jackson, James McAllister, Benjamin Miller, Barry Posen, Gideon Rose, Randal Schweller, Jennifer Sterling-Folker, Gary J. Schaub, Jr., and Stephen Van Evera. Two colleagues in particular, Rose McDermott and

William J. Boettcher, helped me sharpen my treatment of prospect theory and risk behavior.

I presented portions of this book at seminars at the Massachusetts Institute of Technology's Security Studies Program, the University of Virginia's Woodrow Wilson Department of Government, and Harvard University's Center for Basic Research on the Social Sciences. I thank participants in those seminars for many helpful comments. The students in my course on "the rise and the fall of the great powers" at Tufts University not only endured my endless ruminations about Japanese expansion in the 1930s, but also asked questions that helped sharpen the discussion in chapters 4 and 6. I am indebted to Matthias Maas, Christopher Greller, and Ezequiel Reficco for research and translation assistance. The translations by Chaim D. Kauffman and James W. Davis, Jr., of *Die Grosse Politik der Europäischen Kabinette* were invaluable in completing my early research on the 1905–1906 Morocco crisis.

Completion of this book would not have been possible without a junior faculty research grant from the Smith Richardson Foundation, Inc., and a semester-long research leave provided by the Office of the Dean of the School of Arts and Sciences at Tufts University. I did the early research as a graduate associate at Harvard's Center for International Affairs (now the Weatherhead Center for International Affairs). Mellon Dissertation Fellowships and a National Science Foundation Predoctoral Fellowship supported the earlier stages of the project. Raymond Geselbracht, Sam Rushay, and others at the Harry S. Truman Library in Independence, Missouri, were invaluable in gathering archival material on the Korean War. The Political Science Department at Tufts has been supportive over the past five years. One could not ask for better colleagues than Robert Devigne, Richard Eichenberg, Shinju Fujihira, Malik Mufti, Elizabeth Remick, and Vickie Sullivan. Tony Smith, in particular, has been a great adviser and a good friend.

Portions of chapters 1 and 2 appeared as "Security-Seeking under Anarchy: Defensive Realism Reconsidered," *International Security* 25, no. 3 (winter 2000/2001); "Correspondence: Brother, Can You Spare a Paradigm? (Or, Was Anybody Ever a Realist?)," *International Security* 25, no. 1 (summer 2000); and "Power Politics and the Balance-of-Risk: Hypotheses on Great Power Intervention in the Periphery," *Political Psychology* 25, no. 1 (April 2004). Portions of chapter 4 appeared as "Quagmires in the Periphery: Foreign Wars and Escalating Commitment in International Conflict," *Security Studies* 7, no. 3 (spring 1998). I thank MIT Press, Frank Cass Publishers, and Blackwell Publishing for permission to use that material here.

The best part of completing this book is that my family and friends will no longer have to tread gingerly about the timetable for its completion. Shea W. Peacock, and our two "research cats," Sheena and Duncan, have lived with this project longer than anyone else. Without their love, support, and seemingly inexhaustible patience, this book would never have seen the light of day. I dedicate this book to my father, John W. Taliaferro, who has always encouraged me in everything that I have done, and to the memory of my mother, Althea M. Taliaferro, who taught me to never give up and to always have faith.

ABBREVIATIONS

BD	*British Documents on the Origins of the War,* 11 vols. ed. H. P. Gooch and Howard Temperly. London: His Majesty's Stationary Office, 1926–38.
BFO	British Foreign Office
Cab.	Cabinet Papers, United Kingdom
CCP	Chinese Communist party
CDD	*Collected Diplomatic Documents Relating to the Outbreak of the European War.* London: Fisher Unwin, 1915.
CIA	Central Intelligence Agency
CINCFE	Commander-in-Chief, U.S. Forces in the Far East
CINCUNC	Commander-in-Chief, United Nations Command—Korea
COI	Committee on Imperial Defence, United Kingdom
CPVs	Chinese People's Volunteers, Korean War
CPVA	Chinese People's Volunteer Army, People's Republic of China
CPSU	Communist Party of the Soviet Union
CWIHP	Cold War International History Project, Washington, D.C.
CWIHPB	*Cold War International History Project Bulletin*
DA	Department of the Army
DCI	Director of Central Intelligence
DoD	Department of Defense
DoS	Department of State
DPRK	Democratic People's Republic of Korea (North Korea)
DGFP	*Documents on German Foreign Policy, 1818–1945,* Series C and D. Washington, D.C.: U.S. Department of State, 1933–37 and 1937–45.
DSB	U.S. Department of State, *Department of State Bulletin*
FEAF	Far East Air Force, U.S. Air Force
FEC	Far Eastern Command
FRUS	U.S. Department of State, *Foreign Relations of the United*

	States, multiple vols. Washington, D.C.: GPO, various years.
FRUS, Cairo	U.S. Department of State, *Foreign Relations of the United States, 1943:* Conferences at Cairo and Tehran. Washington, D.C.: GPO, 1961.
FRUS, Japan	U.S. Department of State, *Foreign Relations of the United States: Japan, 1940–1941,* 2 vols. Washington, D.C.: GPO, 1943.
FRUS, Potsdam	U.S. Department of State, *Foreign Relations of the United States, 1945: The Conference of Berlin (Potsdam Conference),* 2 vols. Washington, D.C.: GPO, 1960.
GDD	*German Diplomatic Documents, 1871–1914,* 4 vols., ed. E. T. S. Dugdale. London: Methuen, 1928.
GP	*Die Grosse Politik der Europäischen Kabinette, 1871–1914,* 39 vols. Berlin: Deutsche Verlagsgesellschaft für Politik und Geschichte, 1922–1927.
HST	Harry S. Truman Papers, Harry S. Truman Library, Independence, Missouri
HSTL	Harry S. Truman Library, Independence, Missouri
IGHQ	Imperial General Headquarters (Japan)
IJA	Imperial Japanese Army
IJN	Imperial Japanese Navy
IMTFE	*Court Papers, Exhibits, Interrogations, Trial Transcripts, and Judgments of the International Military Tribunal for the Far East, 1946–48.* Washington, D.C.: GPO, 1948.
JCS	Joint Chiefs of Staff
KMAG	Korea Military Advisory Group
KMT	Kuomintang (Chinese Nationalist party)
KPA	Korean People's Army (North Korea)
LC	Library of Congress
MSA	Mutual Security Agency
MSFE	U.S. Congress, Senate, Armed Services and Foreign Relations Committees, *Military Situation in the Far East,* 82nd Cong., 1 session, 1951.
NA	National Archives, Washington, D.C., and College Park, Maryland
NATO	North Atlantic Treaty Organization
NIE	National Intelligence Estimate
NME	National Military Establishment

NSC	National Security Council
NSRB	National Security Resources Board
OIR	Office of Intelligence Research, U.S. Department of State
PLA	People's Liberal Army (People's Republic of China)
PPP: HST	*Public Papers of the President: Harry S. Truman*
PPS	Policy Planning Staff, U.S. Department of State
PRC	People's Republic of China
PRO	Public Records Office, United Kingdom
PS	"Princeton Seminars," Dean G. Acheson Papers, Harry S. Truman Library, Independence, Missouri
PSF	President Secretary's Files, Harry S. Truman Papers, Harry S. Truman Library, Independence, Missouri
ROC	Republic of China (on Taiwan)
ROK	Republic of Korea (South Korea)
SCAP	Supreme Commander for the Allied Powers—Pacific
SE	Special Estimates
SRRKW	Selected Records Relating to the Korean War, Harry S. Truman Papers, Harry S. Truman Library, Independence, Missouri.
USAFIK	U.S. Army Forces in Korea
UN	United Nations
UNC	United Nations Command, Korea
USAKW	U.S. Department of the Army, *United States Army in the Korean War*, 3 vols. Washington, D.C.: GPO, 1961–1972.
WCF	White House Central Files, Harry S. Truman Papers, Harry S. Truman Library, Independence, Missouri
WHO	White House Office Files, Harry S. Truman Papers, Harry S. Truman Library, Independence, Missouri
WIAP	*War in Asia and the Pacific,* ed. Donald S. Detwiller and Charles B. Burdick, 15 vols. U.S. Army Center for Military History: Washington, D.C., 1980.

Note on Translations, Romanization, and Stylistic Conventions

Throughout the text, Japanese proper names appear in Japanese order: surname first followed by given name (e.g., Tōjō Hediki instead of Hediki Tōjō), except in cases of Westerners of Japanese origin. The same rule applies to Chinese and Korean proper names in the text, except in cases of Westerners of Chinese or Korean origin. The one exception to this rule is Syngman Rhee (Yi Sung-man), the founding president of the Republic of Korea. Rhee, who spent over thirty years in the United States before the liberation of Korea in 1945, rendered his name in Western order (given name followed by surname). To simplify locating works cited in the notes, however, the names of Japanese, Chinese, and Korean authors appear in Western order, with the surname last.

In keeping with the Japanese practice of referring to a deceased emperor according to his reign name and not his personal name, I use the term Emperor Shōwa instead of Emperor Hirohito (the name by which he is universally known in the West). The same rule applies to his predecessors: Emperor Taishō (instead of Emperor Yoshihito) and Emperor Meiji (instead of Emperor Mutsuhito). Macrons indicate long vowels in Japanese words and names, except in the case of well-known place names (e.g., Tokyo).

I employ the Pinyin transliteration of most Chinese proper names, places, and organizations (e.g., Mao Zedong, Zhou En Lai, and Beijing, instead of Mao Tse-Tung and Chou En-Lai, and Peking). However, for places, organizations, and persons associated with Nationalist China (1926–49) and the Republic of China on Taiwan (1949–present), I use the Wade-Giles system of transliteration (e.g., Chiang Kai-Shek and the Kuomintang instead of Jiang Jieshi and the Guomintang). The Taiwanese government uses Wade-Giles transliterations in official English language documents.

The given names of Russian and German officials appear in the original language or in the case of Russian, the approximate transliteration into Latin script (e.g., Heinrich instead of Henry or Mikhail instead of Michael). I make an exception in cases where the English translation of a Russian proper name is more common in the scholarly literature (e.g., Tsar Nicholas II instead of Tsar Nikolai II). With the exception of the Russian title *tsar*, the military ranks, government offices, royal and noble titles of all officials appear in English (e.g., the German emperor Wilhelm

II instead of Kaiser Wilhelm II). Furthermore, the English translations of Germanic titles of nobility and rank precede the person's given and surnames in the text instead of coming between the given name and surname (e.g., Prince Bernhard von Bülow instead of Bernhard Fürst von Bülow or Bernhard Prince von Bülow or General Count Alfred von Schlieffen instead of General Alfred Graf von Schlieffen). Finally, in the case of British hereditary peers below the degree of duke or life peers (after 1958), the person's full title appears in the initial reference followed by the courtesy form in subsequent references (e.g., the marquess of Salisbury, the earl of Selbourne, and Viscount Haldane, then subsequently, Lord Salisbury, Lord Selbourne, and Lord Haldane).

BALANCING RISKS

[1]

Power Politics and the Balance of Risk

This book examines a recurrent puzzle in world politics. Great powers frequently initiate risky diplomatic and military interventions in the periphery—regions that do not directly threaten the security of a great power's homeland. They often persist in failing interventions despite mounting political, economic, and military costs. More surprising, great powers often undertake risky strategies toward other great powers in an effort to continue failing interventions in strategically inconsequential regions.

During the cold war, the United States and the Soviet Union expended blood and treasure to defend clients in the Third World. The United States, for example, found itself in an inconclusive and arguably self-defeating war in defense of South Vietnam. President Lyndon Johnson, Secretary of Defense Robert McNamara, Secretary of State Dean Rusk, and other officials repeatedly escalated air and ground operations against Viet Cong guerrillas and North Vietnam, despite credible information that such strategies had a low probability of achieving the war's stated objective: the preservation of South Vietnam.[1] Rather than extricate itself from an expensive and increasingly unpopular war, the Nixon administration extended it into Cambodia and Laos in order to win concessions from North Vietnam.

In December 1979, Soviet General Secretary Leonid Brezhnev, Defense Minister Dmitri Ustinov, the KGB chairman Yuri Andropov, and other Politburo members hoped to use minimal force to secure a stable Soviet-aligned government in Afghanistan. Instead, the Soviet leadership soon found itself in a prolonged guerrilla war against Afghan rebels, which exacerbated tensions with the United States, fueled the Reagan administration's defense buildup, and ultimately contributed to the Soviet Union's collapse.[2]

Great power intervention in peripheral regions is not unique to the cold war. In 1899, for example, Great Britain became mired a bloody war against the Transvaal and the Orange Free State. Joseph Chamberlain, the secretary of state for the colonies, and the marquess of Lansdowne, the secretary of state for war, initially thought that the 25,000-man garrison in the Cape Colony would be more than sufficient to defeat the Boers. The British prime minister, the marquess of Salisbury, and the cabinet eventually deployed 500,000 regular troops to subdue the 80,000-strong Boer militia, thus leaving the British Isles, Afghanistan, and India critically exposed. The war cost £211 million, increased the national debt by 25 percent, resulted in the deaths of 22,000 British troops, and eroded Britain's naval superiority.[3] Other examples abound. Athens' expedition to Sicily during the Peloponnesian War, Britain's involvement in the two Afghan wars in the nineteenth century, Japan's pursuit of economic autarky through empire in East Asia in the 1930s and early 1940s, and France's war against independence movements in Indochina and Algeria in the 1950s are all instances where great powers became entrapped in vastly expensive and arguably self-defeating interventions in the periphery.

This book addresses two questions: First, why do great powers initiate risky diplomatic or military commitments in the periphery? Second, why do great powers persist in peripheral conflicts despite the diminishing prospects of victory and increasing political, military, and economic costs? These questions concern the foreign policies of the great powers, not the international consequences of those policies. A theory of international politics seeks to explain international outcomes—aggregate phenomena resulting from the interaction of two or more actors in the international arena. A theory of foreign policy, on the other hand, seeks to explain why different states or even the same state at different times pursues particular strategies in the international arena.[4]

Two rationalist theories might explain why great powers initiate risky interventions and then continue to pursue failing strategies in tertiary areas. A great power's propensity for peripheral involvement might be a function of its domestic politics. States with highly cartelized political systems—polities where small groups control a disproportionate share of the society's material resources—are prone to risky interventions in peripheral regions. Various domestic interest groups, which often have a material interest in expansion, logroll favored interests, "hijack" political institutions, and then pervert the state's foreign policy. Central decision makers persist in failing intervention strategies because imperialist groups or the public would punish them if they backed down. Liberal democratic great powers, on the other hand, are less prone to imperialist group logrolling, and thus less likely to pursue expansionist policies in the periphery.

Alternatively, great powers intervene in the periphery because they enjoy a favorable international power position and the perceived benefits of intervention outweigh the costs and risks. The international system provides incentives for states to maximize relative power or influence. Increases in relative capabilities cause states to expand their interests abroad. States tend to expand into areas where there is a power vacuum or where they perceive the risks of intervention to be low. They might also intervene or escalate intervention in the periphery to demonstrate resolve, and by doing so deter would-be aggressors in other areas. When the costs associated with a peripheral intervention exceed the marginal benefits, however, great powers will withdraw or dramatically scale back their involvement.

THE ARGUMENT

In the pages that follow, I find that domestic structure and interest group logrolling, on the one hand, and rising power and international opportunity, on the other, are often not the main determinants intervention by the great powers in the periphery or their persistence in failing intervention strategies. Instead, I argue that the aversion of senior officials to perceived losses—in terms of their state's relative power, international status, or prestige—drives great power intervention in peripheral regions. Officials initiate risky diplomatic and/or military intervention strategies to avoid perceived losses. When faced with perceived losses, leaders tend to select more risk-acceptant intervention strategies. Leaders then persevere and even escalate failing peripheral interventions to recoup past losses. Instead of cutting losses, they continue to invest blood and treasure to losing ventures in tertiary regions.[5] These tendencies produce policies driven by concerns about power and security, but still at odds with many variants of political realism. Drawing on the defensive realist literature in international relations and the prospect theory literature in psychology, I construct a theory of foreign policy that I call balance-of-risk theory. The book employs comparative case studies to test rival hypotheses about great power peripheral interventions. The main cases are Wilhelmine Germany's initiation of the 1905–06 Morocco crises; Japan's decisions for war in 1940–41; and the intervention in and escalation of the Korean War by the United States in 1950–51.

The questions this book poses and the answers it offers have policy and theoretical significance. Throughout history, the most powerful states in the international system have often become embroiled in strategically inconsequential regions. Overextension and strategic exposure in the core have been two of the most frequent causes of the relative decline

of great powers.[6] In terms of policy, this topic is relevant to current debates about U.S. national security policy and the criteria for diplomatic
and military intervention. A coherent grand strategy must identify likely
external threats to a state's security and the means to remedy those
threats.[7] In addition to homeland defense, a great power's grand strategy must evaluate the relative importance of different world regions to
national security. Since the collapse of the Soviet Union in 1991, the
United States has enjoyed preponderance in all the underlying components of power: military, technological, economic, and geostrategic capabilities.[8] Nonetheless, the lone superpower does not have infinite resources and must avoid excessive military and economic commitments
in peripheral regions. In the past decade, presidents George H. W. Bush
and William Jefferson Clinton deployed troops to open-ended missions
in Somalia, Bosnia, Kosovo, and Macedonia. Thus far, the actual costs of
such humanitarian military interventions and peacekeeping operations
have been quite low.[9] Nonetheless, a clearer understanding of the causes
of great power intervention in the periphery may help Washington policymakers identify and avoid more costly interventions in the future.

This study is also relevant for how the United States responds to
asymmetric threats posed by so-called rogue states and international terrorism. For example, in response to the 11 September terrorist attacks,
President George W. Bush called for a multifaceted war on terrorism.
Thus far, the war has entailed military action against the Taliban regime
in Afghanistan for harboring training camps used by Al Qaeda and its
leader, Saudi exile Osama bin Laden. Contrary to the predictions of
many pundits and military analysts, the Taliban collapsed after a month
of American bombing and a coordinated ground offensive by the opposition Northern Alliance. In an address to a joint session of the Congress,
the president declared: "Our war on terror begins with Al Qaeda, but it
does not end there. . . . From this day forward, any nation that continues
to harbor or support terrorism will be regarded by the United States as a
hostile regime."[10] Subsequent statements and actions by the Bush administration raise the possibility that the United States may embark on
preventive or preemptive military operations against states that harbor
terrorists or that seek to acquire weapons of mass destruction. A clearer
understanding of why great powers escalate their commitment to risky
interventions may help policymakers avoid possible entrapment in Central Asia, the Caucasus, Iraq, the Philippines, Colombia, and elsewhere.[11]

This book contributes to the scholarly literature in several ways. First,
it advances the debate between two camps of structural realism: offensive realism and defensive realism.[12] Both see international politics as in-
herently conflictual and assume that international outcomes will broadly
match the relative distribution of power among states. They disagree

primarily over whether the international system always generates intense security competition and, therefore, compels states to maximize relative power or maximize security.[13] Consequently, they also disagree over the types of calculations leaders make and the conditions under which they will pursue hard-line or accommodative strategies. Offensive realists have found empirical support for their core proposition: increased relative power and international opportunity causes states to expand their interests abroad. This book responds to the offensive realist challenge by framing and testing defensive realist hypotheses on the foreign policy of great powers.[14] Although this book only examines the question of military and diplomatic intervention by great powers in the periphery, balance-of-risk theory is a general theory of foreign policy. It should generate testable hypotheses about other aspects of states' foreign policies as well.

Second, my analysis provides a firmer foundation for defensive realism. Defensive realism proceeds from the assumption that the international system does not always generate intense competition and war among states. Only under certain conditions will the international system provide incentives for aggressive foreign policies. Examples of such structural conditions include increases in the level of international threat; rapid shifts in relative power; situations where states can exploit the resources of conquered territory; shifts in the offense-defense balance in favor of offensive weapons and technologies; and multipolarity.[15] Defensive realism assumes most states value what they already possess over what they seek to acquire for reasons rooted in the anarchic nature of the international system. Kenneth N. Waltz observes that "in anarchy, security is the highest end. Only if survival is assured can states safely seek other goals, such as tranquility, profit, and power."[16] Joseph Grieco argues that states are defensive positionalists: "Driven by an interest in survival and independence, states are acutely sensitive to any erosion in relative capabilities."[17]

Unfortunately, the defensive realist literature does not fully address the origins of the so-called status-quo bias of states.[18] This bias may have less to do with the anarchic nature of the international system, per se, than with how leaders process information about the international environment and their position relative to that of other states. I seek to build on the foundation of defensive realism, but also improve it by introducing concepts from prospect theory. While I concur with the assumption offered by offensive realists that leaders make cost-benefit calculations, I would modify this assumption with the caveat that the specifics of the situation influence those calculations. In other words, states are not pre-ordained toward intense competition by anarchy itself and objective increases in relative capabilities do not necessarily lead to increased international ambition. Cost-benefit calculations made by leaders will never be objectively efficient or predictable based on systemic incentives alone, since the decision-making process will skew toward loss avoidance. The substance of perceived costs involves both material capabilities and intangible elements (such as loss of status or reputation), which may be particular to each state. Balance-of-risk theory, therefore, is not an alternative to defensive realism but rather a refinement of it.[19]

Third, the empirical question of why great powers become involved in the periphery is underdeveloped in contemporary realism. Part of this inattention stems from a contradiction in Waltz's balance-of-power theory. The main conclusion is that bipolar international systems are less prone to major war or a crisis that risks inadvertent escalation to major (or hegemonic) war than multipolar ones.[20] Two strands of Waltz's theory are relevant here. The first argues that bipolarity is less prone to major war, in part, because each superpower recognizes that the other is the only serious threat to its survival. Since the addition or defection of weaker allies has little impact on the systemic balance-of-power, the superpowers can rely on internal balancing—defense spending and arms production—to ensure their survival. There are no systemic incentives for the superpowers to attract smaller allies or to intervene in peripheral regions. The second strand, however, attributes bipolar stability to each superpower's knowledge that because there are only two of them, each must block the other throughout the world. The acquisition of weaker allies, additional territory, and other material resources increases a superpower's ability to engage in internal balancing. Any increase in relative power for one superpower, by definition, is a decrease in relative power of equal magnitude for the other. Waltz writes, "In a bipolar world there are no peripheries. With only two powers capable of acting on a world scale, anything that happens anywhere is potentially of concern to both of them. Bipolarity extends the geographic scope of both powers' concerns."[21]

The two strands of the theory are equally plausible, but contradictory. Robert Jervis observes that "here Waltz faces a problem that is generic to realism. In arguing that the international environment compels certain lines of behavior, these theories are both descriptive and prescriptive, which means that actions that do not conform embarrass the theory as well as harm the country."[22] If the acquisition of smaller allies and the control of third regions has little impact on the systemic balance-of-power in a bipolar system and if anarchy (regardless of system type) compels weaker states to balance against stronger ones, then what explains American and Soviet propensity for costly military interventions in Vietnam, Korea, Afghanistan, and other parts of the Third World? Waltz ignores the descriptive strand of his argument that sees superpower intervention as stabilizing and systemically driven, and instead focuses on the prescriptive strand—namely the folly of expending blood and treasure in defense of peripheral states, such as South Vietnam. Jervis writes that "while it is true that what happens in third countries [could not] directly influence either superpower, one cannot neglect the indirect and delayed effects which indeed constituted the main rationale—or rationalization—for many American interventions, most notably Vietnam: Defeat would lead other dominoes to fall, endangering the American position in Europe as well as in Asia."[23] Waltz, however, denies the validity of the so-called domino theory and argues that anarchy provides incentives for balancing, not bandwagoning. Instead, he characterizes the American war in Vietnam and the Soviet invasion of Afghanistan as "over-reactions" explained (albeit in a reductionist and ad hoc manner) by domestic politics, miscalculation, and poor leadership.[24]

Following Waltz, many contemporary realists focus only on the prescriptive aspects of great power intervention: Under what conditions should major states intervene in peripheral areas? How might the defense of the periphery contribute to the security of a great power's core interests? Does the Third World matter? Waltz, Stephen Van Evera, Stephen M. Walt, and others warn against American overextension in the periphery. Yet, few defensive realists (or offensive realist for that matter) explicitly address the questions of why and under what conditions great powers intervene, escalate intervention strategies, persist in failing strategies, and ultimately withdraw from peripheral commitments in the first place.[25]

COMPETING THEORIES OF FOREIGN POLICY

Why have great powers intervened so frequently in peripheral regions? Why do they persist in failing intervention strategies far longer than most cost-benefit analyses would suggest? In addition, why have great powers undertaken risky diplomatic and military strategies toward other great powers in an effort to continue failing interventions? Three theories of foreign policy might shed some light on these questions. The first two are rationalist explanations for foreign policy behavior. Logrolling theory predicts that leaders will likely pursue expansionist policies abroad as a rational response to certain domestic incentives. Offensive realism predicts that leaders will likely pursue expansionist policies as a rational response to rising power and international opportunities. By contrast, the third theory, balance-of-risk theory, predicts that leaders will pursue expansionist external strategies when and if those leaders fear an erosion of their states' relative power or reputation. Table 1.1 illustrates the theories.

Logrolling Theory of Imperialism

The literature on imperialism generates one plausible explanation for intervention and risk-taking by great powers in the periphery. J. A. Hobson and Vladimir Lenin hold that monopoly capitalists see expansion in the periphery as a means to export surplus capital, thus forestalling declining returns on investments.[26] As second variant, associated with Joseph Schumpeter, holds that military and feudal elites advocate the pursuit of peripheral expansion to maintain the rationale for their obsolete warrior functions (and thus, their privileged social and political position in industrialized societies).[27] Expansion benefits discreet groups, but it does not benefit society as a whole. Indeed the state apparatus and the general population disproportionately bear the costs of expansion in the form of deficit spending, public borrowing, higher taxation, conscription, and higher prices for consumer goods. Self-serving imperialist groups justify peripheral intervention to the government and the public through appeals to national security concerns. In short, the imperialism literature suggest that great powers often persist in costly and failing peripheral interventions because these policies benefit private imperialist groups. In extreme cases, very powerful or persuasive imperialist groups might cause a great power to engage in self-destructive expansionist policies.

Jack Snyder's logrolling theory of imperialism improves on older theories by specifying the mechanism through which parochial interests translate into expansionist foreign policies.[28] He seeks to explain great power overexpansion, defined as aggressive military and diplomatic strategies that provoke the formation of a hostile coalition or continue to the point where the costs exceed the benefits. Snyder writes, "Counterproductive aggressive policies are caused most directly by the idea that the state's security can be safeguarded only through expansion."[29] Parochial groups in society—industrialists, financiers, traders, and the military and colonial bureaucrats—each have some economic or political interest in an expansionist foreign policy. Expansion may benefit these groups but not society or the state as a whole. These groups' material interests in specific foreign policies, however, are not identical. Individually none of them can influence state policy.[30] They, therefore, engage in logrolling, where "each group gets what it wants most in return for tolerating the adverse effects of the policies its coalition partners desire." Other groups in society, who might oppose expansion, lack the organi-

TABLE 1.1. *Three theories of foreign policy*

Theory of foreign policy	View of international system	View of states	Explanatory variables	Causal logic
Logrolling theory of imperialism	Relatively unimportant; domestic level variables are the primary determinant of foreign policy	Highly differentiated	Domestic structure (Cartelization)	Domestic structure → risk-taking behavior in the periphery
Offensive realism	Very important; system *generally* provides incentives for conflict and aggression. States try to maximize relative power or influence	Undifferentiated	Relative power and international opportunity	Systemic incentives → risk-taking behavior in the periphery
Balance-of-risk theory	Very important; system *rarely* provides incentives for conflict and aggression; States try to maximize security	Undifferentiated	Relative power and elite assessments of gain and loss (relative to their expectation level)	Systemic incentives → elite perceptions of relative gains or losses → risk-taking behavior in the periphery

zation and access to the government needed to successfully lobby for their interests.[31]

These logrolling imperialist coalitions propagate myths of empire, strategic rationalizations for expansion designed to gain broader support for their preferred policies. These myths include the prospective gains of conquest, domino beliefs, "paper tiger" images of the enemy, and the efficacy of "big stick" diplomacy. These strategic beliefs and lessons correlate with the material interests of imperialist groups, not the formative experiences or biases of central decision makers. Imperialist coalitions frequently oversell these myths to domestic constituencies. Over time, these groups and government elites often internalize their own rhetoric. In their own minds, the distinction between sincere strategic beliefs and tactical argumentation blurs, thus creating blowback. Alternatively, imperialist groups and senior officials find themselves politically entrapped in their own rhetoric. "Insofar as the elite's power and policies are based on society's acceptance of imperial myths, its rule would be jeopardized by renouncing the myths when the side-effects become costly. To stay in power and to keep central policy objectives intact, elites may have to accept some unintended consequences of their imperial sales pitch."[32] Blowback creates a dynamic whereby a great power pursues more ambitious expansionist policies or continues to pour resources into ongoing imperial projects. In short, states find themselves entrapped in policies that have long since lost any strategic rationale.[33]

A state's domestic political structure determines its susceptibility to overexpansion. Great powers with highly cartelized political systems are particularly susceptible to logrolling dynamics among parochial groups. The more cartelized a state is, the more "power assets—including material resources, organizational strength, and information—are concentrated in the hands of parochial groups." Snyder writes, "Because imperial and military interests are commonly more concentrated than anti-imperial and antimilitarist interests, a cartelized political system, will give a chair at the bargaining table to imperial interests whereas diffuse groups with diffuse interests, like taxpayers and consumers, are excluded."[34] Wilhelmine Germany (1888–1918) and early Shōwa Japan (1926–45), for example, were both highly cartelized polities; consequently, both fell prey to acute overexpansion.

Conversely, great powers with democratic political system are less prone to overexpansion. "When political power is highly disperse throughout society, as in an electoral system with universal suffrage and administrative institutions beholden to elective officials, diffuse interests will have a stronger voice."[35] Thus the United States and Britain did not fall prey to acute overexpansion. Finally, the theory does not make definitive predictions for "unitary" political systems controlled by one party or individual. The concentration of political power in the hands of a single dictator or a unitary oligarchy eliminates the need for logrolling with other groups. There are no social incentives for overexpansion. At the same time, there are no direct checks on the international ambitions of the leaders. Thus, the theory does not predict when unitary systems are more prone to limited opportunistic expansion (such as the Soviet Union under Josef Stalin or China under Mao Zedong) or reckless, unlimited expansion (such as Germany under Adolf Hitler). The timing of a state's industrialization correlates with the concentration of power within society and the concentration of elite interests.

Snyder's theory attributes intervention in the periphery to domestic politics. However, senior officials, not domestic interest groups, formulate and implement grand strategy. It is therefore necessary to trace the influence of such domestic considerations in the deliberations of central decision makers. The theory suggests that leaders will be highly cognizant of the preferences of domestic interest groups. In democratic regimes, leaders will be less inclined to intervene in the periphery. When democratic leaders do intervene, however, they will be more inclined to adopt risk-averse strategies. In cartelized regimes, leaders will be more inclined toward peripheral intervention and more inclined to pursue risk-acceptant strategies. Over time, blowback and the material interests of imperialist coalitions should make it very difficult for leaders to readjust failing intervention strategies. In cartelized regimes, imperialist group pressure and prior government rhetoric should force leaders to continue or escalate risky intervention strategies. This should be less of a problem in democratic polities, where leaders are less beholden to the interests of imperialist coalitions. Liberal democratic great powers should be, therefore, less likely to persist in failing intervention strategies.

Offensive Realism

Offensive realism explains great power intervention with reference to material capabilities and international opportunity. States strive to maximize relative power or influence, since only the most powerful states can guarantee their survival. When confronted with specific threats to their interests or survival, states will attempt to increase their relative power through expansion or internal mobilization.[36] Even in the absence of specific threats, however, states strive to increase their relative power because they can never be certain where or when the next threat will arise. In short, the mere possibility of international conflict conditions the behavior of states.[37] As John Mearsheimer argues, "States seek opportunities to weaken potential adversaries and improve their relative power positions. They sometimes see aggression as the best way to accumulate more power at the expense of rivals."[38]

Offensive realism does not hold that anarchy forces states to engage in reckless or unlimited expansion, although some states clearly have been driven by this motivation to pursue extreme expansionist policies. Rather, it expects states (or more properly, leaders) to engage in calculated expansion. Eric Labs notes that "successful expanders learn from past mistakes and they try to go about expanding in a manner that draws the least attention of the other great powers. When expansion fails, states rationally adapt. They realize not that expansion does not pay, but that that particular effort at expansion failed for whatever the specific reasons were."[39] Leaders will be sensitive to the marginal costs and benefits of expansion. Negative feedback, in the form of rising costs, diminishing revenues, or the formation of a hostile great power coalition, should force leaders to reevaluate, and if necessary, alter their strategies. Great powers will seize all reasonable opportunities to enhance their relative power through conquest, but will also retract when the international environment is less permissive.

For offensive realists the link between structural incentives and the foreign policy behavior of states is relatively unproblematic. To understand why a state behaves in a particular way, one must examine its relative capabilities and its international environment. Domestic differences between states or the perceptions of national leaders are relatively unimportant because systemic constraints are strong enough to make similarly situated states behave alike. States, or more properly, national leaders, generally adhere to the norms of bounded rationality. As Fareed Zakaria notes, states will expand "in a rational way, measuring risks, opportunities, costs and benefits."[40]

Mearsheimer presents the best-known version of offensive realism. Anarchy compels each great power to strive to become a regional hegemon—the only great power in its part of the globe. "Although a state would maximize its security if it dominated the entire world, global hegemony is not feasible, except in the unlikely event that a state achieves nuclear superiority over its rivals. The key limited factor . . . is the difficulty of projecting power across large bodies of water, which makes it impossible for any great power to conquer and dominate regions separated from it by oceans."[41] Only when another great power appears on the brink of regional hegemony will a geographically distant great power intervene, generally in the form of buck passing, and failing that, through direct military intervention and/or the formation of a war-fighting coalition in the core. Therefore, the United States, the only great power to have successfully achieved regional hegemony, would be better served by pursuing a grand strategy of "offshore balancing" with respect to Europe and Northeast Asia rather than by pursuing a strategy of active engagement.

As another offensive realist, Christopher Layne, points out, there is an inherent contradiction in Mearsheimer's theory. On the one hand, the "stopping power of water" would appear to make continental great powers, such as the United States, and even island great powers, such as Britain and Japan, relatively secure. As Layne puts it, "If by chance a rival emerges in some other part of the world, the regional hegemon should still be safe in its own neighborhood, because geographical distance and water confine regional hegemons to their regions, and stop them from becoming global hegemons. If the stopping power of water really stops, when it comes to worrying about peer competitors in distant areas, regional hegemons ought to be able to base their strategy on Alfred E. Newman: 'What, me worry?'"[42] On the other hand, intervention in distant peripheries would appear to be a viable strategy to weaken potential great power rivals and maximize relative power. Mearsheimer even writes, "Rival hegemons separated by an ocean can still threaten one another by helping to upset the balance of power in each other's backyard. Specifically, a regional hegemon might someday face a local challenge from an upstart state, which would surely have strong incentives to ally with the distant hegemon to protect itself from attack by the neighboring hegemon. At the same time, the distant hegemon might have reasons of its own for collaborating with the upstart state."[43]

Other offensive realists do not share Mearsheimer's qualification about the geographic scope of great powers' ambitions. Layne writes, "On its own terms, the logic of offensive realism should predict that great powers will seek global hegemony, thus solving their security dilemma by establishing themselves as the only great power in international politics"[44] Labs distinguishes between "manual expansion" and "automatic expansion," both of which are rational responses to international opportunities. Manual expansion is the result of a conscious bid for hegemony, whereas automatic expansion is the result of incremental and localized efforts to expand when opportunities arise. "Manual expansion can certainly explain Napoleon's or Hitler's bids for hegemony. It can also explain why their attempts failed: other states realized what they were up to and coalesced against them. Britain's more automatic expansion, however, gave it the greatest empire the world has ever known—one quarter of the land area of the globe."[45] Zakaria contends that systemic opportunity and the level of state power (that is, the ability of a government to extract resources from domestic society) determine the scope of a great power's international ambitions. "Over the course of history, states that have experienced significant growth in their material resources have relatively soon redefined and expanded their interests abroad, measured by their increases in military spending, initiations of war, acquisition of territory, posting of soldiers and diplomats, and participation in great power decision-making."[46]

Under many conditions, great power intervention in peripheral regions is consistent with the power maximizing logic of offensive realism. The acquisition of territory, population, raw materials, and economic resources can augment a great power's relative power, and thereby its relative security. Intervention becomes more likely if decision makers perceive an increase in their state's relative capabilities. If decision makers perceive a favorable balance-of-power (vis-à-vis other great powers) or a power vacuum, they will be more likely to pursue risk-acceptant intervention strategies. Conversely, if they perceive an unfavorable power balance, they are more likely to pursue risk-averse strategies. Leaders will weigh the costs and benefits of withdrawal or a continuation of ongoing intervention strategies, update their preferences in response to new information, and display sensitivity to marginal costs and diminishing returns. Thus offensive realism would not expect leaders to pursue risky diplomatic and military strategies toward other great powers in an effort to continue failing interventions in strategically inconsequential regions.

Balance-of-Risk Theory

Unlike offensive realism, balance-of-risk theory holds that great powers (or more properly, central decision makers) pursue risky intervention strategies in the periphery to avert perceived loss. The necessity of avoiding losses in their state's material power, status, or reputation weighs more heavily in the calculations of leaders than the prospect of gains in those commodities. Senior officials initiate risky diplomatic and/or military intervention strategies to avoid such losses. They then persevere and even escalate failing peripheral interventions to recoup past losses.

Senior officials evaluate anticipated foreign policy outcomes in terms of deviations from an expectation level—a clearly articulated goal (or set of goals) that functions as a baseline for evaluating policy outcomes. The expectation level of these officials serves a heuristic function by framing anticipated outcomes in terms of gains and losses. This, in turn, influences the disposition of senior officials toward risk. Concrete examples of expectation levels include leaders' war aims, territorial aspirations, minimum bargaining positions, and diplomatic expectations.[47]

In the opening months of the First World War, for example, Prime Minister H. H. Asquith and his cabinet adopted the "destruction of

Prussian militarism" as Britain's central war aim in the European theater. This aim not only entailed the decisive military defeat of Germany, but also the discrediting of the *Junker* military caste and possibly the removal of the German emperor Wilhelm II. Therefore, any outcome to the war short of a decisive German defeat and regime change in Berlin, would fail to achieve the aspirations of British leaders.[48] In the Second World War, the unconditional surrender of Germany, Italy, and Japan functioned as an expectation level for British and American leaders. President Franklin D. Roosevelt and Prime Minister Winston Churchill established unconditional surrender as the war aim of the Allied powers at the January 1943 Casablanca Conference. Any termination of the war that did not involve the decisive defeat of the German, Italian, and Japanese armed forces, the surrender of sovereignty, and the military occupation would be unacceptable to Washington and London.

In both world wars, the stated war aims of British and American leaders were more than rhetoric designed to mobilize public support. Instead, the "destruction of Prussian militarism" and the "unconditional surrender" of Germany and Japan were the political ends of wartime grand strategy. One finds repeated references to these ends not only in the public pronouncements of senior officials, but also in elite deliberations, diplomatic communications, and planning documents. Officials repeatedly used these respective war aims as a bench mark against which to measure anticipated outcomes. Likewise, in peripheral conflicts, leaders' war aims also function as an expectation level. In the early to mid 1980s, Brezhnev and other members of the Politburo refused to accept any outcome to the Afghan war short of the establishment of a stable and Soviet-aligned regime in Kabul. Similarly, in the Vietnam War, the Johnson and Nixon administrations refused to accept any settlement short of their expectation level: the preservation of an independent noncommunist South Vietnam.

Expectation levels need not involve the political aims of wartime grand strategy. Leaders may evaluate outcomes in terms of deviations from a desired diplomatic outcome, a sphere of influence, or an inflexible bargaining stance. Consider for example, the behavior of Wilhelmine Germany's leaders following the cancellation of the Russo-German Reinsurance Treaty in 1887. Avoiding encirclement became the baseline from which Chancellor Bernhard von Bülow and other officials evaluated diplomatic developments. The recovery of the Sinai was the overriding strategic objective of the Egyptian president Anwar al Sadat and his military chiefs of staff following the 1967 Six Day War. To recover the Sinai, Sadat risked war on two occasions and eventually went to war in October 1973, despite evidence of overwhelming Israeli military superiority.[49]

Elite perceptions of relative power and anticipated power shifts deter-

mine the selection of the expectation level. If leaders anticipate a diminution of relative power or status, they are more likely to adopt an expectation level that reflects a more desirable international environment. Because the current international environment falls below that expectation
level, elites are more likely to adopt risk-acceptant strategies to avoid,
avert, or recoup anticipated losses. Conversely, if leaders anticipate a relative increase in power, they are more likely to adopt the status quo as
the expectation level. Leaders' ability to revise their expectations in response to adverse outcomes is directly proportional to the length of time
they adhere to a particular expectation level.

Balance-of-risk theory marries defensive realism with a decision-
making model based on prospect theory. Prospect theory is a psychological model of decision-making under conditions of risk. In the late 1970s,
Israeli psychologists Daniel Kahneman and Amos Tversky developed
the theory to explain systematic violations in the behavior predicted by
expected utility theory that they observed in experimental studies.
Prospect theory holds that most individuals tend to evaluate choices
with respect to an expectation level and pay more attention to losses relative to comparable gains. They also tend to overweigh certain outcomes
relative to probable ones; value what they already possess over what
they seek to acquire; and display risk-acceptant behavior to avoid (or recoup) losses, but risk-averse behavior to secure gains. Related experimental studies involving groups find similar behavioral patterns. Furthermore, the intensity of risk-acceptant behavior to avoid loss appears
with greater severity in groups than among individuals. Within group
settings, the responsibility of members for past failed investments increases the likelihood that the group will adopt risk-acceptant strategies
to recoup losses.[50]

Numerous experimental studies have found strong support for Kahneman and Tversky's findings in several contexts: simple gambles, consumer purchasing, health care, natural hazards, corporate and individual investing, and nonfinancial business decisions. Prospect theory has
generated an enormous literature in consumer economics, social psychology, organizational behavior, and the relatively new field of behavioral economics. In the past decade, various scholars have applied
prospect theory hypotheses and concepts to the study of international
cooperation, crisis diplomacy, war initiation and termination, and extended deterrence. Most empirical applications of prospect theory in the
literature seek to demonstrate the theory's utility in explaining political
behavior against expected utility theory or generic rational choice models.[51] However, neither prospect theory nor expected utility, per se, is a
theory of foreign policy or international relations. Instead, they are abstract decision-making models that make no substantive predictions

about political behavior. One can incorporate prospect theory or utility theory decision models into broader theories about political behavior by adding substantive assumptions about actors and the environment in which they operate. To date few works explicitly incorporate prospect theory's insights into existing bodies of international relations theory. The present book undertakes that task.[52]

Balance-of-risk theory proceeds from four assumptions. First, like all other variants of contemporary realism, the theory assumes that the international system—that is, anarchy, the relative distribution of power among states, and power trends—set the broad parameters of international outcomes and the foreign policy of states. Over the long run, international outcomes mirror the relative distribution of material capabilities. Second, like other defensive realist theories, balance-of-risk theory assumes that the international system rarely provides incentives for conflict and aggression.[53] The security dilemma causes states to worry about one another's future intentions and relative power, thus generating spirals of mutual hostility or conflict. States can often achieve security though the pursuit of moderate foreign policies. Under rare circumstances, however, defensive realism expects the international system to provide incentives for states to pursue expansive policies.[54]

Third, balance-of-risk theory assumes a complex and indirect linkage between systemic imperatives and the foreign policy choices of national leaders. In doing so, it seeks to recapture the complexity of foreign policymaking that played a prominent role in the classical realist literature, but which neorealist theories downplay for the sake of parsimony.[55] The classical realism of Hans Morgenthau, Arnold Wolfers, and E. H. Carr did not posit a perfect transmission belt between power and interests, on the one hand, and the foreign policies of states, on the other.[56] The problem with classical realism, as Aaron Friedberg observes, is that "when it comes to explaining how statesmen actually do their difficult job, the classical realists appear to lose interest and move on to other, more tractable subjects."[57] To understand why states undertake particular policies, one must understand how senior officials actually assess relative power and the international environment.[58]

Finally, balance-of-risk theory recognizes that human beings have a limited capacity to process new information about their environment. They therefore rely on prior belief systems and cognitive short cuts to assess the actual distribution of power, anticipate likely power trends, and select appropriate policies. Certain psychological tendencies—namely loss aversion, nonlinear responses to probabilities, and the tendency to value current possessions over comparable acquisitions—systematically bias the types of options most people consider when faced with high-risk situations. This does not suggest that leaders are "irrational" or that their choices are not goal oriented. On the contrary, it suggests that while leaders are extremely goal oriented, the links between structural variables and the actual foreign policies that states pursue are complex. By explicitly incorporating such perceptional variables into realist theories one can better explain instances of foreign policy behavior that seem anomalous from the standpoint of purely structural theories.

RESEARCH METHODS AND PROCEDURES

The book employs a qualitative, comparative case study methodology. Given the questions the book seeks to answer, a qualitative research design offers several advantages. Like large N statistical studies, case studies can establish covariation between observed outcome variables and hypothesized causal variables. More important, case studies allow the researcher to uncover causal mechanisms and test more observable implications of the competing hypotheses.[59] The data for each case consists of archival records—the minutes and, in some cases, the transcripts of high-level meetings, private correspondence, internal government documents, intelligence reports, and diplomatic cables—as well the vast secondary literature in diplomatic history and international relations.

The Cases

The book examines three historical cases in depth: Germany's initiation and escalation of the 1905–06 Morocco crisis; Japan's decisions for war in 1940–41; and the United States intervention in and escalation of the Korean War in 1950–51. In each case, I seek to demonstrate that balance-of-risk theory not only explains the risk-propensity of central decision makers, but that it also provides a superior explanation for the observed behavior than offensive realism or logrolling theory.

In addition to data availability, I chose the principal cases with several aims in mind. First, although the exact nature of diplomatic or military intervention differed, all three constitute critical events in late-nineteenth and twentieth-century diplomatic and military history. Other things being equal, scholars of international politics and foreign policy should prefer to study significant events rather than trivial ones.[60] Although each state arguably intervened in strategically inconsequential regions, the consequences of interventions had broad implications for great power politics and regional security. Germany's initiation of the first Morocco crisis set in motion the chain events that led to the division of Europe into rival alliance blocs, the adoption of rigid war plans, and a vastly expensive race in land armaments, all of which contributed to the outbreak of the First World War. Japan's pursuit of autarky and empire in northern China and later Southeast Asia precipitated the entry of the United States into the Second World War. Finally, the Truman administration's intervention in Korea not only extended the cold war to East Asia but also precluded diplomatic relations between the United States and the People's Republic of China for twenty years. The legacies of that war continue to shape the security environment in East Asia: the forward deployment of American troops in South Korea; the U.S.–Korean and U.S.–Japan security pacts; and the security dilemma across the Taiwan Straits and on the Korean Peninsula.

Second, the cases are sufficiently data-rich to permit process tracing and multiple within-case comparisons.[61] One can easily divide the cases into a number of decision points, thus maximizing the number of observations.[62] The table below shows twenty-one observations across the three cases:

Third, I selected these cases to ensure variation in the factors that allegedly affect risk taking in the periphery: the degree of cartelization; relative power and international opportunity; and elite perceptions of loss and gain (relative to the expectation level). There is variation in the degree of cartelization: Germany and Japan had highly cartelized political systems, whereas the United States in the late 1940s and early 1950s had a less cartelized system. Relative material capabilities and elite perceptions of gain and loss, the explanatory variables of offensive realism and balance-of-risk theory, respectively, also vary within and across these cases.

Fourth, each case has large within-case variation in the dependent variable across time and space. Senior officials adopted risk-averse strategies during some periods and risk-acceptant strategies in others. Moreover, the intensity of their risk aversion or acceptance varied across issue areas within particular periods.[63] Nonetheless, some readers may argue that the research design falls prey to selection bias. They might argue that decision makers took great risks in all of the cases. Furthermore, the book does not examine cases where leaders undertook high-risk intervention strategies that resulted in "success." The pursuit of risky diplomatic and military strategies invariably leads to policy failure (or at least entails greater costs than anticipated): Bülow and his associates may have initiated the 1905–06 Morocco crisis to divide the Anglo-French entente, but their "big stick" strategies led to Germany's diplomatic isolation in the short-run and helped set the stage for the outbreak of war in 1914. Japanese leaders' risky drive for autarky and empire ultimately led to a vastly destructive war. The Truman administration's intervention in defense of South Korea ultimately embroiled the United States in a costly and ultimately inclusive war with China.

TABLE 1.2 *List of observations in the principal cases*

Germany and the first Morocco crisis	Japan and the 1940–41 war decisions	The United States and the Korean War (1950–51)
The Anglo-French entente and Germany's response I: Efforts to secure Anglo-German rapprochement (April-June 1904)	The inauguration of the second Konoe cabinet to the signing of the Tripartite Pact (June-Sept. 1940)	Adverse power oscillations: the Soviet A-bomb and the loss of China (August-December 1949)
The Anglo-French entente and Germany's response II: Efforts to secure a Russo-German alliance and the Dogger Bank incident (July 1904–Jan. 1905)	Continuation of the China incident and negotiation of the USSR-Japan Non-aggression Pact (October 1940–March 1941)	NSC-68 and the Projected Window of Vulnerability: reaffirmation of the defensive perimeter strategy in the Pacific (January–May 1950)
The planning and execution of the German emperor's Tangiers landing (Feb.–March 1904)	The "draft understanding" with the U.S. to the northward advance debate (April–June 1941)	The outbreak of the Korean War and the decision to intervene (June 1950)
The reaction to the Tangiers landing to the fall of Delcassé (April–May 1905)	The decision for the southward advance and the occupation of southern French Indochina (June–July 1941)	The period of the North Korean offensive and the debate over war aims (July–August 1950)
The summer war scare and Rouvier's agreement to a great power conference (June–July 1905)	The freezing of Japan's assets and Roosevelt's deterrent warning (July–August 1941)	The war for rollback I: Inchon and the U.S./UN counteroffensive (September–October 1950)
Negotiations over the conference agenda and a renewed war scare (August–1905)	The resignation of Konoe, the appointment of Tōjō, and the Hull-Nomura talks (September–November 1941)	The war for rollback II: Crossing the Thirty-eighth Parallel and encounters with the CPVs (October–November 1950)
Anglo-French military staff talks and German isolation at the Algeciras conference (December 1905–March 1906)	The failure of the Hull-Nomura talks and the final decision for war with the United States (November–December 1941)	An entirely new war: The Chinese counteroffensive and the limited war strategy (December 1950–January 1951)

The selection bias charges are erroneous on several grounds. As I note above, the dependent variable—the direction of risk-taking behavior—takes different values at different observation points within each case. I compare conditions in the cases to a known average situation: great power nonintervention in the periphery. Great powers have frequently used diplomatic and military strategies to intervene in the periphery.

Like the broader phenomena of interstate war, however, peripheral interventions are not the known average situation in world politics. The
standard injunction against case selection of the dependent variable,
while perfectly acceptable (indeed necessary) to draw causal inferences
from statistical data, is often inappropriate for qualitative research.[64]

Balance-of-risk theory makes probabilistic predictions about leaders'
risk propensity among available policy options; it does not generate predictions about the content of those options, the outcomes of the strategies, or the types of negative or positive feedback officials will likely receive. For example, balance-of-risk theory does *not* predict that when
faced with perceived losses to their state's relative power or status, leaders tend to select intervention strategies that lead to disastrous outcomes. Instead, it predicts that leaders will demonstrate a bias toward
the more risky options.

One major case—Germany's initiation and escalation of the 1905 Morocco crisis—constitutes both a "least likely" case for balance-of-risk theory and a "most likely" case for the alternative theories.[65] This case
seems unlikely to accord with balance-of-risk theory. The German government did not make a major investment of economic or military resources to protect the status quo in North Africa. Moreover, Berlin
backed down when confronted with opposition from the other great
powers. At the same time, one would expect offensive realism and
logrolling theory to provide adequate explanations. Germany enjoyed a
favorable balance-of-power (especially in land forces, population, and
economic capabilities) vis-à-vis its principal continental adversary at the
time, France. Logrolling theory would also predict German opportunistic expansion, given the highly cartelized nature of domestic politics in
the Second Reich. To the extent that the balance-of-risk hypotheses provide a superior explanation for German behavior, the theory will have
passed a rigorous test.

Finally, to explain why great powers pursue (or escalate) risky interventions in the periphery in some instances but not others, I compare the
three principal cases as well as Germany's initiation of the 1911 Morocco
crisis against the following four cases: the Japanese government and military high command's efforts to prevent the escalation of border clashes between the Japanese and the Soviet armies during the 1938 Changkufeng
and the 1939 Nomonhan incidents; and the Truman administration's decision to seek a negotiated settlement to the Korean War in the February-
June and July-November 1951 periods. In these cases, leaders did not initiate risky diplomatic or military commitments in the periphery or
attempted to withdraw from such commitments in the face of mounting
costs. Although the results are not definitive, the cases suggest that great
power nonintervention or deescalation was due to the unwillingness of

leaders to pursue risky strategies to secure gains over and above their expectation levels.

The method for testing the balance-of-risk hypotheses is straightforward. To establish a casual connection between officials' perceptions of gains and losses (relative to their expectation level) and their risk-taking behavior, I employ primary sources and detailed content analysis of elite deliberations. The balance-of-risk hypotheses gain support in a particular observation if the following conditions are present. First, decision makers must evaluate outcomes in terms of the expectation level adopted at T. Second, decision makers must perceive themselves as facing gains or losses relative to that expectation level at $T + N$. Third, the aggregate risk-taking behavior of officials must be in the predicted direction: risk-acceptance for loss and risk-aversion for gain.

I limit my analysis to senior officials who possessed all or nearly all relevant information available to anyone involved in the decision, or could have gained access to it if desired. Such officials include chiefs of state, heads of government, cabinet members, and the ranking uniformed military officers. Limiting the analysis in this manner minimizes the chances of correlation between psychological variables and new information. By doing so one can more easily discern whether or not any changes in decision-makers' risk propensities resulted from loss aversion or simple updating in response to new information.[66] Table 1.3 lists the central decision makers in the three principal cases.

Definitions

Great power intervention in the periphery can take several forms—diplomatic support or posturing, covert operations, arms sales, military advisors, or direct use of force. Each of these strategies (as well as complete noninvolvement) involves a certain level of risk, although in the abstract none of them is necessarily more risky than the other strategies. I use the term *risk* to characterize situations where any action or lack of action may result in serious losses resulting from a great power's own behavior, adversary or third party reactions, or other exogenous events.[67] This definition differs from the distinction between risk and uncertainty found in microeconomics.[68] In economic theory, risk refers only to those situations where the decision maker has perfect knowledge of all possible outcomes associated with an event and the probabilities of their occurrence. Uncertainty refers to situations where the decision maker lacks both information about possible outcomes and the probability distribution of their occurrence. In short, uncertainty connotes a state of incomplete information.[69]

In the study of international politics and foreign policy, the microeco-

TABLE 1.3 *Central decision makers in the principal cases*

Cases	Decision maker	Position and tenure in office
Germany		
The first Morocco crisis (March 1905–April 1906)		
	Count Bernhard von Bülow	Reich Chancellor and Minister-President of Prussia (17 Oct. 1900 to 14 July 1909)
	Baron Friedrich von Holstein	Senior Counselor, Reich Foreign Office (1900 to 13 Jan. 1906)
		Director, Political Department, Reich Foreign Office (13 Jan. to 16 Apr. 1906)
	Wilhelm II	German Emperor and King of Prussia (15 Jun. 1888 to 28 Nov. 1918)
	Baron Oswald von Richtofen	State Secretary for the Reich Foreign Office (19 Oct. 1900 to 16 Jan. 1906)
	Heinrich von Tschirschky und Börgendorff	State Secretary for Reich Foreign Office (23 Jan. 1906 to Sept. 1907)
	Otto von Mühlberg	Under State Secretary for the Reich Foreign Office (19 Oct. 1900 to 1907)
	General Count Alfred von Schlieffen	Chief of the Prussian General Staff (1891 to 1 Jan. 1906)
	Lt. General Count Helmuth J. L. von Moltke	Chief of the Prussian General Staff (1 Jan. 1906 to 14 Sept. 1914)
	Admiral Alfred von Tirpitz	State Secretary for the Reich Navy Office (June 1897 to March 1916)
Japan		
War decisions (July 1940–Nov. 1941)		
	Prince Konoe Fumimaro	Prime Minister (4 June 1937 to 5 Jan. 1939; 22 July 1940 to 18 July 1941; and 18 July to 18 Oct. 1941)
	Lt. General Tōjō Hideki	Minister of War (22 July 1940 to 18 Oct. 1941)
		Prime Minister and Minister of War (18 Oct. 1941 to 22 July 1944)
	Matsouka Yosuke	Minister of Foreign Affairs (22 July 1940 to 30 June 1941)
	Admiral Toyoda Teijiro	Minister of Foreign Affairs (30 June to 10 Oct. 1941)
	Tōgō Shigenori	Minister of Foreign Affairs (11 Oct. 1941 to 1 Sept. 1942)
	Admiral Yoshida Zengo	Minister of the Navy (30 Aug. 1939 to 5 Sept. 1940)
	Admiral Oikawa Koshiro	Minister of the Navy (5 Sept. 1940 to 11 Oct. 1941)

(continued)

TABLE 1.3 *(Continued)*

Cases	Decision maker	Position and tenure in office
	Admiral Shimada Shigetaro	Minister of the Navy (18 Oct. 1941 to 17 July 1944)
	Taki Masao	Minister-of-State and President, Cabinet Planning Board (25 Oct. 1937 to 6 Dec. 1940)
	Hoshino Naoki	Minister-of-State and President, Cabinet Planning Board (6 Dec. 1940 to 4 Apr. 1941)
	Lt. General Suzuki Teiichi	Minister-of-State and President, Cabinet Planning Board (4 Apr. 1941 to 22 July 1944)
	Kaya Okinori	Minister of Finance (18 Oct. 1941 to 19 Feb. 1944)
	Field Marshal Prince Kan'in Kotohito	Chief of the Army General Staff (1 Dec. 1931 to 3 Oct. 1940)
	General Sugiyama Hajime (Gen)	Chief of the Army General Staff (3 Oct. 1940 to 21 Feb. 1944)
	Lt. General Sawada Shigeru	Vice Chief of the Army General Staff (2 Oct. 1939 to 6 Nov. 1940)
	Lt. General Tsukada Osamu (Ko)	Vice Chief of the Army General Staff (6 Nov. 1940 to 6 Nov. 1941)
	Admiral of the Fleet Prince Fushimi Hiroyasu	Chief of the Naval General Staff (2 Feb. 1932 to 9 Apr. 1941)
	Admiral Nagano Osami	Chief of the Naval General Staff (9 Apr. 1941 to 21 Feb. 1944)
	Vice Admiral Kondo Nubutake	Vice Chief of the Naval General Staff (2 Oct. 1939 to 1 Sept. 1941)
	Vice Admiral Ito Seichi	Vice Chief of the Naval General Staff (1 Sept. 1941 to Nov. 1944)

United States

The Korean War (June 1950–May 1951)

Cases	Decision maker	Position and tenure in office
	Harry S. Truman	President of the United States (12 Apr. 1945 to 20 Jan. 1953)
	Dean G. Acheson	Secretary of State (21 Jan. 1949 to 20 Jan. 1953)
	Louis B. Johnson	Secretary of Defense (28 Mar. 1949 to 19 Sept. 1950)
	General of the Army George C. Marshall	Secretary of Defense (21 Sept. 1950 to 12 Sept. 1951)
	James E. Webb	Under Secretary of State (28 Jan. 1949 to 29 Feb. 1952)
	Stephen T. Early	Deputy Secretary of Defense (2 May 1949 to 12 Sept. 1950)

Cases	Decision maker	Position and tenure in office
	Robert A. Lovett	Deputy Secretary of Defense (21 Sept 1950 to 17 Sept. 1951)
		Secretary of Defense (17 Sept. 1951 to 20 Jan. 1953)
	Dean Rusk	Deputy Under Secretary of State (26 May 1949 to 28 Mar. 1950)
		Assistant Secretary of State for Far Eastern Affairs (28 Mar. 1950 to 9 Dec. 1951)
	John D. Hickerson	Assistant Secretary of State for UN Affairs (8 Aug. 1949 to 27 July 1953)
	W. Averell Harriman	Special Assistant to the President (28 Jun. 1950 to 31 Oct. 1951)
	Philip C. Jessup	Ambassador-at-large (2 March 1949 to 23 Jan. 1953)
	H. Freeman Matthews	Deputy Under Secretary of State (5 July 1950 to 11 Oct. 1953)
	Lt. General Walter Bedell Smith	Director of Central Intelligence (7 Oct. 1950 to 29 Jan. 1953)
	Frank Pace, Jr.	Secretary of the Army (12 April 1950 to 10 Jan. 1953)
	Francis P. Matthews	Secretary of the Navy (25 May 1949 to 31 July 1953)
	Thomas K. Finletter	Secretary of the Air Force (24 Apr. 1950 to 30 Jan. 1953)
	General of the Army Omar N. Bradley	Chairman, Joint Chiefs of Staff (16 Aug. 1949 to 16 Aug. 1953)
	General J. Lawton Collins	Chief of Staff, U.S. Army (16 Aug. 1949 to 14 Aug. 1953)
	Admiral Forrest Sherman	Chief of Naval Operations (2 Nov. 1949 to 22 July 1951)
	General Hoyt Vandenberg	Chief of Staff, U.S. Air Force (30 Apr. 1948 to 30 June 1953)

nomic distinction between risk and uncertainty becomes untenable for several reasons. First, the classic conditions for risk and uncertainty rarely exist in the "real world." Central decision makers almost never have complete information about the outcomes associated with a foreign policy option and the probabilities of their occurrence. At the same time, the paucity of information about various outcomes is rarely so great as to make subjective probability estimates impossible. Again, officials can and do estimate (however imperfectly) the likely consequences of pursuing various strategies. Second, the distinction between risk and uncertainty focuses on outcome probability to the exclusion of outcome value. The value of a particular outcome depends on whether the decision maker views its occurrence as desirable or undesirable. Obviously some outcomes will have higher values than others. This in turn will affect the decision maker's preference among various outcomes, and therefore risk propensity.[70] Third, even in situations where decision makers make subjective probability assessments of particular outcomes, there will always be a certain level of uncertainty about exogenous phenomena. In short, the definition of risk in foreign policy must subsume uncertainty.

The definition of risk offered here focuses on the potential for loss or gain. Depending of the situation, losses and gains generally entail objective measures of a state's capabilities, such as military forces and equipment, territory, economic resources, military and civilian casualties. They can also refer to subjective values, such as a great power's reputation for resolve, the credibility of commitments, and prestige, that play a role in leaders' calculations.[71] Risk-acceptant behavior occurs when central decision makers select a policy option that has three characteristics. First, the preferred option must have more numerous and extremely divergent outcomes than the other available options. Second, in selecting that option, central decision makers must perceive that negative outcomes are at least as possible as (and often more probable than) positive ones. Third, decision makers must recognize that their subjective probability estimates may be flawed or completely incorrect. Risk-averse behavior, on the other hand, occurs when central decision makers select an option that has fewer and less divergent outcomes.

Before continuing, I should note two caveats. The definition of risk and the distinction between risk acceptance and risk aversion refer only to leaders' preferences among particular foreign policy strategies. They do not refer to international outcomes, which are phenomena resulting from the interaction of two or more actors in the international system. Risk-acceptant behavior is not synonymous with policy failure, and risk-averse behavior is not synonymous with policy success. It is entirely possible for national leaders to pursue a risk-averse strategy, which through the actions of other actors and systemic variables, produce suboptimal or even disastrous outcomes. Likewise, the pursuit of risk-acceptant foreign policy strategy may result, through the actions of other actors and systemic forces, in a desirable international outcome. Second, risk acceptance is not necessarily synonymous with the threat or use of force. Under many circumstances, military force may entail greater risks than other options under consideration. However, one can easily imagine a scenario where the use of force entails fewer and less divergent outcomes than other available strategies.

Risk acceptance and risk aversion are not dichotomous. Rather, one should conceive of risk behavior as a continuum. A particular policy option is more or less risky relative to other options decision makers identify at the time. It make little sense to rank the "real" risks associated with particular options on a cardinal or ordinal scale because of the difficulties in measuring "objective" utilities and probabilities in foreign policy decision-making. Nor does it make sense to draw a sharp distinction between the "real risks" associated with a particular policy option and its "perceived risks."[72] First, the term "real risk" connotes the probability estimates, costs, and benefits that a fully informed neutral observer would make. This approach, however, raises the danger of coding the relative risks of particular foreign policy strategies based on international outcomes. The theory-driven researcher, who presumably has full knowledge of how history actually unfolded, may code particular foreign policy options that led to disaster as "risk acceptant" and those that led to success as "risk averse."[73] Second, focusing on the perceived risk of particular options poses a harder empirical test.[74] If central decision makers select policy options they perceive as relatively risk acceptant to avoid losses and options they perceive as relatively risk averse to secure gains, then the core balance-of-risk theory hypothesis will have withstood a stronger test.

The term *entrapment* denotes "a decision making process whereby individuals escalate their commitment to a previously chosen, though failing, course of action in order to justify or 'make good on' prior investments."[75] The related concept of *escalating commitment* denotes a tendency to increase the investment of resources in courses of actions where decision makers have experienced past setbacks and where the ultimate outcome of continued investment remains in doubt.[76] In cases of foreign military intervention, sunk costs would include both the material costs of military operations (such as casualties, money, lost equipment, or opportunity costs) and whatever political capital or reputation costs decision makers expended to mount such operations. In the case of diplomatic disputes involving peripheral regions, sunk costs again include both reputation and material considerations.

The *periphery* refers to geographic areas where actual or likely conflict cannot directly threaten the security of a great power's homeland. Whereas others draw a distinction between the periphery and core based solely on geographic distance, I have tried to incorporate the relative distribution of capabilities into the definition. A region is peripheral vis-à-vis a great power based on a combination of: (1) its geographical distance from the core, and (2) the inability of the peripheral state's military forces to inflict damage on the great power's homeland.[77] This is not say that control of peripheral region cannot enhance a state's power. Indeed certain regions are strategically important because they contribute to the defense of the homeland or other intrinsically valuable regions. The Philippines, for example, constituted a periphery for the United States, both because of the islands' geographic distance from the mainland and the tremendous imbalance of relative capabilities. The occupation of the Philippines and the four-decade military presence after independence, however, enhanced American relative capabilities. Specifically it allowed the United States to project naval power in the Pacific.[78]

PLAN OF THE BOOK

I began this chapter by noting that great powers frequently initiate risky diplomatic and military interventions in the periphery. The strongest states in the international system often persist in failing intervention strategies despite mounting political, economic, and military costs. More surprising, great powers sometimes undertake risky diplomatic and military strategies toward other great powers in an effort to continue failing interventions in strategically inconsequential regions. Three theories of foreign policy—the logrolling theory of imperial overexpansion, offensive realism, and balance-of-risk theory—might explain these phenomena.

The next chapter presents the theoretical argument in detail and lays out the competing hypotheses that I evaluate in the rest of the book. Chapters 3, 4, and 5 consist of the principal case studies: the German government's initiation and escalation of the 1905 Morocco crisis; the decisions by the Konoe and Tōjō governments and the Imperial General Headquarters for war in 1940–41; and the Truman administration's intervention in the Korean War in 1950–51. In Chapter 6 I briefly analyze five additional cases—German diplomacy in the 1911 Morocco crisis, Japanese decision-making during and after the hostilities between Japanese and Soviet forces at Changkufeng and Nomonhan in July 1938 and May-September 1939, and the Truman administration's efforts to negotiate an end to the Korean War in 1951—which I use to refine my central argument. Finally, in chapter 7 I summarize the results of the historical cases, describe their theoretical implications, and highlight their policy implications.

[2]

Explaining Great Power Involvement
in the Periphery

This chapter explains how leaders' aversion to perceived losses in their state's relative power, prestige, and international status drives foreign policy. Robert Gilpin observes, "Realism, like liberalism and Marxism, is essentially a philosophical position; it is not a scientific theory that is subject to the test of falsifiability and, therefore cannot be proved or disproved. Testable theories, however, can be derived from realist assumptions."[1]

Balance-of-risk theory represents a fusion of realism's assumptions—the centrality of conflict between groups under anarchy; the relative distribution of material power; positional conflict for scarce resources; and the utility of force—with prospect theory. Prospect theory provides a descriptive and predictive explanation for why leaders are extremely sensitive to losses; value what they possess more than what they seek to acquire; and display different risk propensities when faced with prospective gains or losses. In short, the prospect theory literature suggests that many behaviors associated with defensive realism are not the result of anarchy per se. Rather, the so-called status quo bias of states results from the way in which most human beings process information and select options in situations of risk and uncertainty.[2]

The chapter consists of three sections. The first reviews prospect theory and related branches of the behavioral decision literature that deal with group risk-taking. Along the way, I address some common critiques of prospect theory. The second section explores the implications of these experimental findings for foreign policy and then deduces testable hypotheses. I use historical and contemporary examples to establish the plausibility of each hypothesis and specify the type of evidence that would confirm or disconfirm it. The concluding section summarizes the hypotheses drawn from offensive realism and logrolling theory that might account for the same phenomena I attribute to loss aversion by national leaders.

A DESCRIPTIVE SUMMARY OF PROSPECT THEORY

In the late 1970s psychologists Daniel Kahneman and Amos Tversky developed prospect theory to explain systematic violations in the behavior predicted by expected utility theory observed in repeated experimental studies.[3] Prospect theory consists of two phases: the editing or framing phase and the evaluation phase. The editing phase involves a number of mental operations that simplify the subsequent evaluation and choice of options. These operations consist of the selection of the reference point or expectation level (coding), the framing of outcomes as deviations (losses or gains) from that reference point, the identification of available options, the possible outcomes or consequences of those options, and the values and probabilities associated with them."[4] The encoding of options around the reference point, in effect, functions as a heuristic—a mental short cut that allows the decision maker to quickly process information about the external environment, but with the effect of systematically biasing the decision maker's response.[5] In prospect theory's evaluation phase, the decision maker examines the edited prospects and selects the preferred option. Unlike expected utility theory and other rational choice theories, prospect theory does not purport to be a normative model of decision-making. Rather, it seeks to provide a descriptive and predictive model of how most individuals make decisions.[6]

Since the late 1970s, prospect theory has generated an enormous literature in consumer economics, social and consumer psychology, management science, organizational behavior, and the relatively new field of behavioral economics.[7] Since numerous articles and books reprint the various experiments from which prospect theory derives, there is no need to summarize them here.[8] Instead, I will review those aspects of the prospect theory literature most pertinent to defensive realism in general, and the development of balance-of-risk theory in particular.

Prospect theory provides five main insights. First, most individuals evaluate gains and losses in terms of deviations from a neutral reference point, instead of net levels of wealth. In Kahneman and Tversky's studies, that point is generally the decision maker's subjective understanding of the status quo. Decision makers, however, can also frame options around an expectation level that does not reflect the status quo. For example, when an earlier status or prior outcome is preferable to the status quo, the decision maker will generally adopt the status quo ante as a reference point.[9] The evaluation of outcomes around the reference point or expectation level frames the choice problem as a matter of either achieving a gain or averting a loss. Decision makers view anticipated outcomes that are at or above the reference point as gains; they view outcomes that fall below as losses. A shift in reference point, and by extension the encoding (or framing) of options in terms of gains and losses, can induce a reversal of preferences among equivalent options.[10]

The second insight is loss aversion. Simply put, most people react differently to gains and losses. Losses (no matter how small) hurt more than gains (no matter how large) gratify. For example, the pain of losing $100 exceeds the pleasure of unexpectedly gaining $1000.[11] The oft-cited quotation from tennis player Jimmy Conners nicely illustrates this point: "I hate to lose more than I like to win."[12] Prospect theory suggests the decision-making process will demonstrate a marked bias toward loss avoidance (whether projected or sunken).[13] In simple gambles or lotteries, individuals rarely accept symmetric gambles that involve a 50 percent probability of winning X and a 50 percent probability of losing X.

Third, most people value what they already posses over what they seek to acquire. This endowment effect is a logical outgrowth of the above mentioned loss-aversion phenomenon.[14] The process of acquiring a good enhances that good's value in the eyes of its owner. The gratification of acquiring a new good is less than the pain of losing something already in one's possession. As a result, the minimal compensation people demand to give up a commodity (the selling price) will often be several times higher than the maximum amount they are willing to pay for a comparable commodity. In various experimental studies involving trivial items (such as coffee mugs), valuable commodities (such as real estate), and even proxies for tangible items (such as meal vouchers), the typical ratio of selling prices to buying prices was two to one. These studies also suggest that the endowment effect is instantaneous: people accommodate to perceived gains very quickly. Once in possession of a given commodity, most people rapidly become attached. On the other hand, people do not adjust quickly or easily to losing a commodity initially in their possession.[15]

Fourth, prospect theory suggests that people do not respond to probabilities in a linear manner. Instead they tend to overweigh outcomes considered certain compared with those that are merely probable. A hypothetical game of Russian roulette provides a graphic example of the so-called certainty effect. Players will pay more to reduce the number of bullets in the gun from 1 to 0 than from 4 to 3. Insurance buying behavior provides a second example. People will tend to pay far more to reduce the risk of catastrophic loss from 10 percent to zero than from 20 percent to 10 percent, even though the change in expected utility is the same. Moreover, most people tend to treat extremely probable outcomes as if they were certain. Most variants of rational choice, on the other hand, hold that a decision maker's utility for a given outcome is the product of its expected payoff and probability of its occurrence.[16]

Finally, prospect theory, unlike theories of rational choice, makes definite predictions about individuals' propensity toward risk. Most individuals tend to be risk-averse in their selection of options, if they perceive themselves to be facing gains. For example, a decision maker facing gains would prefer a sure gain of $240 over a gamble involving a 25 percent chance to win $1,000 and a 75 percent chance to win $0. Conversely, individuals tend to be risk-acceptant in their selection of options, if they perceive themselves to be facing losses. For example, a decision maker facing losses (relative to the reference point or expectation level) would prefer a gamble involving a 75 percent chance to lose $1,000, with a 25 percent chance to lose $0, over a sure loss of $750.[17] Thus, situational factors and cognitive dynamics systemically influence most individuals' perception of and disposition toward risk.

Individual versus Group Decision-Making

Most foreign policy decision-making occurs within group settings. Even in totalitarian states, several officials participate in the decision-making process. Prospect theory only provides a probabilistic model of individual choice; one cannot apply the theory to groups. Eldar Shafir argues that prospect theory "is based on specific assumptions regarding people's anticipated pleasure over gains as compared to their pain over losses. . . . All this may be significantly different for groups of individuals."[18] Jack Levy observes that prospect theory (in its current state of development) cannot make predictions about the risk propensities of decision-making groups. He notes, "One problem is that the behavior of groups is not necessary congruent with the aggregation of the risk orientations of individual members as demonstrated by the substantial body of literature in group dynamics on choice shifts."[19] Some critics will further claim that simple behavioral decision theories cannot fully explain the complexities of risk-taking behavior, particularly those involving ill-structured foreign policy problems. Individual-level, group, organizational, cultural, and societal variables, along with state capabilities, and the international environment must all work together to shape risk-taking behavior in foreign policy. Therefore, a theory of foreign policy must take all of these factors into account.[20]

The critics overstate their case for several reasons. First, prospect theory *itself* is not a theory of foreign policy or a theory of international politics. Expected utility theory and prospect theory, by themselves, do not generate substantive predictions about international outcomes or the foreign policy behavior of states. Instead, one must embed concepts from these decision theories into specific theories of foreign policy and international politics.[21]

Second, I reject the so-called "maximalist" approach to theory construction: the practice of including multiple explanatory variables operating at different levels-of-analysis in a single theory. There will always be a trade-off between parsimony and explanatory power. However, theories that posit every conceivable explanatory variable for an outcome do not elucidate potential causal effects.[22] Furthermore, I explicitly pit hypotheses drawn from the theory I develop against the most likely alternatives—offensive realism and logrolling theory. These theories posit variables at the systemic and societal levels of analysis, respectively. Like many social science theories, prospect theory presents a simplified causal relationship; it cannot include all possible variables, which may (or may not) influence risk-taking behavior.

Finally, there is increasing experimental and empirical evidence that prospect theory provides a descriptive model for organizational and group decision-making. These studies suggest that groups, like individuals, tend to evaluate risky prospects in terms of deviations around a common expectation level.[23] They further suggest that the framing of decisions in terms of gains and losses, relative to that expectation level, influences the overall direction of the group's risk propensity.

Escalating Commitment to Recover Sunk Costs

The experimental research on prospect theory sparked renewed attention within the management studies and organizational behavior literature to the problem of escalation of commitment—the tendency for decision makers to persist with failing courses of action despite mounting costs and risks. Contrary to the rational choice assumption that decision-making reflects incremental costs; consideration of sunk costs often leads actors to aim for higher goals as a means to recoup past losses.[24] This has two implications. First, it implies decision makers will persevere in failing ventures far longer than a standard utility calculus would lead one to expect. Expected utility models, on the other hand, suggest that decision makers are more likely to escalate their commitment to an entrapping course of action to the extent that the likelihood of attaining their goal or the perceived value of that goal is high rather than low.[25] Second, in these situations the decision maker will likely continue and even escalate risk-acceptant strategies. Several studies in management sciences and organizational behavior find that these behavioral patterns associated with prospect theory—loss aversion, escalation of commit-ment, and risk-acceptance to avoid loss—occur with greater severity in decision-making groups than among individuals.[26]

Tatsuya Kameda and James Davis found that subjects who had expe-rienced a recent loss were more likely to make riskier choices than those who had not suffered a similar loss before decision-making. They further found that subjects within groups consistently showed riskier personal preferences than did subjects in individual conditions.[27] Max Bazerman examined the effects of escalating commitment in both individual and group decision-making. One hundred eighty-three subjects participated in role-playing exercises in which Bazerman manipulated personal re-sponsibility for an initial decision. A portion of the subjects participated as individuals, while another portion of the subjects were assigned to de-cision-making teams. On making the final allocation decision, all sub-jects completed a questionnaire assessing each of four process variables: commitment, relatedness, confidence, and reversal. As expected, both in-dividuals and the decision-making teams invested additional resources to the failing venture.[28]

. Glen Whyte conducted a similar study on the likelihood and degree of escalating commitment among individuals and groups. He found that the escalating commitment effect within groups appeared with greater frequency and severity than it did among individuals. Moreover, he found that personal responsibility for the consequences of sunk costs magnified the escalation effect.[29] Robert Rutledge conducted a similar study that examined escalating commitment effects in groups and the potential moderating effect of the framing (around an expectation level). He found that overall, management groups had a greater preference for continuing a failing course of action when presented with negatively framed information than when presented with positively framed infor-mation. His findings further suggest that the sense of responsibility for past choices among decision makers exacerbates the loss-aversion phe-nomena within group settings.[30]

These experiments suggest people will escalate their commitment to failing ventures in an effort to recover sunk costs. In other words, deci-sion makers escalate their commitment to an entrapping course of action despite a diminished likelihood of attaining their goal or a diminished value of their goal. More concretely, they will continue to take "bad" gambles—strategies that have a lower likelihood of success—in order to recover their prior investments rather than cut their losses. One finds ex-amples of this phenomenon in a variety of settings. Consider the 1995 collapse of Baring's, Britain's oldest merchant bank. Rather than accept responsibility for losing $24 million on the Japanese futures market, Sin-gapore-based trader Nick Leeson continued to make high-risk investments, despite a diminishing likelihood of recouping the loss. Ultimately Leeson lost an estimated $1.8 billion, precipitating Baring's collapse in February 1995.[31]

Although these and other studies suggest that prospect theory can explain aspects of group decision-making under conditions of risk and uncertainty, there is one caveat. Prospect theory, like most social science theories, provides a *probabilistic* explanation of human behavior, not a deterministic one. Approximately two-thirds to three-quarters of Kahneman and Tversky's research subjects displayed risk-averse behavior with respect to gains and risk-acceptant behavior with respect to losses; the remaining subjects did not.[32] Similarly, in the experiments cited above there was some variation in risk propensity among the members of the decision-making teams. Nonetheless, the overall pattern of group risk behavior was largely consistent with the predictions of prospect theory—risk acceptance to avoid losses and risk aversion to secure gains. The behavior of groups with respect to risky choices is not necessarily an aggregation of the individual risk propensities of its members. A substantial body of literature on "choice shifts" within groups demonstrates this. Experimental studies on "group polarization" suggest that groups tend to move either toward riskier or less risky options, depending on the circumstances.[33]

Clearly, individuals within a group may vary in their propensity toward risk. If the above experimental findings are externally valid, one should expect to see some difference in risk propensities among the members of any decision-making group. The aggregate risk-taking behavior of the group, however, should be largely consistent with prospect theory. Likewise, in foreign policy and international politics, we should expect some variation in risk propensity of individual leaders. The aggregate risk propensity of central decision makers should be in the direction prospect theory predicts: risk aversion for gains and risk acceptance for losses. Explaining this intragroup variation, however, would be beyond the scope of the present study and would entail a vastly different research design.

The Transition from Experiments to the "Real World"

Prospect theory appears to provide an accurate descriptive model of individual and group decision-making in experiments involving gambling, investment, insurance purchasing, and public health. The behavioral patterns associated with prospect theory—loss aversion, the endowment effect, the certainty effect, and the pseudo-certainty effect—appear plausible, albeit counterintuitive. However, the descriptive generalizations that underlie prospect theory emerge from experiments in highly structured settings. Researchers designed experiments that controlled for extraneous variables and ensured prospect theory and expected utility theory would make different predictions. Before one can embed prospect theory insights into foreign policies theories, one must contend with a number of conceptual issues. These issues include the distinction between reference points and expectation levels and the concept of framing choices in terms of gains or losses. I address each in turn.

In the experiments cited above the researchers present subjects with scenarios framed in terms of gains and losses. The status quo, as indicated in the wording of the questionnaire, often served as the default of reference point. The reference point is simply a single point on a utility curve, which in most experiments corresponded to an "objective" status quo. Researchers manipulate the wording of the questions, which in turn induces a change in reference point and thus a reversal of most subjects' preferences among equivalent options.[34] Kahneman and Tversky admitted that their experiments involved choice problems "where it is reasonable to assume either that the original formulation of the prospects leaves no room for further editing, or that the edited prospects can be specified without ambiguity."[35] Thus, much of the experimental literature largely focuses on the evaluating phase of prospect theory and ignores the editing phase.

Many political scientists infer from the prospect theory literature that the reference point and the notion of domain of losses and the domain of gains refer to some objective "state of the world" that the researcher can clearly observe and code. In a similar vein, others have argued that leaders' aversion to losses on the domestic front affects their risk-taking in the international arena.[36] This "objective" approach, however, has major problems. The first concerns terminology. In the experimental literature, outcomes above the reference point fell into the "domain of gains" and those that fell below were in the "domain of losses." The terms *domain of losses* and *domain of gains* refer to specific areas on a utility curve; not actual "states of the world." Instead of using "domain," it is more appropriate to say that decision makers perceive themselves as facing gains or losses, relative to their reference point (or expectation level).

Second, the objective approach also ignores the problems of issue salience. In ill-structured settings, quantitative indicators of material capabilities or popular opinion cannot measure leaders' assessments of what constitutes a relative gain or loss. The researcher may inadvertently identify objective values that have little or no salience to decision makers.[37] Third, and most important, the notion of an immutable and "objective" domain of gains or losses ignores the reality that most aspects of foreign policy are future-oriented. National leaders may enjoy an objectively favorable balance-of-power in the present, but nonetheless fear relative decline in the future.[38] For example, in the decade before World War I, Germany enjoyed a significant margin of superiority in military and economic power. Nonetheless, from 1903 onward German leaders worried about relative decline vis-à-vis a rapidly industrializing Russia and possible encirclement resulting from Britain's rapprochement with France and the existing Russo-French alliance.[39] Leaders who perceive their state as less powerful vis-à-vis a potential adversary might contemplate drastic measures to arrest a widening power gap in the future. For example, Japanese leaders launched a preventive war in 1904 to stem the growth of Russian military power in East Asia. Similarly, in July 1914, fear of the long-term growth in Russian capabilities led Germany, a military preponderant but declining great power, to plunge the international system into major war.[40]

Another problem involves the tendency of international relations and comparative politics scholars to aggregate the costs and benefits associated with different policy arenas into a single domain of gains or losses. Decision makers may not perceive gains or losses in one dimension (for example, domestic politics) as determining values in another dimension (for example, foreign policy). Unless the theory specifies, a priori, which policy dimension the decision maker values more, the determination of "objective" gain or loss becomes post hoc and potentially circular.[41] The theory-driven researcher many inadvertently explain any risk-taking behavior with reference to leaders' desire to avoid objective losses in a completely unrelated area. The decision maker, however, may not view the potential losses in other areas as salient to the primary area of interest. For the sake of theory construction and testing, I will assume that leaders evaluate outcomes relative to a single expectation level, defined for a particular realm of policy, that is, the international arena. This assumption is consistent with an underlying theme of defensive realism: in foreign policy making, international factors weigh much more heavily in leaders' calculations than do domestic politics.[42]

Expectation Levels

Several implications follow from this analysis. In ill-structured and complex settings, such as foreign policy, decision makers are more likely to assess outcomes and contingencies in terms of deviations from an *expectation level*, not a neutral reference point. William Boettcher observes, "Politicians are unlikely to focus on a uni-dimensional reference defined by the status quo. Indeed, foreign policy decisions often research the highest levels *because* the goals or interests at play in the current situation are complex or unclear."[43] Kahneman and Tversky acknowledge that most of their experiments required subjects to evaluate options from a reference point that "usually corresponds to the current asset position, in which case gains and losses coincide with the actual amounts that are received and paid."[44] They later admit that, "although this is probably true for most choice problems, there are situations in which gains and losses are coded relative to an expectation or expectation level that differs from the status quo."[45]

Chip Heath, Richard Larrick, and George Wu conducted several experiments that suggest people evaluate outcomes in terms of deviations from an expectation level or performance goal that does not represent the status quo. Their research integrates prospect theory with expectation level theories and goal-setting behavior literature.[46] The encoding and evaluation of options around a performance goal inherits the behaviors associated with prospect theory's value function: loss aversion, diminishing sensitivity, risk acceptance for gains, and risk aversion for loss. In one experiment, the researchers presented two groups of subjects with a hypothetical cost-cutting program for a company. The choice problem required managers to save costs in their unit for the first quarter of the year. The members of the first group received a fixed performance goal (save $250,000), while the members of the second group received a more general goal ("do your best"). Both groups received two alternatives, both of which were one-time options and were only available during the current quarter. Program M would surely save $120,000 (a sure bet). Program N had an 80 percent chance of saving $50,000 and a 20 percent chance of saving $250,000. The number of people who chose the more risky Plan N doubled when people have a specific aspiration or goal (save $250,000), as opposed to a more general goal ("do your best"). This is consistent with prospect theory's prediction of diminishing sensitivity: most people will pursue risk acceptant strategies when they are below their goal. Furthermore, expectation levels need not entail extrinsic values or additional payoffs (such as promotions or salary increases). Intrinsic expectation levels, such as the goal of completing twenty-five sit-ups or scoring a B on a physics test, divide outcomes into regions of success or failure.[47]

In a related study, Larrick, Heath, and Wu find that specific expectations, challenging "mere" goals—levels of performance that do not entail additional payoffs—increases most peoples' risk-acceptance to avoid loss and risk aversion to secure gain. In one experiment, the researchers presented 136 MBA candidates with a series of choice problems involving gambles and sure bets. All subjects received cash payments based on their decisions. The researchers told the subjects that they had a chance to earn money by choosing one option from a set of options, each of which offered a specific probability of a cash payoff. Further, options with higher expected payoffs had lower expected values. Researchers randomly assigned the subjects to a "goal" condition or a "do your best" condition. They encouraged the first group to select a specific, challenging goal (or aspiration) for the money they would like earn in the exercise. Most subjects chose the goal of winning nine dollars. The second group received a more general instruction to "do their best" to make money. Both groups received fifteen gambles that increased in payoff by fifty cents, ranging from a certain chance (100 percent) to win three dollars and a 21 percent chance to win ten dollars. Each gamble showed the expected values. Expected values decreased by approximately five cents with each fifty-cent increase in absolute payoff. As predicted, participants in the goal condition selected significantly riskier options. Participants in the "do your best" condition, however, preferred the less risky options. For example, 37 percent of the "do your best" group preferred a sure gain of three dollars, as compared to 11 percent of the "goal" group.[48]

Both proponents and critics of prospect theory point to the absence of a "theory of framing" (or more properly, a theory of reference point choice, maintenance, and change) as the principal limitation to the theory's application outside experimental settings.[49] The questions of why and under what conditions decision makers select, adhere, or change a particular expectation level (and thus frame options as gains or losses) are important if prospect theory is to make causal inferences outside controlled settings. Furthermore, one must also address the question of whether that expectation level reflects the current status quo or what the decision maker would like to see arise in the future. In the absence of addressing these questions, one might reasonably argue that prospect theory hypotheses lack predictive power for "real world" behavior. Several works that apply prospect theory hypotheses to the study of foreign policy suggest various mechanisms for reference point selection and change (and thus, framing). While many of these works present interesting descriptive inferences in individual case studies, they are ultimately post hoc. They do not generate and test generalized hypotheses on how national leaders select, change, or adhere to particular reference points or expectation levels.[50] Below, I seek to fill this gap in the literature.

The following section integrates insights from prospect theory into a broader theory of foreign policy. Drawing on the experimental literature discussed above and defensive realism's emphasis on the importance of relative power shifts, I derive testable hypotheses on how elites select, maintain, and change expectation levels. From there, I turn to a discussion of how leaders' aversion to perceived loss drives great power intervention in peripheral regions.

Hypotheses on Great Power Intervention in the Periphery

Defensive realism hold that anarchy does not preordain states toward belligerence. The international system only rarely provides incentives for expansion. Material power can only influence foreign policy through the medium of calculations, perceptions, and forecasts of national leaders. The prospect theory literature portrays a human decision-making process where losses loom larger than gains, risk propensity varies with the situation, existing possessions have a higher value than those not yet acquired, certain outcomes loom larger than probable ones, and sunk costs receive priority over marginal costs. By building prospect theory into defensive realism, we can provide a more accurate descriptive account of elite decision-making and generate predictions about the likelihood, scope, and duration of great power intervention in the periphery.

Systematic incentives filter through an elite decision-making process that systematically skews toward loss avoidance. Thus whether we are attempting to explain particular intervention decisions, predict how a state will behave once it has intervened, or justify particular intervention policies, balance-of-risk theory warns us that policy output can never be perfectly matched to the external input.[51] This decision-making process has observable implications for the foreign policy of great powers. National leaders who seek to avert losses (or recoup past losses) are more likely to adopt the more risk acceptant among available policy options. In other words, they will likely pursue external strategies that could yield more numerous and diverse outcomes, including a high probability of adverse outcomes. At the same time, leaders will recognize that their subjective probability estimates may be flawed or completely incorrect. Conversely, if leaders perceive themselves as facing gains, they are more likely to pursue strategies that offer fewer and less diverse outcomes, and which have a higher probability of positive outcomes. Figure 2.1 illustrates the path balance-of-risk theory posits between systemic imperatives and the disposition of leaders toward risk taking in foreign policy.

Senior officials are acutely sensitive to the relative distribution of power and prestige among the great powers. All else equal, the greater a state's aggregate power—population, industrial resources, territory, military capabilities, and technological resources—the greater a potential threat it can pose to others. A closely related factor is prestige, a state's reputation for having material capabilities or status and using those commodities to achieve its desired aims.[52] The ultimate determinant of prestige is victory in a major (or hegemonic) war. The actual task of assessing relative power and prestige, however, is complicated. The vari-

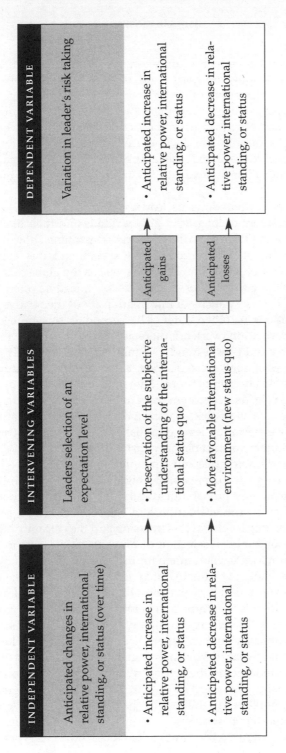

FIGURE 2.1 CAUSAL LOGIC OF BALANCE-OF-RISK THEORY

ous measurements on which leaders rely are often imperfect. The relative distribution of power among states does not remain constant. The so-called law of uneven growth is a recurrent theme in classical realism and contemporary realism.[53] Furthermore, the relative distribution of prestige does not always mirror the actual balance-of-power at any given time. For example, the disjuncture between prestige and actual power balances explains in part the failure of the European great powers to form balancing alliances against Prussia in the wars of German unification.[54]

The central task that confronts leaders in making foreign policy involves the assessment of long-term power trends and their likely implications for a state's future security. Leaders' assessments, however, must take into account short-term trends in specific relative capabilities among particular potential competitors as well as the global distribution of power. In making these assessments, however, leaders often face two dilemmas. The first is a paucity of information about the relative capabilities and intentions of other states. The second is the more common dilemma of information overload: there are simply too many indicators of relative power and power trends.[55] Senior officials must rely on judgmental structures or goals to assess their state's current and future standing relative to likely competitors. Dynamic expectations of relative power and status leads decision makers to focus on a specific aspiration or policy goals as a yardstick against which to measure relative gains and losses. The expectation level establishes the level of relative power or status loss leaders are capable of withstanding.

Prospect theory holds that most people are more sensitive to losses than to gains. They also overestimate high and moderate probabilities and underestimate low probabilities. Although the extant experimental literature focuses on the evaluation and selection of edited prospects, one could reasonably infer that loss aversion and the certainty effect may influence decision makers' selection of an expectation level in the first place. Decision makers who anticipate the erosion of assets over time should be more likely to evaluate outcomes relative to a more favorable position. That expectation level may be a higher performance level or the status quo ante (that is the status quo before the recent loss).[56] For example, consider a situation where a company has made a $10 million profit in the previous fiscal year, but experiences a net $1 million loss in the first quarter of this year. Furthermore, management expects to lose an additional $1 million net in the second quarter. In response to these adverse developments, the board of directors and senior management establish a profit target of $10 million for the present year, thus giving the company two quarters to recover.

Similarly, in foreign policy, national leaders who have experienced a sharp decline in relative power or prestige (real or perceived) will likely adopt the perceived status quo ante as an expectation level. The 1962 Cuban missile crisis provides a dramatic illustration because both Soviet premier Nikita S. Khrushchev and President John F. Kennedy adopted the perceived status quo ante for their respective states as an expectation level. Khrushchev responded to an adverse power oscillation caused by the Kennedy administration's defense buildup and its public disclosure that the "missile gap"—the widespread belief (based upon Khrushchev's boasting) that the American arsenal of intercontinental ballistic missiles (ICBMs) was significantly inferior to the Soviet Union's—was mythical.[57] The successful tests of the first-generation Soviet ICBM, the SS-6, and the launch of Sputnik in 1957 had been technological and propaganda triumphs for the Kremlin. Khrushchev and the Soviet general staff decided not to proceed with the full-scale development of the SS-6, but to await the follow-on missile system. By 1960–61, however, Khrushchev faced a deteriorating strategic balance as the United States proceeded with the full-scale development and deployment of its first generation ICBM, the Minuteman. In fiscal year 1962 alone, the Kennedy defense budget called for the production of 600 Minuteman missiles. The president further requested that 29 Polaris-class submarines and 465 sea-launched ballistic missiles (SLBMs) be operational by June 1965, instead of the 19 submarines and 304 SLBMs requested in the Eisenhower administration's last budget. In light of this adverse power shift, Khrushchev and his advisors adopted a return to the status quo ante—that is, Soviet nuclear parity—as their expectation level.[58]

Coming in the aftermath of the 1961 Berlin crisis and the debacle of the Bay of Pigs invasion, the Soviet Union's deployment of medium-range ballistic missiles to Cuba represented both an adverse shift of the strategic balance and a challenge to the Kennedy administration's resolve. Khrushchev chose to secretly deploy several dozen intermediate range ballistic missiles (IRBMs), medium range ballistic missiles (MRBMs), nuclear warheads, mobile launchers, and over forty thousand Soviet military personnel to an island less than ninety miles from the U.S. homeland, despite recent and repeated warnings by the Kennedy administration not to do so.[59] After U-2 spy planes discovered the missile sites, Kennedy and the Executive Committee of the National Security Council (ExComm) immediately adopted a return to the status quo ante—that is, the complete removal of all Soviet missiles and strategic rocket forces personnel from Cuba—as the expectation level for their deliberations. It is noteworthy that this expectation level did not entail the removal of Cuban president Fidel Castro.[60]

Conversely, if decision makers perceive the current status quo as favorable and do not anticipate negative changes, they evaluate outcomes relative to the status quo or some aspect of the status quo. Similarly, if decision makers anticipate an increase in relative power over time, they will tend to evaluate options relative to the status quo. As a result, they have a longer time horizon. The deliberations and policies of the Eisenhower administration in 1953–54 provide an illustration. Due to the massive defensive buildup called for in NSC-68 and implemented during the Korean War, American defense spending increased from 4.6 percent of GNP in fiscal year 1950 (approximately $13.1 billion) to 12.8 percent of GNP in fiscal year 1954 (approximately $46.6 billion).[61] The United States had a clear advantage over the Soviet Union in the number of atomic bombs, the development of thermonuclear weapons, nuclear delivery systems, and economic capabilities. President Dwight Eisenhower and his advisors perceived the country to be in a much stronger position vis-à-vis the Soviet Union in 1954 than it had been in 1950.[62]

These considerations suggest the following hypothesis:

The perception by senior officials of relative power trends influences the choice of a common expectation level. If officials anticipate a diminution of relative power or status over time, they are more likely to adopt a more favorable international environment as their expectation level. Conversely, if senior officials anticipate a relative increase in power and status over time, they are more likely to adopt the status quo as the expectation level.

If this hypothesis is correct, one should find the following behavioral patterns in elite deliberations. First, and most obviously, national leaders will be attentive to information regarding the present distribution of power and anticipated power shifts. One should find evidence of such power assessments in intelligence reports, diplomatic cables, and internal correspondence. Second, one should find evidence that leaders use these assessments to define an expectation level or baseline of expectations for future policy outcomes. In elite deliberations on the development of specific aspects of grand strategy or the examination of particular policy areas, one should see repeated references to minimum acceptable outcomes. Officials should encode these expectations in planning documents, instructions to diplomats abroad, public statements, and other materials. One should find evidence that senior officials then evaluate specific policy options (and their likely outcomes) relative to the expectation level.

Like the problem of expectation level (or reference point) selection, the existing experimental literature on prospect theory does not directly address the question of how long and what circumstances decision makers adhere to a common expectation level. The literature on the anchoring and adjustment biases suggests that in many situations people make estimates by starting from an initial value and then adjust that value to yield the answer. However, once people decide on that initial value (or an anchor), they are remarkably resistant to adjust it in response to new information, logical and evidential challenges, and alternative modes of reasoning. In an oft-cited experiment, Tversky and Kahneman asked subjects to adjust an arbitrary initial estimate of the percentage of African states in the United Nations. Subjects starting with anchors of 10 percent and 65 percent gave "adjusted" estimates of 25 percent and 45 percent, respectively. The researchers found the same anchoring effects with the initial estimates dictated by the subject's own previous spin of a roulette wheel. This anchoring bias is also evident in situations where people face simple events, conjunctive events, and disjunctive events. People tend to overestimate the probability of conjunctive events (such as drawing a red marble seven consecutive times from a jar containing 90 percent red marbles and 10 percent white marbles). On the other hand, they tend to underestimate the probability of disjunctive events (such as drawing a red marble at least once in seven consecutive tries, with replacement, from a bag containing 10 percent red marbles and 90 percent white marbles).[63]

Anchoring and adjustment biases are also evident in risk perception. Slovic, Fischhoff, and Lichtenstein asked subjects to estimate the frequency of death in the United States from each of forty different causes (including, influenza, cancer, diabetes, heart disease, automobile accidents, and electrocution). Instead of telling one group of subjects that about fifty thousand die annually in automobile accidents, the researchers told them that one thousand die annually from electrocution. When asked to estimate the annual fatality rate across different causes, the electrocution anchor (one thousand deaths) systemically reduced subjects' estimates of the other causes.[64]

Loss aversion and the endowment effect suggest that most people can easily adjust to gains above their reference point (or expectation level), but have great difficulty in adjusting their expectations downward in response to losses. Readjustment to the new (and arguably less desirable) status quo takes a long time and decision makers do not adjust their expectation level downward. Robert Jervis refers to this phenomenon as "renormalization." In an international dispute, renormalization to loss drives leaders' risk acceptance and creates situations where both sides seek to avert (or recoup) losses. He writes, "Thus in the Cuban missile crisis the status quo for the United States was the situation in where there were no Soviet missiles or bombers on the island."[65] Although the extant literature does not address the period for renormalization, it is reasonable to infer that the longer decision makers adhere to a particular expectation level the greater the difficulty they will have in renormalizing for loss.

To return to the historical example, the deployment of Soviet medium-range missiles and bombers to Cuba in October 1962 had the potential to shift the U.S.-Soviet strategic balance in one fell swoop. Khrushchev had only adhered to the aspiration of strategic parity with the United States for several weeks before the Kennedy administration discovered the missile sites. Khrushchev, of course, withdrew the missiles after Kennedy imposed the blockade and agreed to remove Jupiter missiles from Turkey. Jervis speculates the Soviet leader may have "been less accommodating if the installation had been completed and the new status quo [that is, nuclear parity with the U.S.] formalized by an official announcement."[66]

Thirty years later, however, it proved very difficult for Khrushchev's successors to revise their expectation level downward in response to adverse developments in Afghanistan. The breakdown of superpower détente in 1973–75, negative expectations for future U.S.–Soviet security and economic cooperation, Egypt's defection to the Western camp, and the 1978–79 Islamic revolution in Iran, made General Secretary Leonid Brezhnev and the Politburo increasingly wary of future deterioration in the status quo.[67] The maintenance of a friendly regime in Kabul was the expectation level that Soviet leaders adopted long before the actual invasion of Afghanistan in December 1979.[68] When the Afghanistan intervention deteriorated into a quagmire and had negative repercussions across a range of areas in 1982–83, Defense Minister Dimitri Ustinov, KGB Chairman Yuri Andropov, and other Politburo hard-liners found it very difficult to abandon the expectation level. This suggests a second hypothesis:

> *Senior officials' ability to revise their expectation level in response to adverse outcomes will be directly proportional to the length of time they adhere to a particular expectation level. The longer senior officials adhere to a common expectation level, the less likely they will be to revise that expectation level downward in response to adverse policy outcomes.*

If this hypothesis is correct, one should observe several behavioral patterns. Officials who have adhered to a particular expectation level for several months or years will downplay or ignore disconfirming information. They will be resistant to new information that their prior goal is no longer realistic or achievable. One should find evidence that officials challenge and question the reliability of disconfirming information. Records of elite deliberations and internal document should reveal that officials reject less lofty (and presumably more achievable) expectation levels. Conversely, in situations where leaders have only adhered to a particular expectation level for days or weeks, one should find the opposite behavioral patterns. They should be more receptive to disconfirming information. While one should not expect decision makers to immediately abandon their expectation level when initially confronted with adversity, they will gradually realign their aspirations.

The first two hypotheses concern how senior officials select and maintain a common expectation level. To recap, assessments of relative power trends cause senior officials to focus on a specific aspiration or policy goals as a yardstick against which to measure relative gains and losses. The expectation level establishes the level of relative power or status loss leaders are capable of withstanding. Senior officials establish an expectation level in their private deliberations and then encode that baseline of expectations in planning documents, white papers on national security goals and strategies, public pronouncements, instructions to subordinates, and diplomatic communications. The longer senior officials adhere to a common expectation level, the greater the difficulty they will have in adjusting their expectations to adverse outcomes. The next hypotheses directly address the question of great power intervention in the periphery.

Balance-of-risk theory holds that prospective loss in material power, international status, or reputation weighs more heavily in leaders' calculations than prospective gain. When leaders perceive themselves as facing losses relative to their stated expectation level, the avoidance of loss (or the recovery of sunk costs) takes on great importance. They are more prone to engage in worse case thinking, heavily discount the future, and focus on the immediate necessity of avoiding the loss. Decision makers will tend to treat negative but probable outcomes as if they were certain. Adverse developments in areas previously deemed peripheral to a great power's security will suddenly take on tremendous importance in elite deliberations. Central decision makers are more likely to adhere to the so-called domino theory, a set of interconnected beliefs and assertions regarding the interdependence of strategic commitments, the relative prevalence of bandwagoning over balancing in alliance formation, the opportunistic nature of adversary's actions, and the cumulative effect of conquests.[69]

A failure to demonstrate resolve across all issue areas and in all regions will result in the steady erosion of the great power's capabilities and the resolve of its allies. For example, the Kennedy and later the Johnson administrations became increasingly alarmed over the Viet Cong insurgency in South Vietnam and viewed the conflict as part of the global superpower struggle. The survival of South Vietnam, therefore, had implications for the global balance of resolve (ultimately the global balance of power) between the superpowers.[70] It is worth noting that Johnson and his national security team did not see the Vietnam War as an opportunity to *augment* American power or influence in Southeast Asia or elsewhere. On the contrary, their primary concern was to prevent an erosion of American reputation for resolve and, by extension, the undermining of the containment policy worldwide.[71]

Similarly, in 1978–79 many Soviet leaders did not attribute the growing unrest in Afghanistan to the radical economic and land reforms of the new president, Nur Mohammed Taraki, and his ruling People's Democratic Party of Afghanistan (PDPA). Rather, Brezhnev, Ustinov, Andropov, and others attributed the situation to efforts by the United States and its proxies to foment unrest in the Soviet's sphere of influence.[72] Raymond Garthoff notes, "The Soviet leaders decided to intervene militarily in Afghanistan not because they were unwilling to keep it as a buffer, but precisely because they saw no other way to ensure that it would remain a buffer. Intervention was not the next in a series of moves to increase Soviet influence, as in Angola, Ethiopia, and South Yemen, nor the first in a new series involving escalation to direct use of Soviet military power in the Third World."[73]

In situations where leaders perceive themselves as facing losses relative to their expectation level, the pursuit of relatively risky strategies in the periphery becomes more likely. Again, the American intervention in Vietnam is illustrative. In early 1965, the Johnson administration's deliberations on Vietnam demonstrated a strong bias toward the high-risk options, which in that case resulted in the Rolling Thunder air campaign against North Vietnam and the introduction of 100,000 troops. Conversely, in situations where leaders perceive themselves as facing gains (or at least not facing losses) relative their expectation level, the pursuit of risk-acceptant strategies in the periphery becomes less likely. Officials are less prone to engage in worst-case thinking, adopt a longer time horizon, and focus on the attainment of longer-term goals. Leaders will be less willing to tolerate the anticipated costs of risk-acceptant strategies and will prefer those strategies that appear to minimize potential negative outcomes. In short, balance-of-risk theory expects that opportunity is a less powerful inducement for risky intervention strategies than the prospect of loss. These considerations suggest a third hypothesis:

> *Senior officials are more likely to initiate or persevere in risk-acceptant strategies in the periphery to avoid perceived losses. Conversely, senior officials are less likely to initiate or persevere in risk-acceptant strategies in the periphery to secure perceived gains.*

Several behavior patterns would support this hypothesis. Documentary evidence should show that leaders encode potential outcomes as gains or losses relative to their expectation level. Once having encoded potential outcomes as losses, elite deliberation should not only show a marked bias toward intervention in the periphery, but also toward the more risk-acceptant of the available strategies. In other words, officials should demonstrate a bias toward those intervention options that have more numerous and diverse potential outcomes. One should find repeated statements by officials in private deliberations on the need to take drastic action to avert (or recoup) losses in relative power, status, or reputation. Although there might some variation among the risk propensity of individuals, the leadership as a whole should favor and ultimately adopt risk-acceptant options to avoid loss. Evidence that leaders encode potential outcomes as losses and yet adopt less risky options would cast doubt on this hypothesis.

On the other hand, once having encoded potential outcomes as gains, elite deliberations should show a marked bias in the opposite direction. Officials should be less willing to intervene in the periphery, overall. In those instances in which they do contemplate intervention, officials should demonstrate a marked bias toward more risk-averse options. Decision makers should be less susceptible to arguments in favor of drastic actions or arguments that highlight the benefits (or gains) associated with intervention. Officials should be less tolerant of high risks associated with the pursuit of outcomes above their expectation level. Once having intervened in a peripheral region and secured their stated aims, one should not expect leaders to adopt risk-acceptant strategies in the pursuit of additional gains. For example, the expansion of war aims and the pursuit (or escalation) of risk-acceptant options to obtain that new war aim would cast doubt on the hypothesis.

Balance-of-risk theory posits that security concerns, not aggressive motives, are more likely to drive great power intervention. Leaders' aversion to losses to their state's relative power, status, or reputation relative to their expectation level leads to the adoption of risk-acceptant intervention strategies in peripheral regions. This same tendency drives decision makers' calculations about ongoing interventions. Peripheral intervention rarely involves a single once-and-for-all decision. On the contrary, once central decision makers decide on a particular strategy, they will often have several opportunities to continue, modify, or terminate that strategy in response to negative feedback. However, as Jervis observes, "Cutting losses after the expenditure of blood and treasure is perhaps the most difficult act a statesman can take; the lure of the gamble that persevering will recoup the losses is often too great to resist."[74]

Balance-of-risk theory expects leaders to escalate their commitment to recover the sunk costs of prior intervention decisions. Leaders who initially intervened to avert losses in their state's relative power or international status will be quite reluctant to reassess, let alone reverse, strategies that fail to produce desired results (that is, an outcome at or above the expectation level). Instead, officials will likely persist in the investment of resources in courses of actions where they have experienced past setbacks and where the ultimate outcome of continued investment remains in doubt. In these situations, the sunk costs associated with a particular course of action weigh more heavily in leaders' deliberations than the marginal costs of continuing a failing strategy. Such sunk costs include the prior investment of material resources, as well as reputation. Loss aversion drives decision makers to not only persist in failing strategies, but also to take additional risks in the hope of recouping their initial "investment." With respect to interventions in the periphery, great powers (or more properly, their leaders) will likely continue to pursue risk-acceptant (and failing) intervention strategies far longer than a standard cost-benefit analysis would suggest.[75]

Consider, for example, the French war in Indochina. From 1946 to 1954, the Comité de Défense Nationale (CDN) and the French general staff continually escalated their commitment to the defense of Indochina, despite clear costs to France's security interests in Europe. Prosecuting the war against the Viet Minh placed additional strains on the already tight military budget and required the diversion of troops, armaments, and equipment to Southeast Asia. The Johnson and later the Nixon administrations displayed the same behavior in the Vietnam War. Johnson and his national security team repeatedly escalated air and ground operations against the Viet Cong guerrillas and North Vietnam from 1965 until 1968. In 1970, President Richard Nixon and his national security advisor, Henry Kissinger, expanded the increasingly futile and domestically unpopular Vietnam War into neighboring Laos and Cambodia in an effort to win concessions from North Vietnam. These considerations suggest a fourth and final hypothesis:

> *Senior officials will likely continue and even escalate their commitment to risky, and often failing, intervention strategies in the periphery. Therefore, senior officials are unlikely to reassess, scale-back, or terminate ongoing risk-acceptant strategies.*

If this hypothesis is correct, one should find evidence that national leaders refuse to disengage from such conflicts despite available information about diminishing marginal returns. For example, one should find evidence in elite deliberations that officials downplay or minimize the costs of continuing intervention strategies. Furthermore, since most people are more inclined toward risk seeking to avoid loss, we should observe national leaders selecting new risk-acceptant strategies or escalating ongoing strategies. In other words, one should not observe leaders paying attention to the marginal costs (in terms of casualties, military equipment, economic dislocation, and opportunity costs) and the diminishing returns of such conflicts. Thus, the null hypothesis would be that national leaders do not continue peripheral wars longer than a standard cost-benefit analysis would suggest.

Summary of Competing Hypotheses

The following chapters test hypotheses about great power intervention in the periphery drawn from balance-of-risk theory against hypotheses from offensive realism and logrolling theory. These foreign policy theories posit different causal mechanisms and generate divergent predictions about the likelihood, scope, and duration of great power intervention. Before continuing, however, it would be useful to summarize the competing hypothesis. Evidence that would disconfirm the hypotheses appears in parenthesis and italics.

Balance-of-Risk Theory

Balance-of-risk theory holds that central decision makers' aversion to losses in their state's relative power, international prestige, or reputation for resolve drives foreign policy behavior. Situational factors, specifically where officials perceive their state to be relative to their expectation level, are very important determinants of officials' risk behavior. Senior officials are predisposed to pursue risk-acceptant strategies to avert loss and risk-avoidant strategies to secure gains, relative to that expectation level:

1. The perception of senior officials about relative power trends influences the choice of a common expectation level. If decision makers anticipate a diminution of relative power or status over time, they are more likely to adopt a more favorable international environment as their expectation level. Conversely, if officials anticipate a relative increase in power and status over time, they are more likely to adopt the status quo as the expectation level. (*Senior officials pay little or no attention to relative power trends and do not shape their expectations or aspirations accordingly. Senior officials anticipate a diminution of relative power or status, but do not*

adopt a more favorable international environment as their expectation level. Senior officials anticipate a relative power increase and
adopt an expectation level that does not reflect the status quo.)

2. Senior officials' ability to revise their expectation level in response
   to adverse outcomes will be directly proportional to the length of
   time they adhere to a particular expectation level. The longer officials adhere to a common expectation level, the less likely they will
   be to revise that expectation level downward in response to adverse policy outcomes. (Senior officials quickly and easily revise
   their expectation level in response to adverse policy outcomes.)

3. Senior officials are more likely to initiate or persevere in risk-acceptant strategies in the periphery to avoid perceived losses. Conversely, senior officials are less likely to initiate or persevere in risk-
   acceptant strategies in the periphery to secure perceived gains.
   (Senior officials initiate or persevere in risk-acceptant strategies in
   the periphery to secure gains. Senior officials are reluctant to intervene in the periphery to avoid losses; when they do, they will pursue risk-averse strategies.)

4. Senior officials will likely continue and even escalate their commitment to risk-acceptant but failing intervention strategies in the periphery. Therefore, senior officials are unlikely to reassess, scale-
   back, or terminate ongoing risk-acceptant strategies. (Senior officials
   are quite sensitive to the marginal costs and diminishing returns of
   failing intervention strategies in the periphery. Senior officials reassess, scale-back, or terminate such strategies.)

Offensive Realism

Offensive realism holds that great powers will likely intervene in the
periphery when they enjoy a favorable international power position and
the perceived benefits of intervention outweigh the costs and risks. Relative power and international opportunity drives great powers' foreign
policy behavior. Offensive realism is a rationalist theory. As such, it im-
plicitly assumes that leaders treat anticipated losses in their state's relative power the same as they same treat anticipated gains in relative
power. Leaders' expectation level should be irrelevant:

1. Great power intervention in the periphery becomes more likely if
   senior officials perceive an increase in relative capabilities. (Senior
   officials perceive or anticipate relative power loss and yet intervene
   in the periphery. Senior officials intervene in the periphery for se-
   curity-driven reasons, not aggressive motives.)

2. If senior officials perceive a favorable relative power balance (vis-à-vis other great powers) or a power vacuum, they will be more likely to pursue risk-acceptant intervention strategies. Conversely, if they perceive an unfavorable power balance, they are more likely to pursue risk-averse strategies. (Senior officials pursue risk-acceptant strategies despite an unfavorable balance of power. Senior officials perceive a favorable balance of power and pursue risk-averse strategies.)

3. Senior officials weigh the costs and benefits of withdrawal or a continuation of ongoing intervention strategies, update their preferences in response to new information, and display sensitivity to marginal costs and diminishing returns. Thus, offensive realism would not expect officials to pursue risky diplomatic and military strategies toward other great powers in an effort to continue failing interventions in strategically inconsequential regions. (Senior officials appear impervious to the marginal costs and diminishing returns of failing strategies. Senior officials do not reassess the costs and benefits of continuing with failing strategies.)

Logrolling Theory of Imperialism

Logrolling theory attributes the foreign policy behavior of great powers to the composition of its domestic society. Self-serving imperialist groups logroll their various interests, "hijack" political institutions, and pervert the state's foreign policy. Overall, great powers with highly cartelized political systems are more prone to the pursuit of risk-acceptant strategies in the periphery. Great powers with democratic political systems are less prone to the pursuit of such strategies. Like offensive realism, logrolling theory builds on rationalist assumptions. Therefore, leaders and "log rolled" coalitions should not treat anticipated gains in relative power, status, or reputation differently from anticipated losses.

1. In both democratic and cartelized political systems, senior officials will be highly cognizant of the preferences of domestic interest groups. In democratic regimes, senior officials will less inclined to intervene in the periphery since society, as a whole, must bear the costs of such policies. When officials do intervene, however, they will be more inclined to adopt risk-averse strategies. (Senior officials in liberal democratic regimes pursue risk-acceptant intervention strategies with little or nor concern for the costs imposed on society. Senior officials intervene despite strong opposition from various interests in society.)

2. In cartelized regimes, senior officials will be more inclined to intervene in the periphery and pursue risk-acceptant strategies, since doing so furthers the material interests of logrolling imperial coalitions. (Senior officials in cartelized regimes are less inclined to intervene in the periphery. When officials do intervene, they pursue less risky strategies, despite the preferences of logrolling imperialist coalitions.)

3. In cartelized regimes, pressure from logrolling imperial coalitions and prior government rhetoric (so-called "myths of empire") will lead senior officials to persist or even escalate their commitment to failing, risk-acceptant strategies. In democratic regimes, senior officials will be less likely to persist or escalate their commitment to failing risk-acceptant strategies. (In cartelized regimes, senior officials do not escalate their commitment to failing, risk-acceptant strategies, despite pressure from logrolling coalitions. Alternatively, in cartelized regimes, logrolling coalitions do not support the continuation of failing, risk-acceptant strategies and yet senior officials continue to pursue such strategies. In democratic regimes, leaders escalate their commitment to failing, risk-acceptant strategies despite strong electoral disincentives.)

[3]

Germany and the 1905 Morocco Crisis

In March 1905, Germany provoked a crisis over France's efforts to establish a protectorate in Morocco, a country where Germany had few economic or strategic interests. By doing so, it sought to divide the Anglo-French Entente Cordiale—an informal agreement delineating British and French colonies in North Africa. The Reich chancellor, Count Bernhard von Bülow, and his chief foreign policy advisor, Baron Friedrich von Holstein, feared this entente would evolve into a military alliance directed against Germany. They dispatched the German emperor Wilhelm II to Tangier to deliver a speech pledging support for Moroccan independence. Bülow and Holstein hoped this show of resolve would isolate France, which in turn, might cause the collapse of the entente. News of the emperor's speech provoked a crisis that brought Germany and France to the brink of war.

German leaders used the threat of war to extract major concessions, including the dismissal of the French foreign minister and an international conference designed to humiliate the French government for violating the 1880 Madrid Convention on the status of Morocco. They were confident that Britain would not lend diplomatic support, let alone military assistance, to France. They expected support from the United States, Russia, Italy, and Austria-Hungary. Such support never appeared. German leaders' rejection of French concessions and belligerent diplomacy throughout the summer and autumn of 1905 drew Britain and France closer to together. After bringing Europe to the brink of war, Germany faced isolation at the very conference its leaders demanded. Bülow and Holstein's "big stick" diplomacy had the consequence of transforming the entente into an alliance. This crisis resulted in the division of Europe into two alliance blocs and set the stage for a second Morocco crisis five years later.

Balance-of-risk theory predicts officials who anticipate an erosion of relative capabilities over time will likely adopt a more favorable international environment as their level of expectation. Senior officials are more likely to initiate or persevere in risk-acceptant intervention strategies in the periphery to avoid losses relative to that expectation level. Once having intervened, officials will likely continue and even escalate their commitment to risk-acceptant, but failing, intervention strategies. In short, they are unlikely to reassess or terminate such strategies.

In this chapter, I argue that the deliberations and risk-taking behavior of senior German officials during the first Morocco crisis generally supports these balance-of-risk hypotheses. Admittedly, Bülow and Holstein's decision to initiate the crisis in March 1905 is consistent with offensive realism. In initiating the crisis, Bülow and Holstein exploited a favorable balance-of-power and the opportunities created by France's violation of existing treaties. In 1905, Germany enjoyed a large margin of superiority in most underlying components of power—population, per capita industrialization, iron and steel production, gross national product, defense expenditures, and the number of active duty military personnel.[1] France's attempts to establish a Moroccan protectorate not only gave Germany an opening to expand its influence abroad, but also provided a pretext to make Berlin look like the aggrieved party. German leaders calculated that France could not expect strong support from Britain and Russia.

Other than the decision to initiate the Morocco crisis, however, German behavior supports balance-of-risk theory, not offensive realism. From 1904 onward Bülow, Holstein, Wilhelm, and other German officials were obsessed with averting encirclement and relative decline. Specifically, they feared that in the absence of corrective action, the entente would quickly solidify into an alliance. If this happened, overlapping alliance ties and the necessity of supporting great power allies would likely result in Germany's encirclement. France and Russia already had a mutual defense pact, the Dual Entente. The French government would seize the opportunity to negotiate a tripartite alliance. Russia, which was heavily dependent on French loans to fund its industrialization and the modernization of its army, would have an incentive to resolve outstanding disputes with the British. Britain, which had found itself increasingly threatened by the rising power of Germany, would realize that the maintenance of strong Anglo-French ties necessitated a rapprochement with the Russians. Moreover, German leaders feared the growth of Russian power. They estimated that by the middle of the next decade, Russia would overtake Germany as the continent's leading industrial and military power. In short, by failing to break the entente in 1905, Germany would find itself encircled by a hostile and potentially more powerful great power coalition.[2]

Officials in Berlin adopted a more favorable international environment, namely the status quo before the entente, as the expectation level for diplomatic and military strategies. Since the actual status quo was below that expectation level, German officials were willing to adopt risky strategies to avert perceived relative power and status loss. Throughout 1905 and early 1906 German leaders ran the risk that their belligerent strategy would draw Britain and France closer together or even escalate into a military confrontation. Furthermore, balance-of-risk theory explains why German officials persisted in their belligerent strategy for months after Britain pledged diplomatic and military assistance to France.

This chapter consists of four sections. Below I review the reactions of German leaders to the Anglo-French negotiations in 1904, their efforts to seek a rapprochement with Britain, and their first attempt to secure an alliance with Russia. An examination of the March 1905 Tangier landing and the campaign to oust the French foreign minister follows in the second section. The third section examines the height of the crisis in the summer of 1905. The fourth section traces the abortive Björkö treaty in late July, France's effort to seek a bilateral settlement, and the reaction of German leaders to the beginning of Anglo-French military collaboration in December 1905–February 1906. It concludes with an examination of the reaction of German leaders to their diplomatic isolation at the Algeciras Conference in March–April 1906.

WILHELMINE GERMANY AND THE PROBLEM OF ENCIRCLEMENT (1890–1904)

The mere existence of unified Germany fundamentally altered the European balance-of-power, which for three hundred years had rested on the existence of a patchwork of small- and medium-sized Germanic states separating France, Russia, and what became (after 1867) the Austro-Hungarian empire. Despite its relative advantages in population, industrial capacity, and land-based military capabilities, Germany could not easily fight and win a prolonged two-front war. To minimize this possibility, Reich chancellor Otto von Bismarck negotiated a series of overlapping alliances and secret treaties. Chief among these were the 1879 Austro-German Dual Alliance (which became the Triple Alliance when Italy joined in 1882) and the 1887 Russo-German Reinsurance

Treaty.[3] However, the sheer complexity of Bismarck's alliance network proved to be its undoing. By eliminating inconsistent military commitments and pursuing assertive policies in both the core and the periphery, Emperor Wilhelm II and his advisors sought to ensure Germany's place among the great powers. Bismarck's successor, General Leo von Caprivi, who allowed the Reinsurance Treaty to lapse on 18 June 1890, argued that it was inconsistent with the Triple Alliance and the 1890 Heligoland-Zanzibar Treaty with Britain. This gave France, however, an opening to pursue a rapprochement with Russia, which culminated in an alliance, the Dual Entente, in 1894.[4]

By building a blue water navy, German leaders sought to enhance their country's prestige and deter Britain.[5] Admiral Alfred von Tirpitz, the state secretary for the Reich Naval Office, told the emperor that the construction of a North Sea battle fleet would cause Britain to lose "every inclination to attack us and as a result concede to Your Majesty such a measure of naval influence to enable Your Majesty to carry out a great overseas policy."[6] Tirpitz planned to build a fleet of sufficient strength to take the offensive in the event of war with Britain. As the German fleet grew, the British would avoid conflict and might even entertain an Anglo-German alliance. Instead, Britain initiated a major expansion of the Royal Navy.[7] This effort to secure an Anglo-German alliance through intimidation spilled into the colonial sphere. When British and Boer troops clashed in the December 1895 Jameson Raid, Wilhelm sent a telegram to Paul Krüger, the president of the Transvaal, congratulating him on repelling the British raiders. The telegram, which became public on 4 January when the *Times* published it, enraged the British public and Parliament. The Krüger telegram affair and subsequent attempts to influence the Anglo-American dispute over Samoa further alienated British leaders.[8]

Germany began to rely more heavily on the Triple Alliance, which proved to be a greater liability than an asset. Once Germany needed its ties to Austria-Hungary because it had no alternatives, its own freedom of maneuver would vanish; a point that Bismarck fully understood and even his successors began to grasp (albeit belatedly).[9] The Dual Monarchy was the weakest of the European great powers. The Austro-Hungarian navy did not have enough funds to match even the Italian navy, let alone the French navy, in the Mediterranean. The imperial army, one of the few unifying institutions in the empire, could conscript only 30 percent of available manpower due to lack of funding. The army's weapons, particularly its heavy artillery, were out of date and too few.[10] In 1904, the annual army expenditure was an estimated £17,568,152, compared to £38,135,105 in Russia; £31,655,076 in Germany; £26,811,890 in France; and £40,292,214 in Britain.[11] In addition, the Dual Monarchy faced a growing problem of secessionist Serb nationalism within its own borders and the Balkans. Vienna's attempts to thwart the ambitions of Serbia fueled tensions with Russia.[12] Furthermore, Austria had outstanding territorial disputes with Italy. The Triple Alliance did little to facilitate Italy's maritime interests and colonial ambitions. It became apparent to Italy's king, Vittorio Emanuele III, the cabinet, and leading parliamentarians that closer diplomatic ties with France would better serve Italian colonial interests in East Africa.[13]

Pénétration Pacifique *and the* Entente Cordiale

The colonial policies of Théophile Delcassé, the French foreign minister from June 1898, were the catalyst of the first Morocco crisis. An ardent nationalist, Delcassé, sought to enhance his country's status as a Mediterranean power by expanding French colonial rule in North Africa. He envisioned a colonial empire that would stretch from Algeria and Tunisia to the French Congo. Delcassé also saw colonial expansion as a vehicle to improve France's strategic position in Europe and his own political standing.[14]

Morocco enjoyed protected status under the 1880 Madrid Convention, which obligated Britain, France, Germany, Italy, and other signatories to uphold that country's independence. The signatories further pledged to uphold most favored nation status for all foreign powers with economic interests in the country. Any revision to the principle of economic equality of rights or change in Morocco's political status required the consent of all signatories.[15] Delcassé embarked on a campaign to secure the other signatories' approval for a French policy of *pénétration pacifique* (peaceful conquest). He directed the French ambassador in Rome, Camille Barrère, to initiate secret talks on all outstanding Franco-Italian disputes. On 1 November 1902, the French and Italian governments signed an agreement whereby France recognized Italy's political and economic rights in Tripoli. In exchange, Italy recognized French predominance in Morocco. Delcassé also used the negotiations to detach Italy from its allies. Italy's foreign minister Guilo Prinetti agreed that any renewal of the Triple Alliance would contain "nothing hostile" to France.[16]

Officials in Berlin saw the Franco-Italian agreement as a potential threat to the Triple Alliance. Chancellor Bernhard von Bülow pressed the Italian ambassador for assurances that the mutual defense portions of the treaty remained in place.[17] In October 1902, General Count Alfred von Schlieffen, the chief of the Prussian General Staff, reported that his Italian counterpart, General Tancredi Salletta, sought a revision to the long-standing agreement whereby Italy promised to send two army corps to Germany in the event of war.[18] In December of the following year, Schlieffen confided to Baron Oswald von Richtofen, the state secretary for the Reich Foreign Office (Auswärtiges Amt): "I beg to state that I am convinced that not only can we not count on the Italian Third Army, but that we shall have to make up our minds to face the entire French army without any reinforcements from the Alpine frontier."[19] German officials also concluded that Italy, which had a long vulnerable coast, would not dare risk war against Britain and France, the dominant naval powers in the Mediterranean.[20]

After concluding an agreement with Italy, Delcassé turned his attention to improving Anglo-French relations. The 1898 Fashoda crisis was the culmination of the decades-long struggle for supremacy over Egypt and the headwaters of the Nile. Delcassé eventually backed down when the British prime minister, the marquess of Salisbury, refused to negotiate the Egyptian question. Despite his humiliation in this crisis, Delcassé sought a comprehensive resolution to all Anglo-French disputes.[21] In the aftermath of the Fashoda crisis and the Boer War, Prime Minister Alfred James Balfour, Lord Salisbury's successor, concluded that rapprochement with Paris would resolve the Anglo-French colonial dispute in North Africa, and possibly alleviate the Russian threat to Afghanistan.[22]

In mid-1903, Delcassé began talks with the British foreign secretary, the marquess of Lansdowne. The resulting *Entente Cordiale* signed in London on 8 April 1904, provided for Britain's recognition of French pre-dominance in Morocco in exchange for France's recognition of British predominance in Egypt. Each side renounced its economic rights in the other's North African colonies. The entente permitted either side to impose commercial restrictions in Egypt and Morocco at the end of thirty years. The signatories further pledged "to afford to one another their diplomatic support, in order to obtain the execution of the clauses of the present declaration regarding Egypt and Morocco."[23] Delcassé immediately began negotiations with Spain, which culminated in an October 1904 joint declaration of Madrid's adherence to the Anglo-French entente. The Franco-Spanish agreement also contained a secret provision on the eventual partition of Morocco.[24]

Delcassé concluded bilateral agreements recognizing French interests in Morocco with all interested European states, except Germany. He refused to negotiate with the German government because he believed that Bülow would insist that France reaffirm the 1871 Treaty of Frankfurt. He also suspected that the Germans had territorial ambitions in the Mediterranean. Several officials in the French Foreign Ministry, as well as Lord Lansdowne, urged Delcassé to reach an agreement with Berlin, but to no avail. Paul Révoil, the French governor-general in Algeria and one of Delcassé's closest advisors, complained, "The great misfortune is that he [Delcassé] finds it repugnant to have talks with the Germans.' The Germans are swindlers,' he says. But, in heaven's name, I am not asking for an exchange of romantic words or lovers' rings, but for a business-like discussion!"[25]

The German Reaction to the Entente Cordiale

The *Entente Cordiale* violated Germany's rights under the Madrid treaty. On 23 March 1904, Prince Hugo von Radolin-Radolinski, then counselor in the German embassy in Paris (and later the ambassador to Paris), wrote to Bülow: "M. Delcassé carefully avoided the word 'protectorate,' but this does not exclude that the influence sought by France for restoring order in Morocco may be equivalent to a protectorate."[26] On 19 April, Wilhelm wrote to Bülow, "We have considerable economic interests in Morocco and must take care they are not damaged by the Anglo-French agreement."[27] Over the next several months, however, officials in Berlin did little to assert Germany's economic claims in Morocco, despite repeated appeals from consular officials in Fez and Tangier.[28]

In 1904–05, the economic consequences of *pénétration pacifique* were, at best, a secondary concern for German leaders who feared that the entente would evolve into a military alliance.[29] Worse still, Delcassé might eventually convince the British to join the existing Russo-French alliance. If that occurred, Germany would find itself in a minority of two in a great power system of five. Baron Friedrich von Holstein, senior counselor for political affairs in the Reich Foreign Office, observed, "We stand here before a test of strength; a German retreat in the face of Anglo-French resistance would in no way be conducive to German-English relations, but would on the contrary give the English, the French, and the rest of the world practical proof that one gets most from Germany by treating her badly, and that after the conclusion of the Entente, Germany wants to avoid friction with this two powers at any cost."[30] A month later, Bülow informed Radolin that "long hesitation to the Entente would be harmful to our prestige."[31] In a 19 August letter to Bülow, Wilhelm worried that Britain, now assured of French support, "would more and more give a second place to all considerations," relating to Germany.[32] In his reply to the emperor's letter, Bülow wrote, "Without doubt, however, the two powers, by this agreement and their rapprochement, gain in international importance and freedom of action. The force of attraction of the Anglo-French Entente on Italy will be much stronger than was that of each of the two western powers separately."[33]

While German leaders were not sure if the entente contained provisions for military collaboration, they feared the worst. In June 1904, Count Paul Wolff von Metternich, the German ambassador in London, told his superiors that the entente did not commit Britain to lend France military assistance. He wrote, "Lord Lansdowne told me definitely yesterday that England has promised France *désintéressement* in Morocco, but has by no means engaged herself to take France's part in the relations of third parties towards Morocco. Even less will England bind herself in advance of a continental war." At the same time, Metternich warned, "It is not out of the question, although I doubt it, that the British government may have promised France her benevolent neutrality in case France is involved in war on the continent."[34]

From spring 1904 onward, avoiding potential encirclement in Europe became a near obsession among officials in Wilhelmstraße. Bülow, Holstein, Richtofen, and others saw the status quo ante, that is, the more favorable international environment that existed before the entente, as the expectation level for German diplomacy. This supports the balance-of-risk theory hypothesis: If leaders anticipate a diminution of relative power or status, they are more likely to adopt a more favorable international environment as their expectation level.

In 1904, German officials considered at least three options to avert encirclement. These were: (1) the use of coercive diplomacy to challenge French *pénétration pacifique* in Morocco, (2) the resolution of all outstanding diplomatic disagreements with Britain and the possible conclusion of an Anglo-German entente, or (3) direct alliance negotiations with Russia. All three options held the prospect of reversing the adverse trend in great power alignments. In March, Bülow proposed sending three warships to Tangier, as sign of German displeasure. Specifically, he planned to use the murder of a German national by Moroccan bandits as a pretext for this show of naval power.[35] Bülow reasoned that such a confrontational stance would show Britain that the formation of an anti-German bloc would have negative consequences.[36] He also recognized that the proposed deployment might lead to a military confrontation with France. Holstein summarized Schlieffen's estimates as follows: In case of the outbreak of a Franco-German war in 1904, Russian participation would be improbable, but Britain's attitude would be uncertain.[37]

Wilhelm rejected Bülow's proposal for two reasons. First, Germany had few economic or political interests in Morocco; the emperor recently made statements to that effect to his cousin, King Alfonso XIII of Spain, at Vigo, and to his uncle, King Edward VII of Great Britain, at the Kiel Regatta.[38] Six months before the signing of the entente, Richtofen instructed the German ambassador in Madrid, Josef Maria von Radowitz, to tell the Spanish government that Berlin would have no objections to a partition of Morocco among Britain, France, and Spain.[39] Thus, the chancellor's proposal would represent a radical policy shift. Second, Wilhelm feared that the deployment might undermine German credibility. In reply to Bülow's letter, Heinrich von Tschirschky und Bögendorff, the Foreign Office's liaison to the imperial court, wrote: "One-sided bellicose action by Germany . . . would undoubtedly arouse the suspicion of those powers [and] would undermine belief in our repeatedly expressed assurance, reiterated to the king of Spain at Vigo, that we claim no exclusive rights in Morocco, and would put the stamp of duplicity on our policy."[40]

Efforts toward an Anglo-German Rapprochement (1904)

German officials decided to avert encirclement by seeking a rapprochement with Britain, consisting of an arbitration treaty and a colonial settlement similar to the entente. Bülow, Holstein, and Richtofen hoped to accomplish two goals: first, and most important, to decrease the potential threat of the entente by improving Anglo-German relations; and second, to link any Anglo-German colonial agreement with the question of French compensation for German economic interests in Morocco.

Whereas Holstein recommended limiting negotiations to Egypt, Bülow and Richtofen proposed placing all issues on the table. These included disputes over German commercial rights in Egypt, Samoa, and the Transvaal, and the Canadian tariff. If Britain and Germany reached an accord on these issues, even in principle, Richtofen suggested seeking a naval agreement as well. Bülow, however, warned the foreign secretary that naval negotiations "would have to be handled carefully and delicately. But nothing must leak out about it prematurely. With this preparation I am convinced that I can win His Majesty over to the whole transaction."[41] A general settlement offered a high payoff for German leaders, even if such an agreement fell short of an alliance. The resolution of economic disputes might lesson the chance that Britain would side with France in the event of war. Furthermore, a settlement might enhance Germany's standing among the great powers.

On 1 May 1904, the British Foreign Office asked other states with commercial interests in Egypt to approve the changes France's had accepted on 8 April.[42] Metternich approached British officials with a proposal to include the Samoan and Transvaal indemnities and the Canadian tariff issue in any Anglo-German negotiations. Initially, Balfour and Lansdowne refused to broaden the negotiations, preferring instead to resolve the political status of Egypt apart from any other colonial and economic issues. Lansdowne was, however, willing to negotiate over German commercial rights in Egypt.[43] On 28 May, Bülow and Richtofen agreed to confine the negotiations to Egypt, but instructed Metternich to continue informally broaching the other topics. Since, France received compensation in return for renouncing its rights in Egypt, Bülow, Richtofen, and Holstein demanded equal compensation: one-sided freedom of trade in Egypt for thirty years. In late June, the Balfour government agreed to this concession. The bargaining tactics of the German diplomats, however, further alienated British officials.[44]

Efforts to Secure a Russo-German Alliance (1904)

Bülow saw military cooperation between Britain and Russia as improbable, given their competing interests in the Mediterranean, the Persian Gulf, and East Asia. In a letter to Count Friedrich Johann von Alvensleben, the German ambassador in St. Petersburg, he argued, "An understanding between England and Russia would be still harder to attain than one between England and France. . . . Moreover there has so far been no sign on the British side that a rapprochement with Russia would be bought at the price of admitting her into the warm water. Lord Lansdowne's recent speech [in the House of Lords on 5 May 1903] . . . rejects expressly any compromise regarding conditions of sovereignty in the Persian Gulf and [in] neighboring waters."[45]

The outbreak of the Russo-Japanese War on 7 February 1904 provided German leaders a window of opportunity. Bülow believed that the war would likely increase Anglo-Russian antagonism in East Asia. Russia's anticipated victory over Japan would lead to further Russian expansion into Manchuria and Korea. This would force Britain to divert its attention from the North Sea and redeploy several naval squadrons to the Indian and Pacific oceans. Increased Anglo-Russian tension, in turn, would undermine Delcassé efforts to negotiate a general agreement with Britain that might evolve into a tripartite alliance.[46]

Wilhelm went further than Bülow by actively encouraging the Russo-Japanese antagonism. On 3 January 1904, he wrote to his cousin, Tsar Nicholas II of Russia, urging him to go to war with Japan. The effort came to naught, largely because the tsar recognized the weakness of the Russian fleet. Bülow disapproved of the emperor's impulsive intervention, observing, "The surest means of making the Russians conclude a hasty and empty peace with Japan would be by rash German suggestions addressed to the tsar."[47]

From the outset, Holstein doubted whether the Russo-Japanese conflict would rupture the Russo-French Dual Entente or provide an opportunity for Berlin to seek alliance with St. Petersburg. A week before the Japanese attack on Port Arthur, he wrote to Radolin, "The Russians are in a very embarrassing situation because they are isolated. France is quietly remaining neutral. . . . There is tremendous bitterness toward the English in St. Petersburg right now, because they have been inciting the

Japanese ever since it became certain that France will not take part on Russia's side."[48] Throughout 1904, Holstein remained wary about making any commitments. On 22 February, he wrote to Bülow, "And what could possibly cause Germany to stand by Russia and endanger herself? One can admire the bravery and other great qualities of the Russian army and navy. . . . [Nonetheless] if Germany were to take sides, her world trade would be endangered."[49]

The Dogger Bank incident provided Germany an added impetus to seek an alliance. On the night of 21 October 1904, the Russian Baltic Fleet, on its way to the Pacific, mistakenly fired on and sunk British fishing trawlers at the Dogger Bank fishing area in the North Sea. The incident implicated Germany—officially neutral in the Russo-Japanese War—because of the contractual ties between German firms and the Russian navy.[50] For several days, Britain and Russia were on the brink of hostilities. Various British leaders viewed Germany as Russia's de facto ally.[51] In February 1904, the Admiralty reported that "if the Russian navy does emerge from the present war materially weakened, the result will be that the two-power standard must hereafter be calculated with reference to the navies of France and Germany, instead of those of France and Russia."[52] First Sea Lord Admiral Sir Walter Kerr warned the earl of Selbourne, the first lord of the Admiralty, about rising German naval capabilities, the potential threat of a combined Russo-German force in the North Sea, and need to bring additional battleships home from the China Sea.[53] Admiral Sir John Fisher, Kerr's successor, told his superiors that the Germans were behind the Dogger Bank incident; a sentiment shared by other Admiralty officials and some British diplomats abroad.[54] Sir James Clarke, the secretary of the Committee on Imperial Defence (CID), told Balfour that "there is a close understanding between Russia and Germany."[55] The Admiralty announced the redistribution of the Royal Navy's main squadrons, which strengthened the Home Fleet at the expense of the Mediterranean Fleet. Prominent British periodicals advocated a preventive attack on the German fleet at Kiel. Sir Frank Lascelles, the British ambassador in Berlin, told Metternich that "if the German fleet had not been built" the Royal Navy's actions would not have been necessary.[56]

Wilhelm and Bülow felt it necessary to immediately seek an alliance with Russia, and Holstein, who had earlier expressed grave reservations about providing war materials to the Russians, now supported this initiative.[57] On 27 October, Wilhelm telegraphed Nicholas about a possible alliance. The tsar replied that he was interested in undertaking discussions.[58] Bülow drafted a mutual defense pact directed solely against an unspecified European adversary. However, Richtofen, Schlieffen, and Tirpitz all opposed the initiative during a 31 October meeting with

Bülow and Holstein. Tirpitz argued that such an alliance would be of no value in the event of a naval clash between Germany and Britain. Schlieffen argued that if Britain attacked Germany, a Russian move against India would be highly unlikely.[59]

Until December 1904, officials continued to see war with Britain as a distinct possibility. "The preparations for mobilization are going forward at high pressure," Wilhelm wrote to Bülow on 23 November, "and the possibly of being attacked by an overwhelming superior force is imminent."[60] Holstein shared Wilhelm's assessments and wrote, "I now believe—what I did not before—in the possibility of a war with England, in which the attack would come from England."[61] Bülow, on the other hand, doubted the likelihood of a British attack, but agreed to recall Metternich for consultations.[62]

As the prospect of war between Russia and Britain diminished in early November, so did the Russian government's desire for an alliance. Russia's prime minister, Count Sergei Witte, and foreign minister, Count V. N. Lamsdorff, warned about the implications of a proposed alliance for the Dual Entente. Lamsdorff persuaded the tsar to proceed slowly with the negotiations, insist that the treaty have provisions for linking the Dual Entente to any Russo-German defense pact, and to consult Paris before signing any agreement. He also advised Nicholas to insist on a quid pro quo by which St. Petersburg would receive Berlin's support in peace talks with Japan.[63] In short, Lamsdorff wanted a general arrangement, whereas Bülow and Wilhelm sought a temporary war fighting coalition directed at Britain. On 7 December, Nicholas telegraphed Wilhelm to state his opposition to signing any treaty without prior consultation with France. Wilhelm and Bülow were certain that Delcassé would immediately inform Lansdowne about the proposed Russo-German alliance, which would surely increase the British hostility toward Germany.[64] Bülow also came to the share the views of Richtofen, Schlieffen, and Tirpitz that a Russo-German alliance was not worth the risk of war with Britain. By mid December, German leaders abandoned their efforts.[65]

Three themes emerge that have bearing on the subsequent Morocco crisis. First, German officials worried about encirclement as early as 1903–04. Second, the entente was a diplomatic revolution and German leaders perceived it as such at the time. Delcassé took a major step toward ending one of Europe's most enduring rivalries. By signing the entente, France, whose foreign policy since 1871 had oscillated between hostility toward Germany and hostility toward Britain, firmly threw its lot behind the latter.[66] Third, German leaders did not seriously contemplate preventive war in 1904–05. As the panic following Dogger Bank illustrates, they feared that Britain might launch a preventive attack on Germany. In the following months, officials undertook desperate measures to avert encirclement, even at the risk of an unwanted war.

The Tangier Landing to the Resignation of Delcassé (February–June 1905)

From March 1904 onward, senior German officials feared that the Anglo-French entente, along with the Franco-Italian rapprochement and the Franco-Russian alliance, might shift the balance-of-power in Europe against Germany.[67] In a July 1904 letter to Bülow, Holstein complained that German security and prestige had diminished "while our opponents and rivals are on the point of encircling us."[68] Following the failure of the Russo-German alliance initiative in late 1904, these concerns about encirclement and loss of prestige intensified.

Wilhelm II's Tangier Landing and its Aftermath (March–April 1905)

Delcassé's strategy involved forcing a comprehensive plan for public safety, military, and financial reforms on the Moroccan government. French personnel would consolidate their control under the guise of assisting Moroccan officials implement the reforms. In January 1905, Delcassé sent Georges Saint-Rènè Talliender, the French minister in Tangier, to Fez with the instructions to convince the sultan of Morocco, Mulay 'Abdu'l-Aziz, to accept the reform program. The sultan, however, had been in contact with Richard von Kühlmann, the first secretary of the German legation at Tangier, who "unofficially" encouraged him to resist the French proposal.[69] In a second meeting with the sultan and his advisors on 22 February, Talliender asserted that the proposed French reform program already had the approval of all interested European states and that he (Talliender) acted under their mandate.[70] The Talliender mission was the turning point for German diplomacy. Holstein, Bülow, Richtofen, and others came to believe that only a split between Britain and France, prompted by an assertive German stance over Morocco, would reverse the erosion of Germany's status and prestige among the great powers, as well as avert encirclement in the core. Holstein and Bülow decided on a dramatic gesture to demonstrate Germany's displeasure with Delcassé and divide the entente.

Five days later, German newspapers announced that the emperor Wilhelm would stop at Tangier during his annual Mediterranean cruise in March. Bülow outlined the government's objective in a letter to the emperor: "Your Majesty's visit to Tangier will embarrass M. Delcassé, traverse his schemes, and further our economic interests in Morocco."[71] A few days later, he wrote to the emperor: "Apart from the fact that the systematic exclusion of all non-French merchants and promoters from Morocco according to the example in Tunis would signify an important economic loss for Germany, it is also a want of appreciation of our power when M. Delcassé has not considered it worth the effort to negotiate with Germany over his Moroccan plans."[72]

Bülow sent a four-page telegram to Wilhelm on 26 March containing detailed instructions for his upcoming Tangier stopover. Specifically, the emperor was to receive the sultan as a fellow sovereign; publicly state his support for Moroccan independence without mentioning France; and encourage the Moroccan government to continue resisting French encroachments. At the same time, Bülow warned, "The question of whether Your Majesty can risk a war with France for the sake of Morocco cannot be considered at all. On the other hand, it is more doubtful whether the present civil government of France . . . would risk war with Morocco so long as the least possibility exists that Germany might sooner or later interfere. Therefore, we must for the present leave our goal uncertain. We cannot conveniently make an alliance with the sultan." Finally, Bülow gave the emperor instructions on how to respond to questions about Germany's stance on a possible Franco-Moroccan war: "'Germany has no obligations which would prevent her from being guided in that case by her own interests.' This reply sounds disquieting for our opponents [the French] but binds us to nothing."[73]

On 31 March, Wilhelm disembarked at Tangier, rode into the center of the city, and received a public welcome from Abd-el-Melik, the sultan's representative. He then addressed the crowd assembled in the square as follows:

It is to the Sultan in his quality as an independent sovereign that I make my visit today. I hope that, under the sovereignty of the Sultan, a free Morocco will remain open to pacific competition of all nations without monopoly and without exclusion, on the footing of absolute equality. My visit to Tangier is intended to make known that I have decided to do everything in my power to safeguard effectively German interests in Morocco, since I consider the Sultan to be a free sovereign.[74]

Wilhelm reiterated this commitment in private discussions with Moroccan officials, before departing the country.[75] The following day, he met Admiral Prince Louis of Battenberg, the director of British naval intelligence and a nephew-in-law of Edward VII, at Gibraltar. He told Battenberg, "Germany, Great Britain and the United States must make common cause [against France] and [must] march shoulder to shoulder."[76]

When Battenberg inquired about the implications of Germany's Moroccan policy for relations with France, Wilhelm replied: "As to France, we know the road to Paris and will get there again if need be. They [the British] should remember that no fleet [could] defend Paris."[77] The German government made no effort to clarify the emperor's remarks.

One should note several underlying assumptions about German diplomacy and its implementation during this period. First, German officials were concerned with averting further erosion in Germany's prestige and possible encirclement in the core. They did not initiate the challenge to Delcassé's *pénétration pacifique* on behalf of German commercial interests in Morocco. On the contrary, German merchants and companies had shown themselves quite willing to cooperate with French colonial officials. Except for a few references in the exchange of cables between Bülow and Kühlmann, economic considerations, territorial ambitions in North Africa, and pressure from imperialist groups in German society appeared to have played no role in the private deliberations concerning Morocco.[78]

In public pronouncements and communications with foreign capitals, German leaders did, however, stress economic interests and their desire to uphold the "open door" in Morocco. For example, on 29 March, Bülow told the Reichstag that Germany had no aggressive intentions toward Morocco, but did intend to defend its economic interests there.[79] However, one might easily attribute these occasional pronouncements to an effort by German leaders to mask the true aims of their policy—the destruction of the entente.[80] German economic interests in Morocco were minor. German leaders did not seek to acquire territory in North Africa. As Holstein later wrote to Bülow, "You know better than anyone that we defended the Moroccan position not because we were out for acquisitions . . . but merely in order to uphold His Majesty's prestige."[81]

Second, Bülow and other officials assumed they could treat the dispute as a purely Franco-German matter.[82] Richtofen observed, "England is now out of it, for it no longer has any interests in how Germany deals with France over Morocco," following Germany's agreement with Britain over German economic interests in Egypt.[83] Both he and Bülow felt that by challenging France in Morocco, they could always use the pretext of upholding free trade, an argument likely to appeal to American and British leaders. Third, German strategy was incoherent and uncoordinated. Wilhelm, Bülow, Holstein, Richtofen, Mühlberg, and others adhered to a common level of expectation: the status quo before the entente. Beyond that general goal, however, German diplomacy evolved as the events developed. As we will see, throughout the crisis, German leaders frequently worked at cross-purposes.[84]

German Demands for a Great Power Conference (April–May 1905)

Wilhelm's Tangier speech and subsequent statements, along with the Reich Foreign Office's refusal to clarify the objectives of its policy, sparked a crisis with France. As noted above, Bülow and Holstein did not seek to launch a preventive war against France in spring 1905. Nonetheless, they realized Germany's assertive stand on Morocco might inadvertently lead to war. In April 1905, Bülow asked Schlieffen for his estimates on a Franco-German war and the possible intervention of Russia in such a conflict. The chief of the general staff reported that the likelihood of a Franco-German conflict drawing in Russia were low, at least for the time being. Russia, then embroiled in the Russo-Japanese War and revolution at home, could ill afford a war with Germany. The Russian garrison at Port Arthur fell to the Japanese Third Army in January and by the end of May, the Japanese Combined Fleet had sunk the Russian Baltic Fleet to the bottom of the Tsushima Strait. Schlieffen said that the Russian army units in the west were "incapable of standing up to another army, and are completely useless for an offensive. The East Asian war has shown that the Russian army was even less good than had generally be supposed, and as a result of the war it has become worse rather than better. It has lost all spirit, confidence and discipline."[85] He further suggested that Germany might exploit this favorable military situation to press its demands against France and weaken the entente.[86]

Holstein and Bülow concluded that the only way to avert eventual encirclement was to detach Britain from the entente. To do this, however, Germany needed to humiliate France before the other great powers. On 5 April, Holstein seized on a proposal from Kühlmann to convene a conference of the 1880 Madrid Treaty signatories to discuss France's violation of that pact. Holstein argued, "Contractual collectivity is a principle on which we can take a firm stand without ourselves appearing to harbor aggressive intentions. . . . If France refuses the conference, she puts herself in the wrong."[87]

Delcassé's Moroccan policy divided French public opinion and jeopardized support for Premier Maurice Rouvier's government in the National Assembly. Radolin reported that the Morocco controversy had created a breach within the Rouvier cabinet.[88] Bülow wrote to Wilhelm, "In order to strengthen the [domestic] opposition to Delcassé, I am suggesting the following points: (1) negation of territorial claims; (2) demand of equal commercial rights for all states to include not merely freedom of trade or even formal most-favored-nation treatment, but the open door in the fullest sense; (3) a hint—as this is our trump card—that all the European powers, with the United States, have again conferred on the affairs of Morocco and concluded treaties."[89] Wilhelm approved Bülow and Holstein's initiative: Germany would demand an international conference on the status of Morocco and use bilateral diplomatic channels to press for Delcassé's removal. Furthermore, the three agreed to use the hint of war as a means to pressure France into accepting Germany's demands. Accordingly, Radolin delivered a thinly veiled threat to Rouvier: "We sincerely wish for peace but we cannot wait any longer to settle our account, if necessary by force of arms."[90]

Bülow and Holstein expected the United States to support Germany. On 4 April, Bülow wrote to Wilhelm, "I may mention that the American minister, under direct instructions from President [Theodore] Roosevelt to keep in close touch with Your Majesty's representatives, when told of the sentiments regarding the 'open door,' exclaimed: 'That is just exactly what we also want.'"[91] Despite Bülow's optimistic estimates, Roosevelt's support for the open door in North Africa was quite limited, since Washington had few economic interests in the region. In late April, Roosevelt told Baron Hermann Speck von Sternburg, the German ambassador in Washington, that the United States would limit its involvement in the Moroccan dispute to mediating among France, Germany, and Britain.[92] Bülow, on the other hand, interpreted Sternberg's reports to mean that the Washington would unconditionally support a conference.[93]

Bülow, Holstein, and Richtofen further concluded that Britain would not come to France's assistance in the Moroccan dispute. Delcassé had bought off Britain, as he had done with Spain and Italy. The Balfour government, therefore, would have no further interests in the Moroccan situation. Bülow even argued that German policy, disguised as a defense of the open door principle, might even appeal many Britons.[94] However, based on conflicting information, Bülow and Holstein made overly optimistic estimates of British neutrality. In late April, Count Christian von Tattenbach, the German minister in Tangier, reported that his British counterpart, Sir Gerald Lowther, indicated that London would not intervene in the Moroccan dispute.[95] Senior British officials, however, began to express decidedly pro-French sentiments in both their public pronouncements and meetings with German diplomats. Chancellor of the Exchequer Austen Chamberlain denounced both Bülow's diplomacy and Lascelles for not adopting a stronger stance against it.[96] In early April, the Admiralty announced that the British and French fleets would exchange visits that summer. King Edward made a point of meeting Delcassé and French president Emilé Loubet on 6 April, while passing through Paris on his way to the south of France.[97] Lascelles expressed strong disapproval of both Germany's provocative strategy and the conference proposal in a meeting with Otto von Mühlberg, the under state secretary in the Reich Foreign Office.[98] Lansdowne delivered a similar message to Metternich on 19 April: "My impression is that the German government has really no cause for complaint either of us or the French in regard to the Morocco part of the agreement."[99]

The Campaign to Oust Delcassé (April–June 1905)

Wilhelm's remarks at Tangier and the subsequent refusal of the German government to clarify them, made an accurate assessment of German intentions quite difficult for the French government. On 19 April, Georges Bihourd, the French ambassador in Berlin, met with Mühlberg in effort to clarify the Franco-German misunderstanding over Morocco. Mühlberg replied by reiterating his government's demands for a conference of the Madrid treaty signatories.[100]

Meanwhile, Radolin reported widespread anxiety in the press and among French leaders following the Tangier landing. French officials feared the dispute might escalate into a Franco-German war.[101] The French Council of Ministers urged Delcassé to open direct negotiations with Germany. Instead of doing so, however, Delcassé stated he need only dissipate any misunderstandings which . . . may still exist" over French policy in North Africa.[102] Throughout April and May, he made several overtures to German diplomats about the desirability of a Franco-German settlement over access to Moroccan ports, while at the same time instructing French diplomats to continue negotiations with the sultan.[103]

Delcassé remained confident of British support. On 25 April, Sir Francis Bertie, the British ambassador in Paris, delivered an aide-memoire from Lansdowne that suggested Britain would offer diplomatic support.[104] In a letter to Maurice Paléologue, the French chargé d'affaires in Berlin, Delcassé observed, "Germany cannot want war. Her present attitude is no more than a bluff; she knows that she would have England against her. . . . Do you think that Kaiser Wilhelm can calmly envisage the prospect of seeing his battle fleet destroyed, his naval commerce ruined, and his ports bombarded by the English fleet?"[105] Delcassé's fellow ministers did not share his optimism. Rouvier strongly doubted whether Britain would come to France's assistance in the event of war. In a cabinet meeting, he excoriated his foreign minister for precipitating the Morocco crisis, declaring that "[Germany] is disturbed and humiliated by your encirclement of her. In our Morocco dispute she sees an excellent occasion to break the ring." He further criticized Delcassé for bringing Germany and France to the brink of war: "Are we in a condition to sustain a war against Germany? No, No! Even with the aid of the British fleet we should be in for a worse catastrophe than in 1870."[106] Radolin reported that Rouvier threatened to dismiss Delcassé if he failed to reach some accommodation with Germany. Delcassé offered his resignation on 22 April, but withdrew it the next day at Rouvier and Loubet's request. On 30 April, Radolin told Bülow that Rouvier had assumed personal responsibility for foreign policy and that Delcassé's "sole duty was to carry out the decisions of the Council of Ministers."[107] On returning from Paris in early May, Baron Hermann von Eckardstein, informed Bülow that Rouvier desired a general improvement in Franco-German relations and that he was willing to jettison Delcassé.[108]

On 1 May, Holstein sent a letter to Radolin, instructing him to suggest to Rouvier that Delcassé's dismissal was the one obstacle to a peaceful resolution of the Moroccan crisis. He further instructed the ambassador to suggest that Britain hoped to see a Franco-German conflict over Morocco, in order to have a free hand in the Persian Gulf or Ethiopia. He wrote, "This I think is the reason why England is driving the French to speed up their Moroccan action as much as possible. On the other hand, I definitely do not believe . . . that in the case of war the English government would come to the aid of France."[109] At the 6 June meeting of the French Council of Ministers, Delcassé defended his stance on Morocco and suggested that France seek an explicit alliance with Britain to hold Germany in check, while Rouvier argued that such steps would surely lead to war. No other official present supported Delcassé's position and he submitted his resignation that afternoon.[110]

In early 1905, Bülow, Holstein, and other officials pursued two strategies to avert what they perceived as Germany's impending encirclement. The first strategy called for mounting a diplomatic challenge to France's *pénétration pacifique* in Morocco, as a means to divide the entente. The second strategy, which officials adopted in late April, was an extension of the first. German leaders used the threat of war to coerce the French government into convening an international conference and ousting Delcassé as foreign minister.

Sending the emperor to Tangier and then refusing to clarify the scope of German interests was riskier than the options officials in Berlin did not consider: to do nothing or to initiate direct talks with France. First, the "big stick" strategy represented a dramatic reversal of Germany's previous diplomatic stance on North Africa, for the reasons noted above. Such a reversal risked creating uncertainty in other capitals about German motivations. The refusal to clarify the emperor's statements exacerbated that uncertainty. Second, the Tangier landing and the subsequent hints of war were a tortuous means to achieve the policy's stated objective: averting German encirclement. Bülow, Richtofen, Holstein, and others decided to initiate the Moroccan crisis without an indication that doing so would in fact force France to make concessions and divide the entente. On the other hand, in late March and early April, German officials calculated that their Moroccan challenge would likely not escalate into a direct military confrontation with France in the core.

Using the threat of war to force Delcassé's ouster was also a risky strategy. As the evidence above shows, German leaders feared encirclement and future power shifts, but they did not seek a preventive war with France in spring 1905. They certainly did not seek a military conflict with France that might lead Britain to intervene, as the near panic over the Dogger Bank incident a few months earlier indicates. Nonetheless, by hinting that Germany might resort to force and insisting that only Delcassé's removal could resolve the dispute, Wilhelm, Holstein, Bülow, Richtofen, and their surrogates ran the risk of provoking an unwanted military confrontation.

Offensive realism holds that opportunism and a favorable international environment prompted German officials to launch the Morocco crisis and seek Delcassé's ouster in spring 1905. Balance-of-risk theory holds that fear of loss in terms of relative power and international prestige drove German behavior. With respect to the Tangier landing and the campaign to oust Delcassé, the historical evidence is indeterminate. German leaders were preoccupied with averting losses to prestige and were willing to take risks; this much appears consistent with balance-of-risk theory. However, one cannot rule out the strong undercurrent of opportunism and perceptions of a favorable current balance-of-power in Bülow and Holstein's decision to send Wilhelm to Tangier and then to use the threat of war to remove Delcassé.

Since the conclusion of the Dual Entente in 1893, the French General Staff and the Supreme War Council counted on Russian intervention in the event of a German attack; officials in Berlin were quite aware of this. In spring 1905, however, Russia found itself facing defeat at the hands of Japan in East Asia and revolution at home. Bülow also realized that Germany could make France look like the aggressor in Morocco, thus giving the Russian government a pretext to claim that the mutual defense provisions of the Dual Entente did not apply to this dispute.[111] British diplomatic support for France, let alone military assistance in the event of Franco-German war, during this period was also in doubt. The German army enjoyed a dramatic numerical advantage: twenty-one French corps would face the equivalent of thirty-six German corps.[112]

Offensive realism posits a second calculation that may have driven the initiation of the crisis: the desirability of preventive war against France. Russia's preoccupation with the Russo-Japanese War and revolution at home, the absence of a firm Anglo-French alliance, Britain's relative weakness as a land power, and the French army's numerical disadvantage, gave Germany an opportunity to threaten war against France without it escalating into a dreaded two-front conflict. However, the evidence that Holstein and Bülow intended to provoke a war with France in 1905 is largely circumstantial and comes from the memoirs of Baron Oskar von der Lanken-Wakenitz, a junior diplomat in Paris, and Count Anton Monts, the German ambassador in Rome.[113] Holstein and Schlieffen did discuss French and Russian military preparedness in spring 1905. Schlieffen and General Karl von Einem, the Prussian minister of war, did ruminate about using the crisis as a pretext for preventive war against France and possibly Russia. In his memoirs, von Einem recalled that Bülow explicitly asked him if the German army was ready for war in spring 1905, to which the war minister responded in the affirmative: "You may always depend upon it, Herr Graf, and base your policy upon it entirely."[114] Nonetheless, Bülow and Holstein did not intend to provoke a war and the General Staff did not initiate preparations for immediate military action against Russia or France. Although Holstein and Schlieffen did maintain close ties, there was a remarkable lack of coordination between strategic planning and diplomacy throughout the Moroccan crisis.[115]

The Fall of Delcassé to Rouvier's Acceptance of the Conference (June–July 1905)

German leaders saw the resignation of Delcassé as a diplomatic triumph. By adopting an assertive stance on Morocco, Holstein and Bülow had engineered the removal of Germany's arch foe. Writing to his cousin on 16 June, Holstein observed, "Politically we have achieved much in the last six months. In the first place, Delcassé, our cleverest and most dangerous enemy, has fallen. Second, our friend Roosevelt is mediating between Russia and Japan with the secret support of Germany, whereas France and England have long been anxious to play the leading role in the conclusion of the peace."[116] However, Germany's diplomatic triumph would soon prove to be a Pyrrhic victory.

German diplomacy proceeded on two contradictory tracks. On the one hand, officials assumed the Morocco issue would remain a bilateral dispute. On the other hand, Bülow and Holstein made a peaceful resolution contingent on the French government's acceptance of an international conference, where German diplomats would condemn France for violating the Madrid treaty. This second track depended on the actions of the other great powers. By drawing third parties into what appeared to be a Franco-German colonial dispute, there was the possibility that other states might infer that territorial or economic gain drove German policy and support France. Holstein, Bülow, and Richtofen did not plan for this contingency.

In summer 1905, it became increasingly apparent that instead of dividing the entente, German belligerent diplomacy had the opposite effect. As the risk of war increased in late June and early July, the entente increasingly began to resemble a military alliance directed at Germany. The French army mobilized its reserves and preliminary conversations began between the French and British general staffs. German officials, however, continued to assume that France would be diplomatically isolated and that the other Madrid treaty signatories would support an international conference on Morocco.

Rouvier Offers a Bilateral Settlement (June 1905)

Rouvier hoped to secure an agreement with Berlin similar to the ententes Delcassé had negotiated with Italy, Spain, and Britain. In late April, he offered to drop the thirty-year limit on the "open door" embodied in the 8 April Anglo-French declaration. He further offered to seek a general settlement of the Moroccan question through an exchange of notes between France and the other Madrid Treaty signatories.[117] As sign of good faith, he directed Talliender to suspend efforts to impose reforms on the Moroccan government. Berlin's refusal to reach a bilateral settlement puzzled him. On 7 June, Rouvier told Hans von Flotow, the German chargé d'affaires in Paris, that the French government could not accept an international conference, which large segments of the French public and the National Assembly strongly opposed. He added that Britain, Spain, and Italy would also likely reject the conference proposal. Flotow replied that Berlin would not desert the sultan. Two days later, Rouvier offered, through an intermediary, to conclude a general agreement with Germany on Morocco, the Baghdad railway, and East Asia.[118]

In May and June, Bülow and Holstein could not understand why Rouvier had essentially adopted Delcassé's policies.[119] Holstein told Radolin, "We are not in a position to make concessions [to Rouvier] at once, overnight."[120] On 7 June, Bülow wrote to Tattenbach, "Delcassé's fall and his replacement by Rouvier ought to close the acute phase of the Morocco question, whether the conference takes place or not. . . . It will be your task to persuade the Sultan that he has acted rightly for his own interests in rejecting the French program and proposing a conference."[121] At the same time, Bülow privately admitted that Morocco occupied "an infinitely small place" in German foreign policy.[122] Rather, breaking the entente as a means to avert encirclement was the overriding objective of German leaders.

On 14 June, Holstein instructed Radolin, "You can tell Rouvier and his confidants that in all sincerity that we would very much like to get out of the impossible situation in which Delcassé has placed us and arrive at a better relationship with France, but Rouvier must show us a decent way out. We cannot violate the sultan, [and] partition [Morocco between France and Spain] against his will."[123] Radolin cautioned patience and argued that, in time, the French premier would have no option but compromise. He wrote to Holstein, "I do feel that when he [Rouvier] sees that he can do nothing else [than] to accept the conference and he will get no far-reaching concessions from us . . . he will finally yield to the inevitable and formally accept the conference as desired. . . . Here really nobody wants war and that is something one can count on."[124]

The War Scare (June–July 1905)

The Morocco crisis reached its peak in late June and early July. Radolin reported a hardening of the Rouvier cabinet's opposition to a conference and the growing speculation among French elites that the crisis would escalate to war.[125] German officials recognized the heightened risk of war, but nonetheless, generally persisted in their hard-line strategy. Bülow briefed Wilhelm about the deterioration of Franco-German relations and the increased risk of war on 22 June.[126] Holstein observed on 23 June that "it is definitely a great weakness of Rouvier's and shows a lack of logical reflection that he has not realized how, by adopting the Delcassé programme, he is helping Delcassé back to his feet, the man who is now probably his worst enemy."[127] Schlieffen informed Bülow that the French army had called up reservists and issued combat uniforms and four days' rations to the garrisons on the Franco-German border.[128]

On 8 July, Rouvier and Radolin reached an agreement: France would formally accept the sultan's invitation to the conference of Madrid treaty signatories. In exchange, however, Germany agreed to recognize France's "legitimate" interests in Morocco and pledged that the Anglo-French and Franco-Spanish ententes would remain unchanged. Furthermore, the German and French governments agreed to work out a conference agenda, which they would submit to the sultan for acceptance.[129] The fact that Germany and France still had to negotiate the agenda before the conference even convened guaranteed several more months of rancor. Bülow and Holstein's hard line tactics throughout the spring and summer succeeded in alienating Rouvier and others in the French cabinet. Paul Cambon, the French ambassador in London, told Lord Lansdowne, "After all that has happened M. Rouvier was more convinced than ever of the necessity of maintain a close understanding with this country [Britain]. It was, in his view, essential that the two governments treat one another with the fullest confidence, and that no further steps should be taken without previous discussions between us."[130]

Throughout June and July, British officials communicated their disapproval of German policy. On 7 June, Flotow wrote Bülow that the British had made several offers to support Rouvier, including an Anglo-French military alliance.[131] This prompted Holstein to arrange for the publication of a provocative article in the official German press. The article quoted an alleged remark by the emperor: "Germany can only conduct a war with England in France."[132] In a meeting with Metternich, Lansdowne denied that Britain had offered France an alliance, but also warned that in the event of a Franco-German war, he could not be certain of the extent to which British public opinion would demand that the government support France.[133] Two weeks later, Lascelles warned Metternich that "in the event of Franco-German war, . . . the prevailing attitude here is that England would be actively on the French side."[134]

On 22 July, Metternich wrote to Bülow, "There is no doubt at the moment that King Edward is strongly aroused against us and, unfortunately, against the person of the Emperor in particular. . . . In England the Morocco question has come to mean a fight for the friendship of France, and in order to keep this and also to prevent a predominant German hegemony over Europe they would venture on a war." Metternich added, "I must insist that neither King Edward, nor his government, nor even the British people, who are aroused against us, wish for a war with Germany. [Nonetheless,] there are causes [that] might lead to it. The Morocco question has brought us a step nearer to war with England."[135]

As with the earlier decisions to launch the Morocco crisis, offensive realism might explain Germany's continued belligerent diplomacy with reference to a favorable balance-of-power and international opportunity. The entente had not solidified into an explicit military alliance. The likelihood of Russian intervention in a Franco-German war remained low throughout the summer. In fact, the Russian navy suffered a humiliating defeat at Tsushima the week before Delcassé's resignation. Throughout the crisis, the Russian army remained incapable of undertaking offensive operations in the west. During the summer, Wilhelmstra;dse received no intelligence that contradicted Schlieffen's earlier assessment of Russian military collapse. Nonetheless, German leaders did not see 1905 as an opportune time to launch a preventive war against France. Although Germany enjoyed a favorable balance of power, at least in terms of land forces and industrial capacity, there is little evidence to suggest that German leaders were prepared to fight and win a war against France at that time. The level of international opportunity declined as Britain signaled its support for France throughout June and into July. The possibility of British intervention raised the costs and risks associated with Germany's hard-line diplomacy. Offensive realism would expect Wilhelm, Bülow, Holstein, Richtofen, and others to reevaluate their strategy.

Logrolling theory might attribute Germans' saber rattling and insistence on an international conference to the preferences of domestic interest groups. However, as with the earlier decision for the Tangier landing, there is little in the private deliberations of German leaders to support this prediction. Alternatively, German leaders fell victim to blowback, which in turn, prevented them from seeking a bilateral settlement with France. In Wilhelmine Germany, the imperialist coalition and government elites propagated certain strategic myths—the efficacy of "big stick" diplomacy, social Darwinism, "paper tiger" images of the enemy, bandwagoning, and domino theories—to rationalize expansionist policies to the public. Bülow, at least, recognized that the Moroccan gambit might push France and Britain together. However, even after Delcassé's fall, the chancellor and others could not accept French concessions because doing so would call into question existing strategic myths.[136]

The second logrolling theory prediction also has problems. Bülow and Holstein, as well as Wilhelm and other German leaders, made frequent references to bandwagoning and domino dynamics, the efficacy of "big stick" diplomatic tactics, and "paper tiger" images of the enemy in their public pronouncements from 1888 onward and throughout the 1905–06 Moroccan crisis. Logrolling theory runs into problems with its strong claim that such "myths of empire" are purely instrumental. One finds repeated references to such myths in German leaders' private correspondence and deliberations during the height of the crisis. If such beliefs were only strategic rationalizations designed for public consumptions, then why would senior officials make repeated references to them in private?[137]

Balance-of-risk theory suggests that loss aversion and consideration of sunk costs led German leaders to persist in a risky diplomatic strategy after Delcassé's ouster. Officials continued to use the threat of war to extract concessions from France, despite mounting evidence of Anglo-French solidarity and an increased likelihood of unintended war. Although Delcassé's resignation was a diplomatic triumph, it did not meet German leaders' level of expectation. There was still the possibility, however remote, that the entente might evolve into an alliance and that Germany would find itself encircled. Even as the anticipated costs of continuing the Moroccan challenge began to rise in June and July, Holstein, Bülow, and others persisted in a risk-acceptant strategy. As we will see in the next section, most senior German leaders would continue to pursue a belligerent diplomatic strategy throughout the late summer and autumn 1905, despite clear indications that Germany would find itself isolated.[138]

THE BJÖRKÖ TREATY TO THE ALGECIRAS CONFERENCE
(JULY 1905–APRIL 1906)

Had Bülow, Holstein, Richtofen, and others been satisfied with engi-
neering the resignation of Delcassé, the Moroccan crisis might have been
a diplomatic triumph for Germany. Instead, officials in Berlin continued
to call for a conference to humiliate the French government, even at the
risk of provoking an unintended war. Bülow and Holstein decided to
challenge French *pénétration pacifique* in Morocco on the assumption that
Germany would have the tacit support of Austria-Hungary, Spain, Italy,
and Britain. They also expected the United States to support Germany's
defense of the open door principle in North Africa. By mid-July 1905,
each of these expectations proved completely wrong.

While the entente became stronger in the face of the German challenge, the Triple Alliance remained unreliable. Anglo-German relations
had markedly deteriorated since April. Although Roosevelt supported
the open door principle, he and other American officials provided only
tepid support for the German conference proposal. Meanwhile, the pre-
conference negotiations produced further quarrels and ill will. Holstein
complained to Radolin on 20 July, "In verbal exchanges the French politicians show complete understanding for our ideas, but in written exchanges and also in many items appearing in the [official] press one or
other point of the Delcassé programme always reappears."[139] In late July,
while his government persisted in advocating a hard-line stance toward
France even at the risk of hostilities, Wilhelm made an unexpected bid to
break Germany's growing isolation.

The Björkö Treaty (Late July–September 1905)

Tsar Nicholas and Emperor Wilhelm were both on holiday in July
1905: the first in the Finnish Gulf and the second in the Baltic Sea. Without first consulting their respective governments, the two emperors
arranged an impromptu summit on board Wilhelm's yacht in the Bay of
Björkö. On 20 July, Wilhelm cabled Bülow from Björkö to say that he was
on the verge of concluding a Russo-German alliance. He further requested that the Foreign Office send to him "at once and directly the defensive alliance we proposed to the tsar last November 'before it was
mutilated by Count Lamsdorff.'"[140]

Bülow reasoned that Germany now had an opportunity to conclude a
mutual defense pact, before St. Petersburg and Tokyo signed a treaty formally ending the Russo-Japanese War. He feared that once the war

ended, Britain would again seek a rapprochement with Russia. Despite the disastrous conduct of the war, St. Petersburg would likely redirect its attention to Europe and the risks of Russian intervention in a potential Franco-German war would rise. The Rouvier government, therefore, would be less likely to compromise in the Moroccan conference prenegotiations. He told Holstein, "It would be useful if we could commit the tsar to such an extent that Witte and Count Lamsdorff would not be able to initiate a Russo-French-English Entente immediately after the conclusion of the peace. . . . [The] *Novosti* in St. Petersburg and . . . [Georges] Clemenceau in Paris [have recommended this], with the additional comment that this would solve the Morocco question which Delcassé allowed to become acute at the wrong moment."[141]

Holstein, on the other hand, had reservations about the Björkö talks. First, he doubted that the tsar would sign a defense pact that offered Russia few material advantages and that might injure Russo-French relations. A Russo-German alliance would violate the terms of the 1894 Dual Entente. Delcassé and now Rouvier had indicated that France preferred Britain to Germany as a potential third member of existing Russo-French alliance. Second, Holstein knew that even after the Dogger Bank incident, Witte and Lamsdorff strongly preferred a rapprochement with Britain. He speculated that a Russo-German alliance might strengthen the Russian position in upcoming peace negotiations with Japan. However, in order for this to happen, the treaty would have to be made public at the outset. While Holstein did not object to this, he did recommend that Wilhelm allow the tsar to take the initiative in the negotiations.[142] When Bülow incorporated Holstein's arguments against taking the initiative in a telegram to Wilhelm, Holstein dropped all opposition to the proposed alliance.[143]

Wilhelm largely ignored Holstein and Bülow's recommendations and resolved to conclude a Russo-German alliance at all costs. On 24 July, the two monarchs signed a draft treaty that obligated Germany and Russia to lend mutual assistance in the event of an attack by a third state. Without consulting Bülow or Holstein, however, Wilhelm substantially altered the draft from the previous winter, ostensibly to make it more favorable to Germany.[144] He included a provision in the Björkö treaty that would have limited the mutual defense provisions to Europe. To further avoid the possibility that Germany might become involved in the Russo-Japanese War, he arranged that the treaty not come into force until Russia made peace with Japan. Finally, he acquiesced to Nicholas's request for the inclusion of a clause that would have obligated Russia to secure French approval before the Russo-German alliance went into effect.[145]

The Björkö treaty provoked a row within the German leadership. Wilhelm clearly believed that it was in Germany's interests not to assist Russia in East Asia. Bülow, on the other hand, wanted at least the threat of a Russian attack on India, should Germany go to war with Britain.[146] The emperor's effort to be conciliatory directly contradicted Holstein's strategy of compelling the Rouvier government to recognize they could not act in Europe or the periphery without Germany's consent. Holstein complained on 31 July, "What will be the effect if, in the hope of improving French sentiment toward us, we show ourselves very conciliatory and abandon the point of view which His Majesty the Emperor said was his on 31 March? The public, both German and non-German, would regard this as a humiliation for the German emperor and the first great practical success of the Franco-English Entente Cordiale." Nevertheless, Holstein saw the proposed Russo-German alliance as a means to strengthen Germany's position in the Morocco crisis and possibly weaken the Russo-French alliance. The Russian government would pressure France to make concessions in order to avoid war.[147] To further complicate matters, in late July Bülow began to oscillate between Wilhelm's willingness to conciliate France in order to secure Russian ratification to the Björkö treaty and Holstein's advocacy of a continued hard-line stance against France. Like Holstein, Bülow wanted to use the Morocco dispute to win France's acceptance of the Björkö treaty; but like Wilhelm, Bülow also wanted to reduce the probability of war with France.

Count Witte first learned of the Björkö meeting in Paris on 23 July, while en route to peace talks with Roosevelt and the Japanese foreign minister Baron Komura Jutaro at Portsmouth, New Hampshire. In St. Petersburg, Lamsdorff, who was also unaware of substance of the Björkö meeting, assured the French ambassador of Russia's devotion to the Dual Alliance; the tsar did not inform his foreign minister about the Björkö treaty until 30 August.[148] Lamsdorff concluded that the treaty was detrimental to Russia's interests—both because of the terms of the Dual Entente and because of the Russian government's financial dependence on France. Throughout September and October, he and Witte urged Nicholas to abandon it.[149]

On 7 October, Nicholas sent a telegram to Wilhelm to informing him that efforts to bring France into the Björkö treaty had not been successful. Since the treaty conflicted with the Dual Alliance, the former must remain inoperative pending further negotiations with France. The following day, Witte delivered a similar message in letter to Prince Philipp zu Eulenburg-Hertefeld, former German ambassador in Vienna and trusted advisor to the emperor.[150] The tsar wrote to Wilhelm on 23 November to announce his intention to indefinitely postpone further consideration of the Björkö treaty, until his ministers consulted the French government.[151]

Renewed Franco-German Tension (October–November 1905)

Meanwhile, tensions between the German and French governments reignited after their respective negotiators reached agreement on the Moroccan conference agenda on 28 September. In a 3 October interview with the French newspaper, *Le Temps*, Bülow articulate his goals for the conference. "I think the conference, far from dividing [Germany and France], ought to contribute to a rapprochement between us." The chancellor went onto to say, "For that rapprochement, however, one condition is necessary: that French public opinion recognize that the policy of isolating Germany is an object of the past."[152] Other French newspapers did not respond favorably to Bülow's characterization of Rouvier's foreign policy. On 5 October, *Le Martin* published an account of the 6 June meeting of the Rouvier cabinet. According to the article, Delcassé presented his colleagues with a British guarantee to "mobilize her fleet, to seize the Kiel Canal, and to land 100,000 men in Schleswig-Holstein," in the event of a Franco-German war. Delcassé denied having made such a statement and the British Foreign Office denied having made such an offer.[153]

German leaders responded to the *Le Martin* article with an escalation of threatening rhetoric. Wilhelm threatened to recall Metternich from London for an "extended leave of absence."[154] Privately, Bülow may have doubted the accuracy of the article, particularly the claim that Balfour and Lansdowne made a military commitment to France in June. He nonetheless, exacerbated the tension by advising the Reich Foreign Office and the official press to treat the *Le Martin* revelations as true. He wrote, "It is important that the German public understand how grave the international situation is, how necessary it is to be armed, and how wretched, in view of the seriousness of the world situation, party conflicts and usual Philistine pettifogging appear."[155] Holstein complained, "I have the impression that the French have been treated with too much kindness by us from up on high."[156]

Rouvier responded by again offering a bilateral settlement before the conference convened at Algeciras, Spain, in January 1906. On 30 November, Kühlmann informed Holstein that two intermediaries approached him Paris with a secret proposal from Rouvier.[157] The French premier offered the following concessions: First, the open door would continue in Morocco in perpetuity. Second, German firms would participate in 45 percent of all government projects in Morocco. Third, France would both provide Germany with territorial compensation in the French Congo and terminate its right of preference to acquire the Belgian Congo. In exchange, Rouvier asked for recognition of the status quo in Morocco for three to four years, after which if conditions had not improved, Germany would accept French control of the police in the whole country.

Rouvier's secret proposal offered a high material payoff. It would uphold the open door principle and potentially benefit German firms in Morocco. It also offered German leaders gains equal to or greater than the concessions Italy, Spain, and Britain had earlier received from Delcassé. Although the offer initially appealed to Bülow and Holstein, they concluded they could not accept it. Instead, they appeared more concerned with averting a further erosion of Germany's prestige and reputation for resolve. "Our chief object must be to avoid isolation at the conference," Bülow wrote on 23 November. "If we have the majority or all other powers against us on a question upon which we have engaged ourselves, boldness and threats will be of no use since after all that has occurred, our situation would seem almost ludicrous."[158] On 1 December, Holstein informed Tattenbach and Radowitz that he feared Rouvier might discuss the secret agreement's content in a way that would embarrass the German government before the sultan and the other Madrid Treaty signatories. The German government never formally responded to the French premier's offer.[159]

Renewed British Support for France (November 1905–January 1906)

Holstein continued to believe that Britain would offer only limited support to France at the upcoming conference. On 5 December 1905, Balfour resigned as prime minister because of divisions within his ruling Conservative party over the abandonment of free trade. Holstein and Bülow welcomed the appointment of Liberal party leader Sir Henry Campbell-Bannerman as prime minister because they believe he would likely not give the French unconditional support at the conference, let alone pledge military assistance.[160] "The change of government in England is an unexpected stroke of luck for us which we should make use of," Holstein wrote on 23 December. However, he warned Bülow that, "If our relations with England do not improve during this period of grace, if in the meantime England's connection with the [Franco-Russian] Dual Alliance becomes even closer, then the German Reich faces a serious future. Three against one are heavy odds."[161]

After the Liberal victory in the January general elections, Bülow and Holstein become more optimistic about the Algeciras conference. Holstein even concluded that Germany's assertive policy toward France had contributed to the election outcome. He wrote to Radowitz and Tattenbach, "Our London embassy says that the devastating defeat of the Conservatives is in large measures due to the increases in taxes caused by the threat of war, and even that yellow journal the *Daily Mail* says that fear of war was one of the causes." He expected Rouvier's representatives to concede to German demands since "France can hardly hope for English military support for a war of aggression on account on Morocco."[162]

The Algeciras conference met from 16 January to 7 April 1906 with representatives of all the treaty signatories in attendance. As the conference opened, the German government was in turmoil. Lieutenant General Count Helmuth von Moltke (the younger) became chief of the general staff on 1 January, replacing the retiring Schlieffen. Richtofen suffered a fatal heart attack and died on 17 January. Wilhelm appointed Tschirschky as state secretary for the Reich Foreign Office on 22 January.[163]

Meanwhile, the Campbell-Bannerman government made increasingly clear that it would not reverse its predecessor's policy of supporting France. Sir Edward Grey, the new foreign secretary, feared the consequences of a German success in dividing the entente. Unlike Lansdowne, however, Grey was quite explicit in stating Britain's support for France and opposition to Germany in the Moroccan dispute.[164] On 3 January, he warned Metternich that "the British people would not stand [for] France being involved in a war with Germany on account of the Anglo-French agreement, and that if it happened, any British government, whether Conservative or Liberal, would be forced to help France."[165] He repeated this statement to Paul Cambon, the French ambassador in London.[166] Later that month, the British and French general staffs began high-level talks.[167]

On 31 January, Captain Count Friedrich von der Schulenburg, the German military attaché in London, reported: "If war breaks out between Germany and France, England will be on France's side, and hatred of Germany will once again flame up brightly, with the probable result that England will take part in war."[168] In February, Metternich told his superiors about a recent dinner party that his friend Sir Edgar Speyer had attended with members of Campbell-Bannerman's cabinet. The secretary of state for war, Richard Burton Haldane, said that the government fully intended to support the French at Algeciras and thought Rouvier's policies moderate. Baron Tweedsmouth, the first lord of the Admiralty, believed that Germany initiated the Moroccan dispute as a pretext to gain a Mediterranean port. Metternich further reported that First Sea Lord Fisher, who also attended that party, had no objections to a German Mediterranean port, adding, "If we really ever had a war with Germany, we should have something to bombard."[169]

In late January, German newspapers carried reports of troop redeployments in western France in preparation for a possible mobilization. Bülow asked Moltke for his estimates of about the likelihood of war. Moltke reported that the French army had indeed strengthened fortresses along the Franco-German border and redeployed troops from the interior. "In my opinion the French consider that to yield further now on the Morocco question would not benefit the dignity of their country, seeing that they have already given war and allowed M. Delcassé to fall," Moltke noted. He further observed, "They [the French] desire no war and are not themselves dreaming of attacking; but they wish to be armed against a German attack."[170] A month later, Moltke sent Bülow his estimates about Britain's response to a possible Franco-German war: "The change in the distribution of political power which a victorious Germany would occasion in Europe would be so great a national danger for England, that she would be forced to relinquish the neutrality 'which she desires, and which is the intention of the government.'"[171]

Meanwhile, the Algeciras conference remained deadlocked over a French proposal to grant the police mandate in Morocco to France and Spain. Despite growing indications of precautionary operations by the French army and British support for the French position, German officials continued to pursue a hard-line diplomatic strategy. On 12 February, Bülow, acting on Holstein's advice, sent a telegram to German diplomats in London, Washington, St. Petersburg, Vienna, and Rome saying that he saw no need to retreat in the Moroccan dispute. "The principle of sacrificing our interests simply because they stand in the way of another power might lead to such dangerous consequences that in comparison we regard the possibility of the failure of the conference as the lesser evil."[172]

As the conference continued, Wilhelm abandoned his earlier efforts to adopt a conciliatory strategy in favor of the risk-acceptant, hard-line strategy advocated by Holstein. When warned that Germany's refusal to agree to the police mandate might discredit Rouvier and lead to his replacement by Delcassé, Wilhelm replied: "It doesn't matter! That would make the situation all the clearer. It is better to have Delcassé conducting his own policy than to have Rouvier doing it for him! I am standing firmly by my position!"[173] Reports of Franco-Spanish agreement on the police mandate only made the emperor furious with Alfonso. He told Bülow, "I suggest Your Highness let Madrid know quite bluntly that if His Majesty [the King of Spain] does not inform me about the agreement with France over Morocco, and if Spain—by supporting France—helps to jettison the conference, then I will not pay a visit to Madrid this year!"[174]

Finally, Holstein concluded that France would eventually yield to German pressure. "The rapprochement between France and England began immediately after Fashoda when the French saw that they could accomplish nothing against England," he reasoned. "In the same way, the French will approach the idea of a rapprochement with Germany until they see that English friendship . . . is not enough to gain them the agreement of Germany for their seizure of Morocco."[175]

Isolation at the Algeciras Conference (March–April 1906)

In initiating a crisis and demanding a conference of Madrid treaty signatories, German officials assumed that their defense of the "open door" in Morocco would have the support of the United States, Russia, Austria-Hungary, Italy, and Spain. On 7 February 1906, Holstein even wrote to Radolin, "Things are going well for us at Algeciras in that a great many neutrals are coming over to our side . . . I have reason to believe that the French had meet all sorts of disappointments in the Morocco question, for instance in St. Petersburg."[176] These expectations proved completely inaccurate.

The Roosevelt administration began to indicate its displeasure with German diplomacy. Sternberg reported that Roosevelt and Secretary of State Elihu Root saw the resignation of Delcassé the previous June and Rouvier's acceptance of a conference as great concessions. In 7 March meeting with Sternberg, Root urged Berlin to accept the 19 February proposal for joint French and Spanish administration of the Moroccan police. Root added, "I feel that if this arrangement is made, Germany will have accomplished the declared object for her intervention in the affairs of Morocco and for the conference."[177] Holstein instructed Tattenbach and Radowitz to reject the proposal. Eleven days later, Sternburg reported that Root viewed Berlin's hard-line stance as "pettifogging and unworthy of a great nation, and that Germany had quite lost her original strong position at Algeciras and was on the point of losing the world's confidence."[178]

Russia firmly supported France throughout the Algeciras conference. In the closing months of 1905, both Witte and Nicholas had repeatedly urged the German government to adopt a more conciliatory attitude toward France. On 22 February, at the request of the French, Witte urged the German government to settle the Moroccan dispute quickly so that St. Petersburg could more quickly obtain a French loan to combat revolutionary forces.[179] The following day, Baron Wilhelm von Schön, Alvensleben's successor as ambassador to St. Petersburg, informed the Reich Foreign Office that Lamsdorff warned him that "the continued anarchy in Morocco might bring forth bellicose complications at any moment, in which case England would certainly enter on France's side while Russian would remain an inactive witness. . . . A European war would enkindle new revolutionary outbreaks which would also lead to difficult times for Germany." Schön replied that even though Berlin and

St. Petersburg might have to postpone further negotiations to add a third state to the Björkö treaty, the Russo-German accord would remain valid. Lamsdorff flatly stated that Russia would uphold the Dual Alliance and that if France and Germany went to war, the Björkö treaty would collapse.[180]

German expectations for Spanish, Italian, and Austrian support at the conference also proved illusory. As noted above, France and Spain reached an agreement over the police mandate in Morocco in January. Italy found itself in the untenable position of supporting the intransigent position of an ally or supporting the position of the state that could help its colonial ambitions in East Africa. Marquis Viscounti Venosta, the chief Italian delegate, observed that Italy could only hope to "emerge from the conference in the same international position which she had before she went into it."[181]

German leaders knew that Austrian support would be limited, since Vienna had only a marginal interest in Morocco. On 5 February, Count Karl von Wedel, the German ambassador in Vienna, reported that Count Agenor von Golochowski, the Austro-Hungarian foreign minister, offered to support Germany's position on police organization, coastal trade, and ports "through thick and thin."[182] A week later, Wedel warned Bülow that the Dual Monarchy would not risk a war for the sake of Morocco.[183] Toward the end of February, even the Austrians pressured the Germans to yield at Algeciras. The Austrian emperor Franz Joseph told Wedel that his diplomats in Algeciras reported that the British, Spanish, Russian, and possibly the American delegates would support the French position on control of the Moroccan police; the Italians would likely abstain.[184]

At a 12 March meeting, Bülow informed Tschirschky, Mühlberg, Holstein, and Otto Hammann, the foreign office's press chief, that Germany would have to make whatever concessions were necessary to settle the Moroccan crisis and prevent a failure of the Algeciras conference. "With the exception of Hammann," Holstein wrote, in describing the meeting, "we all opposed giving in and point out that if we stood firm we could be certain of mediation by the neutrals because they—Russia, Italy, and even Liberal England—badly needed not only peace but complete calm." The chancellor, however, gave the order to retreat and dictated the main points of a compromise agreement to Mühlberg.[185] The following day, Bülow informed Holstein, in strict confidence, that Wilhelm had forced the decision on him. Bülow claimed the emperor was both worried about German military preparedness and intimidated by news that King Edward had invited Delcassé to lunch. However, since Wilhelm sent a defiant telegram to Roosevelt on 12 March, the day of his alleged surrender in the Morocco dispute, it is more likely that Bülow tried to salvage his own prestige by blaming the emperor.[186]

The final working session of the Algeciras conference met on 31 March and the signing of the final communiqué took place on 7 April. The communiqué recognized the continued sovereignty of Morocco and reaffirmed the open door principle. Spain and France received joint responsibility for training and supervising a Moroccan police force. France, Britain, Germany, and Spain received oversight of a new Moroccan state bank, although the French retained a privileged position on its board of directors. In essence, France emerged from the conference with political and economic predominance in Morocco, while Germany suffered a major diplomatic defeat. The crisis brought Britain and France closer. The conversations between the British and French military staffs that began in January 1906 continued in earnest. Italy moved further away from the Triple Alliance, while Russia renewed its commitment to the Franco-Russian alliance. Only Austria-Hungary remained a steadfast supporter of Germany.

In the months before and during the Algeciras conference, German officials considered at least three options to avert encirclement. The first option entailed a continuation of the strategy of threat and bluster that had begun with the emperor's March 1905 Tangier landing and resulted in Delcassé's ouster in June. The second option involved a renewed effort to secure a Russo-German alliance. The final option involved efforts to conciliate France and seek a bilateral settlement to the Moroccan issue. The analyses of these options is further complicated by the fact that different German officials simultaneously pursued them at different times between June 1905 and April 1906.

A continuation crisis was the most risk acceptant of the three options. By continuing to demand an international conference and sending subtle signals about the use of force, German leaders risked pushing Paris and London closer together. In the summer and autumn of 1905, the Balfour government reiterated its diplomatic support for France in the Morocco dispute. Balfour's resignation, followed by the January 1906 general election, brought to power a Liberal government more willing to coordinate strategy with France. Rouvier made several offers to reach a bilateral settlement with Germany. When German leaders repeatedly rejected his overtures, particularly after October 1905, the French premier became less accommodating.

As in the previous periods, a continuation of this hard-line strategy also risked military confrontation with France and possibility Britain. Furthermore, in late February, the Russian foreign minister warned Berlin that Russia would support France in the event of war. As noted

above, despite its tremendous advantages in economic capacity, population, and the number of troops under arms, Germany was not prepared
for war in 1905–early 1906. Aside from one or two brief remarks from
Schlieffen, senior German officials showed little or no enthusiasm for
war with France. Yet, throughout the period, Holstein and Richtofen
consistently favored this first option, whereas Bülow sporadically favored the first and third options.

The second option, a renewed effort to secure an alliance with Russia,
was less risk acceptant than the first. It also offered a higher expected
payoff. The Björkö treaty would have secured Germany's eastern frontier
and arguably returned Berlin to the position it enjoyed before the 1890
nonrenewal of the Reinsurance Treaty—alliance ties with two other continental powers. Moreover, the proposed alliance offered the chance
(however slight) to improve its relations with France. By linking a Russo-
German alliance to the existing Dual Entente, German leaders would
have secured their western and eastern frontiers in the event of war and
left Britain a minority of one in a great power system of five. Wilhelm favored this option, and even went so far as to sign a draft treaty with
Nicholas at Björkö. Bülow also supported this option, but with the proviso that the alliance not be limited to Europe. Despite his initial misgiv-
ings, Holstein came to support the Russo-German alliance option.

Nonetheless, the Russo-German alliance option also entailed its share
of risks for Germany. First, the pursuit of this option would likely produce a further deterioration in Anglo-German relations. Britain had an
alliance with Japan, Russia's adversary in an ongoing war. Recall that
during the October 1904 Dogger Banks affair, British cabinet ministers
already believed that Germany was Russia's de facto ally. Second, there
was also the strong possibility, which the tsar hinted at the Björkö meeting and Witte and Lamsdorff said explicitly in the autumn, that the Russian government would insist that France have a veto over the proposed
Russo-German alliance. Russia and France, after all, had been allies for
ten years at the time Wilhelm first approached the tsar about an alliance.
Moreover, the Russian government heavily depended in French loans to
finance its war against Japan.

The third option involved seeking a bilateral settlement with Rouvier
and deescalation of the crisis. This is the most risk averse of the three options. In the short term, this option reduced the likelihood of an unintended war with France or Britain. In the longer term, by deescalating
the crisis, even at this late date, German officials might have eventually
paved the way for a rapprochement with France. This, in turn, was a
necessary condition for the conclusion of a Russo-German alliance, as
the final demise of the Björkö treaty in November illustrated. Sequen-
tially pursuing options three (deescalation and eventual rapprochement

with Paris) and then two (alliance talks with Russia) had at least the possibility of averting encirclement. Holstein remained adamantly opposed to a crisis deescalation and bilateral settlement, as did Richtofen. From July 1905 onward, Wilhelm appears to have supported this third option, primarily as a means to also pursue the second option. However, the emperor's interventions in the diplomatic arena were sporadic and generally of a short duration. Arguably, Bülow toyed with the third option as indicated in his 3 October interview with *Le Temps*. After that ensuing uproar in the French press, Bülow largely abandoned this option in favor of the first.

Over all, German leaders' behavior supports two key balance-of-risk hypotheses. First, the longer senior officials adhere to a common expectation level, the less likely they will be to revise that expectation level downward in response to adverse policy outcomes. Recall that Bülow, Holstein, Richtofen, and others adopted the aspiration of breaking the entente as a means to avoid encirclement in April 1904. Throughout the period of study, officials were consistently below their expectation level.

In the months after Delcassé's resignation, most senior officials rejected less ambitious and presumably more achievable expectation levels. They were highly resistant to information indicating the mounting costs of pursuing their initial aspiration—warnings from the Balfour and Campbell-Bannerman governments; the tsar's request for a deescalation of the crisis as a precondition for ratification of the Björkö treaty; news of French military preparations; and the Rouvier government's repeated offers of a bilateral settlement.

Second, balance-of-risk theory holds that senior officials will likely continue or even escalate their commitment to risk acceptant but failing intervention in the strategies in the periphery. Throughout the July 1905–March 1906 period, most German leaders persisted in the most risk-acceptant of the three available options—a continuation of the crisis—despite the marginal costs and diminishing returns associated with that strategy. Bülow only ordered the retreat on 12 March. Offensive realism, on the other hand, would expect leaders to have at least reevaluated the continued efficacy of continuing the crisis, given information about Anglo-French solidarity and French military preparations.

This chapter has shown that fear of relative power and prestige loss generally drove German foreign policy in the 1904–06 period. Wilhelm II, Bülow, Holstein, and other officials feared that the entente might evolve into an anti-German alliance. Since France already had a bilateral alliance with Russia, the formation of an Anglo-French alliance would leave Germany encircled. Initially German leaders sought to forestall encirclement by seeking a rapprochement with Britain and then a defensive alliance with Russia. When both efforts failed, officials initiated a

TABLE 3.1 *Summary of German leaders' risk behavior in the 1905–1906 Morocco crisis*

Observation period	Expectation level (against which leaders evaluated outcomes)	Perceived position relative to the expectation level	Overall risk propensity of leaders	Policy options selected
Anglo-French entente and Germany's initial response I (Apr.–Jun. 1904)	Division of the Anglo-French entente	Loss	Mixture of risk acceptance and risk aversion	Rapprochement with Britain, including all outstanding disputes
Anglo-French entente and Germany's initial response II (Jun.–Dec. 1904)	Division of the Anglo-French entente	Loss	Risk acceptance	Efforts to secure a Russo-German alliance; manipulation of Russo-Japanese tension
The planning and execution of the German emperor's Tangiers landing (Feb.–March 1905)	Division of the Anglo-French entente	Loss	Risk acceptance	Crisis initiation (threat of force to oust Delcassé)
The reaction to the Tangiers landing to the fall of Delcassé (April–May 1905)	Division of the Anglo-French entente	Loss	Risk acceptance	Continued pursuit of belligerent diplomacy
The summer war scare and Rouvier's agreement to a great power conference (Jun.–July 1905)	Division of the Anglo-French entente	Loss	Risk acceptance	Continued pursuit of belligerent diplomacy
Negotiations over conference agenda and war scare (Aug.–Nov. 1905)	Division of the Anglo-French entente	Loss	Risk acceptance	Continued pursuit of belligerent diplomacy
Anglo-French military talks and German isolation at the Algeciras conference (Dec. 1905–March 1906)	Division of the Anglo-French entente	Loss	Risk acceptance	Continued pursuit of belligerent diplomacy

major crisis over the distribution of colonies in the periphery in a desperate gamble to divide the entente.

The decision making process that led to the initiation of the first Moroccan crisis in the third observation period appears equally consistent with offensive realism and balance-of-risk theory. While German leaders feared encirclement and the accompanying damage to Germany's relative power and prestige, it is equally plausible that these officials perceived a currently favorable balance-of-power. By sending Wilhelm II to Tangier in a contrived show of resolve and then demanding the ouster of Delcassé, officials in Berlin exploited an opportunity created by the French foreign minister's violation of the 1880 Madrid Treaty.

Nonetheless, the record of deliberations and the direction of risk behavior by German leaders from Delcassé's resignation on 6 June 1905 until Bülow's order to compromise at the Algeciras conference on 12 March 1906 support several balance-of-risk theory hypotheses. A return to status quo ante, namely the alignment of European powers before the entente, was the expectation level of senior German officials. Bülow, Holstein, and others pursued a risk-acceptant strategy of crisis escalation and threat to divide the entente. Officials knew this strategy might escalate to war with Britain and/or France over the fate of a country where Germany had few economic interests. More surprisingly, officials knew that Germany was not prepared for war. Bülow, Holstein, Richtofen, and others persisted and even escalated their commitment to strategy, even as British leaders voiced increased diplomatic (and possibly military) support for France and Wilhelm's renewed efforts to seek a Russo-German alliance at Björkö foundered. As Table 3.1 shows, the direction of risk-taking behavior by the German leadership is generally consistent with balance-of-risk theory in the seven observation periods.

As noted in chapter 1, the 1905–06 Morocco crisis constitutes a "most likely" case for the logrolling theory of imperialism and a "least likely" case for balance-of-risk theory. Since Wilhelmine Germany is the textbook example of a highly cartelized regime, one might expect a logrolled imperialist coalition of *Junkers*, colonial officials, arms makers, and army officers to have pushed Bülow, Holstein, and others to resist French *pénétration pacifique* in Morocco. As the documentary evidence cited above demonstrates, the preferences of domestic interests groups played almost no role in the decision of German leaders to initiate, escalate, and ultimately end the first Morocco crisis. Thus, by accounting for most of German behavior in the first Moroccan crisis, balance-of-risk theory passes a rigorous test.

[4]

Japan and the 1940–41 War Decisions

From 1931 to 1937 Japan pursued a measured expansionist policy in Manchuria and northern China, with the stated goal of eventually becoming economically self-sufficient and thus less vulnerable vis-à-vis the West and the Soviet Union. In July 1937, a minor clash between Japanese and Chinese troops near Beijing escalated into a full-scale war between Japan and the Kuomintang (KMT) government of Chiang Kai-shek. Despite initial estimates of an easy victory, the Imperial Japanese Army soon found itself in a quagmire. The war imposed tremendous strains on Japan's economy and increased its dependence on the United States, Great Britain, and the Netherlands for oil, steel, tin, rubber, and other raw materials.

Since the United States supported Chiang, the Sino-Japanese war cast a shadow over Tokyo's relations with Washington. From 1938 onward, the Roosevelt administration sought to end the war by gradually imposing economic sanctions. By the summer of 1940, Japanese leaders had essentially two options: They could extricate the army from the war and adopt moderate imperial goals. Alternatively, they could pursue a southward advance into French Indochina and the Dutch East Indies, in an effort to acquire the oil and raw materials necessary to continue the war in China. Although Japan had the military capabilities to execute this southward advance, doing so risked a direct confrontation with the United States.

During the 1940–41 period Japanese elites not only devoted additional resources to a failing war in China, but undertook high-risk strategies in a number of other areas as well. Chief among these were the decisions to: (1) expand the Japanese empire into Southeast Asia and thereby both gain access to oil and raw materials from the Dutch East Indies, (2) use diplomatic and later military means to stop the flow of arms to the KMT through French Indochina, (3) conclude a military alliance with Germany and Italy, and ultimately (4) wage war on the United States—knowing that that Japan could not win a prolonged war and that any war had a high probability of lasting several years.

Why did Japanese leaders continue to pour blood and treasure into a vastly expensive and arguably self-defeating war in China? What caused the cabinets of Prince Konoe Fumimaro and General Tōjō Hideki and the military leadership to pursue strategies that alienated America, Britain, and the Netherlands—Japan's main suppliers of the oil, raw materials, and military equipment required to win the war in China? Ultimately, what drove these officials to launch a war against an adversary of vastly superior economic, industrial and war-making capabilities?

ARGUMENTS ADVANCED, ANSWERS OFFERED

I argue that an aversion to perceived losses of relative power and international status caused Japanese leaders to pursue a series of highly risk-acceptant diplomatic and military strategies in 1940 and 1941, culminating in the decision for war against the United States. Victory against the KMT and the consolidation of Japanese rule in northern and central China was an integral component of the expectation or goal from which Japanese leaders evaluated outcomes. That expectation level was the creation of a New Order in East Asia—a political, economic, and military bloc consisting of the Japanese home islands, Manchuria, northern and central China, and the existing Japanese colonies of Korea, Formosa (Taiwan), and southern Sakhalin. The creation of this sphere would give Japan unlimited access to raw materials, oil, and export markets. This, in turn, would decrease the country's vulnerability by making the Japanese empire economically self-sufficient.

The following analysis of Japan's 1940–41 war decisions provides strong support for several balance-of-risk theory hypotheses. Japanese leaders' perception of relative power trends influenced the choice of an expectation level. They anticipated that future wars would be prolonged attritional struggles and that Japan would experience a deterioration of relative power vis-à-vis the Soviet Union and the West over time. They adopted a more favorable international environment as the expectation level for their grand strategy: the creation of a continental empire that would make Japan economically self-sufficient, and therefore, secure.

In the summer of 1940, Japanese leaders perceived themselves facing losses relative to their expectation level. As balance-of-risk theory would expect, these officials found it extremely difficult, if not impossible, to abandon an expectation level that by all objective measures was no longer achievable. Rather than revise their aspirations downward in response to increasingly desperate military and economic situations, senior officials not only escalated their commitment to a failing war in China, but undertook additional high-risk strategies vis-à-vis other great powers in the region to perpetuate that conflict.

Offensive realism, on the other hand, attributes Japan's 1940–41 war decisions to rising power and international opportunity. This theory does explain the decision to initiate the Sino-Japanese war in July 1937: Japan enjoyed a favorable balance-of-power vis-à-vis China and the chances of third-party intervention were minimal. It also explains the Konoe government's efforts to seek a neutrality pact with the Soviet Union, after the Soviet Far Eastern Army's decisive victory over the Kwantung Army at Nomonhan in August 1939.[1] Offensive realism, however, has problems explaining other aspects of the 1940–41 war decisions. In particular, the theory does not explain why senior officials not only devoted additional resources to a failing war, but undertook risky diplomatic and military strategies vis-à-vis other great powers in the absence of a favorable distribution of capabilities. John Mearsheimer contends that, although Japanese leaders may have miscalculated in the summer of 1937, "Japan's failure to win a victory in China was hardly a catastrophic failure. Nor was the Sino-Japanese War the catalyst that put the United States on a collision course with Japan."[2] Contrary to this sanguine assessment, however, the war wrecked havoc on the Japanese economy, dramatically increased the country's dependence on American raw materials and armaments, and set the stage for a confrontation between Tokyo and Washington in the summer of 1941.

Mearsheimer writes, "The [defensive realist] indictment against Japan for overexpansion boils down to its decision to start a war with the United States, which had roughly eight times as much potential power as Japan in 1941 and went on to inflict a devastating defeat on the Japanese aggressors."[3] Instead, offensive realism portrays Japan's war decisions as a calculated response to an increasingly desperate situation. As the deadline for a negotiated settlement with Washington approached, Japanese leaders chose war, instead of running the risk of "gradual exhaustion."[4] However, the decision for war can only make sense from an offensive realist perspective under three conditions. First, war was a viable option if the service chiefs and the Tōjō government concluded that a preventive attack would likely force an American withdrawal from the western Pacific. Second, if these leaders concluded that any conflict with the United States would be short, then war was a viable option. Finally, if officials concluded that once war began they could negotiate a ceasefire or an armistice with Washington on favorable terms—namely, one that allowed Japan to retain its conquests in Manchuria, northern and coastal China—then the initiation of hostilities was a viable option. As the documentary evidence below shows, Japan's civilian and military leaders did not reach these conclusions. Offensive realism does not provide a convincing explanation for why Japanese leaders not only persisted in a ruinous war in China, but also initiated a war with the United States knowing their country had little, if any, chance of winning and also knowing that any conflict would last several years and likely result in the destruction of the Japanese empire.

Logrolling theory classifies Japan in the late 1930s and early 1940s as a highly cartelized regime. Overexpansion was an outgrowth of the country's route to modernity. The theory holds that competition for scarce resources and budget-share led the imperial army and navy to each base their force requirements on particularly ambitious missions. In order to secure its material needs, however, each service needed the tacit approval of the other. In order to rationalize their preferred policies, the military services employed a repertoire of strategic myths: paper tiger images of the Soviet Union and the United States, bandwagon theories, the turbulent frontier illusion in northern China, window logic, and the like. This produced a logrolling dynamic in which the Japanese military establishment pursued a series of overly ambitious policies that neither the army nor the navy independently desired. Civilian politicians, such as Konoe, and bureaucrats played a peripheral role in Japan's imperialist coalition in the 1930s; they simply acquiesced to the military's expansionist plans for fear of retribution. Self-defeating expansion was due to the logrolling between army and navy elites and to the blowback from their strategic myths. Jack Snyder writes, "Japanese overexpansion, rationalized by the usual repertoire of imperial myths, is best explained as a consequence of Japan's path to modernity, which gave the military a dominant role among Japanese interest groups and truncated the development of democratic forces that might have kept militarism in check."[5]

In 1940–41, Japanese military leaders realized that the pursuit of the southward advance would increase the likelihood of war with the United States. Logrolling theory, however, cannot explain why either military service would ultimately prefer embarking on a self-destructive war to sacrificing some of its institutional resources and influence. It cannot explain the various instances in the late 1930s and early 1940s where the two services checked each other's expansionist tendencies.[6] Finally, as I discuss below, logrolling theory underestimates the central role that civilian politicians, such as Konoe and his foreign minister Matsouka Yōsuke, played in initiating the second Sino-Japanese war in summer 1937 and later embarking on a series of expansionist policies in Southeast Asia that brought Japan into conflict with the United States.

Before turning to the historical evidence, I will briefly discuss another *Innenpolitik* theory. At first glance, the dominance of the Japanese military, particularly the army, would appear to explain the country's slide toward war with China and ultimately with the United States. After a brief period of party government in the reign of Emperor Taishō (1912–26), Japan's limited democracy collapsed and a highly divided army became the dominant political force. The ultranationalist *Kōdō*, or "imperial way" faction, led by generals Araki Sadao and Mazaki Jinzaburō, sought the end of parliamentary government, the "restoration" of actual political power to the emperor, and immediate preparations for war against the Soviet Union. The *Tōsei*, or "control" faction, whose leaders included generals Tōjō, Sugiyama Gen, Nagata Tetsusan, Umezu Yoshijirō, and Ishiwara Kanji, favored expansion in Manchuria and central China, centralized planning, and the comprehensive mobilization of the Japanese economy over several years for eventual war with the Soviets.[7] A series of assassinations and abortive coups, all linked to this interarmy rivalry, intimidated politicians and rendered the Imperial Diet (parliament) irrelevant. Chief among these were the fatal shooting of Prime Minister Hamaguchi Yūkō on 14 November 1930 by an opponent of the 1929 London Naval Treaty; the assassination of Prime Minister Inukai Tsuoyoshi by *Kōdō* members on 15 May 1932; and the abortive 26 February 1936 rebellion, where fourteen thousand soldiers from the *Kōdō* seized control of central Tokyo for several hours and assassinated several high-ranking officials.[8] Fear of civil war or a coup ultimately drove the Konoe and Tōjō cabinets to expand into Southeast Asia, conclude an alliance with Germany and Italy, and finally launch a preventive war against the United States.[9]

While the military was extremely powerful force in early Shōwa Japan (1931–45), the contention that fear of a civil war, military coup, or assassination drove officials' decisions in 1940–41 does not stand up to empirical scrutiny. The 26 February 1936 rebellion nearly toppled the government because the plotters had the active support of senior army officers and ties to several members of the imperial family, most notably Prince Chichibu, the eldest brother of Emperor Shōwa (Hirohito).[10] After the rebellion's failure, the army arrested and tried the plotters, resulting in the execution of seventeen and the life imprisonment of five others. It also transferred or retired five generals associated with the *Kōdō*, including Araki. Political assassinations ceased after 1936. There is little evidence to suggest the senior or mid-level army officers would have supported such a coup in 1940–41, particularly since the *Tōsei* members held the top posts in the War Ministry and the Army General Staff, as well as the major field commands.[11]

The chapter consists of four sections. The first section briefly discusses the origins of "total war" planning in the interwar Japanese military, the Kwantung Army's invasion of Manchuria in 1931, and the outbreak of the second Sino-Japanese war in July 1937. The second section begins with an examination of how civilian and military leaders came to adopt the creation of the New Order in East Asia as the expectation level for Japanese grand strategy in 1937–38. It then examines the strategies undertaken by the second Konoe government and the service chiefs to perpetuate war in China from June to December 1940. An examination of officials' decisions from January 1940 to June 1941 follows in the third section. The fourth section examines the collapse of Konoe's third cabinet, the Tōjō cabinet and the service chiefs' efforts to negotiate with the Roosevelt administration, and the final decision for war in the autumn of 1941.

BACKGROUND: JAPAN'S QUEST FOR SECURITY THROUGH AUTARKY (1931–37)

The notion that Japan could best provide for its long-term security through empire and autarky had its origins in the lessons military planners drew from Germany's defeat in the First World War. Since future wars would likely be attritional conflicts, a state's ability to win would largely depend on its ability to mobilize economic resources. The short-term military balance-of-forces would be a less important determinant of victory that the ability of the belligerents to support several years of intense warfare. This would require the complete mobilization of national economies for warfare and dramatic increases in the extractive capacity of government vis-à-vis society.

States that were not self-reliant in raw materials, especially oil, iron ore, rubber, tin, and foodstuffs, were acutely vulnerable to economic blockade. Victory would no longer depend on Japan's ability to mobilize troops or to construct battleships and artillery pieces. Instead, victory would depend on secure access to the materials required by vital war industries. Japan's home islands and its existing colonies lacked the natural resources required to fight a prolonged modern war. Expansion into resource-rich regions, such as Manchuria, followed by several years of intense industrial development in peacetime seemed the most reasonable means to attain economic self-sufficiency and enhance Japan's strategic position in East Asia.[12] In the mid-1920s, a clique of "total war" army officers, many of whom had studied in Germany, began to lobby for territorial expansion abroad and coordinated industrial planning at home to attain economic self-sufficiency and thus security.[13] Paradoxically, despite widespread expectations that future wars would resemble

the World War I, both the Japanese Imperial Army and the Japanese Imperial Navy adopted offensive military doctrines and largely ignored defensive missions. The army focused on offensive operations against Soviet forces in Manchuria and northern China, while the navy failed to
prepare for the defense of Japan's commercial sea-lanes, despite the devastating effect of German U-boat attacks on Allied shipping in 1916–18.

The Mukden Incident and the North China Autonomy Movement (1931–37)

On 18 September 1931, a contingent of soldiers from the Kwantung
Army blew up a section of the South Manchuria Railroad at Liutiaokou,
near the city of Mukden (Shen-yang), and then blamed the explosion on
Chinese subversives.[14] Then Lieutenant Colonel Ishiwara Kanji and then
Colonel Itagaki Seishirō, both officers on the Kwantung Army's general
staff, orchestrated the incident without the prior knowledge or approval
of their superiors. The Japanese prime minister at the time, Viscount
Saito Makoto, and his cabinet, had little choice but to sanction the *fait accompli*.[15] The Kwantung Army proceeded to create a puppet state in
Manchuria (Manchukuo), with the deposed Qing emperor of China,
Hsuan-tung (Henry Pu Yi) installed as provisional chief of state (from 9
March) and later as emperor under the reign name Kang-Te (from 20 January 1934). In reality, the Kwantung Army ruled Manchukuo and controlled all aspects of its economic development. Direct control of
Manchuria would both protect the army's future source of raw materials
and facilitate offensive military operations against the Soviet Union.

Kwantung Army officers saw Manchukuo as the Japanese empire's
lifeline on the continent, but it could only supply part of the army's raw
materials requirements.[16] To deal with this situation, they began to look
toward the northern provinces of China—Hopei, Chahar, and Shantung—which had large reserves of iron, coal, cotton, wood, and salt. In
1933, the Kwantung Army, again acting without authorization from superiors in Tokyo, repeatedly engaged KMT forces in Hopei province.
Over the next two years, the Kwantung Army extracted economic and
political concessions from Chiang, while actively subverting his authority in northern China.[17]

The China Quagmire (July 1937–onward)

On 7 July 1937, Japanese troops stationed at Feng-Tai, southwest of
Beijing, exchanged fire with troops from the Chinese Twenty-Ninth
Army while conducting night exercises near the Lugou Qiao, or Marco
Polo Bridge, in Beijing.[18] After the initial confrontation, the local Japan-
ese and Chinese commanders sought a negotiated settlement. Japan's

prime minister, Prince Konoe Fumimaro, informed the emperor that while the army would send reinforcements to the continent, the government would try to confine the conflict to the area between Beijing and Tientsin.[19] General Sugiyama Gen, then the minister of war, and Field Marshal Prince Kan'in Kotohito, the chief of the Army General Staff, confirmed this policy in an audience with the emperor on 14 July.[20]

Unlike the 1931 Mukden incident and the Kwantung Army's subsequent incursions into northern China, the decision to escalate the Marco Polo Bridge incident into a full-scale war originated at the highest levels of the Japanese government and military. Sugiyama estimated that three months, three divisions, and ¥100 million would be sufficient to clear the Beijing-Tientsin area, rout the KMT armies, and force Chiang to sue for peace. In early August, the Army General Staff recommended the mobilization of fifteen divisions and a supplemental allocation of ¥2.5 to ¥3 billion for munitions. The War Ministry's Military Affairs Bureau reported that the current budget could only sustain three divisions in northern China.[21] An extraordinary Diet session approved a ¥2 billion supplemental defense appropriation (three-quarters of it for the army) in early September. Combined with supplemental appropriations earlier in the year, Japan spent more than ¥2.5 billion on military operations in China, even though the entire Japanese budget for fiscal year 1937–38 had initially been only ¥2.77 billion. The following year, defense spending increased to ¥4.86 billion, out of ¥8.36 billion in total government expenditures.[22] On 17 November, the emperor approved the creation of an Imperial General Headquarters (IGHQ) to coordinate the expanding military operations in China.[23] A week later, Konoe convened the first liaison conference between the cabinet and IGHQ in an effort to better coordinate Japan's diplomatic and military strategy in China.[24]

By December 1937, the Imperial Japanese Army had deployed 16 divisions and 700,000 troops—approximately the number of troops in the standing army—to China and Manchuria. Furthermore, war left other Japanese strategic interests exposed. The Kwantung Army had 5 infantry divisions, 250 aircraft, and 150 tanks, with a total strength of 200,000 troops. The Intelligence Bureau of the Army General Staff estimated that the Soviet Far Eastern Army had 20 rifle divisions, 3 cavalry divisions, 1,500 tanks, 1,560 aircraft, and approximately 370,000 troops in Siberia.[25] Colonel Inada Masazumi, the chief of war plans in the Operations Bureau, later admitted, "The Kwantung Army was confronting the Russians with a bluff, in a sense."[26] Between 1937 and 1939, the number of active-duty Soviet divisions rose from 24 to 34, and the number of active-duty army personnel swelled from 950,000 to 1.6 million.[27]

The undeclared Sino-Japanese war, which the army and the Konoe government called the "China incident" (or *Shina jihen*), developed into an economically ruinous conflict for Japan. Defense spending rose from 6 percent of net domestic product in 1936 to 19.3 percent of net domestic product in 1939.[28] The economy reached full capacity in 1937 and the dramatic increase in defense spending created inflationary pressures. Between 1937 and 1941, total new government bond issues reached ¥29.9 billion, with an annual average of ¥5.9 billion. This represented a radical departure from the annual average of ¥700 million in the 1932–36 period.[29] To meet the army's demand, the government imposed draconian reductions on raw materials allocations to the civilian section. In 1938 alone, the civilian sector's allotment of steel fell from 5 million to 3.5 million tons. The imported fuel quota fell from ¥556 million to ¥510 million. Factories had to reduce their fuel consumption by 37 percent and their shipping by 10 to 15 percent.[30]

At the same time, the war dramatically increased Japan's economic dependence on the West, particularly the United States. Military and civilian officials hoped to extract raw materials from China. The fighting, however, ravaged the Chinese economy, destroyed one-fourth of the country's cultivated land, and made industrial development virtually impossible. At the same time, Japan's imports of oil, scrap, iron, rubber and other materials needed to sustain the war effort increased until they comprised more than 40 percent of total imports from the United States. During 1938 alone, Japan imported 4 million kiloliters of crude oil from American sources.[31]

From the start, Japan's undeclared war caused a deterioration in its relations with the West.[32] In 1936, Britain had an estimated $1.08 billion invested in China—almost 57 percent of all foreign direct investment in the country—and the United States followed with $220 million.[33] The United States, on whom Japan depended for 70 percent of its oil supply, openly supported Chiang. In addition, the Nanjing massacre and the sinking of the U.S.S. *Panay* on the Yangtze River in December 1937 exacerbated anti-Japanese sentiment in Congress and the press.[34] The Roosevelt administration protested Japan's expansionist policies by gradually imposing economic sanctions. This began with a ban on the sale of aircraft to Japan in mid-1938. On 16 July 1939, Secretary of State Cordell Hull informed the Japanese government that Washington would abrogate the 1911 U.S.-Japan Commerce and Navigation Treaty in six months.[35]

THE TRIPARTITE PACT TO THE OCCUPATION OF NORTHERN INDOCHINA (JUNE–NOVEMBER 1940)

By June 1940, Japan faced a curious strategic and economic condition. While the army remained mired in China, Japan's pursuit of autarky through expansion alienated the West.[36] The war effort continued to wreck havoc on the Japanese economy. At the same time, the army and navy's demand for raw materials, particularly oil and petroleum products, increased dramatically. In short, to secure victory in China, and thus become economically independent and secure vis-à-vis the West, the Japanese armed forces needed oil, steel, and other raw materials from the United States. The Roosevelt administration, however, demanded a cessation to the Sino-Japanese war and a return to the status quo before the Marco Polo Bridge incident. Despite these mounting costs, Japanese leaders not only continued to pour additional blood and treasure into the conquest of China, but undertook risky strategies in other areas as well. From summer 1940 to late spring 1941, the Japanese government and IGHQ authorized the occupation of northern French Indochina, used the threat of force to extract additional oil, rubber and mineral shipments from the Dutch East Indies, signed a defensive alliance with Germany and Italy, and concluded a five-year neutrality pact with the Soviet Union.

Offensive realism would predict an escalation of the China incident and the pursuit of other risky diplomatic and military strategies only if Japanese cabinet ministers and the IGHQ perceived an increase in Japan's relative power. The theory would further predict that Japanese leaders would seize various opportunities created by German military victories in Western Europe to expand the Japanese empire into Southeast Asia. Logrolling theory would predict a continuation of the China incident if resource competition and logrolling dynamics between the army and the navy became particularly intense. Evidence that senior officials were cognizant of these institutional pressures and acted accordingly would tend to support logrolling theory.

Balance-of-risk theory predicts that Japanese officials would persist in the China incident, despite the mounting costs and diminishing returns. Victory in this conflict and the consolidation of Japanese control in northern and central China were integral parts of the expectation level from which the second Konoe government and the IGHQ evaluated options. This was the goal of creating the New Order in East Asia.[37] Expectations of adverse power shifts vis-à-vis the Soviet Union and the West led the first Konoe government and IGHQ to adopt this expectation level as the baseline for Japanese grand strategy in 1937–38. On 3 November 1938, Konoe declared, on behalf of the cabinet, that Japan would not oppose China's participation in the establishment of a New Order in East Asia, if the Chinese government were reconstituted. Specifically, Japan sought the establishment of a new government in central and northern China under the titular leadership of Wang Ching-wei (Wang Jingwei), the sometime president of the Executive Yuan (the equivalent of prime

minister) and one of Chiang's rivals for the KMT leadership. The proposed new northern Chinese regime, which would exclude any representatives of Chiang's government and the Chinese Communists, would
work with Japanese officials to suppress anti-Japanese sentiment among
the populace.[38]

The creation of a continental empire would give Japan access to the
raw materials needed to fight a prolonged modern war. Manchukuo and
northern China would form a closed trading bloc where the Japanese
military and private firms would take the lead in developing heavy industry and exploiting the region's raw materials. Autarky would make
Japan less vulnerable to economic pressure from the West and provide
the resources necessary to fight a major war in the future. As noted earlier, Japanese military planners saw war with the Soviet Union, the
United States, and possibly Britain as highly likely in the next several
years.[39] In addition, the presence of pro-Japanese regimes in Manchuria
and northern China and the forward deployment of the army would reduce the potential Soviet threat to the Japanese home islands.

By the summer of 1940, however, the pursuit of autarky through empire became an end unto itself. Senior officials began to equate Japan's
very survival with the creation of a New Order in East Asia, which
would bring the resource-rich regions of Manchuria and northern and
central China under Japanese rule. As balance-of-risk theory would expect, in 1940–41 the members of the second Konoe government and the
service chiefs had tremendous difficulty in abandoning hopes to create
the New Order, the stated aspiration of Japanese grand strategy since
November 1938.

Principles for Coping with the Changing World Situation

Konoe became prime minister for the second time on 22 July 1940.
The first liaison conference on 27 July approved a document entitled, the
"Outline of the Principles for Coping with the Changing World Situation." The document reaffirmed the New Order in East Asia, including
victory in China, as the aspiration for Japan's grand strategy. The key operational provisions were as follows: (1) Japan would seek a defensive alliance with Germany and Italy, (2) seek a nonaggression pact with the
Soviet Union, (3) adopt a firm posture toward the United States, (4) pressure French Indochina to discontinue aid to Chiang and allow Japanese
troops passage through the colony, and (5) pressure the Dutch East Indies to increase exports of oil, rubber, tin, and other raw materials to
Japan.[40]

This document resulted from extensive negotiations between representatives of the army and naval sections of the IGHQ in the summer of 1940. Despite this collaboration, the two services had fundamental differences over the military consequences of a southern advance and the efficacy of a formal Japanese-German alliance. The army's draft war plan assumed the navy could defeat the remnants of the Royal Dutch Navy defending the Malay Barrier.[41] It further assumed that Japan deal separately with the United States and Britain.[42] Prince Kan'in and War Minister Tōjō estimated that Germany would invade Britain before the end of the year.[43] This would force the United States to withdraw from the Pacific to concentrate its fleet in the North Atlantic, allowing Japan to move into Southeast Asia unopposed. General Sawada Shigeru, vice chief of the Army General Staff, reported to the emperor on 29 July that the army's proposed war plans depended entirely on a continuation of German victories in Western Europe.[44]

The Naval General Staff's estimates contrasted sharply with those of the army. In May 1940, the Naval War College staged maneuvers to see if amphibious units from the Fourth Fleet could occupy the oil fields of Borneo and other "resource zones" under Dutch control. These maneuvers demonstrated that "the strategy of attacking only the Dutch East Indies while taking every precaution to avoid hostilities with the United States, resulted ultimately in war with the United States, Britain and the Netherlands, developing into an attack on Malaya and protracted war with the U.S. navy, whose base was in Hawaii."[45] The official report on the maneuvers concluded:

1. If American exports of petroleum are totally banned, it will be impossible to continue the [projected] war unless within four months were are able to secure oil in the Dutch East Indies and acquire the capacity to transport it to Japan.

2. Even then, Japan would be able to continue the war for a year at most. *Should the war continue beyond one year, our chances of winning would be nil.*[46]

Vice Admiral Yoshida Zengo, the minister of the navy, and Admiral of the Fleet Prince Fushimi Hiroyasu, the chief of the Naval General Staff, concluded that war against Britain and the United States would be ill advised under these circumstances.[47] Yoshida told the liaison conference: "The Japanese navy can continue the fight against the United States for one year—is this not a very unreliable navy?"[48] At the 10 August imperial conference, Prince Fushimi told the assembled cabinet ministers, military officers, and the emperor that Japan could not win a prolonged naval war against the United States.[49]

The "Southern Problem"—Dutch East Indies and
Indochina (July–September 1940)

Japan's total oil imports had averaged 5,370,00 tons annually from 1937 to 1940. Since the outbreak of the China incident, Japan's dependence on oil and petroleum from the United States increased dramatically. In 1935, Japan received 67 percent (2.3 million kiloliters) of its total oil supply from U.S. sources. By 1939, that figure had increased to 90 percent (4.4 million kiloliters).

Officials in Tokyo recognized the possibility that the Roosevelt administration would place a total embargo on oil shipments to Japan at some point in the future. Hoshino Naoki, chief of the cabinet's Planning Board, told his colleagues that "since it is impossible to meet army, navy, government and civilian needs from production within the yen bloc and by drawing our stockpiles, it will ultimately be necessary to work out a way of obtaining oil from northern Sakhalin, the Netherlands East Indies and other places."[50] In August 1940, the Navy Ministry's Munitions Bureau estimated that, should the United States impose an embargo, stocks of aviation fuel would last only one year from the outbreak of any war. Supplies of nickel, cooper, zinc, aluminum, and crude rubber would last a year and half. Another report to the navy minister, this time from Commander Toyoda Soemu, the chief of ship procurement, read: "Such a situation would finish us. . . . The navy could barely fight for one year."[51]

Planning for the so-called southward advance—as Japanese military and planning board officials termed the expansion into Southeast Asia—actually began before the second Konoe government took office. Since the outbreak of European war, the Japanese government had negotiated with colonial officials in the Dutch East Indies to purchase fixed amounts of oil, tin, rubber, industrial shale, and other commodities. From 1937 to 1940, Japan imported 5.37 million tons of oil annually, of which 650,000 tons of oil came from the East Indies.[52] The army and naval staffs concluded that their respective services needed at least 3.5 million tons of oil annually.

The German conquest of France and the Low Countries in May 1940 prompted both the American and British governments to warn Japan against undertaking any provocative actions against the European colonies in Southeast Asia.[53] Later that month, President Franklin D. Roosevelt ordered the continued stationing of the Pacific Fleet in Hawaii to deter any Japanese military operations against the Dutch East Indies. Joseph Grew, the American ambassador in Tokyo, warned the Japanese

Foreign Ministry that the United States would not compromise with aggressors or their allies.[54]

On 25 July, three days after the second Konoe cabinet took office, the Roosevelt administration prohibited the export of oil and scrap iron to Japan, without prior government approval. The following day, the administration imposed restrictions on the export of aviation gasoline, aeronautical lubricants, tetraethyl lead, and other petroleum products to Japan. Roosevelt signed an executive order on 31 July that banned the export of aviation fuel to countries outside the Western Hemisphere.[55] Despite these sanctions and various diplomatic warnings, the liaison conference concluded that Japan had no alternative to securing oil from the Dutch East Indies.[56] Senior officials resolved to use diplomacy (backed by the hint of force) to accomplish this end. They further agreed to use force against the Dutch East Indies only if the negotiations broke down.[57]

At the same time, the IGHQ and cabinet realized that military operations against the colony might destroy the very oil wells and refineries that Japan needed. Furthermore, some officials, particularly Yoshida and Prince Fushimi, feared that any military action in the region would likely result in a total oil embargo by the United States and Great Britain, and possibly war.[58] At the 19 September imperial conference (convened to approve the proposed alliance with Germany and Italy), the prince asked Hoshino and Foreign Minister Matsouka Yōsuke: "Are we to understand that we have no guarantee on the acquisition of oil? I would also like to add that we cannot rely too much on oil supplies from the Soviet Union, and therefore, the only way is to obtain it from the Dutch East Indies." War Minister Tōjō Hideki replied, "The army pays as much attention to oil as does the navy. The question of oil can be equated with the question of the Dutch East Indies. . . . We have already decided that for the time being we will try to secure essential resources from the region through diplomatic means, but we will resort to force if necessary."[59]

In mid August, the planning board completed a policy outline on economic relations with the Dutch East Indies. The outline called for granting substantial concessions to Japanese private and government-owned corporations in the oilfields, rubber plantations, and mineral mines in the islands.[60] On 12 September, Konoe sent Kobayashi Ichizo, the minister of commerce and industry, to negotiate the concessions with Dutch officials. Hubertus Van Mook, the director of economic affairs in Batavia, rejected the proposal for further concessions. This forced Kobayashi to negotiate purchases. Mukai Tadaharu, the chief executive of Mitsui Trading and a member of the Kobayashi mission, presented Batavia with a

request for 3.15 million long tons of aviation-grade crude oil and dis-
tilled products. The Dutch responded that this request would require additional production or the cancellation of existing contracts. Furthermore, Western oil companies (most notably Standard Oil and Royal
Dutch Shell) were reluctant to sell any grade of crude, preferring instead
to use their oil refineries in the colonies and deal in distillates.

On 8 October, Dutch officials offered and Mukai and Kobayashi accepted the sale of less than 1.5 million tons of crude and distillates.
Moreover, the Dutch limited the terms of the contract to six months, effective 1 November 1940, and refused to sell high-grade petroleum to
Japan (in keeping with an understanding with Britain and the United
States). The Dutch East Indies oil contract represented less than half of
the 5.37 million tons Japan imported annually in 1937–40; for the remainder of its oil requirements, Japan remained dependent on the
United States.[61]

The KMT supply lines in northern French Indochina constituted the
second part of Japan's "southern problem" in the summer of 1940.[62] "The
Principles to Cope with the Changing World Situation" and related documents called for using diplomacy, backed by the threat of force, to secure the acceptance of the Vichy government and the French colonial
government in Hanoi for the stationing of Japanese troops in French Indochina. The deployment of troops in the colony would allow the army
to send reinforcements to the Chinese theater of operations from the
south and stop the flow of arms and materials to the KMT.

On 1 August, Matsouka sent an aide-memoire to the Vichy French
government demanding the right to transport Japanese troops through
Indochina, construct and operate military air bases, and station Japanese
troops to guard military installations.[63] Japanese troops crossed into
northern Indochina on 22 September and the U.S. State Department formally denounced the occupation the following day.[64]

The Tripartite Pact (August–September 1940)

The liaison conference hoped to resolve the "southern problem," and
thus the China incident, without provoking a military confrontation
with the United States. A military alliance with Nazi Germany and Italy
would be a means to that end. Two assumptions guided the Japanese
leadership's decision to seek this alliance. First, proponents of an alliance
assumed that Germany would either reach a negotiated settlement ending the European war or invade Britain within the next few months. The
second assumption concerned the Roosevelt administration's possible
response to an explicit German-Japanese alignment. A mutual defense
pact with Nazi Germany, the most powerful of the great powers in 1940,

would deter the United States from interfering with Japan's efforts to obtain raw materials from Southeast Asia and settle the China incident.[65]

The Tripartite Pact was an outgrowth of the 1936 Anti-Comintern Pact. In 1938, the German foreign minister Joachim von Ribbentrop began talks with Major General Oshima Hiroshi, the Japanese ambassador to Berlin, toward strengthening the Anti-Comintern Pact. However, the conclusion of the 25 August 1939 German-Soviet Nonaggression Pact and the Anglo-French declaration of war following the German invasion of Poland, forced Prime Minister Baron Hiranuma Kiichirō to terminate these talks. The German ambassador to Tokyo, Eugene Ott, continued to make overtures to the governments of General Abe Nobuyuki and Admiral Yonai Mitsumasa in 1939–40.[66] In summer 1940, the Konoe government undertook steps to finalize an alliance despite clear indications that this move would likely exacerbate relations with Washington. Matsouka first raised the topic with Ott in early August. At the same time, he instructed Kurusu Saburō, Oshima's successor, to raise the topic with Richard von Weizaecker, the state secretary in the Reich Foreign Office. After two months of secret negotiations, Ribbentrop, Kurusu, and Count Galeazzo Ciano, the Italian foreign minister, signed an alliance treaty in Berlin.

Under the terms of the Tripartite Pact, Japan agreed to recognize German and Italian leadership in establishing a "new order" in Europe. In exchange Germany and Italy recognized Japanese leadership in establishment of a New Order in East Asia, including Japan's right to: (1) settle the China incident and consolidate its control in northern and central China, (2) stop the flow of arms to the KMT via French Indochina, and (3) obtain oil and raw materials from the Dutch East Indies. The treaty further stipulated that "these countries shall pledge themselves to take every political, economic, and military measure to assist each other when any one of the signatories is attacked by a country not participating in the European war or in the China incident."[67]

On 26 September Konoe told the investigation committee of the Privy Council that "not only Germany and Italy but Japan also hopes to avoid conflict with the United States. . . . The original aim of this [Tripartite] treaty is the maintaining [sic] of peace, but we must be prepared for any eventualities."[68] Prince Kan'in and Tōjō expressed support for the alliance, along with an improvement in relations with the Soviet Union.[69] Foreign Minister Matsouka argued:

America's attitude toward Japan has deteriorated to such a degree that it will not [improve] merely by our assuming a pleasing attitude. Only a firm attitude on our part can prevent war with the United States. . . . If we do not conclude an alliance [with Germany

and Italy] and if, as a result, the worst happens and we become involved in a war with the United States, our national economy will
suffer. In order to avoid these difficulties, it would not be totally
impossible to ally with Britain and the United States as well as Germany and Italy. However, to do so we should have to settle the
China incident as the United States tells us, give up our hope for a
New Order in East Asia, and obey Anglo-American dictates for at
least half a century to come. . . . *In short an alliance with the United
States is unthinkable. The only way left is to ally with Germany and
Italy.*[70]

Prince Fushimi and other navy officials worried about how the proposed alliance would affect Japan's ability to obtain raw materials from
the West.[71] During the 19 September imperial conference the prince observed, "As a result of this alliance our trade with Great Britain and the
United States will undergo a change; and that if worst comes to worst, it
will be increasingly difficult to import vital materials. . . . What are the
prospects for maintaining our national strength in view of the present
situation, which finds our national resources depleted because of the
China incident?"[72] Hoshino tried to reassure the prince: "I do not think
other countries will place an embargo upon Japan at the same time the
United States does. . . . Even if the United States further intensifies its
economic pressure on Japan in the future, the most effective means have
already been exhausted." Matsouka suggested that Japan might use the
Tripartite Pact as a means to seek a rapprochement with the Soviet
Union, which in turn, might allow Japan to obtain a considerable
amount of oil from Soviet sources.[73]

Prince Fushimi also feared that the United States would soon enter
the European war. If this happened, the Tripartite Pact would obligate
Japan to enter the conflict on the side of Germany and Italy. A few days
earlier, the prince told his liaison conference colleagues that "war with
the United States must be avoided. The chances of victory cannot be estimated."[74] Vice Admiral Kondō Nubtake, the navy vice chief of staff,
added, "We cannot expect a victory such as we achieved in the Russo-
Japanese War. Even if we win, considerable losses can certainly be expected."[75] At the 19 September imperial conference, Fushimi observed:
"Even if Japan should be compelled to participate in the European war
because the United States participates in it, it is essential for us to chose
independently our own time for beginning hostilities." Matsouka
replied, "It is clear that Japan is obligated automatically to enter the war.
However, the determination of whether or not the United States has participated in the war will be made by consultation among the three countries [Germany, Italy, and Japan]."[76]

Navy Minister Yoshida supported closer diplomatic ties with Germany based on the 1936 Anti-Comintern Pact, but feared that an overt German-Japanese military alliance would needlessly provoke the United States and Britain. His strongly opposed the alliance until his forced resignation on 3 September.[77] Vice Admiral Oikawa Koshiro, Yoshida's successor, equivocated on both the likely effects of the Tripartite Pact and the navy's ability to fight the United States, if necessary. On 26 September, Oikawa told the Privy Council that "today our fleets are completely equipped and in no way inferior to those of the United States." "But," he added, "If the war is protracted, we would have to make more complete preparations, as the United States would certainly augment its naval armaments." When Baron Hara Yoshimichi, the president of the Privy Council, raised questions about the risks of such an alliance, Oikawa replied, "There is a chance we shall pick Germany's chestnuts out of the fire. [Nonetheless,] the United States will hesitate to wage war. I think it is probably safe."[78]

The elite deliberations from this period support the balance-of-risk hypothesis: senior officials will likely continue and escalate their commitment to risk-acceptant but failing intervention strategies in the periphery. Throughout these months, the Konoe cabinet and the IGHQ continued a risk-acceptant strategy on the continent. Initially the China incident offered the prospect of unlimited access to northern China's raw materials—thus enabling Japan to achieve security through autarky. By July 1940, the army's hope of a decisive victory had long since vanished. The war resulted in greater dependence on the United States for oil and other materials, diverted troops from other areas, and wreaked havoc on Japan's economy. The Roosevelt administration abrogated the 1911 commerce treaty and placed restrictions on the export of scrap metal, steel, nickel and other materials.[79] These considerations did not prompt Japanese leaders to reevaluate the feasibility of their objectives in China. Instead, they continued to insist on the defeat of the KMT, the control of central and northern China, and international recognition of Manchukuo.

By 1940, a continuation of the Sino-Japanese war was a particularly risk-acceptant option for Japan. Over the long run, the war risked a depletion of the military's stockpiles and a complete cutoff of American imports, which the Japanese military would need to win the war. Access to resources in Southeast Asia would then become critical to fueling the Japanese war machine. Using force or coercive diplomacy to extract resources and cut off the KMT supply routes, however, ran the risk that the Roosevelt administration would retaliate by imposing additional export restrictions. This would almost certainly worsen Japan's economic predicament in the short-run. There was no guarantee that raw materials from Indochina and the East Indies could equal, let alone surpass, the amounts previously obtained from the United States.

Arguably, two options that never received serious consideration in 1940—direct negotiations with Chiang or the unilateral withdrawal of Japanese forces from China proper—might have been less risky. Either option, over the long run, would have reduced the army's consumption of oil, steel, and other raw materials required to fight the war. This, in turn, would have made Japan less vulnerable to American pressure, since its demand for war materials would decrease. Second, a cessation of the China incident would have eliminated the necessity of a south-ward advance. This, in turn, would have prevented the diversion of scarce military and economic resources to Southeast Asia.

Efforts to secure oil from the Dutch East Indies through diplomatic in-timidation constituted a moderately risk-acceptant policy. Yoshida, Kondo, and Prince Fushimi argued that a military southern advance would bring Japan into conflict with both Great Britain and the United States. Furthermore, the navy's estimates indicated that, given available resources, Japan could not win a prolonged war with the United States. Although Japanese forces could easily defeat the remnants of the Dutch navy, decision makers rejected using military force for fear of destroying the oil wells and refineries. Furthermore, officials believed that a direct attack risked drawing the United States and Britain, both of which sup-ported the Dutch government-in-exile, into the dispute. However, by pressuring Dutch officials to increase the flow of oil and other raw mate-rials for the China war effort, decision makers risked further alienating the United States, Japan's current principal oil supplier.

The occupation of northern French Indochina constituted a risk-ac-ceptant strategy. Western supply routes through the territory provided up to 80 percent of the supplies for Chiang's army. The German conquest of France in May 1940 gave Japanese decision makers an opportunity to solve this problem. Again, the main risks in this strategy revolved around Washington's assessments of Japanese intentions and the likely U.S. response. From a tactical standpoint, sending Japanese troops to cut off KMT supply routes made a great deal of sense. However, from a po-litical standpoint, this action provided Roosevelt, Hull, and administra-tion officials with further proof of Japan's expansionist intentions.[80] The occupation of northern Indochina, therefore, offered the possibility of damaging the Chinese war effort but ran a high risk of tightening the economic noose around Japan.

Finally, the liaison conference's decision to conclude the Tripartite Pact constituted a risk-acceptant strategy in several respects. First, the pact's effectiveness as a deterrent depended on continued German victo-ries in Europe. Second, Matsouka, Konoe and others assumed that the leaders in Washington would recognize the pact as a purely "defensive" arrangement. However, by aligning with Europe's revisionist states, Japanese leaders appeared to be capitalizing on the defeat of France and the Netherlands. Third, the alliance's effectiveness as a deterrent rested on the assumption that the Roosevelt administration would be more responsive to implied threats than explicit promises.

Logrolling theory attributes the Konoe cabinet and IGHQ's decisions during this period to intense competition and bargaining between the two military services. The army refused to disengage from China for fear that it would lose budget share and raw materials allocations to the navy. Indeed, the army leadership advocated the conclusion of the Tripartite Pact primarily as a means to deter the United States and the Soviet Union, and thus enable Japan to achieve its aims in China. The navy went along with the southward advance and the Tripartite Pact rather than lose resources to the army.[81] On closer examination, however, logrolling theory does not fully explain these decisions.

First, while there had been widespread support within the Army General Staff and the War Ministry for an alliance with Germany since 1937, the two officials instrumental in concluding the Tripartite Pact were civilians. Konoe, a former president of the House of Peers (the upper house of the Imperial Diet), had no military experience, although he enjoyed good relations with the army, civilian politicians, and the throne. In fact, Konoe resigned the premiership on 3 January 1939 over the protraction of the China incident and disputes with the army and division within the cabinet over strengthening the existing Anti-Comintern Pact.[82] Before becoming foreign minister, Matsouka had been vice president and later president of the South Manchurian Railway Company. One might ask why the Abe cabinet (30 August 1939 to 14 January 1940), in which active duty officers held the premiership, the war, navy, and foreign affairs portfolios, had not signed the alliance. This suggests that external forces, instead of interservice logrolling, was the crucial factor in determining the timing of the renewed alliance initiative.[83]

Second, it is not quite accurate to say that naval leaders completely dropped their opposition to the Tripartite Pact in the late summer and early autumn of 1940. Admittedly, the revised version of the alliance treaty that Kurusu, Ribbentrop, and Ciano signed on 20 September provided Japan greater leeway in deciding whether to enter the world war than the original version.[84] Nonetheless, Navy Minister Yoshida opposed the alliance until his ouster on 3 September. Prince Fushimi repeatedly voiced concerns about the strategic implications of the alliance until the treaty's final ratification by the Privy Council. Navy Minister Oikawa gave very qualified estimates in response to questions about the pact's likely implications for U.S.-Japan relations.

Third, the logrolling hypothesis does not explain why the navy leadership would prefer the Tripartite Pact and increased diplomatic pressure on French Indochina and the Dutch East Indies, knowing that such policies would likely further alienate and possibly risk war with the United States in the near future. Specifically, narrow material interests do not seem to account for the circular reasoning evident and predisposition toward risky strategies present in the liaison conference deliberations and the planning documents of the two general staffs: Japan would be vulnerable to blockade and strangulation by the West and the Soviet Union in the next war. Such a war was inevitable in the next ten to twenty years. Japan could become secure through the pursuit of autarky and empire in Manchuria and China. The pursuit of this strategy increased Japan's short-term dependence on the U.S., Britain, and the Netherlands for the materials required to conquer China. Pursuit of the southward advance and the Tripartite Pact, however, would raise the probability of conflict with the United States in the short-run, and thus harm the material interests of both services.

As noted above, offensive realism would only expect the second Konoe cabinet and IGHQ to pursue risk-acceptant strategies—the continuation of the China incident, the Tripartite Pact, the stationing of troops in northern French Indochina, or the use of diplomatic pressure to increase shipments from the Dutch East Indies—if these officials perceived both a favorable distribution of power and international opportunity. The record of the summer and autumn 1940 liaison and imperial conferences, however, reveals that senior officials were quite aware of Japan's precarious international position and the risks associated with these options.

Without a secure and reliable source of oil, Japan could not win the war against the KMT and consolidate control in central and northern China. There was no guarantee that diplomatic pressure on Dutch officials in Batavia or the outright occupation of the Dutch East Indies would produce sufficient oil and other resources to meet the demands of the Japanese armed services. While Japanese leaders did not expect any appreciable opposition from Britain (let alone Vichy France or the Netherlands) they also realized that diplomatic and possibly military pressure on European colonies in Southeast Asia risked an unwanted military confrontation with the United States. Prince Fushimi, Yoshida, and other officials from the Naval General Staff estimated that Japan would likely lose such a conflict. Oikawa equivocated on the navy's prospects in a trans-Pacific war. It is difficult to sustain offensive realism's claim that Japan continued the China incident, concluded the Tripartite Pact, and began the southward advance because its leaders' perceived an increase in relative power or exploited international opportunity.

A Neutrality Pact with the Soviet Union

An improvement of relations with Moscow also played a key role in Japanese elites' deliberations during the autumn and winter of 1940 and 1941. Over the past two years, the Kwantung Army operations against the Chinese Communists in northern Manchuria resulted in several border clashes with the Red Army. The two most serious border incidents, at Changkufeng and Nomonhan in the summers of 1938 and 1939, respectively, risked escalation to full-scale war with the Soviet Union. As I discuss in greater length in chapter 6, in both incidents, the Kwantung Army, acting without the authorization of the Army General Staff or the knowledge of the cabinet, engaged Soviet forces near the disputed borders of northeastern Korea and the Soviet Union (in the case of Changkufeng) and Manchukuo and the Mongolian People's Republic (in the case of Nomonhan). In both incidents, the Soviet Far Eastern Army decisively defeated elements of the Kwantung Army.

Matsouka and Konoe hoped a nonaggression pact with the Soviet Union would accomplish three objectives. First, they hoped that a pact would prevent a possible rapprochement between Washington and Moscow. Second, a Japanese-Soviet rapprochement would discourage continued resistance by the KMT in China. Finally, and most important, a pact would allow Japan to pursue the southern advance without fear of a Soviet attack in the north. These plans assumed that the Soviet Union and Germany would honor the 1939 nonaggression pact for at least the next two to five years.[85]

In late March 1941, Matsouka embarked on a European tour, ostensibly aimed at coordinating Japan's foreign policy with those of its Axis allies. Originally, he had planned to ask the German government to mediate comprehensive Soviet-Japanese negotiations to resolve boarder disputes in Manchukuo and Inner Mongolia. He told the 19 September 1940 imperial conference, "We should like Germany to act as mediator in the adjustment of our relations with the Soviet Union. Germany is willing to do this, inasmuch as the adjustment of Japanese-Soviet relations would be to its advantage."[86] Matsouka also hoped that the conclusion of the Tripartite Pact would eventually pave the way for a four-power entente consisting of Germany, Italy, Japan, and the Soviet Union.

Chief among the issues the Japanese foreign minister hoped to resolve in negotiations in Berlin and Moscow were: (1) a Japanese purchase of northern Sakhalin, and barring that, Japanese abandonment of its northern Sakhalin concessions in exchange for 2.5 million tons of oil for the next five years; (2) Japanese recognition of the Soviet position in Sinkiang and Outer Mongolia in return for Soviet recognition of Japan's position in northern China and Inner Mongolia; (3) a cessation of Soviet aid to Chiang Kai-shek; (4) Soviet recognition of Japan's New Order in East Asia; and (5) pledges by Germany and Italy to restrain the Soviet Union and immediately attack the Soviets if the latter attacked Japan or Manchukuo. The liaison conference approved Matsouka's proposal and his planned European tour on 8 February 1941.[87]

Unfortunately for Matsouka, his grandiose plans were completely at odds with the reality of Soviet-German relations in early 1941. Unbeknown to officials in Tokyo, on 18 December 1940, Adolf Hitler signed the "top secret" directive for Operation Barbarossa, which instructed the German army to prepare for an attack on the Soviet Union in spring 1941, even if Britain remained undefeated.[88] Japanese diplomats began to report the deterioration of Soviet-German relations in late 1940. Tōgō Shigenori, then the Japanese ambassador in Moscow, told Konoe on 5 November that, "It will be impossible to force the Soviet Union to recognize German and Italian leadership in Europe. German-Soviet relations have recently deteriorated, and it may be said that they were worse than our relations with the Soviet Union."[89] The timing of the Japanese foreign minister's European tour coincided with mounting tension between the Soviets and the Germans in the Balkans.

Matsouka made a brief stopover in Moscow on 23 March on his way to Berlin. There, he briefly raised the topic of a nonaggression pact with CPSU General Secretary Josef Stalin and Soviet Peoples' Commissar for Foreign Affairs Vyacheslav Molotov. The Soviet Foreign Ministry, however, had informed Molotov that the 1937 Soviet-Chinese nonaggression pact prohibited Moscow from concluding a similar one with Japan. Matsouka did not wish to begin negotiations with Stalin and Molotov before conferring with German officials to ascertain their views on a four-power entente. Nonetheless, by raising the topic, he hoped to lay the groundwork for future negotiations.

On 26 March, Matsouka arrived in Berlin for three days of meetings with Hitler, Ribbentrop, and other German officials. His primary concern was a Japanese-Soviet rapprochement, but Ribbentrop showed no interest in a four-power entente or mediating Japanese-Soviet negotiations. Furthermore, the German foreign minister later warned his Japanese counterpart against concluding a nonaggression treaty with the Soviet Union, noting a sharp deterioration in Soviet-German relations following Bulgaria's (forced) admittance to the Tripartite Pact on 1 March and the entry of German troops into the Bulgarian territory on their way south to Greece the following day.[90] Ribbentrop said that he could not assure the Japanese emperor, "that a conflict between Germany and Russia was inconceivable. On the contrary, as matters stood, such a conflict, though not probable, still would have to be designated as possible."[91]

Returning to Moscow on 7 April, Matsouka immediately began talks with Molotov. The Soviet foreign minister refused to sell north Sakhalin to Japan and insisted that liquidation of Japanese concessions on the island were a precondition for any nonaggression pact. Furthermore, Molotov insisted that a neutrality pact, instead of a broader nonaggression pact would be the more appropriate treaty, since Japan and the Soviet Union still had a dispute over northern Sakhalin.[92] Matsouka accepted the neutrality pact formula, but insisted that negotiations and signing of such a pact take place before his scheduled departure for Japan. On 13 April, the two foreign ministers signed a five-year neutrality pact and a supplementary declaration pledging mutual respect for the territorial integrity and inviolability of Manchukuo and Outer Mongolia.[93] Matsouka also sent a letter to Molotov that pledged the Japanese government "to solve in a few months the question of the liquidation of the concessions in northern Sakhalin."[94] Matsouka presented the treaty for ratification by Privy Council on 24 April, which approved it the same day.

Arguably, the decision to conclude a neutrality pact with the Soviet Union constituted a risk-averse strategy. By stabilizing the Manchurian-Soviet border, the pact decreased the likelihood that a minor border dispute might erupt into a full-scale war. War with the Soviet Union, in addition to the China incident, would only increase Japan's economic dependence on the West, and thus its vulnerability. The removal of the Soviet military presence near Manchukuo was never part of Japanese elites' conception of the New Order in East Asia. However, while the decision to conclude the neutrality pact may be consistent with balance-of-risk theory, this move is equally consistent with offensive realism. Specifically, international opportunity (namely, Stalin's desire to stabilize his eastern frontier) and an unfavorable balance-of-forces in Inner Mongolia and along the Soviet-Manchukuo border gave Japanese leaders a strong incentive to minimize the chances of another conflict with the Soviets.[95]

THE "DRAFT UNDERSTANDING" TO THE NORTHWARD ADVANCE DEBATE (APRIL–JUNE 1941)

Relations between Tokyo and Washington continued to deteriorate in the spring and summer of 1941. The Konoe government and the IGHQ reiterated their commitment to establish a New Order in East Asia, but they hoped to avoid war with the United States. Three questions faced Japanese leaders: Could Japan resume normal economic relations with the United States without abandoning the goal of creating a New Order in East Asia? Under what circumstances and by what means would Japan pursue the southern advance? Finally, should Japan join in Germany's invasion of the Soviet Union?

The stalemate in negotiations with the Dutch East Indies led decision makers to seek a rapprochement with Washington that would still allow Japan to establish its New Order in East Asia. Matsouka instructed Admiral Nomura Kichiasaburō, the Japanese ambassador in Washington, to initiate discussions with Hull and Roosevelt on the state of U.S.-Japan relations. Hull insisted that Japan adhere to "four principles," which remained virtually unchanged throughout the negotiations: (1) respect for the territorial integrity and sovereignty of other states, (2) support for the principle of noninterference in the internal affairs of other states, (3) support of the principle of equality, including equality of commercial opportunity, and (4) no change to the status quo in the Pacific.

In practical terms, Hull's four principles required Japan to do the following: First, Japan would have to recognize that the United States acted in self-defense by aiding Britain, and promise not to enter the war should the United States go to war with Germany. Second, Japan had to withdraw all forces from China (including Manchukuo). Finally, Japan had to agree not to use force against European colonial possessions in Southeast Asia.[96] In short, the Roosevelt administration's preconditions for negotiations made it essentially impossible for Japanese leaders to meet their expectation level.

Events in late 1940 and early 1941 pushed senior Japanese officials closer to authorizing a military southward advance. Negotiations with the Dutch East Indies failed to provide the oil and other raw materials the Konoe government and the military had hoped.[97] In May 1941, Dutch officials even reduced the amount of tin and rubber sold to Japan, as relations between Batavia and Tokyo deteriorated. Decision makers recognized that using force to extract resources from the Dutch East Indies would probably lead to war with the United States. Japan's foreign policy moved in two opposite directions: (1) continued negotiations with the United States and (2) preparations for the southern advance. The probable reaction of Washington and London toward Japan's southward advance entered heavily into deliberations of the Japanese elite during this period. Matsouka felt that a Japanese invasion of Indochina would provoke Washington.

Sugiyama, who had succeeded Prince Kan'in as chief of the Army General Staff on 3 October 1940, disagreed with the foreign minister's conclusions. He argued, "If we are strong, I believe the other side will re-

frain from action." Admiral Nagano Osami, who had succeeded Prince
Fushimi as chief of the Naval General Staff on 9 April 1941, argued: "We
must build bases in French Indochina and Thailand in order to launch
military operations. We must resolutely attack anyone who tries to stop
us. We must resort to force if we have to."[98]

Northward Advance or Southward Advance?

In early June, German diplomats officially informed Tokyo of Hitler's
impending invasion of the Soviet Union. This was not a complete surprise for the Konoe government and the IGHQ, who had received earlier
reports of Hitler's plans. Recall that Hitler and Ribbentrop had warned
Matsouka about the sharp deterioration in German-Soviet relations in
late March and early April. The planned German invasion, however,
posed a fundamental dilemma for Japanese decision makers. On the one
hand, Japanese forces could launch the southward advance to obtain the
oil and raw materials necessary to win the China incident. Alternatively,
Japan could join in the German attack on the Soviet Union from the east,
with the hope of eliminating the potential Soviet threat to Japan. During
late June and early July a debate raged within the government and
IGHQ over what course Japan should take.

Matsouka, who had signed a neutrality pact with Stalin two months
earlier, now favored sending Japanese forces northward to attack the Soviets. He believed that if Japan first attacked the Soviet Union and then
moved south quickly, the United States, confronted with a *fait accompli*,
would not intervene.[99] The leaders of the two armed services, however,
had strong reservations about a northward advance, but for different
reasons. Tōjō argued, "We should not put our complete faith in Germany." He further stated that victory in the China incident continued to
be the top priority of the army and War Ministry.[100] Sugiyama worried
about the risks associated with a Japanese attack on the Soviet Union. He
noted, "Future developments in the German-Soviet war will have a considerable effect on the United States. If the Soviet Union is defeated
quickly, the Stalin regime is likely to collapse, and the United States will
probably not enter the war. If something goes wrong with German calculations, the war will be prolonged and, the probability of American
entry into the war will be increased."[101] Army leaders also raised the logistical problems with the northward advance. Sugiyama told his colleagues: "It will take forty to fifty days to get the Kwantung Army ready.
It will take additional time to organize our present forces for war and get
them ready to take the offensive."[102] The army vice-chief of staff, General
Tsukada Ko, told the liaison conference both options—the northward
advance or the southward advance—would require a major diversion of

troops and equipment from the Chinese theater of operations.[103] Later at the 2 July imperial conference, Sugiyama explained the situation affecting the Kwantung Army: four of the thirty Soviet Far Eastern divisions shifted westward, but the Soviet Union retained "an absolutely overpowering force, ready for strategic deployment."[104]

Oikawa and Nagano wanted unrestricted access to oil and other resources in the Dutch East Indies, and therefore, vehemently opposed the so-called northward advance. Oikawa raised the possibility that a German attack on the Soviet Union might prompt the United States to enter the war. He observed that "the Navy is confident about a war against the United States and Britain, but not confident about a war against the United States, Britain, and the Soviet Union."[105] Whereupon Matsouka asked the navy minister: "You say that you are not afraid of war with Britain and the United States, so why is it that you do not wish to see the Soviets enter the war?" Oikawa replied, "If the Soviets come in, it means fighting an additional country, doesn't it?"[106] However, they also recognized that military operations against European colonies in the region would likely bring Japan into armed conflict with the United States.[107]

As with the earlier decision to conclude a neutrality pact with Moscow, the postponement of the northward advance appears an anomaly for my hypothesis. Balance-of-risk theory posits that decision makers will adopt risk-acceptant strategies to avoid losses relative to their expectation level. When faced with gains, relative to their expectation level, it expects decision makers to be risk-averse. The elimination of the Soviet military presence in northeast Asia was not part of Japanese leaders' conception of the New Order in East Asia. Indeed, had Germany and Japan quickly defeated the Soviet army and toppled Stalin, then the outcome would have been far above Japanese decision makers' expectation level.

Pursuit of the northern advance would have been a risk-acceptant move for several reasons. This option offered Japanese leaders a high payoff, namely the elimination of the Soviet military presence in East Asia. On the other hand, this option risked Japanese forces becoming embroiled in a protracted land conflict in Siberia.[108] The success of the northern advance would depend, in part, on strategic cooperation between German and Japanese forces. Given Hitler's tendency to spring surprises on friend and foe alike, such cooperation would have been difficult under the best of circumstances.[109] Plans for joint German-Japanese military operations did not exist. The Soviet Union's vast area separated German and Japanese leaders, thus making land communication and supply impossible. The postponement of the northward advance, therefore, constituted a more risk-averse strategy.

The overall direction of the liaison conference's risk taking is consistent with the core hypothesis of balance-of-risk theory—risk acceptance for loss and risk aversion for gains. Nonetheless, the decision to postpone the northward advance is equally consistent with offensive realism. The liaison conference principals did not perceive an increase in Japan's relative power vis-à-vis the Soviet Union. The military members of the liaison conference evaluated the so-called northward advance in terms of the value trade-off it would entail; namely the diversion of troops and resources from the war against the KMT and from the proposed southward advance. The liaison conference's deliberations on northward advance appear fully consistent with standard cost-benefit analysis.

The Southward Advance and Washington's Reaction (July–August 1941)

On 15 July, the Japanese Foreign Ministry issued the Vichy French government what was, in effect, an ultimatum. The French would permit Japan to dispatch the "necessary" land, sea, and air forces to southern Indochina in order to prevent further interference from British, U.S. and Free French (Gaullist) forces. Japan would occupy two air bases and two naval bases in Indochina.[110] Japanese occupation forces moved into southern Indochina ten days later. In response, Roosevelt signed an executive order freezing all Japanese assets in the United States, effective the following day. The British and Canadian governments froze Japanese assets in their respective countries on 26 July, as did the Dutch East Indies on 28 July. On 1 August, the State Department announced an embargo on all exports to Japan, except cotton and foodstuffs. These actions amounted to a worldwide embargo, since the war had already cut off Japan's trade with Europe.[111]

The Konoe cabinet and IGHQ decided to proceed with the southward advance despite clear deterrent warnings from Washington. Throughout July, the Roosevelt administration continued to warn Japanese officials that the occupation of southern Indochina and the Dutch East Indies would provoke a strong American response.[112] Decision makers received additional warnings about the likely American response via the diplomatic corps and military intelligence.[113] Even third parties tried to force Japanese leaders to face up to their predicament. In April, British prime minister Winston Churchill sent the following message to Matsouka: "Is it true that the production of steel in the United States of America in 1941 will be nearly 75 million tons and in Great Britain about 12.5 million tons, making nearly 90 million tons? If Germany should happen to be defeated as she was last time, would not the 7 million tons of steel production of Japan be inadequate for a single-handed war?"[114]

Reports from both Japanese military and government planners suggested that even unrestricted access to Indochina and the East Indies would not solve Japan's resource deficiencies. The War Preparations Section of the War Ministry produced an assessment of Japan's material strength in March 1941. The report stated: "It cannot be denied that the empire's material strength would be insufficient for a long war. While we have munitions sufficient to defeat the enemy within a period of two years, by the end of the second year liquid fuels will become short at least temporarily, and should war be further prolonged, our economic capabilities might be strained."[115] Furthermore, there was no guarantee that merchant marine could safely transport oil from the East Indies to where the army and navy needed it. In a report to Tōjō, that section's chief warned: "We must pay attention to the situation with respect to marine transport, which is the foundation of the economy. If we lose too many ships or if we cannot maintain a balance between transportation for war operations and transportation for general materials mobilization, we will be unable to continue the war." He concluded, "We are no match for the United States and Britain in the event of war."[116] During the 1 July liaison conference discussion on whether to strike north or south, Minister of Commerce and Industry Kobayashi warned: "I do not think we have sufficient strength, so far as resources are concerned, to support war. Both the army and navy can resort to force, but we do not have materials for war on both land and sea."[117]

Despite available information and the military's own sobering assessments, most senior officials were willing to risk the southward advance. During the 12 July imperial conference Sugiyama stated: "I believe that in order to hasten our settlement of the [China] Incident it will be absolutely necessary for our empire to increase its direct pressure on the Chungking regime, and at the same time move southward and sever the links between the Chungking regime and the British and American powers, which support it from behind and strengthen its will to resist."[118] Similarly, Nagano told that conference: "I believe that under the present circumstances our empire, in order to secure our defenses in the south and attain a position of self-sufficiency within the Greater East Asian Co-prosperity Sphere, must take immediate steps and push steadily southward by coordinating military and political action with reference to key areas in the south."[119]

As the date for the southward advance approached, some liaison conference members realized that their actions toward French Indochina likely would lead to the imposition of further economic sanctions by the United States, and possibly war. Sugiyama admitted, "Our occupation of Indochina will certainly provoke Great Britain and the United States."[120] In late July, the new foreign minister, Admiral Toyoda Teijirō, told his colleagues, "The occupation of Indochina will exert an influence on the

United States; they will adopt a policy of putting an embargo on vital goods, freezing Japanese funds, prohibiting the purchase of gold, detaining Japanese vessels."[121] Nagano also concluded that the southward advance would provoke a total embargo against Japan, but believed further negotiations with Washington would be futile. He therefore advocated a preemptive strike against the United States before the Roosevelt administration froze Japanese assets on 25 July (26 July in Japan).[122]

The southward advance was clearly a risk-acceptant strategy. Japanese occupation of southern French Indochina offered the possibility of halting arms shipments into China and thus weakening the KMT. This, in turn, might increase the Imperial Army's chances of winning a decisive victory and ending the China incident on terms favorable to Japan. However, the pursuit of this strategy would almost certainly tighten the economic noose around Japan, which still depended on the United States for 90 percent of its oil supply.

Offensive realism would expect decision makers to update their preferences and strategies in response to new information. Since 1939, the Roosevelt administration, along with the British, had responded to Japan's expansionist policies by gradually imposing economic sanctions. Throughout the spring and early summer of 1941, officials in Tokyo received credible information that further military action against the European colonies in Southeast Asia would provoke a strong reaction from Washington. Both Toyoda and Nagano warned that the Roosevelt administration would most likely sever economic relations, thereby depriving Japan of the resources required to win the China incident and establish the New Order in East Asia. Despite these considerations, the liaison conference members decided to send troops into southern French Indochina. Both the pursuit of the southward advance strategy, and the deliberations that produced it, are consistent with the balance-of-risk hypothesis.

THE "CLEAN SLATE" DEBATE (SEPTEMBER–OCTOBER 1941)

The occupation of southern Indochina and the Roosevelt administration's total embargo set Japan and the United States on a collision course. A liaison conference convened on 3 September to discuss a policy document entitled, "The Essentials for Carrying out the Empire's Policies." This document stipulated that Japan would continue negotiations with the United States and simultaneously prepare for war. If the negotiations did not produce favorable results by the last ten days of October, Japan would go to war with the United States, Britain, and the Netherlands.[123]

By August 1941, however, all available information suggested that
Japan's military and diplomatic actions were producing encirclement.
From an offensive realist perspective, the decision to go to war with the
United States would only make sense under three conditions. First, war
was a viable option if Japanese leaders believed that the United States
would withdraw from the Pacific when attacked. Second, if decision
makers in Tokyo believed that a conflict with the United States would be
short, then war was a viable option.[124] Finally, if decision makers believed that once war began they could negotiate a cease-fire with Washington on terms favorable to Japan, then the initiation of hostilities was a
viable option. As the documentary evidence below suggests, however,
Japanese leaders did not reach these conclusions.

During the summer and autumn of 1941 senior officials had no reason
to conclude that a preventive military strike would destroy American resolve and prompt the Roosevelt administration to seek a negotiated settlement. In late August, the then foreign minister, Toyoda Teijirō, urged
restraint in dealing with the United States. He argued: "During Matsouka's time, we tried to deter America with strong language. This
aroused the Americans' hostility, and in the end, they severed communications with Japan. Accordingly, we have to think carefully about the
pros and cons of getting the United States even more excited. . . . [Japan]
cannot help but give some thought to the question of whether it is better
to watch quietly . . . or to go on a rampage."[125] During the late summer,
Konoe proposed seeking a rapprochement with the United States. Tōjō,
however, blocked any movement in this direction. He argued that the
government had stated "it would not change national policies that had
already been decided. . . . Moreover, both the war minister and the navy
minister have demanded in cabinet meetings that there be no relaxation
in national policies."[126]

Both civilian and military leaders agreed that any war with the
United States would likely become a protracted conflict. In May 1941,
Matsouka told his liaison conference colleagues, "If the United States
participates in the war, it will last a very long time."[127] During the 6 September imperial conference, Admiral Nagano stated, "I think it will
probably be a long war. Hence, we must be prepared for a long war. We
hope the enemy will come out for a quick showdown; in that event there
will be a decisive battle near us, and I anticipate our chances of victory
would be quite good. But I do not believe that the war will end with
that."[128] The other participants agreed that "a war with the United States
and Great Britain will be long, and will become a war of endurance."[129]
Major General Suzuki Teiichi, who had replaced Hoshino as the president of the cabinet's planning board in April, observed that "our liquid
fuel stockpile, which is the most important, will reach bottom by June or

July of next year, even if we impose strict wartime control on civilian demand."[130] Moreover, Nagano told the imperial conference that "as to our predictions of the way military operations are likely to go, the *probability is very high* that they [the United States] will from the outset plan on a long war. Therefore, it will be necessary for us to be reconciled to this and to be prepared militarily for a long war."[131]

The China incident remained the main area of disagreement between Tokyo and Washington. On 10 September, Ambassador Grew gave Toyoda a note that clearly stated the Roosevelt administration's position on the subject. The note insisted on the following: (1) a fair and just settlement between Japan and China; (2) an end to Japanese discrimination against American business interests in China; (3) and recognition of Washington's right to aid countries resisting aggression. In essence, the Roosevelt administration insisted on an independent China under Chiang.[132]

Konoe realized that he could not break the impasse in the liaison conference. Reluctant to lead Japan into a major war, Konoe formally resigned as prime minister on 15 October.[133] On 17 October, the emperor, acting on the advice of Marquis Kido Kōichi, the lord keeper of the privy seal, and the *jūshin*, appointed Tōjō prime minister. Tōjō submitted a list of ministers that included Tōgō Shigenori as foreign minister, Admiral Shimada Shigeru as navy minister, and Kaya Okinori as finance minister. He also took the unprecedented step of retaining the War Ministry portfolio for himself. After the imperial audience, Kido informed Tōjō that it was the emperor's desire that the new government "wipe the slate clean." In other words, the imperial conference decisions of 6 September, which set the end of October as the deadline for a negotiated settlement or war with the United States, Great Britain, and the Netherlands, need not bind the new cabinet.[134] From 24 October to 2 November, liaison conferences met continuously to consider eleven questions on Japan's capabilities and the prospects for war against the United States, Britain, and the Netherlands. The questions, which the IGHQ and the relevant ministries prepared, concerned Japan's economic resources, operational prospects, likely support from Germany and Italy, and the likely impact of a U.S.-Japan war on the China incident.[135]

In light of the American embargo, the questions concerning Japan's industrial capabilities and access to raw materials played a key role in the deliberations. Officials realized that Japan's steel production capacity was only one-thirteenth that of the United States and that Japan could not produce all the ships needed to win a war. Although the Japanese government and the armed services made efforts to build up domestic oil reserves, at best Japan's oil supply would last for only eighteen months. Nagano argued, "The navy is consuming 400 tons of oil an hour. The situation is urgent. We want it decided one way or the other quickly." Navy Minister Shimada Shigetaru estimated that "the navy will require a budget of ¥9.4 billion in 1942 and ¥9.5 billion in 1943, and ¥10 billion annually after that."[136]

Suzuki told his colleagues that Japan's "ability to supply the natural resources needed in 1942 will probably be 90 percent of our ability in 1941. In doing this, we will be using up all our stockpiles. However, only in the case of raw cotton can we manage until 1943 by using what is left in our stockpiles and by buying some from China."[137] Finance Minister Kaya Okinori also had dire economic forecasts in the event of war with the United States. During the October 28 conference he observed that if Japan went to war "the navy budget will be ¥9 billion. Hence the army will probably demand ¥15 billion. . . . We would then need more than twice that [amount] in material resources."[138] Even Tōjō agreed with these dire long-term forecasts, noting: "We can manage somehow in 1942 and 1943 if the army has the same [steel] allocation as before. . . . We do not know what will happen after 1944."[139]

CONTINUE TO NEGOTIATE, BUT PREPARE FOR WAR (NOVEMBER–DECEMBER 1941)

On 1 November, Tōjō told the liaison conference members that they had to make a final choice among three alternatives: (1) avoid war and undergo great hardships, (2) go to war with the United States immediately and focus on political and military strategies to that end, or (3) continue negotiations in an effort to reach a compromise agreement, but prepare for war in the event those negotiations fail. The first proposal, which required Japan to make concessions to the United States, never received serious consideration. Foreign Minister Tōgō Shigenori suggested that Japan should offer to withdraw its troops from southern Indochina immediately and from China over the next five years. Sugiyama and Tsukada vehemently objected to any concessions. Tōjō, hoping to broker a compromise, suggested that Japan withdraw its troops over a twenty-five year period. Tsukada strongly objected, arguing that to mention any timeframe would be a sign of weakness.[140]

Both Kaya and Tōgō argued that Nomura should continue negotiations with Hull, in the hope of averting war. Suzuki, on the other hand, argued, "In 1943 the materials situation will be no better if we go to war. We have just been told that with the passage of time the supreme command's strategic position will deteriorate."[141] Nagano stated, "The basic issue that I would like you to understand and appreciate in particular today is that the time for Japan to go to war against the United States is now. Should we miss this opportunity to wage war it will not present it itself again."[142] Vice Admiral Itō Seichii, the vice-chief of the Naval General Staff, warned that given current oil consumption efforts to reach a negotiated settlement could only continue until 20 November.[143] Despite the IGHQ's desire for an immediate decision, senior military officers were not optimistic about a Japanese victory. Tsukada admitted, "In general, the prospects if we go to war are not bright."[144]

The liaison conference decided that midnight 30 November (Tokyo time) would be the absolute deadline for negotiations. If the talks produced a favorable settlement by the deadline, the Naval General Staff would call off military operations against the United States. In the meantime, the foreign minister would instruct Nomura to continue his negotiations with Hull.[145] Tōgō offered two proposals for the conduct of those negotiations. Proposal A would set the basis for a comprehensive settlement between the United States and Japan.[146] Specifically, it reiterated the Japanese pledge to act "independently" in the interpretation and implementation of the Tripartite Pact. Japan would endorse the principle of nondiscriminatory trade and relinquish its long-standing claim to a special trading relationship with China. Finally, the restoration of peace between Japan and China would prompt the immediate withdrawal of all Japanese troops in French Indochina. Within two years of the Sino-Japanese peace agreement, Japan would withdraw all forces from China, except those forces stationed in northern China, Inner Mongolia and Hainan. These forces would remain for a twenty-five year period.

Tōgō intended proposal B to be a modus vivendi, should Hull and Nomura fail to reach an agreement based on proposal A. Specifically, this second proposal sought to avoid war by restoring Japanese-American relations to their condition prior to the asset freeze in June. Tōgō favored proposal A, but recognized the diminishing chances of reaching a comprehensive settlement within the thirty-day time limit. However, he opposed any settlement that required a unilateral Japanese withdrawal from China or which endangered the creation of the New Order in East Asia. He told the conference, "I would like to narrow the area of negotiation, settle just the Southern question. . . . We cannot allow the United States a voice in the China question."[147] Both Nagano and Shimada favored proposal A, but again noted the inevitability of war with the United States. Sugiyama and Tsukada advocated that negotiations proceed based on proposal A and that proposal B be dropped from further consideration. While Nomura made a final attempt to reach an acceptable settlement with the United States, the Imperial Navy would prepare for war.[148]

Nomura presented proposal A to Hull on 7 November.[149] Eight days later, the secretary of state rejected it. Hull gave Nomura a statement proposing a reduction in trade barriers—thus, restoring American-Japanese trade to a "normal" basis—if Japan demonstrated its commitment to equality of commercial opportunity. There was one caveat: for the duration of the "present international emergency," each country could restrict the export of war-related materials to the other.[150] Nomura presented proposal B to Hull on 20 November. Six days later Hull gave Nomura a note that not only rejected proposal B, but rescinded many of the concessions the secretary of state had made in the 27 June "oral statement."[151] The 30 November deadline passed without a settlement and the liaison conference drafted an imperial rescript declaring war on the United States, Great Britain, and the Netherlands. In his opening statement to the 1 December imperial conference Tōjō noted:

> Not only has the United States not conceded an inch in its original demands . . . it has applied new conditions—such as demanding the unconditional and total withdrawal of troops from China, the repudiation of the Nanking government, and the transformation of the Tripartite Pact between Japan, Germany, and Italy into a dead letter—and has importuned the Empire for unilateral concessions. If the Empire were to submit to these, not only would the Empire lose its authority and be unable to anticipate concluding the China incident; the very existence of the Empire would also be in jeopardy.[152]

During these last two periods (October–November and November–December 1941), offensive realism posits the following. The Roosevelt administration's freeze on Japanese assets in the United States and its total oil embargo presented Japanese decision makers with three basic alternatives: negotiation, gradual exhaustion, or war. In the early autumn Japanese officials tried to reach some sort of accommodation, which the Roosevelt administration rejected. The second option meant certain defeat. The third option, however, offered a remote chance of success. Senior officials concluded that, given available resources, the navy and army could fight a short war with the United States. In this scenario, Japan might be able to negotiate a peace settlement with Washington without abandoning its eventual goal of security through autarky and empire.

The documentary evidence does not support the offensive realist hypothesis. The members of the Tōjō cabinet and the chiefs of staff knew that any war with the United States would be lengthy and that Japan's prospects for a favorable outcome would certainly diminish over time. There was also no information to suggest that once war began, Japan could negotiate a favorable settlement with the United States. Reports from Naval General Staff, the finance ministry, and the planning board all indicated that Japan did not have the material resources needed for war with the United States, even with unrestricted access to the Dutch East Indies, Manchuria, and Indochina.

I submit that the balance-of-risk hypotheses set forth in chapter 2 provide insights into Imperial Japan's slide toward the Pacific War that the offensive realism and logrolling theory do not. The refusal of the Konoe and Tōjō cabinets and the IGHQ to consider any alternative short of victory in the China incident and the creation of the New Order in East Asia appears anomalous from the standpoint of offensive realism. Furthermore, throughout the 1940–41 period Japanese elites had credible information that their strategies had not only increased Japan's economic dependence on the United States, but were leading to encirclement. Balance-of-risk theory posits that senior officials will be risk averse for gains and risk acceptant for losses, relative to the expectation level from which they operate. Furthermore, Japanese leaders in 1940–41 were incapable of abandoning or scaling down their aspiration of creating a New Order in East Asia, the stated objective of Japanese grand strategy since October 1938. This behavior is consistent with the balance-of-risk hypothesis: The longer officials adhere to a common expectation level, the less likely they will be to revise that expectation level downward in response to adverse policy outcomes.

Obviously, some members of the leadership displayed higher levels of risk acceptance. In particular, Matsouka would appear to be the most risk-acceptant participant in the liaison conference deliberations. He was the most forceful advocate of the northward advance in the spring and summer of 1941, despite the Army General Staff's reservations about a full-scale war against the Soviet Union. Earlier, he was the most forceful advocate of an alliance with Germany to deter the United States. Others involved in the deliberations, particularly Prince Fushimi, expressed grave reservations about the efficacy of that type of deterrent diplomacy. In the fall 1941 deliberations Sugiyama, Tsukada, and Nagano were more risk acceptant than the other liaison conference participants. They each saw a window of opportunity in attacking the United States, despite credible information about American military capabilities, Japan's oil and raw materials deficiency, and the high likelihood that any war would be a long one. Other officials, most notably Konoe, Toyoda, Kaya, and Tōgō had great reservations about war with the United States. Nonetheless, the aggregate direction of the liaison conference members' risk behavior is consistent with balance-of-risk theory across the observation periods.

As table 4.1 below illustrates, in six of the eight observation periods, both the documentary record of liaison conference deliberations and the

TABLE 4.1. *Summary of Japanese leaders' risk behavior in the 1940–41 war decisions*

Observation period	Expectation level (against which leaders evaluated outcomes)	Perceived position relative to the expectation level	Risk propensity of central decision makers	Policy options selected
The inauguration of the second Konoe cabinet to the signing of the Tripartite Pact (June–Sept. 1940)	Creation of New Order in East Asia	Loss	Risk acceptance	• Continuation of China incident • Conclusion of Tripartite Pact • Occupation of northern French Indochina
Continuation of the China incident and negotiation of the USSR-Japan Nonaggression Pact (Oct.1940–Mar. 1941)	Creation of New Order in East Asia	Loss	Risk acceptance	• Continuation of China Incident • Coerce Dutch East Indies to increase oil shipments
The "draft understanding" with the U.S. to the northward advance debate (April–June 1941)	Creation of New Order in East Asia	Loss (with respect to China war) Gain (with respect to the USSR)	Risk acceptance Risk aversion	• Continuation of China Incident • Nonaggression pact with USSR.*
The decision for the southward advance and the occupation of southern French Indochina (June–July 1941)	Creation of New Order in East Asia	Loss (with respect to China war) Gain (with respect to the USSR)	Risk acceptance Risk aversion	• Continuation of China Incident • Postponement of northward advance (indefinitely)
The freezing of Japan's assets and Roosevelt's deterrent warning (July–Aug. 1941)	Creation of New Order in East Asia	Loss	Risk acceptance	• Continuation of China Incident • Southward advance: occupation of southern French Indochina and the Dutch East Indies
The fall of Konoe, appointment of Tōjō as premier, and the Hull-Nomura talks (Sept.–Nov. 1941)	Creation of New Order in East Asia	Loss	Risk acceptance	• Continuation of China Incident
The failure of the Hull-Nomura talks and decision for war (Nov.–Dec. 1941)	Creation of New Order in East Asia	Loss	Risk acceptance	• Continuation of China Incident • War with the United States*

*The decision to conclude a neutrality pact with the Soviet Union is equally consistent with offensive realism.

direction of aggregate risk taking support my balance-of-risk hypothesis. In two periods, however, the documentary evidence and direction of risk-taking is equally supportive of the offensive realism. Both the decision to seek a neutrality pact with the Soviet Union and the later decision to postpone the so-called northward advance constituted relatively risk-averse options. In both instances, relative power imbalances and international opportunity drove the calculations of the Konoe cabinet and IGHQ. Since the balance-of-risk hypothesis does not provide a superior explanation for these decisions, then offensive realism wins in those two periods.

In the remaining eight periods, the documentary evidence supports the balance-of-risk hypothesis. Here the liaison conference members undertook risk-acceptant strategies (such as the Tripartite Pact, pressuring the Dutch East Indies, the southward advance), despite their own subjective estimates about the likely negative outcomes of such moves for U.S.–Japan relations. There was no evidence to suggest that a defensive alliance with Germany would deter the Roosevelt administration. Similarly, in June 1941 officials decided to proceed with the southward advance despite clear indications that the Roosevelt administration would impose a total trade embargo. Furthermore, they estimated that alternative sources of oil and raw materials could not make up the shortfall caused by a total cessation of trans-Pacific trade. Throughout 1940–41, Washington demanded that Japan halt its war against the KMT in China. Senior officials in Tokyo refused and continued to evaluate outcomes relative to their aspiration of establishing the New Order in East Asia, which Japan did not have the capabilities to achieve.

[5]

The United States and the
Korean War (1950–51)

During the cold war, the United States fought two costly land conflicts in East Asia. The stated rationale for both was the need to preserve the credibility of American commitments around the world. Most realists see the Vietnam War as a case of self-defeating overextension. The Korea War is a more debatable case that deserves reexamination for three reasons.

First, the Truman administration faced far greater risks in Korea than the Johnson and Nixon administrations later faced in Vietnam. Intervention not only risked entrapment in the periphery, but war with the People's Republic of China (PRC) and possibly the Soviet Union as well. Second, the Korean War expanded the geographic scope of the cold war and precluded diplomatic ties between Washington and Beijing for two decades. The United States strengthened its ties to the North Atlantic Treaty Organization (NATO) and forged alliances with Australia, the Philippines, New Zealand, Japan, South Korea, and Taiwan. At home, the war drove the Democrats from the White House for the first time since 1933, removed previous constraints on defense spending, and forged a consensus for military containment.[1]

Third, unlike their decisions regarding the war in Vietnam, the American leaders engaged in dramatic shifts in war aims and risk-taking behavior during the Korean conflict. After years of excluding South Korea from the American defensive perimeter in the Pacific, President Harry S. Truman and his advisors sent troops, nominally under the auspices of the United Nations, to repel a North Korean invasion in June 1950. The stated aim was the restoration of the border at the Thirty-eighth Parallel. In late August and early September, officials escalated the war aim from containment to rollback: the destruction of the North Korean army and the military reunification of Korea. They did so despite warnings that China would enter the war if U.S. troops crossed the Thirty-eighth Parallel. A month later, despite the presence of thousands of Chinese "volunteers" in North Korea, officials approved an offensive to the Yalu River proposed by General Douglas MacArthur. After a Chinese counteroffensive drove American and UN forces southward, officials abandoned rollback in favor of a restoration of the prewar status quo—a decision that ultimately led Truman to remove the bellicose MacArthur in April 1951.

This chapter addresses the following questions: What explains the dramatic changes in the Truman administration's overall policy in East Asia and its specific war aims in Korea between June 1950 and January 1951? Why did officials allow MacArthur to continue his drive to the Yalu despite evidence of an imminent Chinese counteroffensive? To what extent did Truman and his advisors contemplate the expansion of the conflict beyond Korea or the use of nuclear weapons?

ARGUMENTS ADVANCED, ANSWERS OFFERED

I argue that loss aversion caused the Truman administration to reverse its long-established policy and intervene in the Korean War in June 1950. Officials' perceptions of relative power trends influenced the selection of an expectation level, which in this case was the preservation of the territorial status quo. In 1949–50, a series of adverse developments—the Communist victory in the Chinese civil war, the Sino-Soviet alliance, and the Soviet atomic bomb—produced a profound sense of vulnerability among decision makers. Failure to check the projected growth of the Soviet bloc's power would result in the steady of erosion of American power and influence by the mid-1950s. However, if the administration took immediate steps to reverse this trend—mainly through increased defense spending and stronger military ties to Western Europe and Japan—the United States would remain preponderant. In the meantime, however, Truman and his advisors concluded that major war during the American window of strategic vulnerability (1950–53) would be disastrous. Consequently, they sought to avoid any action that might precipitate a direct superpower confrontation, while reaffirming the priority of European defense and the defensive perimeter in the Pacific consisting of Japan, the Ryukus, and the Philippines.

The North Korean invasion represented a dramatic challenge to the status quo. As balance-of-risk theory would expect, Truman and his advisors adopted the risky strategy of committing troops to defend South

Korea, a country that officials deemed "strategically insignificant" weeks earlier. Intervention was riskier than other options, given the strength of the U.S. armed forces in June 1950 and the possibly that the invasion was a diversion. Once American troops crossed the Thirty-eighth Parallel in early October, Truman and his advisors sought to re-cover the sunk costs of their previous policies. They were insensitive to the marginal costs associated with MacArthur's offensive—namely the increasing likelihood that China would enter the war. After the Chinese counteroffensive sent American and allied forces reeling in November and December 1950, the administration opted to wage a limited war, de-spite widespread calls at home for a unilateral withdrawal and calls from the allies for an immediate negotiated settlement.

Offensive realism suggests that increased relative power and interna-tional opportunity drove the 1950–51 Korean War decisions. The theory does explain the escalation of American war aims from containment to rollback in August–September 1950. The retreat of the North Korean army, the diminished likelihood of Soviet intervention, and China's per-ceived military weakness, gave the administration a window to reunify the Korea at a low cost. Offensive realism, however, does not explain the officials' intervention decision in June and their subsequent refusal to halt the Yalu offensive despite the increasing likelihood of a Chinese counteroffensive.[2]

Logrolling theory attributes the Korean War decisions to coalition building between two factions. The Europe-first internationalists, who included secretaries of state George Marshall and Dean Acheson and State Department policy planning director George Kennan believed that denying the Soviet Union control of the major industrialized and re-source rich areas of Eurasia was the overriding security concern. The Asia-first nationalists had a less coherent conception of vital interests. Some, such as Ohio senator Robert Taft, the leader of the Republican party's isolationist wing, argued that atomic bombs and airpower alone would be sufficient to defend the U.S. homeland. Other Republicans, such as California senator William Knowland and Minnesota represen-tative Walter Judd were harshly critical of Truman's China policy. Nei-ther faction necessarily sought a war in East Asia. Instead, intervention in Korea resulted from a tacit logroll between the two factions: to secure support for containment in Europe, the Europe-first internationalists needed to appease the Asia-first nationalists in Congress. The adminis-tration's sudden reversal of its Korea and Taiwan policies was merely a strategy to defuse congressional criticism and to preserve domestic sup-port for containment in Europe.[3]

Logrolling theory faces two problems. The first concerns the value of the explanatory variable: the degree of cartelization. Liberal democratic great powers should be less susceptible to risky interventions in the periphery than great powers with highly cartelized political systems, such as Wilhelmine Germany. Jack Snyder admits, "In America, cartelization was merely a transitory aspect of the handling of some foreign policy issues, caused by a temporary pattern of factionalism and partisanship. The political system as a whole was democratic." The second problem is the lack of empirical proof. There are few explicit references to the preferences of congressional voting blocs in the private deliberations of Truman and his advisors.[4]

The chapter consists of five sections. The first provides background to the war and examines the Truman administration's reaction to adverse power oscillations in 1949–50.[5] The second examines the 25–30 June 1950 intervention. An examination of officials' escalation of war aims in August-September and their refusal to halt the Yalu offensive in October-November follow in the third and fourth sections, respectively. The final section examines the reaction to the Chinese intervention and subsequent efforts to limit the conflict in December 1950 and January 1951.

CONTAINMENT AND DEFENSIVE PERIMETERS (1947–50)

The Korean War had its origins in the final days of World War II. The Allies agreed that Korea, a Japanese protectorate since 1905 and a colony since 1910, would regain its independence. President Franklin Roosevelt proposed a four-power trusteeship—with the Soviet Union, China, the United States, and Great Britain acting as trustees—to prepare Korea for independence. He obtained the approval of British prime minister Winston Churchill and Generalissimo Chiang Kai-Shek at the November 1943 Cairo conference. Soviet General Secretary Josef Stalin subsequently agreed to the trusteeship, with the proviso that American and Soviet forces jointly occupy the peninsula.[6] Roosevelt's plan faced two major problems. First, China lacked the capabilities to play the role of regional guarantor. Second, Harry Truman and his advisors feared that Stalin would exploit the power vacuum created by Japan's collapse and renewed civil war between Chiang's Kuomintang (KMT) and Mao Zedong's Chinese Communist party (CCP). The Kremlin declared war on Japan on 8 August and units of the Soviet Twenty-fifth Army crossed into northern Korea and Manchuria the following day. Colonel Charles Bonesteel, policy section chief in the War Department's operations division, and his deputy, Lieutenant Colonel Dean Rusk, proposed dividing the Soviet and American zones at the Thirty-eighth Parallel; a plan which Stalin and Truman approved on 15 August.[7]

U.S.-Soviet Occupation and the Creation of Two Koreas (1945–49)

The joint occupation began without agreement on its nature or duration. Lieutenant General John R. Hodge, the commander of U.S. Army Forces in Korea (USAFIK), faced the task of balancing the widespread desire for independence against the need for an orderly transition from colonial rule. The rapid influx of 1.5 million refugees and food shortages sparked riots. Fearing that left-wing parties would use the unrest as an opportunity to seize power, Hodge welcomed the repatriation of right-wing Korean politicians, including seventy-seven-year-old Syngman Rhee.[8] Meanwhile, Stalin concluded that a unified Korea under Rhee would jeopardize Soviet access to natural resources. The creation of a friendly North Korean regime, however, would both guarantee access and allow for troop withdrawals.[9] In October 1945, Soviet officials took the first step in this direction by creating the Korean Workers' party (KWP) and installing Kim Il-sung, a former leader of anti-Japanese guerrillas in Manchuria, as its leader.[10]

In August 1947, the Truman administration sought to extricate itself from the costly occupation.[11] After intense lobbying, the UN General Assembly passed a resolution that called for a Temporary Commission on Korea (UNTCOK) to supervise national elections. When Soviet and KWP officials denied UNTCOK entry to the northern zone, the commission staged elections in the south on 10 May 1948. The conservatives won a majority in the new national assembly, which immediately drafted a constitution for a Korean republic and elected Rhee as president. The Republic of Korea (ROK), with its capital in Seoul, came into existence on 15 August. On 3 September, the Soviets established the Democratic People's Republic of Korea (DPRK) with its capital in Pyongyang and Kim as premier. Ten days later, Moscow announced that Soviet forces would leave the DPRK by 31 December. The last USAIK troops withdrew on 23 June 1949, leaving behind a five hundred-person Korea Military Advisory Group (KMAG) to train an army and national police force.[12]

American and Soviet forces left a situation ripe for civil war. Rhee and Kim declared their intent to topple the other and unify the peninsula. Clashes broke out along the Thirty-eighth Parallel in late 1948 and 1949.[13] A March 1949 report to the National Security Council (NSC) said that the South Korean military consisted of 114,000 American trained and equipped troops: 65,000 in the regular army, 45,000 in the national police force, and 4,000 in the coast guard. In reality, the army was collection of police units that lacked heavy artillery, tanks, combat aircraft, and reserves.[14] General of the Army Douglas MacArthur, the commander-in-chief of U.S. forces in the Far East (CINCFE), told his superiors that "the United States did not have the capability to train and equip [South] Korean troops to the point where the [South] Koreans would be able to cope with a full-scale invasion accompanied by internal disturbances fomented by the Communists."[15] Meanwhile, the Soviets supplied the (North) Korean People's Army (KPA) with 1,600 mortar and artillery pieces, 258 T-4 tanks, automatic weapons, and several detachments of naval vessels.[16] The KPA also had an advantage in combat experience, since Kim had sent thousands of troops to assist the Communists in the Chinese civil war in 1946. By June 1950, battle-tested veterans comprised half of the estimated 110,000 KPA regular troops.[17]

The Truman administration drew a distinction between the strategic importance of South Korea, which it considered negligible, and the symbolic value of the country's survival.[18] Walton Butterworth, then director of the State Department's Office of Far Eastern Affairs, stressed the importance of maintaining "sufficient flexibility" in the army's planned withdrawal from South Korea.[19] In March 1948, Secretary of State George C. Marshall "expressed grave doubts as to the feasibility of building up a native Korean force in south in the time allotted which would be at all comparable to the forces existing north of the Thirty-eighth Parallel." Marshall, Butterworth, Undersecretary of State Robert A. Lovett, and others urged a postponement of the troop evacuation to provide some additional time for the training of ROK troops.[20]

Despite South Korea's symbolic importance, the army could ill-afford to continue a substantial troop presence. Fear of inflation and congressional opposition to new taxes led Truman to impose a $14.4 billion ceiling on defense spending for fiscal year 1949. Secretary of Defense Louis Johnson and the Joint Chiefs of Staff (JCS) favored withdrawal because of their conviction that Korea would not provide favorable terrain on which to fight.[21] Nor were the prospects of redressing the military imbalance any better. In January 1949, MacArthur told the JCS, "The threat of invasion possibly supported by Communist armies from Manchuria, will continue for the foreseeable future," and "that in the event of any serious threat to the security of Korea, strategic and military considerations will force the abandonment of any pretense of military support."[22]

NSC-68 and the Projected Window of Vulnerability

In the months before the Korean War, Truman and his advisors confronted a series of international setbacks. In early September 1949, intelligence sources detected traces of radioactivity over the northern Pacific and concluded that the Soviet Union had detonated an atomic bomb, several years ahead of the estimates of the Central Intelligence Agency

(CIA).[23] Truman announced the end of the American nuclear monopoly on 23 September. Officials did not see the Soviet atomic bomb as heralding an immediate power shift. Rather, they worried about the psychological impact on allies and the long-term implications of a growing Soviet arsenal of atomic and eventually hydrogen bombs. In January 1950, Paul H. Nitze, director of the Policy Planning Staff (PPS) at the State Department, concluded: "Nothing about the moves indicates that Moscow is preparing to launch in the near future an all-out . . . attack on the West. They do however suggest a greater willingness than in the past to undertake a course of action, including a possible use of force in local areas, which might lead to an accidental outbreak of general military conflict. Thus, the chance of war through miscalculation is increased."[24] However, the Soviet nuclear capability ended the United States' fifty-year reliance on its vast mobilization capacity to either deter Eurasian great powers from initiating a global war or to defeat that challenger should war break out. Once the Soviets had a sufficient number of atomic bombs and long-range bombers, the continental United States would be vulnerable to a preventive or preemptive attack.[25]

The administration faced additional setbacks, including the flight of Chiang and the KMT army to Taiwan, Mao's proclamation of the People's Republic of China (PRC) on 1 October 1949, and the conclusion of the Sino-Soviet alliance treaty on 14 February 1950. As early as 1947, Marshall and others at the State Department concluded that the United States could do little to influence the outcome of the Chinese civil war.[26] In the letter of transmittal to the ill-fated August 1949 *China White Paper*, Secretary of State Dean Acheson wrote: "Nothing that this country did or could have done within the reasonable limits of its capabilities could have changed the result; nothing that was left undone by this country has contributed to it."[27]

Despite this recognition, officials saw the impending "loss of China" as indicative of an adverse power trend. In May 1949, the CIA acknowledged that while a Communist victory might shift the regional balance of power, China would remain heavily dependent on foreign aid and the "superior ability to provide such assistance belongs to the U.S., not the USSR."[28] The JCS reiterated their view that a CCP victory would enhance Soviet influence throughout East Asia, but recognized the futility of additional military aid to Chiang. "The loss of China to the Communists," argued then Deputy Undersecretary of State Dean Rusk, "has marked a shift in the balance-of-power in favor of Soviet Russia and to the disfavor of the United States."[29]

At home, Republicans denounced the administration's China policy. In January 1950, Taft accused Truman of handing China to the Communists. A month later, Wisconsin senator Joseph McCarthy accused Acheson of harboring 205 Communists in the State Department. New Hamp-

shire senator Henry Styles Bridges called for the secretary's resignation.[30] In an effort to placate critics, Truman replaced Butterworth with
the more hawkish Rusk as assistant secretary of state for Far Eastern Affairs on 28 March. On 18 May, Truman named Republican John Foster
Dulles as special advisor to Acheson, with responsibility for negotiating
a Japan peace treaty.[31]

Truman and his advisors concluded that the balance of power would
shift against the United States in the absence of corrective action. On 31
January 1950, Truman authorized the secretaries of state and defense "to
undertake a reexamination of our objectives in peace and war and of the
effect of these objectives on our strategic plans, in the light of the probable fission bomb capability and possible thermonuclear bomb capability
of the Soviet Union."[32] Acheson and Johnson assembled a study group
composed of members of the PPS and the Joint Strategic Survey Committee (JSSC), with Nitze as chair. After two months of deliberations, the
group presented its report, eventually designated NSC-68.[33]

Three themes run throughout the document. First, despite the adverse
power oscillation, the United States could remain preponderant. The
CIA warned the "West now lagged behind the USSR in terms of total
gain of political, economic and military strength."[34] With four times the
Soviet GNP, however, the United States could reverse this trend through
a dramatic increase in defense spending and by shifting its military doctrine from minimal deterrence and reliance on atomic air power to a full
war fighting posture.[35] NSC-68 reiterated the conclusion of the NSC-7 in
1948: "Between the United States and the USSR there are in Europe and
Asia areas of great potential power which if added to the existing
strength of the Soviet world would enable the latter to become so superior in manpower, resources, and territory that the prospect for the survival of the United States as a free nation would be slight."[36] In addition
to a separate peace treaty and a security pact with Japan, the report
called for a military commitment to NATO, expanded efforts to promote
Western European political and economic integration, and the further integration of West Germany into the western bloc.[37]

Second, efforts to redress the power oscillation would take several
years. In 1950–53, however, Washington faced a window of vulnerability. "On the basis of current programs, the United States has a large potential military capability but an actual capability which, though improving, is declining relative to the USSR, particularly in light of its
probable fission bomb capability and possible thermonuclear bomb capability. . . . If war breaks out in 1950 or in the next few years, the United
States and its allies, apart from a powerful atomic blow, will be compelled to conduct delaying actions, while building up their strength for a
general offensive."[38] Officials did not believe that the Soviet Union
would initiate a general war in 1950–52. Still, they feared that growth in

the Soviet atomic arsenal and long-range bombers could tempt Stalin or his successors into undertaking bolder diplomatic moves or precipitating international crises.[39]

Third, as balance-of-risk theory would expect, NSC-68 reaffirmed the necessity of maintaining the territorial status quo during the window of vulnerability. After the proposed military buildup, the United States would have the capabilities to "induce a contraction of the Kremlin's power and influence."[40] In the short-term, however, NSC-68 and related documents reaffirmed the defensive perimeter strategy in the Pacific. Since Western Europe was the primary theater of the cold war, it made sense to confine the U.S. military presence to East Asian islands capable of defense by sea or air—the Ryukus, the Philippines, and Japan. Holding these would facilitate access to the strategic raw materials of India and Southeast Asia, particularly if the Suez Canal were closed.[41]

While there was consensus on Japan, the Philippines, and the Ryukus, there was considerable debate over Taiwan. Johnson, Rusk, and Dulles favored an explicit commitment to defend the island. General Omar N. Bradley, the chairman of the Joint Chiefs of Staff, told Johnson in December 1949 that "a modest, well-directed and closely supervised program of military aid to the anti-Communist government of Taiwan would be in the security interests of the United States."[42] On the other hand, Acheson concluded that Taiwan would probably fall within the year and wanted to use the prospect of diplomatic recognition to drive a wedge between Moscow and Beijing. He wrote to Truman, "U.S. military assistance enabling the Chinese Nationalist government to continue the fight on Formosa would turn Chinese anti-foreign feelings against us and place us in the position of subsidizing attacks on a government [in Beijing] that would soon be widely recognized. We have now extricated ourselves from the Chinese civil war and it is important that we not be drawn into it again."[43] On 5 January 1950, Truman announced that the United States would neither intervene in the Taiwan Straits, nor provide military assistance to the belligerents in the Chinese civil war.[44] This statement was controversial and led to considerable debate over the next several months.[45] However, at the time no senior official in the administration contemplated a military commitment to South Korea. Acheson's infamous 12 January speech at the National Press Club, in which he excluded Korea from the defensive perimeter, was simply an articulation of long-established policy.[46]

Outbreak of the Korean War (June–July 1950)

The setbacks of the previous months made the Truman administration sensitive to any further deterioration in relative power and credibility. The North Korean invasion on 25 June 1950 came as a complete shock, despite periodic border clashes and the military imbalance on the peninsula. By 30 June, Truman and his advisors, who had sought to avoid an East Asian land war, sent troops to defend South Korea and the Seventh Fleet to block the Taiwan Straits. Balance-of-risk theory predicts that aversion to perceived losses in terms of their state's relative power and reputation for resolve drove the decisions of American leaders.

At 4:00 a.m. on Sunday 24 June (local time), North Korean tanks and infantry launched a surprise attack across the Thirty-eighth Parallel. The State Department received the first news in a cable from John Muccio, the U.S. ambassador in Seoul, at 9:16 p.m. (EDT). Rusk and John D. Hickerson, the assistant secretary of state for U.N. Affairs, immediately telephoned Acheson at his farm in Maryland. Acheson directed Hickerson to arrange for an emergency meeting of the Security Council the following day. He then telephoned Truman, who was in Independence, Missouri. The president agreed to return to Washington the following morning.[47]

Truman convened a meeting of top advisors at Blair House on the evening of 25 July. The participants included Acheson; Rusk; Hickerson; James E. Webb, the undersecretary of state; Philip C. Jessup, the ambassador-at-large; Johnson; Stephen T. Early, the deputy secretary of defense; Frank Pace, Jr., the secretary of the army; Francis P. Matthews, the secretary of the navy; Thomas K. Finletter, the secretary of the air force; Bradley; and the other JCS members—Admiral Forrest P. Sherman, the chief of naval of operations; General J. Lawton Collins, the army chief of staff; and General Hoyt S. Vandenberg, the air force chief of staff. After briefing the others about the latest battlefield developments, Acheson recommended that the president authorize MacArthur to supply ROK troops with weapons and equipment beyond the levels authorized in the 1949 Mutual Defense Assistance Act. He further proposed that the Far East Air Forces (FEAF) provide cover for retreating ROK troops and assist in the evacuation of American dependents in Seoul, with authorization to fire on any KPA tank that interfered. Finally, he recommended the immediate deployment of the Seventh Fleet to the Taiwan Strait to deter both sides in the Chinese civil war from attacking the other.

Bradley agreed with Acheson's proposals, noting "the Korean situation offered as good an occasion for action in drawing the line as anywhere else." Sherman added that "the Russians do not want war now, but if they do they will have it." Pace expressed doubts about the advisability of sending ground troops to Korea. Vandenberg agreed that the United States had to stop the North Korean invasion, but warned against basing policy on the "assumption that the Russians would not fight." When Truman asked if FEAF planes could "take out" Soviet bases near Korea, Vandenberg replied yes, but noted that doing so might require

atomic bombs. Finletter added that "our forces in the Far East are sufficient if the Russians do not come in." The president ordered the air force
to prepare plans "to wipe out all Soviet air bases in the Far East." He approved all of Acheson's recommendation, but also emphasized the importance of making careful estimates of other potential sites for Soviet-
backed aggression.[48]

At this point, officials simply assumed that the North Korean invasion was part of a coordinated campaign of Soviet-backed aggression or
subversion. Stalin had likely intended the invasion as a diversion for a
Soviet move elsewhere or a probe of American resolve.[49] On 25 June, Truman told his aide George Elsey that "Korea is the Greece of the Far East.
If we are tough enough now, if we stand up to them [that is, the Soviets]
like we did in Greece three years ago, they won't take any steps."[50] Paul
Kirk, the U.S. ambassador in Moscow, cabled Acheson to say that the
North Korean invasion represented "a clear-cut Soviet challenge which
the U.S. should answer firmly and swiftly as it constitutes a direct threat
to our leadership of the free world."[51] A 28 June CIA report stated that
"the invasion of the Republic of Korea by the North Korean army was
undoubtedly undertaken at Soviet direction. . . . By choosing Korea as
the area of attack, the USSR was able to challenge the U.S. specifically
and test the firmness of U.S. resistance to Communist expansion."[52]

On 26 June, the Security Council met at Lake Success and unani-
mously passed a resolution calling for the immediate cessation of hostilities and the withdrawal of North Korean forces. Yaacov Malik, the Soviet ambassador to the United Nations, was not present to veto the
resolution; he had boycotted council meetings since January 1950 to
protest its refusal to admit PRC representatives and expel the representatives of Chiang's government-in-exile. Meanwhile, the military situation
deteriorated. MacArthur initially reported that ROK troops could hold
the line, but it soon became readily apparent to embassy officials in
Seoul and the Far Eastern Command (FEC) Headquarters in Tokyo that
the KPA would capture Seoul. By the morning of 27 June (the afternoon
of 26 June in Washington), KPA tanks had reached striking distance of
Seoul and Rhee's government fled the capital.[53]

Acheson, Hickerson, Rusk, Jessup, Johnson, Pace, Finletter, Matthews,
Bradley, and the other chiefs, joined by Deputy Undersecretary of State
H. Freeman Matthews, met with Truman on the evening of 26 June at
Blair House. Acheson proposed suspending all restrictions on the use of
naval and air power in the area and using U.S. planes to "offer the fullest
possible support to the South Korean forces, attacking tanks, guns,
columns, etc. of the North Korean forces in order to give a chance for the
South Koreans to reform." Pace asked whether the president would permit military aircraft to fly north of the Thirty-eighth Parallel, to which

Truman replied, "not yet." Acheson further recommended that the administration tell Chiang to desist from any military operations against the Chinese mainland and that the Seventh Fleet remain in the Taiwan Strait. Rusk informed the meeting that George Kennan, the State Department's counselor and Nitze's predecessor as PPS director, estimated that Taiwan would likely be the next target. Bradley warned that if the president were to "commit ground forces to Korea, we cannot at the same time carry out other commitments without [a general] mobilization," a view also shared by Collins. The three service secretaries raised operational questions about the introduction of ground troops, but nonetheless supported direct military intervention. In concluding his report, Acheson observed "that it is important for us to do something even if the effort were not successful."[54]

On 27 June, the president met with the congressional leadership at the White House. Truman said that he and advisors unquestionably believed that "if we let Korea down, the Soviets will keep right on going and swallow up one piece of Asia after another. . . . If we were to let Asia go, the Near East would collapse and no telling what would happen in Europe." He informed congressional leaders that Hickerson and Warren Austin, the U.S. ambassador to the United Nations, would submit a second resolution to the Security Council calling for the restoration of peace and security in Korea. Democratic leaders at the meeting supported the administration's actions. However, Nebraska senator Kenneth Wherry, the Republican leader, argued that the president had an obligation to consult Congress before committing troops to Korea.[55] Other Republicans, including Knowland, Taft, James Kem of Missouri, and Arthur Watkins of Utah, raised similar concerns on the Senate floor.[56]

At the 28 June NSC meeting, Acheson stated that the deployment of ground and naval forces did not necessarily constitute "a decision to engage in a major war with the Soviet Union if Soviet forces intervene in Korea." However, he observed: "The decision regarding Korea . . . was undertaken in the full realization of a risk of war with the Soviet Union."[57] Likewise, Truman continued to worry about possible Soviet intervention in Korea or an attack elsewhere. He ordered the CIA, the State and the Defense departments to review all position papers affecting the entire Soviet perimeter. Ambassador Averell Harriman, Truman's new special assistant for foreign affairs, reported on the favorable European reaction to the steps the administration had already taken.[58] Britain, Australia, New Zealand, and Canada offered combat aircraft, troops, and naval forces in support of the American effort in Korea. Truman said that he welcomed military assistance from other UN members.[59] Finally, against the advice of Finletter and Vandenberg, the president refused to let the air force operate north of the Thirty-eighth

Parallel, only to reverse that decision the following day. Truman ordered troops to secure the airfields and port facilities at Seoul and Pusan.[60]

MacArthur flew to the front on 29 June (30 June in Seoul) and soon reached the conclusion that the North Korean army would conquer the south in the absence of external intervention. In a cable to the JCS, he recommended the immediate deployment of a regimental combat team, followed by two army divisions stationed in Japan.[61] On the morning of 30 June, Truman discussed MacArthur's recommendations with Acheson, Johnson, Early, Harriman, Pace, Finletter, Matthews, and the JCS. At this meeting, the president decided to commit ground forces to South Korea, permit bombing missions north of the Thirty-eighth Parallel, and establish a naval blockade of the entire Korea coast.[62]

Truman established a limited war aim: the preservation of an independent South Korea and a restoration of the Thirty-eighth Parallel.[63] Some officials, however, were skeptical about the wisdom of military intervention. Deputy Undersecretary Matthews suggested that the administration was devoting "too much attention to Korea and not enough attention to the effects of the Korean War on other parts of the world." Jessup argued that the main danger in Korea was not Soviet intervention, but rather Chinese intervention. Charles E. Bohlen, one of the State Department's leading Soviet experts, warned that it would be dangerous for the United States to become deeply committed in Korea "without replacing military units which were called up from other areas."[64]

The 25–30 June intervention decisions support balance-of-risk theory. Truman and other officials considered four options: (1) the continuation of existing policies, (2) the use of airpower to provide cover for retreating South Korean troops and the deployment of the Seventh Fleet to the Taiwan Straits, (3) the use of airpower above the Thirty-eighth Parallel to disrupt North Korean supply lines, and (4) full-scale intervention by ground, naval, and air forces to reverse the North Korean invasion. The administration quickly abandoned the first option and then pursued the remaining three in succession. No option was completely free of risk and each entailed difficult trade-offs. However, given the administration's oft-stated desire to avoid an entrapment in an East Asian ground war or a confrontation with the Soviets in the near term, the two latter options entailed high risks. As the theory expects, officials pursued risk-acceptant intervention options in the periphery as a means to avoid perceived losses to reputation for resolve and relative power.

A continuation of technical assistance and weapons sales to Rhee's government would have resulted in the almost certain conquest of South Korea. Nonetheless, existing policies would have avoided the possible entrapment of understrength army divisions in an East Asian war and enabled the United States to focus on the short-term defense of Western

Europe. One might argue that nonintervention was a risky strategy because a unified Korea under Kim would pose a direct threat to Japan and Taiwan. However, the CIA confirmed on 19 June, that the North Korean navy had few ships and no experience in amphibious warfare.[65] Despite the post–World War II demobilization and defense spending constraints, the U.S. Navy was the most powerful in the world. The Seventh Fleet could defend strategic East Asian islands with minimal effort. While a North Korean victory would have been blow to U.S. reputation for resolve, it is not clear whether the fall of South Korea would have altered the balance of power in East Asia. In sum, nonintervention would have meant a sure loss, but one whose magnitude officials had difficulty in estimating.

The use of airpower to provide cover for retreating ROK troops and deployment of the Seventh Fleet to the Taiwan Straits entailed higher risks. Specifically, the air cover option ran the risk that air force and naval pilots might become combatants or prisoners of war. The Seventh Fleet's deployment was a policy reversal. Truman, Acheson, and the JCS saw the neutralization of straits as essential to preventing a CCP attack on Taiwan or a KMT effort to retake the mainland. However, while the administration might declare its neutrality and decline Chiang's offer to send troops to fight in Korea, there was the distinct possibility that Mao would interpret the naval presence in the straits as a sign of Washington's continued support for the KMT. This, in turn, would make it more difficult to exploit tensions between Beijing and Moscow, at least in the short-run.[66]

The use of airpower in North Korea entailed greater risks than simply allowing the air force to provide cover for retreating ROK troops. If, as officials suspected in the 25–30 June period, Moscow orchestrated the invasion and sent weapons, equipment, technical and military personnel to North Korea, then FEAF planes might inadvertently fire on Soviet personnel stationed north of the Thirty-eighth Parallel. This ran the risk of a direct confrontation with Soviet forces. Furthermore, as Vandenberg noted on 25 June, any effort to cripple Soviet air bases near Korea would likely require the use of nuclear weapons. The United States had nearly three hundred atomic bombs and more than 260 aircraft capable of delivering them to Soviet territory in June 1950, whereas the Soviet Union had exploded its first nuclear device tenth months earlier and only had eight to ten atomic bombs in its arsenal at that point. Yet, officials also recognized that America was vulnerable to a retaliatory nuclear strike. The Soviet air force had 300 to 400 TU-4 medium range bombers capable of undertaking one-way missions to deliver atomic bombs to targets in North America. Alternatively, the Soviets could smuggle nuclear weapons into U.S. harbors aboard merchant ships. In short, the use of air power above the Thirty-eighth Parallel entailed some risk of inadvertent escalation.[67]

Troop deployment was arguably the riskiest of the four options given the uncertainty about Soviet intentions in June 1950 and the state of American conventional forces. In the 25–30 June period, Truman, Acheson, Rusk, Johnson, the JCS, and others assumed that North Korean invasion was part of a calculated Soviet plan to probe American resolve in East Asia or a diversion for a possible Soviet move elsewhere. Stalin's reluctance to risk a clash with the United States in Korea or to launch a limited probe elsewhere did not become apparent until early July.

The army's authorized strength was 630,201 troops, as opposed to its actual strength of 591,000 troops (including reserves) in June 1950. Approximately 360,000 troops were in the United States, with the remaining 231,000 assigned to overseas commands, most performing occupation duties. Slightly under half of the overseas troops, 108,000 soldiers, were under the jurisdiction of the FEC. MacArthur commanded only four understrength divisions with little combat experience and seven antiaircraft artillery battalions on the Japanese main islands and one infantry regiment and two antiaircraft battalions in Okinawa. The Eighth Army, the main combat arm of the FEC, had 45,451 troops (of whom 26,494 were combat ready) out of an authorized strength of 87,215 troops.[68] The CIA and army intelligence estimated that the Soviet army had twenty-five combat-ready divisions stationed in East Germany and Poland, with an additional fifty to sixty divisions ready to provide support at a moment's notice. If the North Korean invasion had been a diversion, the army would not have been able to quickly redeploy its troops to other theaters.[69]

Offensive realism holds that rising power and international opportunity leads states to pursue risky interventions in the periphery. As the documentary record reveals, officials did not perceive an increase in relative capabilities or see the war as an opportunity to expand American influence. The United States had yet to translate its overwhelming advantage in potential and economic power into military power. Truman did not ask Congress for a $10 billion supplemental defense appropriation until 19 July. In various meetings, the JCS and the service secretaries worried about whether the forces-in-being would be sufficient to simultaneously reverse the North Korean invasion and defend other areas.

Domestic politics no doubt entered into officials' calculations, although the documentary evidence is sparse. Truman and his advisors realized that they could not expect Republican support for containment in Europe and military intervention in South Korea, if they simultaneously allowed the Chinese Communists to conquer Taiwan. As Thomas Christensen observes, "Truman and Acheson had learned the lesson that, because of domestic constraints on grand strategy, nothing significant could be done in Europe, let alone Korea, without assistance to Chiang and public hostility toward Beijing."[70] Nonetheless, this is hardly strong support for the logrolling theory hypotheses introduced in chapter 2. There is little, if any, discussion of the preferences of the Asia-first nationalists in the documentary record. Indeed, support among Senate Republicans for military intervention in Korea was tepid. According to one account of the 24 June meeting at Blair House, Webb raised the likely implications of the Korean conflict on the Democrats' prospects in the upcoming congressional elections. Truman chastised Webb and forbade any further discussion of domestic politics in high-level meetings.[71]

From Containment to Rollback (August–October 1950)

Truman and his advisors established the restoration of the status quo in Korea as their expectation level. However, from late August onward, rollback—the destruction of the KPA and the military reunification of Korea—became the administration's expectation level. Officials began to receive signals that Beijing would not tolerate the presence of U.S. troops above the Thirty-eighth Parallel. This poses an anomaly for balance-of-risk theory, which expects leaders to pursue risky intervention strategies in the periphery to avoid perceived losses relative to their expectation level. Instead, policymakers not only adopted a risky strategy to secure gains over their initial expectation level, but they also adopted new expectation level. Offensive realism, on the other hand, provides a compelling explanation for this escalation of war aims.

The Debate over War Aims (July–August)

The first American troops arrived in South Korea on 1 July. Six days later, the Security Council passed a resolution establishing a combined command under U.S. leadership. Truman designated MacArthur as the commander-in-chief of the United Nations Command in Korea (CINCUNC), in addition to his post as CINCFE, the following day. Rhee placed all South Korean forces under the United Nations Command (UNC) on 15 July. The Eighth Army, under Lieutenant General Walton Walker, managed to hold the line against the KPA offensive at Pusan, some 150 miles south of Seoul. By mid August, Britain, France, the Netherlands, Belgium, Greece, Turkey, Canada, Australia, New Zealand, Argentina, Brazil, South Africa, Pakistan, Thailand, and the Philippines had all contributed troops to the UNC.[72]

Initially, Truman insisted that the United States only sought the restoration of the status quo ante. Ground operations north of the Thirty-eighth Parallel risked direct Soviet and Chinese intervention, a point that he and Acheson reiterated in late June and early July.[73] In a 12 July letter to Nitze, Acheson said that the United States had to drive the KPA back to the Thirty-eighth Parallel. After reoccupying South Korea, the United States would have to garrison it, but under no circumstances should the war expand into China.[74] Furthermore, Truman wanted to avoid any step that might bring the Russians into the conflict. Accordingly, he rejected a suggestion by the director of central intelligence, Rear Admiral Roscoe Hillenkoetter, to seek Security Council sanction for the use of atomic bombs even if doing so could not guarantee that the Soviet Union would restrain North Korea and China.[75]

The president made two decisions, however, that set the stage for an escalation of war aims. First, on 17 July, he ordered the NSC, the CIA, the State and the Defense departments to undertake a comprehensive review of options once the UNC forces reached the Thirty-eighth Parallel.[76] Second, on 19 July, he requested that Congress increase defense spending by $10 billion to fund an immediate conventional force buildup. Johnson had already approved plans to increase the number of army personnel from 630,000 to 834,000, the number of navy combat ships from 238 to 282, and the number of air force wings from 48 to 58. At the 28 June NSC meeting, Truman requested departmental estimates for the implementation of NSC-68 by 1 September.[77]

John Allison, director of Northeast Asian Affairs at the State Department, first raised the issue of rollback with his superior, Rusk, on 1 July. He wrote, "I am convinced that there will be no permanent peace and stability in Korea as long as the artificial division at the Thirty-eighth Parallel continues." Later he wrote, "At the very least we should destroy the North Korean army, through force if necessary, or by disarmament under UN auspices as result of an offer of peace."[78] Allison and John Paton Davies, an East Asian expert on the PPS, explicitly linked rollback in Korea to the containment strategy codified in NSC-48 and NSC-68: "Since a basic policy of the U.S. is to check and reduce the preponderant power of the USSR in Asia and elsewhere, then UN operations in Korea can set the stage for the non-Communist penetration of areas under Soviet control."[79] Dulles expressed similar views. On 14 July, he wrote to Nitze, "The Thirty-eighth Parallel was never intended to be, and never ought to be, a political line. The United Nations has, from the beginning, insisted that justice and equality required a united Korea. . . . If we have the opportunity to obliterate the line as a policy division, certainly we should do so."[80]

Bradley and the service chiefs argued that it made little sense to halt at the Thirty-eighth Parallel, a line that "from the point of view of military operations . . . had no more significance than any other median." The failure of UNC forces to move forward would guarantee a return of military instability on the Korean Peninsula. Furthermore, the elimination of North Korea would provide "the United States and the free world with the first opportunity to displace part of the Soviet orbit." This, in turn, would disturb "the strategic complex that the USSR is organizing between its own Far Eastern territories and the contiguous area."[81] Johnson not only favored rollback in Korea, but also stronger military ties to Taiwan. However, the defense secretary's equivocation on a presidential order to have MacArthur retract an inflammatory 26 August statement to the Veterans of Foreign Wars, as well as his bitter rivalry with Acheson and conniving with the administration's Republican critics, led Truman to dismiss him on 12 September.[82] Truman nominated former secretary of state and former army chief of staff, General of the Army George Marshall, to replace him. Marshall, in turn, asked Robert Lovett to return to government as deputy secretary of defense. Like their predecessors, the new Pentagon team strongly favored rollback in Korea, if the chance of Soviet or Chinese intervention remained low.[83]

The main argument against rollback centered on the likelihood of large-scale Soviet or Chinese intervention. Opponents also stressed the need to stabilize Korea as quickly as possible and then deploy U.S. troops to more vital areas. During a 30 June meeting with Matthews, Jessup, and Hickerson, Bohlen warned that it "would be dangerous for us to become committed more deeply in Korea without replacing military units which were called up from other areas." Jessup noted that the main danger of external intervention in Korea came from the Chinese Communists.[84] Nitze warned, "The risks of bringing on a major conflict with the USSR or Communist China, if UN military action north of the Thirty-eighth Parallel is employed in an effort to reach a 'final' settlement in Korea, appear to outweigh the policy advantage that might be gained from such further military action."[85] In mid August, the CIA estimated that, "although an invasion of North Korea by UN forces could, if successful, bring several important advantages to the U.S., it appears at present that grave risks would be involved in such a course of action."[86] Kennan, who planned to leave government in late August, wrote to Acheson: "It is not essential to us to see an anti-Soviet Korean regime extended to *all* of Korea for all time. . . . It is beyond our capabilities to keep Korea out of the Soviet orbit."[87]

British prime minister Clement Atlee warned Truman on 6 July that sending coalition troops over the parallel might provoke more direct Soviet or Chinese assistance to North Korea. Likewise, British foreign secretary Ernest Bevin told Acheson that Beijing might see military operations near the Sino-Korean border as a provocation and that an escalation of the war would divert resources from European defense.[88] On 9 July, the Indian prime minister Jawaharlal Nehru proposed that, in return for the Truman administration's support for the admission of the PRC to the United Nations, Beijing and Moscow would support an "immediate cease-fire" in Korea, the withdrawal of North Korean troops to the Thirty-eighth Parallel, and UN mediation toward the creation of unified independent Korea. Acheson rejected Nehru's proposal, arguing that the Korean conflict and China's admission to the UN were completely unrelated issues.[89]

MacArthur weighed into the debate with a third option, which never received serious consideration: the deliberate expansion of the war into China. On 13 July, MacArthur told Collins and Vandenberg (who were visiting Tokyo) that he intended "to destroy and not [just] drive back the North Korean forces. I may need to occupy all of North Korea."[90] Later, MacArthur's repeated calls to help the KMT retake the Chinese mainland, prompted Truman and Acheson to send Harriman to Tokyo in early August to explain the administration's policy to the Far East commander.[91]

NSC 81/1, which Truman approved on 11 September, argued that Korean reunification had military advantages for the United States and that actions to bring this about were consistent with the June and July Security Council resolutions. The report stipulated that American troops should only cross the Thirty-eighth Parallel and occupy North Korea if neither the Soviet Union nor China intervened or threatened to intervene. Under no circumstances should military operations extend to Soviet or Chinese territory. Furthermore, only South Korean troops would approach the Sino-Korean border. In the event of Soviet or Chinese intervention, MacArthur should stabilize the front at "the most favorable possible position," without risking escalation to general war. The president, not MacArthur, would make a final decision in light of "any action of the Soviet Union or the Chinese Communists, consultations and agreements with friendly members of the United Nations, and an appraisal of the risk of general war."[92]

Battlefield Developments and Systemic Opportunities

Between late August to early October 1950, battlefield developments and systemic opportunities combined to make rollback an increasing attractive goal for the Truman administration. These opportunities included: (1) MacArthur's successful landing at Inchon and the subsequent UNC counteroffensive, (2) the decreased likelihood of Soviet intervention in Korea or provocative moves elsewhere, and (3) China's perceived military weakness.

In early August, MacArthur proposed staging an amphibious landing at the port city of Inchon, near the Thirty-eighth Parallel. The JCS expressed strong reservations, but grudgingly approved the plan on 28 August. On 15 September, troops from the X Corps, under Lieutenant General Edward Almond, landed at Inchon and within eleven days managed to cut off North Korean supply lines and recapture Seoul. On 29 September, Marshall wrote to MacArthur: "We want you to feel unhampered tactically and strategically to operate north of the Thirty-eighth Parallel."[93] The General Assembly adopted a U.S.-sponsored resolution on 7 October that endorsed "all appropriate steps be taken to ensure conditions of stability throughout Korea . . . including, the holding of elections, under the auspices of the United Nations for the establishment of a unified, independent, and democratic government in the sovereign state of Korea."[94]

Soviet circumspection contributed to the Truman administration's growing risk acceptance. On 11 August, Kirk cabled Acheson to report that the Kremlin had made no apparent preparations for an offensive in Western Europe or intervention in Korea.[95] Malik ended his Security Council boycott on 1 August and, contrary to expectations, did not demand that that PRC representatives receive the permanent seat on the council still occupied by KMT representatives. Instead, over the next few weeks, Soviet diplomats sent out strong signals that they were interested in negotiations on Korea. Soviet foreign minister Andrei Vynshinsky delivered a comparatively restrained speech at the opening session of the General Assembly on 21 September, in which he expressed concern about the Korean conflict.[96] Later Malik and Vynshinsky approached Austin and Jessup to discuss the possibility of Korean peace talks. Moreover, the Soviet foreign ministry filed only mild diplomatic protests in response to FEAF bombings of targets near the Soviet-Manchurian border.[97] By mid October, the CIA concluded, "Soviet leaders will not consider that their prospective losses in Korea warrant direct military intervention and a consequent grave risk of war. They will intervene in Korean hostilities only if they have decided . . . that it is in their interests to precipitate a global war at this time."[98]

Senior officials further concluded that crossing the Thirty-eighth Parallel would likely not lead China to enter the war. First, and foremost, they perceived the PRC as militarily weak. The Joint Intelligence Committee (JIS) concluded that Mao would be preoccupied with internal security and that the People's Liberation Army (PLA) was not prepared for conventional combat. The CIA reported that Beijing's "domestic problems are of such magnitude that the regime's entire domestic program and economy would be jeopardized by the strains and the material damage which would be sustained in war with the United States . . . the regime's very existence would be endangered."[99] Officials inferred that Soviet restraint in Korea would likely mean that China would avoid intervention as well. Although Acheson had initially hoped to drive a wedge between Beijing and the Kremlin, by late summer 1950 he and most officials simply assumed that Mao took orders from Stalin. On 12 October, the CIA concluded that open Chinese intervention "would be extremely costly unless protected by powerful Soviet air cover and naval support" and that there was little evidence that such assistance was forthcoming.[100]

Finally, officials assumed that the Sino-Soviet treaty merely papered over the rivalry between Moscow and Beijing. In early October, Acheson concluded that Chinese invention in Korea would be "sheer madness" given Soviet pressure in the north.[101] The CIA reported that "acceptance of major Soviet aid would make [Beijing] more dependent on Soviet help and increase Soviet control in Manchuria to a point probably unwelcome to the Chinese Communists. . . . While full scale Chinese Communist intervention in Korea must be regarded as a continuing possibility, a consideration of all known factors leads to the conclusion that barring a Soviet decision for global war, such action is not probable in 1950."[102]

Deterrent Signals from Beijing (September–October)

As the debate continued in Washington, various Chinese officials warned that U.S. military operations above the Thirty-eighth Parallel would prompt the PRC to enter the war. The absence of diplomatic ties between the PRC and the United States, which still recognized Chiang's regime in Taipei as the legitimate Chinese government, forced both sides to communicate their intentions through third parties.

At the 7 July NSC meeting, Pace, noting FEC intelligence reports about the presence of some 200,000 PLA troops along the Sino-Korean border, worried that a possible Chinese intervention could force the withdrawal of UNC forces from the peninsula.[103] Yet, on 20 and 21 September, the State Department received, via the U.S. embassy in New Delhi, the estimate of Sardar K. M. Pannikar, the Indian ambassador to Beijing. Based on recent conversations with the Chinese premier and foreign minister Zhou En Lai, articles in the official press, and the absence of even "precautionary precaution against [U.S.] air raids" in Beijing, Pannikar concluded that Mao would not intervene. He reported that, "in these circumstances, direct participation of China in Korean fighting seems beyond the range of possibility, unless of course a world war starts as a result of UN forces [passing] beyond the Thirty-eighth Parallel and the Soviet Union [intervening]."[104] James Wilkinson, the American consul-general in Hong Kong, reported, based on mainland sources that, because Mao and Zhou desired entry into the United Nations and remained preoccupied with domestic affairs, the PRC would not attack Taiwan and would only provide token support to North Korea.[105]

On 27 September, sixteen days after Truman approved NSC 81/1, the State Department began to receive more disturbing messages. Hubert Graves, counselor in the British embassy in Washington, met with Livingston Merchant, Rusk's deputy. Graves presented Merchant with copies of three telegrams obtained from the British embassy in New Delhi. Based on his recent conversations with Zhou and General Nie Rongzhen, the acting chief of staff of the PLA, Pannikar now expected China to pursue a strategy of "indirect intervention" in North Korea. Nie was particularly alarmed by FEAF violations of Manchurian airspace and told Pannikar that the China "would not take such provocations lying down." In a 21 September meeting, Zhou told Pannikar that, "since the United Nations had no obligations to China, China had no obligations to the United Nations." The third telegram was a personal appeal by Nehru to Bevin urging that UN forces halt their advance at the Thirty-eighth Parallel.[106] In a 3 October meeting with Web and Matthews, Merchant urged that the administration treat the telegrams with "extreme seriousness and not discount it as a bluff."[107]

At midnight on 3 October, Zhou summoned Pannikar to the Chinese Foreign Ministry and gave him a message to pass to Washington: if American troops crossed the Thirty-eighth Parallel, China would enter the war. However, China would not intervene if only South Korean forces crossed the parallel.[108] The State Department received the message the following day. Edmund O. Clubb, director of the Office of Chinese Affairs, warned Merchant that the Zhou "demarche cannot safely be regarded as a mere bluff," and that "if China and the USSR are prepared now to accept the danger of war with the UN in Korea, this means they are prepared to risk the danger of World War III, and feel ready to meet that danger, given present comparative military strengths." In light of these signals, U. Alexis Johnson, Allison's deputy, suggested to Rusk that only South Korean troops cross the Thirty-eighth Parallel.[109] Most officials, however, dismissed the Zhou ultimatum. They assumed that the most opportune time for Chinese intervention had passed.[110] Furthermore, officials questioned the reliability of Pannikar. The CIA viewed him has a Communist sympathizer and an unwitting medium for a Chinese bluff. Rusk and Jessup thought that Pannikar was "temporarily following the party line for ulterior motives," a view shared by Acheson, Webb, and Hickerson.[111] Finally, having received mixed messages from different segments of the CCP in the past year, officials doubted the authority of Zhou to speak on behalf of Mao and the Politburo.[112]

In the period from 1 July to 7 October, Truman and advisors considered two options; neither was completely free of risk and both entailed difficult trade-offs. Containment would secure the expectation level set during the 25–30 June meetings: the restoration of the status quo. The pursuit of this limited objective would have avoided a possible escala-tion of the war. However, by only restoring the Thirty-eighth Parallel and allowing North Korea to rearm, the administration would find itself back in the position it had been in before 1949: providing military and economic aid to South Korea at the expense of commitments elsewhere. Acheson later observed: "In the longer run, if we should succeed in reoc-cupying the South, the question of garrisoning and supporting it would arise. This would be a hard task for us to take on, and yet it seemed hardly sensible to repel the attack and then abandon the country."[113]

Rollback, if successful, would have achieved an outcome far above the 30 June expectation level. Korean reunification would eliminate the need for long-term military and economic aid to South Korea. By late August, the subjective probability of Soviet intervention in the war or a move against Western Europe had diminished. Available information sug-gested the China was militarily weak and would likely not intervene militarily. Warnings from Zhou and Nie were not credible, in part be-cause of the lack of direct channels between Washington and Beijing.

Nonetheless, rollback was the riskier of the two options. There was still a chance that China would enter the war. This would require the possible deployment of additional troops to Korea, place additional strain on a tight defense budget, and force officials to consider a possible expansion of the war into China. An expanded war would likely work to the Soviet Union's advantage by creating dissention between Washing-ton and its allies. This would delay plans for the defense of Western Eu-rope. Furthermore, the armed forces were overstretched and under-strength. While the outbreak of the Korean War mobilized public support for higher defense spending, Congress had not yet enacted the massive spending increases recommended in NSC-68. As NSC 71/4, which Truman approved on 26 August, warned Soviets leaders would avoid general war or provocative diplomatic moves until they had calcu-lated that "the United States had reached the point of maximum diver-sion and attrition of its forces-in-being."[114]

The expansion of war aims poses an anomaly for balance-of-risk the-ory. Both the direction of elite risk-taking, risk-acceptant behavior to se-cure gains above the initial expectation level and the content of private deliberations and planning documents are more consistent with offen-sive realism. Rusk, Johnson, Marshall, Lovett, the JCS, and others stressed the opportunity to resolve the long-term problem of South Korea's defense. Soviet introspection, perceived Chinese weakness, and the success of MacArthur's Inchon operation provided the administration with the systemic and battlefield opportunities necessary for the United States to expand its influence in East Asia.

Logrolling theory, however, fares less well. National polls showed strong public support for a military effort to reunify in Korea, a position also supported by many members of Congress.[115] However, there is no evidence in primary sources to suggest that officials expanded the war's aims as means to secure congressional funding for higher defense spending, as logrolling theory would expect. While there was strong popular and congressional support for rollback, particularly after Inchon, Truman and his advisors began discussing the military reunification of Korea in mid July—when the Eighth Army was still trapped on the Pusan pocket.

THE YALU RIVER OFFENSIVE (OCTOBER–NOVEMBER 1950)

The ROK Second Corps crossed the Thirty-eighth Parallel on 1 October, followed by the Eighth Army six days latter. Unbeknown to officials in Washington, Mao made the initial decision to enter the war on 2 October; nothing short of a unilateral withdrawal of American troops from North Korea and the withdrawal of the Seventh Fleet from the Taiwan Straits would dissuade the PRC chairman from entering the war.[116] Within a week, Chinese People's Volunteers (CPV) began secretly crossing the Yalu River into North Korea. Despite the growing likelihood of Chinese intervention, Truman and his advisors simply did not reassess the feasibility of achieving the new expectation level codified in NSC 81/1. Instead, they gave MacArthur authorization to begin an offensive to the Yalu River.

The administration's behavior during this period is consistent with balance-of-risk theory. Senior officials escalated their commitment to a risky strategy in an effort to recover the sunk costs of their prior decisions. Those sunk costs involved the substantial investment of money, troops, weapons, and American prestige to the defense of South Korea (from 30 June). Since most officials expected UNC forces to conquer North Korea and to do so relatively easily, they saw anything short of the outcome of that goal as a loss. As the subjective probability of an adverse outcome increased—namely Chinese intervention possibly leading to an expanded war in East Asia—Truman and his advisors rejected repeated pleas by the British, French, and Indian governments to stabilize the front and seek a negotiated settlement. The continuation of MacArthur's drive northward was risk-acceptant relative to other options. The record of deliberations from 7 October to 27 November contains repeated references to the need to recoup the sunk costs of military operations.

Changing Assessments of Chinese Intentions and Capabilities

The JCS and Lovett proposed an addendum to the 27 September directive. The addendum, approved by Truman on 8 October, stated: "Hereafter in the event of the open or covert employment anywhere in Korea of major Chinese Communist units, without prior announcement, you [MacArthur] should continue the line of action as long as, in your judgment, action by forces now under your control offers a reasonable chance of success." The order forbade MacArthur from expanding military operations into Chinese territory without explicit authorization from Washington.[117]

On 15 October, Truman, Rusk, Pace, Jessup, and Harriman, flew to Wake Island to meet MacArthur. When the president asked about the likelihood of Chinese or Soviet military involvement in Korea, MacArthur replied that such intervention was unlikely since Chinese could get only fifty thousand to sixty thousand troops across the Yalu River. He noted that China had no air force and that the FEAF had air superiority in Korea. While the Soviets could provide air support, they would have problems coordinating their planes with Chinese ground operations.[118] The discussions merely reinforced the basic policy decision Truman and his advisors made weeks earlier: to continue the drive to the Yalu River, if the likelihood of Soviet or Chinese intervention remained low.

American and South Korean troops captured Pyongyang on 19 October, while Kim moved his seat of government to Sinjuiju, on the Yalu River. Meanwhile, reports of Chinese soldiers in North Korea and PLA troop concentrations in Manchuria increasingly concerned the administration. By 25 October, South Korean troops throughout the northwestern and northeastern sectors had encountered resistance from Chinese guerrillas.[119] Lieutenant General Walter Bedell Smith, the director of central intelligence, wrote to Truman on 1 November that "this pattern of events and reports indicates that Communist China has decided, regardless of the increased risk of general war, to provide increased support and assistance to North Korean forces."[120] On 3 November, FEC intelligence put the number of Chinese troops in Korea between 16,500 and 34,000, only to revise the number upward to 34,500 four days later.[121] On 6 November, MacArthur responded to the infiltration by ordering the bombing of the bridges connecting Sinjuiju to the city of Antung in Manchuria.[122] The following day, the CPVs broke contact with American and South Korean troops, thus adding further uncertainty about Chinese intentions and capabilities.

The administration wanted to avoid drawing China into the war, but not at the expense of achieving rollback in Korea. With the approval of Truman, the JCS overruled MacArthur's order and directed the suspension of all air operations within five miles of Sino-Korean border. This was consistent with an earlier promise Acheson made to Sir Oliver Franks, the British ambassador in Washington, to consult London before taking any action that might affect Manchuria. In a meeting with Acheson and Lovett, Rusk voiced concerns about the consequences for Anglo-American relations. He noted that the British cabinet would meet that morning "to consider their whole attitude toward the Chinese Communist government and . . . ill-considered action on our part might have grave consequences."[123]

Finletter and Vandenberg, while not wanting to initiate a full-scale war with China, told Rusk they felt "very strongly that the whole world should understand the great problem created by forces which are in position to attack UN forces from within a safe haven."[124] Truman lifted the bombing suspension on 8 November, but in a manner that satisfied no one. MacArthur had authority to bomb only the Korean side of the bridges. FEAF planes could not bomb Chinese dams and hydroelectric plants. Furthermore, "hot pursuit" of Chinese aircraft was impermissible and American pilots were to "avoid violation of Manchurian territory and airspace and to report promptly hostile action from Manchuria."[125]

The NSC met on 9 November to consider a possible alteration of MacArthur's mission. Smith presented a new National Intelligence Estimate (NIE) that put the number of Chinese troops in Korea between 30,000 and 40,000. In addition, the PLA could mobilize 350,000 troops within thirty to sixty days for sustained ground operations in Korea, without jeopardizing CCP control in Manchuria or China proper. The NIE further concluded that Chinese troops were capable of forcing a "U.N. withdrawal to defensive positions further south through a powerful assault."[126] A JCS option paper stated that "the Chinese Communists are presently in Korea in such strength and in a sufficiently organized manner as to indicate that, unless withdrawn, they can only be defeated by a determined military operation. . . . From the military standpoint, the continued commitment of U.S. forces in Korea is at the expense of more useful strategic deployment of those forces elsewhere." The report outlined three alternatives: (1) withdrawal of UN forces from North Korea; (2) the establishment of a defensive line at the present location of UN troops and (3) a continuation of MacArthur's advance northward. The JCS, Marshall, and Lovett flatly rejected the first two options. Instead, they recommended that the State Department explore the idea of a negotiated settlement with Beijing via third parties. In the meantime, MacArthur's mission would remain unchanged. Acheson, Webb, Rusk, Jessup, Hickerson, and Harriman did not object.[127]

Acheson made overtures to Chinese leaders through Sweden, but with no success.[128] He also hoped that the PRC delegation, enroute to Lake Success to participate in Security Council deliberations on Taiwan, would have the authority to discuss Korea. On 8 November, Secretary General Lie invited the PRC delegation to participate in upcoming Security Council discussions on Chinese intervention in Korea, but Zhou rejected the invitation.[129] Chinese diplomats did not arrive in Lake Success until 24 November; the day MacArthur began his "end-the-war" offensive. Meanwhile, Truman, Acheson, and Rusk publicly and repeatedly stated that the administration had no territorial objectives beyond Korea.[130]

The Allies Enter the Debate

As American and South Korean troops began to encounter CPVs in October, the allies and various neutral countries became apprehensive. Atlee proposed halting MacArthur's drive south of the Yalu and creating a demilitarized zone under joint UN and PRC administration. Bevin's 13 November proposal for a UN resolution in support of a buffer zone received a cool reception in Washington. In reply, Acheson wrote, "Giving up the part of Korea we do not yet occupy would at this time undoubtedly be interpreted as a sign of weakness."[131]

French foreign minister Robert Schuman proposed a General Assembly statement promising that UNC air forces would refrain from bombing Yalu River installations. On 14 November, the Netherlands' foreign minister, Dirk Stikker, warned that his government feared that violations of Manchurian airspace would prompt China to enter the war. Stikker also reported the presence of 500,000 Chinese troops in Manchuria, in addition to the 160,000 Chinese troops already in North Korea. The Dutch embassy in Beijing also reported that the PRC leadership wanted to avoid a clash with UNC troops, but only if they stayed at least fifty miles from the Sino-Korean border. The Canadian, Australian, and New Zealand foreign ministers expressed similar concerns to U.S. diplomats, as did Sir Girja S. Bajpai, the secretary-general of India's Ministry of External Affairs.[132]

Marshall and the JCS refused to accept any proposal that did not include provisions for a demilitarized zone on the Chinese side of the Yalu. On 8 November, Truman and Marshall approved a draft Security Council resolution which stated that U.S. and UN forces would not violate the Manchurian border "unless Chinese Communist continued their actions in Korea." The French felt the final condition was a veiled threat (which it was) and the State Department tried to modify it. Acheson and Marshall agreed on a comprise resolution that promised to hold the Sino-Korean border "inviolate," while also calling "attention to the grave danger which the continued intervention of Chinese forces would entail for the maintenance of such a policy."[133]

A Few Voices of Caution

Like the allies, a few mid-level officials in the State Department began to express reservations about MacArthur's planned offensive. Clubb warned Rusk that the probability of China's entry into the war had increased. "Although firm information to reach conclusions is still lacking," he wrote, "it would be hardly safe to assume other than that (1) the Chinese Communists, if they are intervening directly in Korea, propose to do so in considerable force, and (2) the Soviet Union would be behind that intervention in accordance with an overall military plan which presumably would . . . [inflict] defeats on the UN forces generally and perhaps the U.S. forces particularly." Similarly, on 18 November, Davies proposed a temporary halt to MacArthur's offensive and a withdrawal of UNC forces to the area north of Pyongyang and Wonsan. "The bulk of evidence," he argued pointed, "to the probability that the Kremlin and [Beijing] are committed to at least holding the northern fringe of Korea—and, that, against our present force they have the military capability of doing so."[134] Among officials, however, only Jessup supported a buffer zone. He wrote to Acheson on 20 November that the objective of "unity and independence of Korea . . . does not necessarily require the military occupation of all Korea to its northernmost boundaries. . . . At least ninety percent of the Korean population is in territory under the control of UN forces."[135]

A meeting of State and Defense department officials convened on 21 November at the Pentagon. Lovett reported that he received no information from MacArthur to suggest that his forces could not accomplish its mission. Marshall expressed "satisfaction that Mr. Acheson had stated his belief that General MacArthur should push forward with the planned offensive." He also expressed doubts about "the establishment of the [buffer] zone and assumed that if one were established south of the river another would have to be established to the north." Lovett questioned whether instead of negotiations for a buffer zone, it would better if MacArthur simply withdrew to a defensive line after completing his offensive to the Yalu River.[136]

Acheson argued that the administration needed to find some way to end the Chinese intervention, but he also acknowledged the difficulties inherent in establishing a buffer zone. Vandenberg doubted whether any solution would satisfy the Chinese, given Acheson's interpretation of their long-term fears. Collins suggested, and the other participants agreed, that after the beginning of the Yalu offensive, MacArthur "could announce that it was his intention only to go forward to destroy the North Korean units (in Manchuria) and that he intended to hold the high ground overlooking the Yalu with ROK forces." None of the participants supported the buffer zone proposal.[137]

From 7 October to 21 November, Truman and his advisors considered two options. The first was to proceed with the offensive to Yalu River. This option had a high potential payoff for policymakers, but it was also the more risk acceptant of the two. A continuation of the drive to the Yalu had the potential to destroy the remnants of the KPA and reunify Korea. This would fulfill the expectation level codified in NSC 81/1. At the same time, officials recognized that this option entailed a heightened risk of direct military confrontation with China. Recall that NSC 81/1 also called for an immediate withdrawal to the Thirty-eighth Parallel if China or the Soviet Union intervened. Although Truman and his advisors perceived China as militarily weak, they also recognized that a full-scale PLA counteroffensive might push MacArthur's forces out of North Korea or perhaps off the Korean Peninsula altogether. Even if the UNC forces managed to hold their positions above the Thirty-eighth Parallel in the face of the Chinese attack, the administration would likely find itself embroiled in a prolonged (and possibly expanded) land war in East Asia during the American window of vulnerability.

The second option, a cessation of the offensive and the establishment of a buffer zone between UNC forces and the Sino-Korean border, admittedly had a lower potential payoff for officials determined to reunify Korea. However, given the information available to officials in Washington at the time, this option had a higher likelihood of averting a full-scale Chinese counteroffensive. Establishing a demilitarized zone, either just south of the Yalu or above the Pyongyang-Wonsan line, may have given the administration more time to establish additional channels of communication with Beijing, reassess the relative capabilities of the PLA and the forces under MacArthur's command, or perhaps begin negotiations toward an armistice.[138]

Offensive realism does not explain the decision to continue MacArthur's drive to the Yalu River. By late October, the administration had abundant evidence of the presence of thousands of CPVs in North Korea and large PLA troop concentrations in Manchuria. Systemic opportunities—the low likelihood of Chinese intervention and the perceived weakness of Chinese military capabilities—were no longer present. Here, offensive realism would expect officials to adapt their war aims in light of changing strategic realities. It would further expect them to adopt the less risky alternative of halting the offensive and establishing a demilitarized zone. Likewise, logrolling theory finds little support in this period. As with the earlier decision to cross the Thirty-eighth Parallel, there is little evidence to suggest that the need to appease Asia-first nationalists in Congress or avoid electoral retribution drove the Truman administration's decision to proceed with the Yalu offensive. Although the Democrats lost four Senate seats and twenty-nine House seats in the 7 November election, no senior official raised the political repercussions of halting MacArthur's northward advance.[139]

Before considering the balance-of-risk theory hypothesis, one must consider another variant of *Innenpolitik* that attributes the decision to pursue the "end the war" offensive to the domestic prestige and influence of MacArthur. Proponents contend that MacArthur's reputation as a brilliant field commander, seniority, close ties to important segments of the Republican Party, and vocal criticism of the administration's European-centric grand strategy led Truman and others to defer to his judgment. The Inchon operation, which the JCS initially opposed, proved decisive in defeating the KPA and driving most its remnants back across the Thirty-eighth Parallel. Furthermore, the general's ill-concealed presidential ambitions made it very difficult for an embattled Democrat president to overrule him. When MacArthur downplayed the likelihood of Chinese intervention, no one questioned his judgment. Later, when he purposed the Yalu offensive, despite growing evidence that China would enter the war, officials acquiesced. In short, from 15 September until the PLA launched its counteroffensive on 28 November, no one in the administration or the Joint Chiefs dared question the judgment of the "sorcerer of Inchon."[140]

Clearly, Inchon enhanced MacArthur's already considerable reputation. However, proponents of this argument overstate his influence on the Truman administration's risk taking. First, before and after the Inchon, the president and his advisors frequently overruled the general's calls for an expanded war and the use of KMT troops. Second, there is no evidence to suggest that MacArthur deliberately downplayed the likelihood of Chinese intervention. On the contrary, his estimates during the Wake Island conference were similar to those recently reported by the CIA and army intelligence. Certainly, officials took advantage of MacArthur's unwise and grandiose statements after China entered the war.[141] In early November 1950, however, the Yalu offensive had the enthusiastic support of all but a handful of officials. Far from being a quixotic crusade by an ambitious general, this operation was consistent with the war aims the Truman administration officially adopted on 11 September.[142]

Instead, balance-of-risk theory provides the most persuasive explanation for the decision to proceed with the offensive. The theory holds that officials will likely continue and even escalate their commitment to risk-acceptant strategies in the periphery, in an effort to recover sunk costs. In this instance, the administration had still not achieved the expectation level codified in NSC 81/1 or recouped the costs of four months of military operations. The Yalu offensive was riskier than the alternatives because it entailed an increasingly high probability of an expanded war with China—an outcome that Truman and others sought to avoid. Even the most vocal supporters of the offensive acknowledged the presence of several thousand CPVs in North Korea and large PLA troop concentrations in Manchuria. Nonetheless, they refused to halt the offensive. Marshall, Lovett, Pace, and the JCS appeared more concerned with avoiding the operational and tactical difficulties inherent in establishing a defensive line than with averting an expanded war. Since most officials expected to complete the conquest of North Korea quickly and with little difficulty, they began to view any outcome short of that as a loss.

Epilogue: An Entirely New War (December 1950–January 1951)

The Chinese counteroffensive on 28 November plunged the United States into the most serious cold war crisis to date. During the next three months, the Truman administration again escalated its commitment to achieve the war aim originally established on 25 June 1950: the restoration of the Thirty-eighth Parallel and the preservation of an independent South Korea.

The Chinese Counteroffensive and Washington's Reaction

The UNC offensive to the Yalu River began on 24 November as scheduled. Instead of concentrating his forces, MacArthur deployed the Eighth Army, under Walker's command, along the western front and the X Corps, under Almond's command, in the central highlights. Together the two forces had slightly more than 110,000 troops in the field, but no substantial reserves of supplies or personnel. The following night, 256,000 Chinese and 10,000 North Korean troops launched a massive counteroffensive across the Yalu. Units of the Chinese People's Volunteer Army (CPVA) enveloped the X Corps and pushed the Eighth Army southward. On 30 November and 1 December alone, the Eighth Army's casualties exceeded 11,000.[143]

MacArthur asked for immediate reinforcements and authority to expand the war. On 28 November, he wrote to the JCS: "We face an entirely new war . . . it is quite evident that our present force strength is not sufficient to meet this undeclared war by the Chinese with the inherent advantages to them. The resulting situation presents an entire new picture which broadens the potentialities to world embracing considerations beyond the sphere of decision by the theater commander."[144] The following day, he proposed a four-point plan: (1) a naval blockade of the Chinese coast; (2) the use of air and naval bombardment to destroy China's industrial capacity to wage war; (3) the use of Nationalist Chinese troops to reinforce the Eighth Army and the X Corps; and (4) "unleashing" Chiang to attack the Chinese mainland. The JCS initially deferred acting on, and later rejected, MacArthur's plan.[145]

As the extent of the battlefield reversals for the UNC coalition became clear, recriminations flew. The constraints the president and the JCS placed on the conduct of the war, MacArthur told correspondents from the *New York Times* and *U.S. News and World Report* on 2 December, were "an enormous handicap, unprecedented in history."[146] Privately, officials blamed MacArthur for the Yalu debacle. Lovett said that the general's complaints to reporters were "among the most extraordinary things" he had ever seen. A furious Truman issued an order requiring all civilian and military personnel to clear any public statements on military and foreign policy through the State or Defense departments, respectively.[147]

Despite pleas from Truman and Acheson for national unity, several Republicans excoriated the administration for its conduct of the war. Senator Harry Cain of Washington declared that the field commander should "be given the right to strike wherever military necessity dictates, behind the Yalu River, or anywhere else." In a 2 December telegram to the president, McCarthy demanded to know why Truman allowed the "crimson clique in the State Department" to "run amuck with the lives of American soldiers." He further demanded the dismissal of Acheson and Marshall, and threatened impeachment proceedings against Truman if the administration did not use KMT troops in Korea.[148]

In a 30 November press conference, Truman mentioned that the use of nuclear weapons in Korea had always been under consideration and implied (incorrectly) that the decision on nuclear use rested with MacArthur. Although the administration quickly clarified its position— namely, that the only the president could authorize the use of nuclear weapons—Truman's ill-advised remarks produced a panic in Western European capitals and elsewhere. Within hours of the press conference, Atlee requested a face-to-face meeting with the president in Washington. Schuman and French premier René Pleven rushed to London to coordinate strategy with Atlee and Bevin.[149] Meanwhile at the United Nations, Austin reported that diplomats from Western Europe and the British Commonwealth appeared "greatly shocked" and feared that use of nuclear weapons in Korea would "inevitably start World War III."[150]

Limit the War to Korea, But Prepare for Global Conflict

In the first six days of the crisis (28 November to 4 December), the Truman administration reached consensus on a number of issues. The Chinese counteroffensive increased the likelihood of a regional war or even a general war with the Soviet Union. Moreover, this heightened risk during the window of vulnerability. At an emergency NSC meeting on 28 November, Acheson warned of the danger of general war and asked his colleagues to "remember that the Soviet Union had always been behind every [Chinese and North Korean] move." While the secretary of state recommended a six-power UN resolution branding the Chinese as aggressors, both he and Marshall agreed that the administration should avoid publicly branding the Soviets as an aggressor, at least for the time being.[151] Later that afternoon, Truman told his cabinet that "the situation is very dangerous and can develop into complete involvement in total war." The "possibly cannot be disregarded," the CIA concluded on 2 December, "that the USSR may already have decided to precipitate global war in circumstances most advantageous to itself through the development of general war in Asia."[152]

Truman and his advisors also agreed that for the moment, UNC forces should attempt to hold the line in North Korea. On 28 November, Acheson argued that an immediate withdrawal would be "disastrous." Rusk and Kennan, who had returned to Washington for emergency consultations, drew an analogy between the current crisis in Korea and Britain's decision to fight Nazi Germany alone after the fall of France in May 1940.[153] As the military situation grew worse over the next several days, Acheson, Marshall, Lovett, Jessup, and others argued that American prestige would suffer a terrible blow if MacArthur's forces withdrew from Korea before it became a military necessity. On 1 December, Marshall sent Collins to inspect the front in Korea and to confer with MacArthur. The administration and the JCS also decided that MacArthur and his field commanders would have to hold the line without major reinforcements. No new U.S. divisions could reach the combat theater until mid-March 1951. Bradley and Pace advised against the deployment of National Guard or regular army units to Korea, given strategic commitments elsewhere.[154] This commitment to hold the line, however, was conditional. On 29 December, the JCS wrote to MacArthur that: "[A] successful resistance to Chinese-North Korean aggression at some position in Korea and a deflation of the military and political prestige of the Chinese Communists would be of great important to our national interests, if this could be accomplished without incurring serious losses."[155] Two weeks later, the chiefs advised MacArthur to withdraw his forces if the costs of staying were too high: "Should it become evident in your judgment that evacuation is essential to avoid severe losses of men and materials you will at that time withdraw from Korea to Japan."[156]

At the same time, the president and his advisors were determined to avoid a wider war with China, if possible. This meant confining military operations to the Korean Peninsula and adjacent waters, unless the PLA and North Korean forces drove the UNC coalition from the peninsula altogether. During the 28 November NSC meeting, Bradley reported the presence of approximately three hundred PLA aircraft in Manchuria, including two hundred two-engine bombers. While Chinese aircraft could strike a severe blow against retreating American and UN forces in North Korea, he and the other chiefs did not recommend giving MacArthur authority to bomb Chinese bases in Manchuria. Bradley observed that "the situation [in Korea] may change in a week of two. The JCS feel just as strongly as the service secretaries that we should not be pulled into a war with the Chinese." Marshall also warned against air operations in Chinese territory: "If we enter Manchuria it would be very hard to stop and very easy to extend the conflict. If we were successful in Manchuria, the Russians probably enter to aid their Chinese ally without considering it war with us. . . . One imperative step is find a line [in Korea] and hold it." Likewise, Acheson argued that the "great trouble is that we are fighting the wrong nation. We are fighting the second team [China], whereas the real enemy is the Soviet Union."[157]

Truman and his advisors rejected the use of nuclear weapons, unless the PLA launched large-scale air strikes on American troops or if the UNC forces had to withdraw from the Korean peninsula altogether. In any other circumstance, the costs of nuclear weapons use outweighed any political or military benefit. The JCS recommended that Truman tell Atlee that the United States had "no intention" of using nuclear weapons in Korea unless they should be needed to protect the evacuation of UNC forces or to prevent a "major military disaster."[158] After inspecting the front and meeting with MacArthur in Tokyo on 5–7 December, Collins publicly announced that he saw no need to use atomic bombs in Korea and that military situation was not nearly as bad as had been feared.[159] To reassure the British and other allies, the communiqué following the Truman-Atlee meetings (4–8 December) stated that the president "hoped to keep the prime minister at all times informed of developments" that might lead to the use of nuclear weapons.[160]

Finally, the Truman administration saw the Korean conflict as inextricably linked to its overall national security strategy. During the 28 November NSC meeting, Stuart Symington, the chairman of the National Security Resources Board (NSRB), argued that an expanded or pro-

longed East Asian war would divert resources from the buildup of economic and military capabilities called for in NSC-68. Lovett concurred
and suggested that the administration use the Chinese intervention as a
means to increase the fiscal year 1952 defense budget, if this resulted in
"peaking and dropping back later."[161] On 1 December, Truman asked
Congress for a $16.8 billion supplementary defense appropriation and
$1 billion for the Atomic Energy Commission (AEC). The Atlee-Truman
communiqué stressed the need for a rapid buildup of American and
NATO military capabilities, the early completion of an integrated force
in Western Europe, and the appointment of a NATO supreme commander. Two weeks later, Truman approved NSC 68/4, which called for
fulfillment of 1954 rearmament goals by mid 1952.[162]

By late February 1951, the Truman administration had abandoned
any serious consideration of recapturing North Korea or expanding the
war, unless Chinese and North Korean forces drove the Eighth Army
and the X Corps from the peninsula. The administration reverted to its
original expectation level: the restoration of the prewar borders at
roughly the Thirty-eighth Parallel and the preservation on an independent, noncommunist South Korea. Officials were willing to risk further
blood and treasure to restore the status quo, but they were not willing to
accept a cease-fire line south of the Thirty-eighth Parallel or unilaterally
withdraw from Korea altogether. Nor was the administration willing to
risk an expanded war with China or to risk major war over a country as
unimportant as Korea, despite pressuring the UN General Assembly to
pass a resolution condemning Beijing as an aggressor on 1 February.[163]
As Acheson wrote to Truman on 23 February: "A decision to press for the
unification of Korea by military action would constitute a vast increase
in our present military commitments, would almost certainly require the
extension of hostilities against China, would increase the risk of direct
Soviet participation, and would require a major political effort to obtain
the agreement of directly interested governments."[164] MacArthur, on the
other hand, raised the possibility of full-scale war with China, even as
the Eighth Army and the X Corps abandoned Seoul in the face of a renewed Chinese and North Korean offensive south of the Thirty-eighth
Parallel on 1 January. He again advocated preventive war once the
Eighth Army retook Seoul on 15 March and later when UNC forces advanced to the Thirty-eighth Parallel on 3 April. MacArthur's repeated insubordination and public opposition to the limited war strategy led Truman to relieve him of his various commands on 11 April and to appoint
in his place Lieutenant General Matthew B. Ridgway, the commander of
the Eighth Army.[165]

In December 1950 and early January 1951, the Truman administration
considered three options. The first, and the most risk acceptant, was the

deliberate escalation of the war into China, up to and including the tactical use of nuclear weapons. Officials quickly concluded that this entailed both wildly divergent potential outcomes and low potential payoffs. If the administration had chosen to escalate the conflict, it would have done so without the support of the NATO members and other UN members, a point that Atlee emphasized in his 4–8 December meetings with Truman and Acheson. More important, as Bradley and Marshall noted, a blockade of the Chinese coast, the conventional bombing of PLA bases in Manchuria, and "unleashing" Chiang and the KMT to attack the mainland could lead to a prolonged U.S. military involvement in a secondary theater of the cold war, as well as possible Soviet military intervention. The use of nuclear weapons against Chinese troops would certainly provoke condemnation in the United Nations and among the NATO allies. It would also increase the likelihood of Soviet military intervention. Furthermore, there was no guarantee that conventional or nuclear escalation would achieve the Truman administration's war aim—the preservation of South Korea and a restoration of the prewar border. In short, escalation of the war beyond the Korean Peninsula risked escalation to regional war or a general war during the window of vulnerability.

The second option was a limited war strategy in Korea. This involved having the Eighth Army and the X Corps hold the line against the Chinese counteroffensive. In the meantime, the FEAF would refrain from bombing Manchuria or expanding the conflict into Chinese territorial waters. After UNC forces stabilized the front, the United States would seek cease-fire and eventually armistice negotiations with Beijing with the objective of restoring the Thirty-eighth Parallel and guaranteeing South Korea's independence. If, however, Chinese troops drove American forces from Korea, the administration reserved the option of escalating the conflict. Limited war was arguably less risky than an escalation of the war. Nonetheless, this strategy also entailed great risks. Chief among them was the probability that UNC forces would have to fight a prolonged ground and air war against Chinese and North Korean forces on the peninsula, during the American window of vulnerability. Although the Truman administration and the Joint Chiefs refused MacArthur's requests for reinforcements, a continuation of the war would likely require the deployment of additional troops to the battle zone. In short, even a limited war in Korea would require the diversion of troops, military equipment, and resources from the defense of Western Europe—the administration's overriding security concern.

The third and arguably least risky option was a unilateral withdrawal from Korea. This option was consistent with the strategic priorities embodied in NSC-68 and the now discarded defensive perimeter strategy in the Pacific. Withdrawal would permit the deployment of existing conventional forces to the defense of more strategically important regions. A deescalation of war and possibly concessions on Chinese admission to the United Nations as well would have allowed the Truman administration to devote its full energies to the rapid mobilization of U.S. military and economic capabilities. Most important, this option would have avoided the entrapment of an understrength and overburdened armed forces in a prolonged conflict.

Clearly, a unilateral withdrawal would have been a great humiliation. Primary sources show that officials genuinely feared that any concessions in Korea would lead the members of NATO and Japan to conclude that Washington lacked resolve. At home, Republicans would have excoriated the president and called for Acheson's resignation. Nonetheless, proposals for withdrawal resonated with the American people. In a national poll during the third week of January 1951, 66 percent of those interviewed thought that the United States should withdraw. Earlier, in December, Lovett found little support for limited war among members of the Senate Armed Services Committee. Republicans had been consistently critical of the administration's foreign policy and its lukewarm support for Chiang and the KMT for the past three years. They had shown little enthusiasm for the initial intervention in Korea in June, pressed for the expansion of war aims from containment to rollback in August and September, and then harshly criticized the administration for restricting MacArthur's freedom of action once China entered the war in November-December 1950. The Truman administration was in a classic "damned if it did and damned if it did not" predicament.[166]

Logrolling theory finds some empirical support in this period. The Asia-first nationalist coalition whose support the administration needed to fund its rearmament program, strongly opposed Beijing's admission to the United Nations and the withdrawal of American protection for Taiwan in exchange for a Korean cease-fire. During the Truman-Atlee meetings in December, Acheson was quite clear on this point. Nonetheless, officials had decided on the limited war option before Atlee arrived on 4 December, thus suggesting that Truman, Acheson, Marshall, Bradley, and others used the summit meetings as an opportunity to justify its policies and mobilize allied support.[167]

Offensive realism would expect leaders to be more risk-averse, if they perceive an unfavorable power balance or the disappearance of systemic or battlefield opportunity. The Chinese counteroffensive eliminated the systemic opportunities the Truman administration had enjoyed since late summer and the battlefield opportunities that MacArthur's forces had enjoyed since Inchon. Soviet intervention in support of China could shift the balance of power against the United States in Europe.[168] Here the theory would expect leaders to not only revert to less ambitious war aims of 30 June, but also to pursue less risky strategies in the conduct and termination of the war. Thus officials rejected MacArthur's calls for a preventive war against China. However, given the immediate priority of Western European defense, offensive realism would expect officials to more receptive to cease-fire negotiations with the Chinese in this period. The Truman administration refused to unilaterally withdraw from the Korean Peninsula or enter into negotiations with China until American and allied forces had stabilized the front near the Thirty-eighth Parallel.

Balance-of-risk theory may provide a more persuasive explanation for the contraction of the administration's war aims and willingness to fight a limited war in Korea. The Chinese counteroffensive was a tremendous setback for the Truman administration. However, since rollback had only been the administration's expectation level since late August and early September, officials had little difficulty in revising that expectation level downward. Despite the heightened danger of regional and possibly general war in December 1950, officials still anticipated an increase in relative power over the next several years. If Congress authorized the defense increases called for by NSC-68, the United States would be more capable of defending Western Europe in 1953–54 than it had been in 1950–51. As balance-of-risk theory expects, the administration persevered in a risk-acceptant strategy—the conduct of a limited war to restore the Thirty-eighth Parallel and preserve an independent South Korea.

This chapter generally supports the book's contention that leaders' aversion to losses in their state's relative power or reputation drives great powers to undertake risky interventions in peripheral regions. As balance-of-risk theory expects, the administration intervened in Korea to avert perceived losses to American reputation and international standing. Military intervention involved high risks, given the strength of the armed forces and the possibility that the North Korean invasion was a diversion.

The escalation of the administration's war aims and the decision to send troops across the Thirty-eighth Parallel in August and September 1950 poses an anomaly for balance-of-risk theory. The content of the decision-making process and the direction of the administration's risk taking—risk-acceptant behavior to secure *gains* over the initial expectation level—is consistent with offensive realism. Soviet introspection, perceived Chinese weakness, and the rapid collapse of the KPA offensive provided the United States with systemic and battlefield opportunities to eliminate the long-term threat of North Korea. Balance-of-risk theory, however, provides a more persuasive explanation than either logrolling theory or offensive realism for the administration's risk-behavior after UNC troops crossed the Thirty-eighth Parallel in October. Officials

TABLE 5.1 *Summary of Truman administration's risk behavior in the Korean War, 1950–51*

Observation period	Expectation level (against which leaders evaluate outcomes)	Perceived position relative to expectation level	Overall risk propensity of leaders	Policy options selected
NSC-68 and the projected window of vulnerability: (January–May 1950)	Territorial status quo	Gain	Risk aversion	• Reaffirmation of the defensive perimeter strategy in the Pacific • Devotion of a larger share of economic and potential power to defense
The outbreak of the Korean War and the decision to intervene (June 1950)	Territorial status quo (in Korea, restoration of the Thirty-eighth Parallel)	Loss	Risk acceptance	• Use of airpower to provide cover for ROK troops • Deployment of the Seventh Fleet to the Taiwan Straits • Use of airpower above the Thirty-eighth Parallel to disrupt North Korean supply lines • Full-scale intervention by ground, naval and air forces to reverse the North Korean offensive
The period of the North Korean offensive and the debate over war aims (July–August 1950)	Territorial status quo	Loss	Risk acceptance	• Full-scale intervention by ground, naval, and air forces to reverse the North Korean offensive

The war for rollback I: Inchon and the U.S./UN counteroffensive (September–October 1950)	Status quo/shift to rollback in Korea*	Gains (Relative to the initial expectation level)	Risk acceptance	• Authorization of ground and air operations above the Thirty-eighth Parallel
		Loss (Relative to the new expectation level)	Risk acceptance	
The war for rollback II: Crossing the Thirty-eighth Parallel and encounters with the CPVs (October–November 1950)	Rollback in Korea	Loss	Risk acceptance	• Authorization of MacArthur's offensive to the Yalu River
An entirely new war: The Chinese counteroffensive (December 1950–January 1951)	Territorial status quo	Loss	Risk acceptance	• Continued use of ground, air, and naval forces to restore the prewar border at the Thirty-eighth Parallel

* This observation poses an anomaly for balance-of-risk theory, which expects leaders to pursue risky intervention strategies in the periphery to avoid perceived losses relative to their expectation level. Instead, policymakers adopted a risky strategy to secure *gains* over their initial expectation level. At the same time, the expectation level shifted from the restoration of the status quo to rollback in Korea. Offensive realism, on the other hand, provides a compelling explanation for this escalation of war aims.

began to see a failure to liberate North Korea as a loss. Consequently, they were insensitive to the marginal costs associated with MacArthur's proposed Yalu River offensive—namely the increasing likelihood that China would enter the war.

As table 5.1 below shows, the record of deliberations and the aggregate direction of the Truman administration's risk behavior is generally consistent with balance-of-risk theory: risk aversion to secure gains and risk acceptance to avert (or recoup) losses relative to officials' expectation level. Again, the escalation of war aims from containment to rollback and the decision to send UNC forces over the parallel pose an anomaly for the theory. In all observation periods, there was variation in risk propensity among the members of Truman's national security team. For example, Acheson, Rusk, Truman, and Bradley displayed a stronger preference toward the riskier options during the 24–30 June 1950 period—the use of airpower above the Thirty-eighth Parallel to disrupt KPA supply lines and a full-scale intervention by ground, naval, and air forces to reverse the North Korean invasion—than did Johnson, Finletter, Matthews, and Pace. Similarly, during the debate on whether or not to allow MacArthur to proceed with the Yalu offensive, Marshall, Lovett, Bradley, and Collins displayed greater acceptance of the inherent risks than did Acheson, Rusk, or Jessup.

The Korean war decisions differ from the book's two other major cases, the 1905–06 Morocco crisis and Japan's 1940–41 war decisions, in that here the subjective expectation level against which leaders evaluated outcomes changed not once, but twice. First, in August and early September, Truman and his advisors escalated their war aims from a restoration of the Thirty-eighth Parallel to rollback. Since officials expected the UNC forces to cross the parallel and eliminate the remnants of the North Korean army quickly and without large-scale Chinese or Soviet intervention, they coded anything less than this outcome as a loss. Second, after the PLA counteroffensive drove UNC forces back across the Thirty-eighth Parallel, Truman and his advisors reverted to the expectation level established in the 25–30 June meetings, the restoration of the prewar border at the Thirty-eighth Parallel and the preservation of an independent South Korea. Whereas, in November, officials saw the failure to conquer North Korea as a loss, by January, they saw it as foregoing a gain. In both instances, the shift in leaders' expectation level preceded any change in risk-taking behavior.

[6]

The Limits of Great Power Intervention
in the Periphery

The previous chapters focused on the conditions under which great powers will likely initiate risky diplomatic or military interventions in the periphery and the circumstances under which great powers persist in failing intervention strategies despite mounting political, economic, and military costs. Does balance-of-risk theory have explanatory power beyond these cases? Does it explain attempts by great powers to deescalate or terminate risky intervention strategies? Does it account for instances where great powers do not initiate risky interventions or decline to pursue risky strategies vis-à-vis other great powers to perpetuate ongoing and often failing peripheral interventions?

This chapter addresses these questions by examining three cases: Germany's initiation of the 1911 Agadir crisis; Japan's efforts to prevent the escalation of border clashes between the Japanese and the Soviet armies during the 1938 Changkufeng and the 1939 Nomonhan incidents; and the United States' decision to seek a negotiated settlement to the Korean War in the February–June and July–November 1951 periods. Each case supports the basic claims of the book: Great powers are more likely to initiate or persevere in risk-acceptant strategies in the periphery to avoid perceived losses. Conversely, they are less likely to initiate or persevere in risk-acceptant strategies in periphery regions to secure perceived gains.

WILHELMINE GERMANY AND THE AGADIR CRISIS (1911)

The Agadir crisis was the outgrowth of the 1905–06 Morocco crisis. The 1906 Algeciras conference preserved the "open door" principle and Morocco's de jure sovereignty, while granting France and Spain de facto

TABLE 6.1 *Central decision makers in the control cases*

Cases	Decision maker	Tenure in office
Germany		
Agadir crisis (1911)		
	Wilhelm II	German Emperor and King of Prussia (15 Jun. 1888 to 28 Nov. 1918)
	Theobold von Bethmann-Hollweg	Reich Chancellor, Minister-President and Foreign Minister of Prussia (14 July 1909 to 13 July 1917)
	General Helmuth von Moltke the younger	Chief of the Prussian General Staff (1 Jan. 1906 to 14 Sept. 1914)
	Alfred von Kiderlen-Wächter	State Secretary for the Reich Foreign Office (17 June 1910 to 30 December 1912)
	Admiral Alfred von Tirpitz	State Secretary for the Reich Naval Office (June 1897 to 15 March 1916)
Japan		
Changkufeng incident (1938)		
Nomonhan incident (1939)		
	Prince Konoe Fumimaro	Prime Minister (4 June 1937 to 5 Jan. 939; 22 July 1940 to 18 July 1941; and 18 July to 18 Oct. 1941)
	Baron Hiranuma Kiichirō	Prime Minister (5 Jan. to 30 Aug. 1939)
	Admiral Yonai Mitsumasa	Minister of the Navy (4 June 1937 to 5 Jan.1939)
	General Ugaki Kazunari (ret.)	Minister of Foreign Affairs (26 May to 30 Sept. 1938)
	Arita Hachirō	Minister of Foreign Affairs (29 Oct. 1938 to 30 Aug. 1939)
	General Sugiyama Gen (Hajime)	Minister of War (4 June 1937 to 3 June 1938)
	Lt. General Itagaki Seishirō	Minister of War (3 June 1938 to 30 Aug. 1939)
	Lt. General Tōjō Hideki	Vice Minister of War (May to Dec. 1938)
	Lt. General Yamawaki Masataka	Vice Minister of War (Dec. 1938 to 14 Oct. 1939)
	Vice Admiral Yamamoto Isoruku	Vice Minister of the Navy (December 1936 to 30 August 1939)

Cases	Decision maker	Tenure in office
	Field Marshal Prince Kan'in Kotohito	Chief of the Army General Staff (1 Dec. 1931 to 3 Oct. 1940)
	Lt. General Tada Hayao (Shun)	Vice Chief of the Army General Staff (August 1937 to 1939)
	Lt. General Nakajima Tetsuzō	Vice Chief of the Army General Staff (To 2 Oct. 1939)
The United States Limitation of the Korean War and early negotiations (May–Dec. 1951)		
	Harry S. Truman	President of the United States (12 Apr. 1945 to 20 Jan. 1953)
	Dean G. Acheson	Secretary of State (21 Jan. 1949 to 20 Jan. 1953)
	General of the Army George C. Marshall	Secretary of Defense (21 Sept. 1950 to 12 Sept. 1951)
	James E. Webb	Under Secretary of State (28 Jan. 1949 to 29 Feb. 1952)
	Robert A. Lovett	Deputy Secretary of Defense (21 Sept 1950 to 17 Sept. 1951) Secretary of Defense (17 Sept. 1951 to 20 Jan. 1953)
	Dean Rusk	Assistant Secretary of State for Far Eastern Affairs (28 Mar. 1950 to 9 Dec. 1951)
	John D. Hickerson	Assistant Secretary of State for UN Affairs (8 Aug. 1949 to 27 July 1953)
	W. Averell Harriman	Special Assistant to the President (28 Jun. 1950 to 31 Oct. 1951)
	Philip C. Jessup	Ambassador-at-large (2 March 1949 to 23 Jan. 1953)
	H. Freeman Matthews	Deputy Under Secretary of State (5 July 1950 to 11 Oct. 1953)
	Frank Pace, Jr.	Secretary of the Army (12 April 1950 to 10 Jan. 1953)
	General of the Army Omar N. Bradley	Chairman, Joint Chiefs of Staff (16 Aug. 1949 to 16 Aug. 1953)
	General J. Lawton Collins	Chief of Staff, U.S. Army (16 Aug. 1949 to 14 Aug. 1953)
	Admiral Forrest Sherman	Chief of Naval Operations (2 Nov. 1949 to 22 July 1951)
	General Hoyt Vandenberg	Chief of Staff, U.S. Air Force (30 Apr. 1948 to 30 June 1953)

control over the police and national bank. Still the Moroccan government was bankrupt and a major insurgency broke out among the various Bedouin tribes. In late 1908, the European powers recognized Abdu'l Hafiz, who had forced the abdication of his brother, Abdu'l Aziz, in January of that year, as the new sultan of Morocco. The desertion of five German nationals from the French Foreign Legion in September 1908 and the resulting arbitration at the Hague Tribunal prompted Germany and France to clarify their activities in Morocco. Diplomats signed an accord at Casablanca on 8 February 1909, whereby France agreed to "safeguard economic equality" in Morocco and not to "hinder German commercial and industrial interests there." In exchange, Germany declared that it recognized French "special political interests" in Morocco. Both sides declared "that they [would] not pursue or encourage any measure of a nature to create in their favor or in the favor of any power whatsoever, an economic privilege."[1]

Neither the 1906 Act of Algeciras nor the 1909 Casablanca accords settled the Moroccan problem. In January 1911, the Zair tribe staged a revolt that culminated in the murder of five French army officers. The killings, along with a request from the local French commander for reinforcements, gave the French government of Premier Ernest Monis a pretext to extend its control over Morocco beyond the terms of the existing agreements. On 28 April, citing the need to protect its nationals, the French Council of Ministers announced the dispatch of an armed column to Fez and Rabat in order to punish those responsible for the murders.

German Expectation Level: Preservation of the Status Quo

Germany's second Moroccan challenge was the work of one official: Alfred von Kiderlen-Wächter, the state secretary for the Reich Foreign Office. When the French ambassador, Jules Cambon, informed him of the possibility of intervention on 28 April 1911, Kiderlen warned that Germany would regard the occupation of Fez and Rabat as a violation of the Algeciras Act. This would restore Germany's freedom of action to protect its economic interests in Morocco.[2]

Kiderlen was not alone in expressing concerns about the proposed French occupation of Fez and Rabat. The Spanish government warned in April that any occupation of Fez would alter the status quo and leave Spain free to occupy the zone accorded to it in the secret protocol to the October 1904 Franco-Spanish accords.[3] Similarly, British prime minister H. H. Asquith worried that a failure to support France would lead the Monis government to seek a rapprochement with Germany, thus undermining the effectiveness of the Triple Entente, the tacit alliance among Britain, France, and Russia concluded in August 1907. Foreign Secretary

Sir Edward Grey informed Paul Cambon, the French ambassador in London, that Britain would support the occupation of Fez.[4]

On 3 May, Kiderlen wrote a lengthy memorandum on the deteriorating Moroccan situation and the consequences of a French occupation of Fez. He recognized that "the sultan, who can only maintain his authority in the land with the help of French bayonets, no longer provides guarantees for the independence of his country, and this was the object of the Act of Algeciras." Germany would have to recognize the changed circumstances and to adjust its colonial policies accordingly. However, a French annexation of Morocco would be detrimental to German economic interests, as well as harmful to Germany's prestige among the great powers. He wrote:

> The occupation of Fez would pave the way for the absorption of Morocco by France. We should gain nothing by protesting and it would mean a moral defeat [that would be] hard to bear. We must therefore look for an objective for the ensuing negotiations, which shall induce the French to compensate us. If the French, out of anxiety for their compatriots, settle themselves at Fez, it is our right, too, to protect our compatriots in danger. We have large German firms at Mogador and Agadir. German ships could go to those ports and protect the firms. They could remain anchored there quite peacefully—merely with the idea of preventing other powers from intruding into these very important harbors of southern Morocco. . . . In possession of such a pledge we should look confidently at the further development of affairs in Morocco and see whether France will offer us proper compensation in her own colonial possessions, in return for which we could abandon the two ports [Mogador and Agadir].[5]

This memorandum established an implicit expectation level for German policy: the status quo as established by the 1909 Algeciras Act. Fear of relative economic losses in North Africa and damage to German prestige among the great powers led Kiderlen to adopt this as an expectation level.[6] In spring 1911, Kiderlen and others saw the status quo in Morocco as deteriorating. The sultan had effectively lost control, while French penetration of Morocco's finances, police, and economy increased. Kiderlen realized that Algeciras was effectively dead. In the absence of a return to the status quo ante, only compensation in the French Congo would maintain German prestige among the great powers. However, if France established a protectorate with impunity, German prestige would diminish.

Kiderlen did not seek to gain a Moroccan port or capitalize on the dis-

order to secure a unilateral advantage vis-à-vis the other Algeciras signatories.[7] He certainly did not want to go to war over Morocco, a view
shared by Wilhelm II and the Reich chancellor, Theobold von Bethmann-
Hollweg. Yet Kiderlen and Bethmann, at least, were convinced that Germany had to risk war to get France to agree to compensation in the
Congo, and thus preserve Germany's prestige. Kiderlen, however, did
not consult the General Staff or Prussian War Ministry about his plans,
let alone Reich Naval Secretary Admiral Alfred von Tirpitz, who happened to be on holiday at the time.[8] As General Franz von Wandel, the
chief of the General War Department in the Prussian War Ministry, wrote
in August 1911: "In this case too, as so often before, the dispatch of our
warships seems to have been a matter not of a carefully evaluated decision with all of its consequences considered, but rather a sudden im-
pulse." Wandel went onto to lament that Kiderlen had not consulted the
Prussian war minister, General Josias von Heeringen, or the chief of the
General Staff, General Helmuth von Moltke the younger.[9]

German Risk Acceptance to Avert Loss—The Coup d'Agadir

Kiderlen planned to allow the French to occupy Fez and then assert
Germany's demands for compensation by dispatching cruisers to two
ports on Morocco's Atlantic coast where German firms claimed interests:
Mogador and Agadir.[10] He concluded that France would not receive assistance from its allies. Russia, which had no economic interests in Morocco, would hardly risk war with Germany in defense of French colonial claims. Britain would not support France in the dispute, since most
British firms had investments along Morocco's Mediterranean coast.
Kiderlen wrote, "The importance of choosing those ports [Mogador and
Agadir], the great distance of which from the Mediterranean should
make it unlikely that England would raise objections, lies in the fact that
they posses a very fertile hinterland, which ought to contain important
mineral wealth as well."[11] Indeed, on 23 May, Bethmann reported that
Emperor Wilhelm had discussed Germany's interests in Morocco as well
as the possibility of dispatching a German naval vessel to Agadir, with
his cousin King George V during a private visit to London earlier in the
month. The king raised no objections, according to the German emperor,
who also told Bethmann that "France's action in Morocco is much dis-
liked in England."[12]

On 21 May, French troops occupied Fez and the French Foreign Ministry announced that the occupation would be temporary. Meanwhile,
there were strong indications that the French government was willing to
negotiate territorial concessions for Germany, if not in Morocco, then

elsewhere in Africa. Baron Wilhelm von Schön, the German ambassador in Paris, wrote Bethmann on 7 May that "recently there have been various suggestions in the press that Germany should be granted colonial and trade concessions in return for letting France have a free hand in Morocco. Amongst other possibilities it is proposed to satisfy us handing over the French Congo in return for us giving up Togoland."[13]

Bethmann met with Jules Cambon, the French ambassador to Berlin, on 10 and 11 June. He encouraged Cambon to travel to Bad Kissingen so that he might confer with Kiderlen, who was visiting the spa to "expiate his table excesses."[14] Kiderlen reiterated his willingness to accept a French protectorate, provided Germany received compensation for any rights relinquished. Cambon noted that French public opinion would not support a division of Morocco between France and Germany, but added that "one [Germany] might seek compensation elsewhere" and promised to raise the issue with his government. The meeting ended with Kiderlen saying, "bring us something from Paris."[15] Cambon had barely arrived in Paris when the Monis government collapsed. A new cabinet, under the leadership of Joseph Caillaux, did not take office until 27 June.[16] Meanwhile, Kiderlen and Bethmann secured the emperor's approval for the dispatch of cruisers to Morocco's Atlantic coast. The cruiser *Panther*, en route to Germany from Southwest Africa, weighed anchor in the harbor at Agadir on 1 July. The Reich Foreign Office informed other European capitals that the ship's mission was to "to lend, in case of need, aid and succor to her subjects and protégés as well as the considerable German interests engaged in the environs."[17]

The arrival of the *Panther* transformed a minor colonial dispute into a great power crisis. The Caillaux government opened bilateral negotiations with Germany, rejecting a proposal by the new foreign minister, Justin de Selves, to send warships to Morocco. By mid July, the talks deadlocked over the territory France would have to cede to Germany in exchange for a "free hand" in Morocco. Kiderlen wanted the majority of the French Congo, specifically the region extended from the Atlantic to the Sangha River. Cambon balked, noting that the Congo parcel was larger than Morocco.[18] Kiderlen decided that the best way to ensure territorial compensation in Congo was to confront the Caillaux government with the prospect of war. Bethmann backed Kiderlen, arguing that a failure to get compensation meant that German "credit in the world, not only for the moment, but for all future international actions, suffers an intolerable blow." If Germany accepted only minor territorial adjustments, France would become "so haughty that we must, sooner or later, take her to task."[19] The German emperor eventually went along with the plan.[20]

Lloyd George's Mansion House Speech and the War Scare

The British government had a restrained, but resolute, reaction to the arrival of *Panther*. On 4 July, Grey warned German ambassador Count Paul Wolff von Metternich that Britain would not recognize any new Moroccan settlement negotiated without its participation.[21] When talks between Kiderlen and Cambon reached an impasse in July, the Asquith government decided to signal its support for France. On 21 July, David Lloyd George, the chancellor of the exchequer, delivered a major address at the Lord Mayor of London's annual banquet at Mansion House. Reading from a text approved by Asquith and Grey, Lloyd George declared:

> It is essential in the highest interests, not merely of this country, but of the world, that Britain should at all hazards maintain her place and prestige among the Great Powers of the world. Her potent influence has many a time been in the past, and may yet be in the future, invaluable to the cause of human liberty. It has more than once in the past redeemed Continental nations, who are sometimes too apt to forget that service, from overwhelming disaster, and even from national extinction. I would make great sacrifices to preserve the peace. I conceive that nothing would justify a disturbance of international goodwill except questions of the gravest national importance. But if a situation were to be forced upon us in which peace could only be preserved by the surrender of the great and beneficent position Britain has won by centuries of heroism and achievement, by allowing Britain to be treated, where her interests were vitally affected, as if she were of no account in the Cabinet of nations, I say emphatically that peace at that price would be a humiliation intolerable for a great country like ours to endure.[22]

Although the Mansion House speech contained no specific mention of Morocco, the Reich Foreign Office saw it as a demarche.[23] The British government had advertised the speech as a major foreign policy statement. The following day, several British and French newspapers lauded Lloyd George's remarks and attacked Germany's foreign policy. Kiderlen told Bethmann: "We have lost our reputation abroad, we must fight!"[24] Acting on instructions from Berlin, Metternich told Grey that "the more [Germany] received threatening warnings the more determined would be our actions." He assured Grey that no German troops had landed at Agadir, but warned the British foreign secretary not to disclose this information in the House of Commons, lest it appear that Germany had capitulated after the Mansion House speech. The French occupation of Fez had abrogated the Act of Algeciras, Metternich warned, and therefore Germany would secure "by all means . . . full respect by France of German treaty rights."[25] Metternich's words so disturbed Grey that he immediately called for Lloyd George and Home Secretary Winston Churchill and reported, "I have just received a communication from the German ambassador so stiff that the [British] fleet might be attacked at any moment. I have sent for [First Lord of the Admiralty Reginald] McKenna to warn him."[26]

The Mansion House speech and the German reaction to it provoked a war scare that lasted for the remainder of the summer. While the British Admiralty prepared for possible operations against the German High Seas Fleet, in August, Viscount Haldane, the secretary of state for war, and General Sir William Nicholson, the chief of the Imperial General Staff, began a detailed study of military strategy in a possible European war for the Committee on Imperial Defense (CID).[27] In an effort to defuse the crisis, Asquith delivered a speech to the House of Commons on 31 July in which he withdrew his government's demands for four-power talks on Morocco, reiterated its support for France, and promised to support "territorial arrangements [for Germany] considered reasonable by those who are more directly interested." Although the German government responded favorably to Asquith's speech, the threat of war did not abate.[28]

The French war minister Adolphe-Marie Messimy worried that German maneuvers near Metz might be the prelude to an invasion. The new chief of the French General Staff, General Joseph-Jacques-Cèsaire Joffre, did not complete his preliminary plans for a full-scale offensive deployment along the Franco-German border until mid-September 1911.[29] However, when the French army recalled troops from Champagne on 31 July, rumors of French mobilization caused Berlin to fear an imminent war.[30] Franco-German tensions flared again in August. The Caillaux cabinet threatened to dispatch French and British men-of-war to engage the *Panther*, which promoted a counter-threat by Kiderlen to end the negotiations altogether. The French government withdrew its threat and the talks resumed.[31]

The German leadership was reasonably confident of the army's prospects in a war against France alone. However, they were less sanguine about a war against France, Britain, and possibly Russia. German naval leaders recognized the difficulties in simultaneously fighting the French navy in the Mediterranean and the British Royal Navy in the Atlantic and the North Sea. Quite aware that the Royal Navy still enjoyed an overwhelming superiority despite the 1908 naval law, Tirpitz feared losing the German battle fleet in a war before it was ready to challenge the British. Similarly, Admiral Karl Alexander von Müller, the chief of the naval cabinet, advised Wilhelm and Bethmann "to postpone this war which was probably unavoidable in the long run until after the completion of the [Kiel] canal."[32]

The German General Staff was similarly apprehensive about the prospects of a major war in 1911. Moltke warned that Germany could not assume Russian neutrality in a Franco-German war, even if such a conflict ignited over a colonial dispute in North Africa.[33] Throughout the crisis, Russia equivocated in its support for France. In mid August, the acting Russian foreign minister, Aleksander Izvolsky, informed de Selves that "he was officially charged with telling me that, if as a result of the failure of our [that is, the Franco-German] negotiations we were to end up in a conflict with Germany, Russia would give us not only diplomatic but also military assistance against it." Later that month, Izvolsky retreated from that pledge. The chief of the Russian General Staff, General Iakov Zhillinski, assured his French counterpart that St. Petersburg would fulfill its alliance obligations, but added that "under these conditions Russia does not seem to be in a state to sustain a war against Germany with the certainty of success for at least two years. It would be capable of warding off blows, but perhaps less so of delivering any."[34]

German intelligence reports during the Agadir crisis suggested that the Russian army would mobilize if necessary. Unlike the 1905–06 Morocco and the 1908 Bosnia-Herzegovina crises, by 1911, the Russian army had sufficiently recovered from its defeat in the Russo-Japanese War to pose a credible threat to Germany's eastern frontier. In late 1910, the Russian war minister, Vladimir Sukhomlinov, instituted a major reorganization of the army that increased the number and the effectiveness of the reserves. Although the full impact of the reforms would not appear for several years, the German General Staff concluded that the Russian reorganization constituted a "significant increase in readiness" and a "stronger threat." Furthermore, any German military action against France would likely result in Russian intervention under the terms of the 1894 Franco-Russian Dual Entente.[35]

The Agadir crisis ended when the Caillaux government promised to maintain the "open door" principle in Morocco and to cede approximately 263,000 square kilometers of territory in the French Congo to Germany. France also retained control over the Moroccan state bank. In exchange, Germany agreed to recognize the establishment of a French protectorate in Morocco and to withdraw the *Panther* from the waters off Agadir. The 4 November 1911 Franco-German treaty abrogated the 1906 Algeciras and the 1909 Casablanca accords, while simultaneously protecting the economic and political interests of both signatories. The German press and the opposition parties in the Reichstag excoriated Bethmann and Kiderlen for their handling of the crisis once the final compromise became public, but Germany had in fact secured the objectives set forth by Kiderlen on 3 May.[36] Nonetheless, the perceived "defeat" in the Agadir crisis was the major catalyst for the German government's decision to embark on an extraordinary buildup of land armaments in expectation of a future war.[37]

When informed of the French government's intention to deploy troops to Fez and Rabat, the German leadership had two options. The first option, and arguably the more risk averse of the two, was the diplomatic option. This would involve negotiations with Paris for the protection of German economic rights in Morocco consistent with the terms of Algeciras and the 1909 Franco-German accord. While events in Morocco may have rendered Algeciras irrelevant, and while it was quite clear that the French column would occupy Fez indefinitely, the Monis government and the press also indicated a willingness to provide Germany territorial compensation in May. In short, it was quite likely that through bilateral negotiations with the Monis and later the Caillaux governments Kiderlen could have acquired territorial compensation in French Congo and preserved German prestige among the great powers, without a resort to force or big stick diplomacy.

The second and riskier option involved a demonstration of German naval prowess and resolve. By dispatching the *Panther* to the port of Agadir after his meetings with Cambon at Bad Kissingen, Kiderlen risked a major crisis with France and Britain. The circumstances in spring 1911 were quite different from those in spring 1905. In April and May 1911, the French government had indicated its willingness to discuss compensation for the German government and private German firms. Britain and Spain had also voiced their displeasure with the Monis government's decision to dispatch an armed column to Fez and to occupy Rabat. Therefore, Germany was not alone in seeing its economic interests threatened by the creation of a French protectorate in Morocco. Whether or not France would have granted Germany all of the Congo territory that Kiderlen wanted as compensation in the absence of threats is debatable. Nonetheless, there was room for negotiation and it reasonable to assume that Bethmann and Kiderlen could have preserved German prestige without resorting to big stick diplomacy.

The deployment of the *Panther* to Agadir was also risky given the state of German military preparedness in summer 1911 and the likelihood that a Franco-German conflict might have drawn in Britain and Russia. Clearly, Kiderlen, Bethmann, Wilhelm, and others saw Germany as encircled by a hostile great power coalition. Yet no German leader seriously contemplated a major war in an effort to break that encirclement in 1911.

Although not consulted by Kiderlen before the crisis erupted, Moltke and Tirpitz consistently urged caution, particularly after Lloyd George's Mansion House speech.

Balance-of-risk theory contends that Kiderlen and Bethmann pursued a risky strategy of diplomatic confrontation in an effort to avert losses to German prestige and economic interests in Morocco created by the impending French annexation of the sultanate. As Kiderlen's 3 May memorandum set forth, by spring 1911, he and other German officials saw the status quo in Morocco and German prestige as deteriorating. They recognized that the sultan was not capable of governing the country and that the establishment of a French protectorate was nearly certain. At the same time, senior officials did not seek to acquire territory or compensation over and above what Germany would have lost once the French consolidated their control over the country. As the theory expects, Kiderlen and Bethmann gravitated toward the riskier option—the deployment of the *Panther* to Agadir—in an effort to avert those perceived losses.

Offensive realism suggests that German leaders exploited the favorable balance-of-power on the continent and the international opportunity to gain territory in the French Congo. Germany was preponderant militarily. The chances of Russian or British intervention appeared low. The French occupation of Fez, which clearly violated the Algeciras and Casablanca accords, provided Kiderlen an opportunity to gain concessions in the Congo. When Britain signaled its support for France and the probability of war increased, however, Kiderlen and Bethmann retreated. Yet, at no time during the crisis did Kiderlen, Bethmann, or Wilhelm contemplate war, despite a balance-of-forces that favored Germany and ambiguous British support for the French position until Lloyd George's 21 July speech. Furthermore, Kiderlen did not seek a unilateral advantage over other European powers by gaining an additional Moroccan port or by forcing the French government to cede territory and economic concessions in the Congo that exceeded the value of German economic interests in Morocco. Given this favorable balance-of-power and international opportunity, the puzzles for offensive realism become: why were Kiderlen's goals so modest and why did he and other German leaders not take greater risks?

Likewise, logrolling theory ought to have few problems in explaining German "big stick" diplomacy in this crisis. Bethmann and Kiderlen, like their predecessors Bülow and Holstein, were beholden to a logrolled coalition of landed *Junkers,* German industrialists and merchants, military officers, colonial officials, and nationalist political organizations who had a material interest in overseas expansion. Moreover, Bethmann and Kiderlen cynically employed certain strategic myths—the efficacy of "big stick" diplomacy, social Darwinism, "paper tiger" images of the

enemy, bandwagoning, and domino theories—to rationalize expansionist policies to the public. Officials provoked the crisis at the behest of the
logrolled coalition and then, once the venture began to sour, persisted in
hard-line diplomatic tactics for fear of domestic retribution.

There is little evidence to suggest that this logrolled coalition pushed
German leaders to initiate the Agadir crisis. Instead, once having
hatched the plot to secure French compensation for German losses in
late April, Kiderlen encouraged the Pan German League (Alldeutscher
Verbund) and the Naval League (Flottenverein) to mobilize public support for the government's Morocco policy.[38] As Wolfgang Mommsen observes, "The move against France over Morocco did not come about as a
result of pressure from economic interest groups. Indeed, the Mannes-
mann brothers, who had a financial stake in southern Morocco, had deliberately been kept out of the plot."[39]

LIMITS OF JAPAN'S QUEST FOR A NEW ORDER:
CHANGKUFENG AND NOMONHAN (1938–39)

In the Changkufeng (July–August 1938) and the Nomonhan (May–
August 1939) incidents, local Japanese army commanders took it upon
themselves to punish border incursions by Soviet troops near the juncture of the contested borders of Japanese-ruled Korea and Manchuria
(Manchukuo) with the Soviet Union and Outer Mongolia. These border
clashes threatened to embroil Japan in a two-front war against the Soviet
Union in the north and against Chiang Kai-Shek's Chinese Nationalist
Army and Mao Zedong's People's Liberation Army in the south and
west. Once large-scale fighting broke out, senior military and civilian
leaders in Tokyo moved quickly to break off these engagements and to
negotiate with Moscow, over the vehement objections of local commanders.

At first glance, Japan's conduct appears to contradict my argument.
After all, elements of the Japanese army undertook tremendous risks to
punish border violations by Soviet troops and to seize additional territory. I contend, however, that the cabinet of Prince Konoe Fumimaro and
the Imperial General Headquarters (IGHQ) in the 1938 Changkufeng incident and the cabinet of Baron Hiranuma Kiichirō and the IGHQ in the
1939 Nomonhan incident were actually loath to take risks to secure potential territorial gains over the immediate expectation of establishing
the New Order in East Asia. The seizure of Soviet territory and the elimination of the Soviet military presence in the Far East were not parts of
the Konoe and Hiranuma cabinets' and IGHQ's conception of that New
Order. As noted in chapter 4, the consolidation of Japanese rule in

Manchuria and northern and central China, followed by several years of rapid industrialization and exploitation, were part of a scheme to prepare Japan for an eventual war against the Soviet Union that army planners and many civilian leaders had long seen as inevitable.[40]

Operations against Soviet forces along the Soviet-Manchukuoan-Korean borders in summer 1938 and along the Outer Mongolian-Manchukuoan border in summer 1939 were clearly not the preferred strategy of the senior leadership. As I discuss below, with the exceptions of War Minister Itagaki Seishirō and Army Vice Chief of Staff Tada Hayao during the Changkufeng incident, most senior military and civilian officials in Tokyo strongly opposed any military operation that risked a full-scale war with the Soviet Union. During the Changkufeng incident, Emperor Shōwa took the unusual step of refusing the imperial sanction for a proposed operation to evict Soviet troops. In both incidents, local army commanders acted in direct contravention of orders from Tokyo and pursued escalatory strategies. In both instances, the Japanese cabinet and the IGHQ acted to avoid further escalation.

Offensive realism may explain why senior officials in Tokyo decided to seek a negotiated settlement with Moscow after the Soviet Far Eastern Armies decisively defeated Japanese forces at Changkufeng and later at Nomonhan. The theory attributes Japan's behavior to a favorable balance of power and systemic and battlefield opportunity. Senior officials in Tokyo allowed the Nineteenth Division and the Kwantung Army to punish border incursions by Soviet and Mongolian troops because they perceived those forces as weak, in large part due to Josef Stalin's purge of the Soviet army the previous year. Furthermore, they perceived Moscow as preoccupied with the rising threat of Nazi Germany in Europe. The defeats at Changkufeng and Nomonhan removed all doubt about the actual balance of power and Soviet resolve. As John Mearsheimer notes, "It is true that Japan had picked fights with the Red Army in 1938 and 1939 and lost both times. But as a result, Japan stopped provoking the Soviet Union and the border between them remained quiet until the last days of World War II, when Japan's fate was clearly sealed."[41]

A closer examination of Changkufeng and Nomonhan incidents, however, reveals problems for offensive realism. First, to the extent that senior civilian and military leaders in Tokyo perceived the regional balance of power as favorable to Japan and concluded that the Kremlin would be preoccupied with the rising German threat, then offensive realism predicts that those leaders would seize additional territory near the disputed Korea-Manchukuo-Soviet and the Manchukuo-Mongolia borders. Instead, during the Changkufeng and Nomonhan incidents, they advocated nonenlargement and tried to restrain local commanders. Insubordinate field commanders, not senior leaders, provoked the two crises. If officials did in fact perceive a favorable power balance vis-à-vis the Soviets in 1938–39, then their efforts to restrain the Korea Army and the Kwantung Army are anomalous.

Second, the extent to which Japanese leaders actually perceived the Soviet Union as militarily weak in the late 1930s is open to dispute. In the public statements, senior army officers downplayed Soviet military capabilities. For example, after returning from Moscow in mid 1937, Major General Honma Masaharu, the chief of the Army General Staff's Intelligence Bureau, boasted that Stalin's executions of Marshal Mikhail Tukhachevsky and dozens of other generals had so weakened the Soviet military that it faced disintegration and destruction. According to Honma, the Japanese "had no need to fear the Soviet army."[42]

Privately, however, the Army General Staff was less sanguine. In 1936, the Intelligence Bureau estimated that the Soviet Far Eastern Armies enjoyed a three-to-one advantage in the number of troops, a four-to-one advantage in infantry divisions, and a six-to-one advantage in aircraft. The imbalance of forces grew wider in 1937–38.[43] Furthermore, the outbreak of the China incident in July 1937 and the ensuing war against the Kuomintang (KMT) and the Chinese Communists required the Japanese army to shift the bulk of its forces away from the northern border. Despite these dire estimates and the necessity of shifting resources to the China theater, the leadership of the Kwantung Army, the Japanese empire's first line of defense against the Soviet Union, believed that superior morale and fighting spirit of its troops alone were sufficient to defeat better armed and numerically superior Soviet forces.[44]

Logrolling theory attributes Japanese overexpansion on the Asian mainland to logrolling among army and navy officers, as well as the civilian politicians who needed to build and sustain governing coalitions. Factional splits within the army contributed to the uncontrolled character of Japanese expansionism overall, and no doubt contributed to the outbreak of the Changkufeng and Nomonhan incidents. The ultranationalist *Kōdō*, or "imperial way faction," stressed the immediate Soviet threat, short-run necessity of a forward defense on the Asian mainland, and immediate preparations for war. As historian and diplomat Sadako Ogata observes, "Fear of the Soviet Union was 'necessary' for the army, which had built up its forces on the basis of a possible war with Russia."[45] The *Tōsei*, or "control faction," advocated controlled expansion in Manchuria and central China, centralized economic planning, and the comprehensive mobilization of the Japanese economy over several years for eventual war with the Soviet Union.[46] In order to maintain support for its war against the Kuomintang and radical economic planning at home, the *Tōsei* and civilian politicians such as Konoe and Hiranuma had to allow the *Kōdō* to pursue punitive expeditions against Soviet forces at Changkufeng and Nomonhan, despite the heightened risk that Japan would become embroiled in a two-front war.

Logrolling theory correctly identifies the factional dynamics within the Japanese army and sheds light on how those dynamics contributed to repeated acts of insubordination by the Kwantung Army in the 1930s. As in the 1931 Mukden incident, at Changkufeng and Nomonhan field commanders took it on themselves to initiate military operations. However, logrolling theory does not account for the ultimate success of senior civilian and military leaders in containing the Changkufeng and Nomonhan incidents and reaching a settlement with Moscow, despite the vehement objections of the Kwantung Army leadership.

The Changkufeng Incident (July–August 1938)

Although Japanese army planners had identified Russia as a likely opponent from 1907 onward, the Soviet Union pursued a relatively conciliatory policy toward Japan in the late 1920s and early 1930s. Weakened by revolution and later civil war, the Soviet government sold its rights to the Eastern Chinese Railway and redeployed troops to the Amur River, marking the border with Manchuria. At the time of the 1931 Mukden incident, the Soviet army only had 100,000 troops stationed east of the Urals and no fortifications along the Soviet-Manchurian border.[47]

After 1934, numerous incidents—shootings, kidnappings, border violations, and hijackings—broke out along the disputed borders of the Soviet Union, Manchukuo, and Korea, but local Soviet and Japanese commanders moved quickly to contain them.[48] The Army General Staff estimated that the number of Soviet divisions in the Far East rose from eight in 1933 to twenty in 1937 and the number of combat aircraft from 350 to 2,000 in the same period. Soviet troop levels in the region increased from approximately 230,000 to 370,000 between 1934 and 1937. Throughout the 1930s, the Kwantung Army could only count on reinforcement by the two infantry divisions.[49] Relations between Japan and the Soviet Union deteriorated with the outbreak of the China incident on 7 July 1937. Recognizing the heightened threat to the Soviet Maritime Provinces, the Kremlin signed a five-year nonaggression pact with China on 21 August 1937.[50]

The Changkufeng incident began on 13 July 1938, when some forty Soviet soldiers occupied the summit of Changkufeng, a hill to the west of Lake Khasan near the conjuncture of the borders of Korea, Manchukuo, and the Soviet Union. General Koiso Kuniaki, the outgoing commander of the Korea Army, promptly reported the Soviet troop presence to the IGHQ in Tokyo. However, Koiso and his superiors decided not to divert attention and resources from the upcoming campaign against the KMT at Hankow. Instead, the Korea Army would attempt to negotiate with the Soviets and ask them to withdraw, but if that effort failed, it would expel them to the area east of Lake Khasan. Kwantung Army headquarters at Hsinching (Changchun) recommended that the Korea Army expel the Soviet troops by force. With the encouragement of the Kwantung Army staff, Lieutenant General Suetaka Kamezō, the commander of the Nineteenth Division of the Korea Army, began preparations to launch an attack on Soviet positions on or about 21 July.[51]

Initially, the army section of the IGHQ, along with the majority of the Konoe cabinet and the War Ministry, agreed that the Hankow campaign was the priority and that the Korea and Kwantung armies should not take actions that might provoke a Soviet retaliation. Lieutenant Colonel Arisue Yadoru and Major Kōtani Etuso of the Operations Bureau went to Hsinking to deliver the imperial order to that effect on 15 July. However, radical young officers on the Army General Staff, with the support of the chief of operations and war plans, Colonel Inada Masazumi, and the army vice chief of staff, Lieutenant General Tada Hayao, favored military action. Eventually, Inada and Tada succeeded in persuading most of the army section and bureau chiefs, as well as General Itagaki Seishirō, the war minister, to support a limited punitive expedition to Changkufeng.[52]

Chief of the Naval General Staff Prince Fushimi Hiroyasu and other naval officers opposed any offensive ground operations, citing the navy's inability to transport troops to the Asian mainland via the Korea Strait or the Tsugaru Strait in the event of Soviet-Japanese hostilities. Vice Admiral Yamamoto Isoruku, the vice navy minister, was particularly apprehensive lest the Soviet leadership misunderstand Japanese intentions.[53] Navy Minister Yonai Mitsumasa and Foreign Minister Ugaki Kazushige strongly opposed the use of force during the Five Ministers Conference on 19 July.[54] Konoe observed, "We have absolutely no intention of making trouble with the [Russians]. This is quite a different situation from the Marco Polo Bridge. My only great fear concerns what the Soviet central authorities have in mind."[55] Ugaki insisted that it was "not appropriate to give up too soon and to move forces in the midst of diplomatic negotiations."[56] At a full cabinet meeting on the morning of 20 July, he warned, "We are in the midst of the China incident, where we need to achieve desired results swiftly, applying all our strength. . . . It would be extremely dangerous to exacerbate matters with the USSR in addition. . . . Would it not be better to resolve the Changkufeng affair by diplomacy?" Konoe and Finance Minister Ikeda Seihin shared this sentiment.[57]

Meanwhile, Inada and the Army General Staff prepared a draft IGHQ order directing the Korea Army to evict Russian troops from the Changkufeng area. Confident that the draft order would receive the necessary imperial sanction, the staff officers briefed the incoming Korea Army commander, Lieutenant General Nakamura Kōtarō, in Tokyo. However, Yonai, Ugaki, and Yausa Kurahei, the lord keeper of the privy seal, conveyed their opposition to military action directly to Emperor Shōwa. Angered by the army's high-handed behavior, the emperor strongly opposed the use of force at Changkufeng. When Itagaki and Prince Kan'in Kotohito, the chief of the Army General Staff, went to the palace on the afternoon of 20 July to obtain imperial sanction for the draft IGHQ order, the emperor refused to grant it. During the audience, the emperor asked if the draft order had the support of the foreign and navy ministers, to which Itagaki replied that it did. The emperor, who knew that Ugaki and Yonai actually opposed the Changkufeng operation, reprimanded Itagaki saying, "The methods of army in the past have been unpardonable. In the Manchurian incident and also in the doings at the Marco Polo Bridge . . . there was complete disobedience of central orders." Denouncing army officers who had abused the throne's constitutional prerogative of supreme command, he declared, "Hereafter, not even a single soldier may be moved without our express orders."[58]

The emperor's admonition seemed to have some effect, since later on 20 July Inada wired Korea Army headquarters not to engage the Soviets. Inada's cable read, in part, "There is no prospect of obtaining an imperial order for the use of force. As for the conduct of the Changkufeng incident hereafter, it is veering toward the following policy: though we shall promote diplomatic negotiations, they will be cut off promptly if there is no hope of success. Have the concentrated forces wait for a while at their present locations, and return the main body to their original positions as soon as possible. The situation has been reversed 180 degrees."[59]

Suetaka ignored the imperial order to disengage. On 29 July, several Soviet soldiers crossed the border to construct positions near Shatsaofeng, a mountain about two kilometers north of Changkufeng. Suetaka used this as pretext to order the Nineteenth Division and the Seventy-Fifth Infantry Regiment, under Colonel Satō Kōtoku, to attack Soviet positions at dawn on 31 July. The Satō regiment dislodged approximately three hundred Soviet soldiers at Changkufeng, before defeating an additional three hundred Soviet soldiers at Shatsaofeng. In his report to the IGHQ on 1 August, Suetaka tried to justify the operation by asserting that "since the enemy near Shatsaofeng staged an advance, the Satō unit [the Seventy-Fifth Infantry Regiment] dealt them a counter attack."[60]

Tada went to the imperial villa at Hayama on 31 July to brief the emperor. He told him that Japanese soldiers had not crossed the international border and had acted in a purely defensive manner. This was untrue, since the Seventy-Fifth Regiment had crossed to launch their attack. Much to Tada's surprise, the emperor acquiesced to the *fait accompli*, but warned that under no circumstances should the fighting spread beyond Changkufeng and that all operations should cease once Soviet troops evacuated the area.[61]

The Five Ministers Conference met on 1 August and decided to adhere to a policy of nonenlargement. A subsequent meeting of Yonai, Itagaki, and Ugaki on 5 August reconfirmed this policy. The Korea Army would refrain from further military operations, as long as Soviet troops took no further provocative actions. In the event that negotiations failed, however, the government and the army would maintain the situation along that border. Imperial Order No. 163 stated: "The Korea Army commander will, for the time being, occupy approximately the present forward lines in the Changkufeng-Shatsaofeng area and will also be on strict guard along the Soviet-Manchukuo frontiers, from which front that army is responsible."[62] The IGHQ ordered the Second Air Wing of the Korea Army stationed at Hoeryong not to undertake offensive operations, despite the presence of some 150 Soviet warplanes in the area and repeated requests from Suetaka for the use of air power. Nonetheless, most senior officials remained steadfast in their determination to avoid entrapment or escalation at Changkufeng.[63] One of the chief advocates of deescalation and a unilateral withdrawal was the vice minister of war, Lieutenant General Tōjō Hideki, who had previously served as Kwantung Army chief of staff. Eventually Tada, the only member of the senior leadership to have consistently supported the use of force from the outset, prepared to issue the order to withdraw if and when the opportunity arose through negotiations with Moscow.[64]

The Soviets withdrew eastward following the Sato regiment's attack on 31 July. General Georgi Shtern, the chief of staff of the Soviet Far Eastern Army, responded by sending several regular divisions, several hundred tanks, bombers, and heavy guns to the area. The Army General Staff knew that Suetaka possessed only twelve infantry battalions compared to an estimated twenty-seven battalions available to the Soviets. The Russians enjoyed a three-to-one troop advantage near the Manchukuoan-Soviet border; the Soviet Far Eastern Army deployed 21,000 troops compared to the 7,000 to 7,300 combat troops in Suetaka's Nineteenth Division and attached units from the Korean Army.[65] Soviet forces launched a counteroffensive on the night of 2 August, accompanied by air strikes. Suetaka requested authorization to launch a counteroffensive. The IGHQ forbade any expansion of the conflict for fear that full-scale war would erupt with the Soviet Union, which would divert equipment and personnel from the Hankow campaign. On 11 August, the Japanese ambassador in Moscow, Shigemitsu Mamoru, reached an agreement with Soviet Foreign Minister Maxim Litvinov whereby Japan consented to withdraw its troops to within one kilometer of Changkufeng in exchange for a cease-fire.[66] Publicly, the War Ministry claimed 158 killed and 740 wounded during the Changkufeng incident. Classified Japanese records, however, provide a final toll of 526 killed and 913 wounded, or 21 percent of all forces listed as officially engaged.[67]

The Konoe cabinet and the IGHQ considered two basic options: the use of force to evict Soviet troops from Changkufeng or the use of diplomacy to convince the Soviets to voluntarily leave the area. The second option was arguably the less risky of the two. The borders separating Manchukuo, the Soviet Union, and Korea have never been clear. According to the Army General Staff's estimates, the Soviet Far East Army had a decisive advantage in troops, planes, tanks, and heavy artillery. There was no guarantee that negotiations would result in the Soviets agreeing to Japan's view of the border. However, the forfeiture of several desolate hills on the eve of a major military campaign in China was certainly preferable to a simmering border dispute that might erupt into a full-scale war. With the exceptions of Tada and Itagaki, this was the preferred option of senior civilian and military leadership from 13 July onward. The Five Ministers Conference on 1 August reiterated its support for negotiations and nonenlargement.

The use of force was the riskier option because of the higher likelihood that Japan would find itself fighting a two front war against the Soviet Union and China. Specifically, by authorizing the Korea Army to evict the Soviet troops from the hill and to restore the border, senior officials would run the risk that the fighting would spread beyond the Changkufeng area. Given the numerical imbalance between the opposing forces, the IGHQ would have to send reinforcements to the region should the fighting spread. This would divert resources on the eve of the Hankow offensive. If the Soviet army responded to the escalating border skirmishes by launching a major offensive across the Soviet-Manchukuoan or Soviet-Korean borders, there was real possibility that Japan might lose Korea and Manchuria, even if the China Expeditionary Army halted the Hankow campaign and marched north to reinforce the Korea and Kwantung armies.

The Nomonhan Incident (May–August 1939)

Less than a year after Changkufeng, a more serious clash between Japanese and Soviet forces erupted along the disputed border between Manchukuo and the Mongolian People's Republic. For centuries, Outer

Mongolia had been a buffer between Russia and China, although the country had been under Chinese suzerainty. Under agreements concluded in 1913 and 1915, the Russian government forced the fledgling Chinese Republic to accept Mongolian autonomy. The 1917 Bolshevik revolution and the 1919–22 Russian civil war gave Chinese warlords an opportunity to reestablish control over Mongolia, and the Chinese Republic dispatched troops to the area in 1921. Following the Bolshevik victories over White Russian forces and the Red Army's occupation of the Mongolian capital of Urga in July 1921, Soviet Russia again became the dominant external force in Mongolia. Local Communists seized power in 1924 and proclaimed a Mongolian People's Republic (MPR). Japanese expansion in Manchuria after 1931 led to closer Soviet-Mongolian diplomatic and military ties. Mongolia signed a ten-year mutual assistance pact with the Soviet Union on 12 March 1936.[68]

On 11 May 1939, anywhere from thirty to seven hundred horsemen from the Mongolian People's Republic Army (MPRA) crossed the Halha River in an area fifteen kilometers south of the village of Nomonhan and clashed with the Manchukuoan army garrison there.[69] The exact border between Manchukuo and Mongolia had never been clear. The Kwantung Army claimed that the Halha River was the boundary. The Mongolians, on the other hand, claimed that the boundary ran to the east of the Halha (called Khalkhin-gol by the Russians). Lieutenant General Komatsubara Michitaro, the commander of the Twenty-Third Division stationed at Hailor, immediately reported the border violation to his superiors at Kwantung Army headquarters at Hsinking.[70]

The Changkufeng incident the previous year reinforced the hard-line views of many Kwantung Army officers toward border incursions, as well as contempt for the IGHQ in Tokyo. In April 1939, the Kwantung Army had adopted a new operations order entitled, "Principles for the Settlement of Soviet-Manchurian Border Disputes." The order stipulated that only resolute and thorough punishment could prevent future Soviet border incursions. Accordingly, the guiding principle of any operation would be to neither invade Soviet or Mongolian territory nor to allow Soviet and Mongolian troops to cross the border. If the exact border were unclear, however, the local commander would have the authority to temporarily cross the Soviet border or to lure Soviet forces across the border into Manchukuo and engage them there. These orders had the full support of General Ueda Kenkichi, the commander of the Kwantung Army.[71]

On 13 May, Komatsubara sent a regiment under the command of Lieutenant Colonel Azuma Yaozo to repel the raiders. The Mongolians pulled back to the western shore of the Khalkhin-gol. Azuma's regiment then pulled back on the night of 16 May, leaving behind Manchukuoan troops. On 28 May, a detachment of one thousand Japanese soldiers under the command of Colonel Yamagata Takemitsu moved near the river where they came under sustained heavy artillery fire from the left bank. Over the next two days, Soviet light tanks and heavy artillery annihilated Azuma's cavalry regiment, while the Yamagata detachment retreated across the river. It quickly became clear that the opposing units were not Mongolians, but rather Soviet troops. After this engagement, Soviet forces remained in the disputed zone and proceeded to fortify their positions. On 18 and 19 June, Soviet planes bombed Japanese positions at Hailaerh, Aerhsan, and Kanchuerhmaio (all well inside Manchukuo), while regular infantry penetrated Nomonhan, under the cover of Soviet artillery and mechanized forces.[72]

During this period, a senior Soviet official publicly and repeatedly pledged to defend the Mongolian border. In an address to the Supreme Soviet on 31 May, Foreign Minister Vyacheslav Molotov warned Japanese and Manchukuoan authorities that "by virtue of our treaty with Mongolia, we shall defend its frontiers as energetically as our own [;] . . . patience has its limits." Molotov, one of Stalin's chief lieutenants, issued a similar warning to Japanese Ambassador Tōgō Shigenori on 19 May.[73]

Until this point the Kwantung Army had acted in accordance with orders adopted in April: to punish Mongolian border incursions and retaliate in the case of attack, but not to expand the situation beyond the tactical level and seek local settlements. The standing orders were consistent with the policies that the army high command and the first Konoe cabinet had adopted in the Changkufeng incident a year earlier. The Hiranuma cabinet, which took office following Konoe's resignation on 5 January 1939, was primarily concerned with the successful completion of the China incident; most ministers did not relish the prospect of a second front against the Soviets.[74] Furthermore, the emperor instructed Prince Kan'in to localize and settle the incident with a clearer demarcation of the Manchukuoan/Mongolian border to avoid similar incidents in the future.[75]

However, in the aftermath of the 28–30 May engagement and the 18–19 June bombings, Komatsubara and Kwantung Army staff officers began planning a massive ground and air offensive to drive Soviets forces out of the Khalkhin-gol region. General Ueda and the Kwantung Army chief of staff, Lieutenant General Isogai Rensuke, decided that the entire available strength of that army—150,000 troops, including 12 infantry battalions, 120 anti-tank guns, 70 light tanks, 400 vehicles, and 180 planes—would take part in this operation. Specifically, the Twenty-Second Division and the main body of the Second Air Group would join a detachment commanded by Lieutenant General Yasuoka Masaomi, two regiments of medium and light tanks, one motorized artillery regiment, and one regiment from the Seventh Infantry Division. In an effort to forestall retaliation by Soviet-Mongol air forces, the Kwantung Army would launch strikes on the Tamsagbulag airfield, deep in Mongolia. Ueda and his staff attempted to conceal the planned air strikes from superiors.[76]

The proposed ground offensive would begin on 1 July; the airstrikes would begin on 30 June. On 25 June, Ueda sent telegrams to Lieutenant General Nakajima Tatsuzō, the vice chief of the Army General Staff, and Lieutenant General Yamawaki Masataka, the vice war minister, requesting that the deployment of thirty fighter planes to supplement the ninety fighters already assigned to the Kwantung Army should hostilities with the Soviets spread. Ueda made this request despite receiving a telegram from Nakajima the previous day instructing the Kwantung Army to prevent the fighting from spreading and prohibiting any offensive air operations in Mongolia. The Army General Staff learned of the planned air offensive when a Kwantung Army staff officer inadvertently mentioned it during a mission to Tokyo. Most officials in the War Ministry opposed the planned offensive, arguing that it made no sense to deploy a strategic-sized unit to a minor border dispute in Outer Mongolia, while the bulk of the Japanese army remained mired in China.[77]

Major General Hashimoto Gun, the chief of the Operations Bureau, and Colonel Inada supported a limited ground operation against the Soviets, mostly out of deference to Ueda. War Minister Itagaki came to share this view, which effectively ended the debate within the ministry. However, Itagaki did not necessarily support a major offensive that risked full-scale war with the Soviet Union. Even Hashimoto and Inada moved to halt the proposed offensive when they learned that the Kwantung Army planned air strikes deep into Mongolia.[78] Prince Kan'in dispatched Lieutenant Colonel Arisue Yadoru of the General Affairs Bureau to Kwantung Army headquarters with instructions to halt all air operations. Before Arisue arrived in Hsinking, however, Kwantung Army staff officer Tsuji Masanobu gave the order to start the air assault on the Tamsagbulag airfield on 27 June, three days ahead of schedule. Kwantung Army headquarters reported that its planes had shot down ninety-nine Soviet aircraft and destroyed a further twenty-five on the ground.[79]

The Kwantung Army's unauthorized offensive provoked a furious reaction among senior officials in Tokyo. Prime Minister Hiranuma and members of his cabinet opposed the escalation, but lacked any authority over field armies. Unlike the Changkufeng incident, where Prince Kan'in and Itagaki requested imperial sanction for the use of force, in this instance the Army General Staff sought (albeit unsuccessfully) to restrain the Kwantung Army. Nakajima went to the Imperial Palace to report the Tamsagbulag bombing to the emperor. An irate monarch castigated the

Kwantung Army for violating the imperial prerogative of supreme command. He further instructed Nakajima and Prince Kan'in to punish Kwantung Army leaders for violating orders to cease hostilities. IGHQ Army Order No. 320, issued on 29 June, forbade the Kwantung Army from attacking enemy air bases in Outer Mongolia. The order read, "depending upon the situation, areas where boundaries between neighboring countries and Manchukuo are in dispute and where the use of force is inconvenient need not be defended by force."[80] Prince Kan'in also issued specific instructions for the handling of the Nomonhan incident: "(1) Ground operations will be limited to the border region between Manchukuo and Outer Mongolia, east of Lake Buyr; (2) enemy bases will not be attacked by air."[81]

Despite orders from Tokyo to deescalate, on 2 July, the entire Twenty-Third Division and a regiment from the Seventh Infantry Division crossed the left bank of the Halha River and began to push southward. In the interim between the May engagements and the start of the Japanese offensive, the Soviet Far East Army sent reinforcements to the Nomonhan area, so that by July its forces consisted of three rifle divisions, five mechanized and armored regiments (with 860 tanks and armored vehicles), and two Mongolian cavalry divisions. The main Japanese infantry force came under heavy Soviet tank and artillery fire and retreated across the river on 3 July. The Yasuoka detachment, pulled back on 3 July, but resumed the offensive with the Twenty-third Division on 5 July. However, from 11 July onward, Japanese forces could barely hold their ground in the face of Soviet 47 mm. antitank guns and some four hundred Soviet heavy tanks.[82] On 16 July, Soviet planes bombed Fulaerhchi, a suburb of the Manchurian city of Tsitsihar. Although there were no Japanese causalities, the Kwantung Army unsuccessfully lobbied the IGHQ to rescind the 29 June prohibition on bombing targets in Mongolia.[83]

Throughout July, the Hiranuma cabinet and the IGHQ in Tokyo continued to oppose escalation. After the Fulaerhchi bombing on 16 July, Itagaki suggested to Foreign Minister Arita Hachirō that the time was ripe for a diplomatic settlement. The following day, the five ministers conference decided to retain the nonenlargement policy regarding Nomonhan, and then to open negotiations with the Kremlin at an appropriate time. The Japanese Foreign Ministry instructed Ambassador Tōgō in Moscow to seek a suitable opportunity to broach the Nomonhan incident with Molotov, but to take care not to convey the impression that Tokyo was overly eager for a settlement.[84] On 21 July, Colonel Doi Aiko, the military attaché in Moscow, reported to the War Ministry, that the Soviets were reinforcing their forces in the Martine Provinces. The Intelligence Bureau, as well as the Kwantung Army's intelligence section, reported that

Soviet-Mongolian forces would launch an offensive in mid August, although the size of the operation remained uncertain. Staff officers at Hsinking, along with the Operations and the Intelligence Bureaus in Tokyo, estimated that the peak of the fighting at Nomonhan had passed and would now become a war of endurance.[85]

The Army General Staff summoned Isogai to Tokyo on 20 July. In the presence of senior War Ministry and general staff officers, Nakajima urged Isogai to unilaterally end the Nomonhan incident and then handed him a new directive, "Principles for the Settlement of the Nomonhan Incident." The directive called for an early end to hostilities. While the Twenty-Third Division and supporting units would hold the right bank of the Halha, the Japanese Foreign Ministry would enter into negotiations with Moscow. If these negotiations were not successful, the Kwantung Army would withdraw to the boundary claimed by the Soviet army before the start of winter. Isogai objected to any evacuation, arguing, "We cannot abandon a region where controversy has erupted and where thousands of heroes' lives have been sacrificed."[86] Eventually, he promised to have Kwantung Army headquarters study the document, whereupon (at Isogai's urging) they ignored it.[87]

The Kwantung Army reacted strongly to a draft proposal for a cease-fire developed by the Japanese Foreign Ministry. The plan called for both Soviet and Japanese forces to suspend operations and pledge that neither would cross the Halha. Failing this, both sides would agree to a cease-fire along the line of control as of 11 July or pull back an equal distance from a preagreed cease-fire line, as of an agreed-upon time. In a 30 July telegram to Nakajima, Isogai strongly opposed any intimation that Japan would seek a cease-fire.[88] Instead, to prepare for a possible Soviet offensive, Ueda and Isogai set up a new Sixth Army under Lieutenant General Ogisu Ryūkei on 10 August to provide a unified command for the Twenty-third Division and associated units deployed to the Nomonhan area.[89]

On 20 August, the Soviet Far East Army, now under the command of General Gregori Zhukov, launched a massive offensive with 450,000 troops, equipped with approximately 350 tanks, 340 armored cars, 210 heavy field guns, and 200 aircraft. The Japanese, on the other hand, had only 56,000 troops, no heavy tanks, no heavy field guns, and limited air support.[90] Soviet tanks outflanked and annihilated Komatsubara's Twenty-third Division. According to that division's own records, of the 15,975 officers and enlisted personnel who participated in the fighting, 30 percent died in action, 34 percent were wounded, 4 percent were missing, and 8 percent were ill—for a combined loss ratio of 76 percent. Before the end of August, casualties for the Sixth Army and supporting units rose to 8,440 killed and 8,766 wounded, or approximately 79 per-

cent of its entire strength. By the time War Minister Hata Shunruko, Itagaki's successor, visited Manchuria on 9 December 1939, the official
causalities during the Nomonhan incident (May to September) stood at a
little under 18,000—8,000 killed, 8,800 wounded, and 1,200 sick—or 32
percent casualties—out of a total of 75,738 troops. By contrast, at
Changkufeng, Japanese infantry casualties amounted to only 24.7 percent, while overall casualties amounted to 21 percent.[91]

Meanwhile, to avoid further confrontations between the IGHQ and
the Kwantung Army, the Japanese Foreign Ministry decided to conceal
its desire for a peaceful settlement at Nomonhan by not empowering
Tōgō to initiate talks with the Soviet government. Instead, on 22 August,
two days after the beginning of the ignominious defeat of the Twenty-
Third Division, Soviet deputy foreign affairs commissar Solomon Lo-
zovsky mentioned the Kremlin's desire for a negotiated settlement at
Nomonhan to Tōgō during a meeting ostensibly called to discuss the
long-standing Soviet-Japanese dispute over Sakhalin. However, the ambassador did not receive permission from Tokyo to begin negotiations
until 28 August, four days after the Soviet Union unexpectedly signed a
five-year nonaggression pact with Nazi Germany, which precipitated the
resignation of the Hiranuma cabinet. Tōgō did not receive detailed instructions from the Foreign Ministry until 8 September, by which time
Zhukov's forces had completed their objectives and the German invasion
of Poland plunged Europe into the Second World War.[92] The final cease-
fire agreement signed by Tōgō and Molotov on 15 September, called for
the suspension of all military action by Japanese-Manchukuoan and Soviet-Mongolian forces at 2:00 a.m. (Moscow time), followed by a withdrawal to the line of control at 1:00 p.m. (Moscow time) on 15 September.
The two sides agreed to exchange prisoners of war and to set up a commission composed of Japanese, Soviet, Mongolian, and Manchukuoan
representatives to determine the final border.[93]

Humiliated by its defeat at the hands of Zhukov's forces, the Kwantung Army headquarters unrealistically planned for a renewed offensive
in mid September. On 27 August, it proposed a paper entitled, "Counter-
measures to Deal with the Changing European Situation," which called
for the incorporation of the Second, Fourth, Seventh, and Eighth divisions into the battered Sixth Army, as well as heavy artillery and rapid-
fire guns, in preparation for an immediate attack. This would only be a
prelude to a full-scale war with the Soviet Union in spring 1940. Kwantung Army staff officer Terada Masao sent the plan directly to Inada,
while another staff officer, Isomura Takesuke, flew to Tokyo to brief the
Army General Staff. The IGHQ finally decided that the time had come to
act and to replace the Kwantung Army leadership.

Nakajima flew to Hsinking on 30 August and again on 4 September to deliver Imperial Orders No. 343 and No. 349 that called for the localization of the fighting and a unilateral withdrawal of Japanese forces from the disputed Nomonhan region. On 6 September, Ueda asked the Army General Staff for permission to clear the battlefield of Japanese corpses and threatened to resign if permission were not forthcoming. The following day, Prince Kan'in removed Ueda and named General Umezu Yoshijirō as Kwantung Army commander. The army conducted a top to bottom purge of officers associated with the Nomonhan debacle: Lieutenant General Iimura Yuzuro replaced Isogai as Kwantung Army chief of staff; Hashimoto, Isogai, Nakajima, and Ueda were "involuntarily" retired from active duty in September 1939; Komatsubara and Ogisu voluntarily retired in January 1940; and Terada, Hattori, and Tsuji received other assignments. Lieutenant General Sawada Shigeru replaced Nakajima, but seventy-five-year-old Prince Kan'in continued as army chief of staff for another year, due largely to his special position as an imperial prince.[94]

In the Nomonhan incident, the Hiranuma cabinet and the IGHQ faced the same two options that the Konoe cabinet and the IGHQ had faced the previous year: localization of the dispute and negotiations or escalation of the dispute at the risk of full-scale war with the Soviets. Localization and negotiation was the less risky of the two options. The border between Outer Mongolia and Manchuria was unclear. Unlike Changkufeng, which had some strategic value from a purely local standpoint, the village of Nomonhan and the Halha had no strategic value whatsoever. A deescalation of the dispute along the Halha and direct negotiations with the Soviets would have allowed the IGHQ to concentrate military resources on the China incident, and thereby fulfill the goal of establishing the New Order in East Asia. Furthermore, this option would minimize the chances that the incident would escalate to full-scale war with the Soviet Union, a conflict that Japan was not prepared to fight in 1939–40. The second and riskier option entailed giving the Kwantung Army the authority and the resources necessary to punish Soviet-Mongolian border incursions. Operations across the Manchukuoan-Mongolian border would have demonstrated Japanese resolve and possibly secured control of the Halha area, but at the risk of a full-scale war. This option would certainly divert resources from ongoing military operations in China.

In the Changkufeng and Nomonhan incidents, balance-of-risk theory predicts that Japanese leaders would prefer the relatively risk-averse option. In both cases, officials declined an opportunity to secure territorial gains near the Manchukuoan-Mongolian and Soviet-Manchukuoan-Korean borders. The fact that local commanders decided to escalate the Changkufeng and Nomonhan disputes does not necessarily pose an anomaly for balance-of-risk theory. Recall that the theory purports to explain the risk behavior of a state's senior political and military leaders—in most instances the perceptions and calculations of senior officials, not local army commanders. Explaining the breakdown of IGHQ control over the Kwantung and the Korea armies is beyond the scope of the theory. Nonetheless, throughout the two incidents, most members of the first Konoe cabinet, the Hiranuma cabinet, and the IGHQ consistently preferred the less risky strategy: localization of the conflict and a negotiated settlement.

The Truman Administration and the Korean War Negotiations (February–November 1951)

The Truman administration's efforts to end to the Korean War in two periods—February to June 1951 and July to November 1951—are the final control cases in this chapter. Despite the failure of the large-scale offensives by the Chinese and North Korean forces in April and May 1951, and the despite dramatic increase in the United States' military capabilities over the past year, President Harry S. Truman and his advisors rejected calls by Major General James Van Fleet, the commander of the U.S. Eighth Army in Korea, to seize additional territory north of the Thirty-eighth Parallel. Instead, officials decided to negotiate an armistice with the People's Republic of China (PRC) and the North Korea that would preserve an independent South Korea. Once talks began in July 1951, the Truman administration insisted the postwar border be the actual battle line between the American-led United Nations forces and Chinese Communist and North Korean forces, not the Thirty-eighth Parallel.

I contend that loss aversion drove the Truman administration's behavior in the two periods. Truman, Secretary of State Dean G. Acheson, Secretary of Defense George C. Marshall, Marshall's deputy and successor Robert A. Lovett, and other senior officials, after having invested blood and treasure in defense of a country they previously deemed "strategically insignificant," adamantly refused to accept any outcome below their expectation level: the preservation of an independent, noncommunist South Korea. Although the administration insisted on a military demarcation line (MDL) that was north of the Thirty-eighth Parallel in most places, that line merely represented the actual line of contact between UN force and Chinese Communist and North Korean forces in spring 1951. Moreover, it offered strong defensive positions against a renewed North Korean attack on the South. As balance-of-risk theory expects, senior officials were extremely reluctant to take additional risks to secure a territorial settlement over that expectation level. Truman and his advisors did not act on Van Fleet's calls to crush the Chinese and North Korean armies and to seize additional territory north of the battle line in the spring of 1951. In short, they did not pursue risk-acceptant strategies in the pursuit of territorial gain.

Offensive realism expects decision makers to pursue risk-acceptant strategies in the pursuit of territorial gains in the periphery. The failure of the spring offensive by the Chinese and the North Koreans demonstrated the limits of their military capabilities. The chances of Soviet intervention on behalf of its Chinese Communist and North Korean allies remained low, so long as the United States did not expand the conflict into China. Finally, between June 1950 and June 1951 there was a tremendous increase in American capabilities. The army grew from ten to eighteen divisions, from eleven to eighteen regimental combat teams, and from 56 to 100 antiaircraft battalions. The air force, which had 48 combat wings and 8,687 combat aircraft in June 1950, had 87 combat wings and 12,870 combat aircraft in June 1951. The total number of naval vessels rose from 647 to 1,037 and the number of combatant ships (aircraft carriers, destroyers, cruisers, battleships, and submarines) rose from 237 to 342 in the same period. Although the administration had not achieved its target of fulfilling its fiscal year 1954 defense targets by the beginning of fiscal year 1952, in terms of relative military power, the United States was stronger in spring 1951 than it had been in spring 1950.[95]

While offensive realism would not necessary expect that the Truman administration to resume the previous November's drive to the Yalu River or to expand air and ground operations into Chinese territory (a move perceived as having a high risk of escalation to major war), the theory would expect senior officials to exploit an increasingly favorable balance-of-power to push the "line of contact" as far north of the Thirty-eighth Parallel as possible. On the POW issue, offensive realism predicts that the administration would demonstrate greater flexibility. Recall that the theory expects decision makers to be sensitive to the marginal costs and risks of their intervention strategies in the periphery. By 1952, the war degenerated into a bloody stalemate as the truce talks stalled. The window of opportunity to seize additional territory closed in late November 1951, as the Chinese began a major buildup of ground and air forces, including the deployment of 258,000 troops from the Peoples' Liberation Army (PLA) and three North Korean divisions in Manchuria, and the appearance of Russian MIG-15 jet fighters over Korean airspace.[96]

Logrolling theory would expect the Truman administration to have shown much greater reluctance to enter into negotiations with the Chinese and the North Koreans in spring 1951. The theory contends that a tacit logroll between the Europe-first internationalists in the executive branch and the Asia-first nationalists in Congress led to the adoption of a hard-line stance toward the PRC and continued support for Chiang Kai-Shek and the KMT on Taiwan. Moreover, given the need to maintain the support of powerful Asia-first nationalists for containment in Europe, the theory would also expect the Truman administration to have been more receptive to Van Fleet's calls to seize additional North Korean territory. Ohio senator Robert A. Taft argued that anything less than "complete triumph" was evidence that the administration had wasted "140,000 casualties and billions of dollars." Members of the so-called China lobby, particularly Republican senators William F. Knowland of California, Styles Bridges of New Hampshire, and Richard M. Nixon of California seized on any concession as evidence of the administration's perfidy and claimed that a truce at the Thirty-eighth Parallel would be "appeasement."[97] Finally, although not an Asia-first nationalist per se, Republican senator Joseph McCarthy of Wisconsin continued his vitriolic attacks on Acheson, Ambassador-at-large Philip C. Jessup, and the State Department (as a whole) throughout 1951–52.

Decisive Victory or Truce Talks? (February–June 1951)

In February 1951, the Truman administration identified five possible courses of action with respect to the Korean War: (1) a unilateral withdrawal of U.S. and UN forces from the Korean Peninsula; (2) a renewed effort to reunify Korea by force; (3) the extension of the hostilities to China; (4) acceptance of an indefinite stalemate along the current line of control between UN and Chinese Communist and North Korean forces; or (5) immediate steps toward a negotiated settlement, with the recognition that neither side had the capabilities to drive the other out of Korea.[98]

As noted in the previous chapter, senior civilian and military officials effectively ruled out the first option in late January. The fourth option was not desirable, in part because of the unpopularity of the Korean War at home, and in part because the Truman administration's Eurocentric strategic priorities. Given the United States' finite resources and military commitments elsewhere, an early termination of the Korean War was desirable. Furthermore, the acceptance of an indefinite stalemate along the current battle line would fall short of the administration's stated expectation level—the preservation of an independent, noncommunist South Korea below the Thirty-eighth Parallel. The second option, a renewed effort to reunify Korea and eliminate the North Korean regime, was simply not possible, given the military realities on the ground in 1951. The second and third Chinese offensives (24 November to 24 December 1950 and 31 December 1950 to 8 January 1951) succeeded not only in halting

General Douglas MacArthur's march to the Yalu, but sent the UN forces under his command reeling to the southern tip of the Korean Peninsula. After abandoning Seoul on 4 January and Inchon the following day, the Eighth Army and the X Corps halted the Chinese offensive on 14 January and then managed to retake the South Korean capital on 14 March.[99] While the elimination of the North Korean regime and the military re-unification of the peninsula were out of the question in spring 1951, the United States had the capabilities to retake territory north of the prewar border at the Thirty-eighth Parallel.

Despite an effort by British prime minister Clement Atlee to secure a commitment to halt operations at the Thirty-eighth Parallel, Truman announced on 16 February that the decision to cross the line would lie with MacArthur.[100] The following day, in a private briefing for representatives of countries who had troops in Korea, Assistant Secretary of State for Far Eastern Affairs Dean Rusk admitted that the Chinese counteroffensive eliminated the possibility of a military reunification of Korea. When the question of crossing the parallel became a "more immediate problem," the United States would consider the issue "in depth" and in consultation with the other states fighting under the UN flag. Meanwhile, American-led UN forces would conduct an "aggressive defense," including tactical thrusts into North Korea.[101] On 23 February, Acheson reiterated the point: UN forces should avoid a general advance north of the Thirty-eighth Parallel, he wrote Marshall, because of the "risk of extending the Korean conflict to other areas and even into general war at a time when we are not ready to risk a general war."[102]

The third option, the extension of air, naval, and ground operations into Chinese territory, had the strong support of MacArthur and some of his Republican allies in Congress. However, this option had no support within the administration or the JCS in spring 1951. An expansion of the Korean conflict risked major war with the Soviet Union during the United States' window of vulnerability (1950–53). Truman wrote MacArthur on 13 January 1951 that "pending the build-up of our national strength, we must act with great prudence in so far as extending the area of hostilities is concerned."[103] The previous day, General Lawton Collins, the army chief of staff, wrote: "Since the United States is not now prepared to prepared to engage in global war, and will not be ready before 1 July 1952, we should take all honorable means to avoid any action that is likely to bring Russia into open conflict with the United States prior to that date."[104] Offensive air strikes on targets in Manchuria would enable Beijing to invoke the mutual defense clause of the 1950 Sino-Soviet alliance treaty.

At the same time, Washington received indications that the Soviet army had moved three divisions into Manchuria and positioned other forces for a possible attack on Japan. On 6 April, JCS Chairman Omar N. Bradley brought Truman the latest reports of the Soviet buildup and the chiefs' recommendation that MacArthur receive authority to retaliate against Shantung and Manchuria in the event of a "major attack" on UN forces originating from outside the Korean Peninsula. Director of Central Intelligence Walter Bedell Smith confirmed these reports and apparently discussed the feasibility of preemptive versus retaliatory air strikes on Soviet bases. In response to the Soviet buildup and to signal American resolve, Truman sent B-29 bombers, armed with complete atomic bombs, to the island of Guam.[105] A 10 May NIE indicated the Soviet Union had the ability to "ensure successful defenses of the Chinese mainland against any of our forces." In June, Air Force Chief of Staff General Hoyt Vandenberg concluded that the balance-of-forces in the air over China favored the Soviets: "These [Far East Air Force] groups that we have over there now doing this tactical job are really about a fourth of our total effort that we could muster today [but] four times that amount of groups in the area over the vast expanse of China would be a drop in the bucket." By contrast, the Soviet air force could launch two thousand planes.[106]

MacArthur's public advocacy of expanding the war caused considerable anxiety among the coalition members. The NATO allies and the other states that contributed troops in Korea, however, adamantly opposed any expansion of the war. Indeed, throughout spring 1951 there were efforts by various members of the UN coalition and neutrals to facilitate cease-fire talks.[107] On 23 March, MacArthur released a statement claiming that China lacked "the industrial capacity to provide adequately many crucial items essential to the conduct of modern war." He warned that Beijing "must by now be painfully aware that a decision of the United Nations to depart from its tolerant effort to contain the war to . . . Korea through expansion of our military operations to [Chinese] coastal areas and interior bases would doom Red China to the risk of imminent military collapse."[108]

Although Truman promptly disavowed MacArthur's 23 March statement, Norwegian and Indian diplomats asked Warren Austin, the U.S. ambassador to the United Nations, for a clarification of the Truman administration's war aims.[109] Belgian, Canadian, Dutch, French, and Philippine diplomats met with Assistant Secretary of State for United Nations Affairs John Hickerson on 6 April to express their governments' concerns about a draft presidential directive granting MacArthur authority to bomb Chinese airbases in Manchuria in the event an air attack on UN forces. Later that day, Sir Oliver Franks, the British ambassador in Washington, expressed similar concerns to Bradley and Paul H. Nitze, the director of the Policy Planning Staff.[110]

MacArthur's repeated acts of insubordination culminated in a 20 March letter responding to a query from Massachusetts Representative Joseph W. Martin, Jr., the Republican leader of the House of Representatives. In the letter, MacArthur expressed support for a speech that Martin gave, which strongly criticized the Truman administration's conduct of the war and proposed that Chiang Kai-Shek receive American support for an attack on the Chinese mainland. Martin read the general's reply during a House floor debate on the afternoon of 5 April. After conferring with Acheson, Marshall, Deputy Secretary of Defense Lovett, and the JCS, Truman dismissed MacArthur from his various commands on 11 April and named as his replacement, Lieutenant General Matthew B. Ridgeway, the commander of the Eighth Army in Korea.[111]

As UN forces poised to push north of the Thirty-eighth Parallel for a second time in mid March 1951, the Chinese and North Koreans appeared to be readying a massive ground offensive. While there was consensus within the Truman administration that the long-term policy objective of the United States was "to bring about the establishment of a unified, independent, and democratic Korea," there was considerable debate over the short-term military objectives of UN forces. Initially, Acheson, Rusk, and most senior officials in the State Department concluded that the United States could compel the enemy to negotiate immediately (option five). Doing so, however, would require the administration to explicitly state what American-led UN forces would do once they reached the Thirty-eighth Parallel for the second time.[112]

Marshall, the JCS, and others in the Defense Department, however, resisted efforts by the State Department to clarify the United States' stance on the Thirty-eighth Parallel, believing that only a strong military posture in Korea—including giving CINCUNC authority to engage in tactical operations north of the parallel—and the imposition of direct economic and military pressure on China could lead to a negotiated end to the war. Bradley wrote Marshall on 27 February that restoration of the prewar border would "permit the Communists to build up north of the thirty-eighth parallel, either overtly or covertly, such a concentration of military forces at to jeopardize the safety of present or contemplated United States and United Nations forces in Korea."[113] During a 16 March meeting with State Department representatives, Collins and Chief of Naval Operations Admiral Forrest Sherman suggested the possibility that UNC forces might advance as far north as Pyongyang or at least the narrow neck of the Korean Peninsula.[114] A JCS report to Marshall and Lovett dated 27 March stated that "from a military point of view . . . an armistice agreement of itself would not, even temporarily constitute an acceptable solution to the Korean situation."[115] Writing on behalf of the JCS on 5 April, Vandenberg insisted that any viable Korean armistice would have to include a demilitarized zone "on the order of 20 miles in width, centered at or north of the thirty-eighth parallel," and that in the meantime, "preparations should be made immediately for naval and air forces against the mainland of China."[116]

United Nations forces pushed the Chinese Peoples' Volunteer Army (CPVA) and the North Korean People's Army (KPA) back to the Thirty-eighth Parallel in March 1951. Ridgeway, at the time Eighth Army commander, proposed that his forces should attempt to seize and fortify the high ground just north of the parallel in anticipation of a renewed enemy offensive. Specifically, Ridgeway proposed two defensive lines—Line Kansas and Line Wyoming. The former began at the junction of the Han and the Imijin rivers (thirty miles north of Seoul) and ran northeastward and eastward for 115 miles to Yangyang on the coast of the Sea of Japan (some eight miles north of the parallel). The latter ran some twenty miles north of Line Kansas and intersected the towns of Chorwon and Kumhwa at the southern base of the so-called Iron Triangle. If CPVA and KPA forces counterattacked, the Eighth Army would resist along Wyoming Line and if necessary, fall back to the better fortified Kansas Line.[117]

Marshal Peng Dehaui, the CPVA commander, launched a fifth offensive on 22 April with the aim of retaking Seoul, committing nine armies of about 250,000 troops. Six Chinese armies struck UN positions along the Wyoming and succeeded in pushing those forces south of the parallel. The Eighth Army, under the command of Lieutenant General James Van Fleet, stopped the offensive north of Seoul by 30 April. The Chinese and the North Koreans suffered an estimated 70,000 casualties, some ten times that of the UN forces, despite the fact they enjoyed a force ratio of three-to-one. The Chinese began a planned sixth offensive on 16 May, with twenty divisions—fifteen CPVA and five KPA—of approximately 175,000 troops. Van Fleet, on the other hand, commanded approximately 270,000 U.S. Army, Marines, and allied troops, in addition to 235,000 South Korean troops. The Eighth Army not only held the line north of Seoul but also pushed the enemy back across the Thirty-eighth Parallel and recaptured territory as far north as Line Kansas. During the 16–23 May offensive, the Chinese and the North Koreans suffered an additional 35,000 casualities, compared to only 900 UN casualties. Approximately 10,000 CPVA and KPA soldiers surrendered to the Eighth Army.[118] The capture of enemy equipment—mortars, heavy artillery, and automatic weapons—exceeded anything previously taken since the outbreak of the war in June 1950. Food shortages and logistical problems weakened the morale of CPVA troops. In a 30 May report to the JCS, Ridgeway judged that "a plainly evident disorganization now exists among both the Chinese Communist forces and the North Korean People's Army forces."[119]

Van Fleet proposed an advance against Chinese and North Korean forces, citing their stunning defeat at the hands of the UN forces and the South Korean army during the March and April offensives. The JCS and Ridgeway disagreed, concluding that an offensive risked overextending UNC supply lines, while shortening those of the Chinese and the North Koreans. Conversely, halting the advance near the Kansas Line would actually increase pressure on the enemy, since the further south the CPVA and KPA tried to maintain themselves, the more vulnerable their supply lines would be to air interdiction by the U.S. Far Eastern Air Forces (FEAF).[120] Instead of authorization for Van Fleet's proposed general advance, Ridgeway received a new directive on 1 May that restricted ground operations by UN forces and forbade any "air or naval action against Manchuria, against USSR territory, or against North Korean electrical power complex including the Yalu River power installation" without the prior authorization of the JCS and the president. The Eighth Army would not move north of Kansas-Wyoming lines, but would instead assume a defensive posture and inflict "maximum personnel losses" on Chinese and North Korean forces.[121]

On 17 May, Truman approved NSC 48/5, that reaffirmed the United States' long-term political objective, "as distinguished from military means," was a "solution of the Korean problem which would provide for a united, independent, and democratic Korea." With respect to short-term political objectives, however, Washington would seek a negotiated settlement. Any armistice would have to preserve the Republic of Korea with a border no further south than the Thirty-eighth Parallel; provide for the timely withdrawal of all non-Korean forces from the peninsula; and give South Korea sufficient military capabilities to deter a renewed North Korean attack. At the same time, the United States would "seek to avoid the extension of hostilities in Korea into a general war with the Soviet Union, and seek to avoid the extension beyond Korea of hostilities with Communist China, particularly without the support of our major allies."[122] NSC 48/5, however, did not resolve a number of practical matters with respect to Korea.

Bradley raised the question of whether Ridgeway had authority to defend UN positions as far north as the Yalu or the Thirty-eighth Parallel, or at some point between them during a 29 May meeting of the JCS with State Department representatives. Furthermore, it was unclear whether Ridgeway had to obtain JCS approval before sending troops north of the line running east to west through the Hwachon reservoir, or whether that line should be further north at Pyongyang or Wonsan,

as Sherman suggested. Rusk responded saying that he and his colleagues in attendance—Nitze, Freeman Matthews, and Averell Harriman—worried about advancing too far north and provoking the Soviets. Sherman conceded that the "risks would definitely increase if one
went north of Pyongyang." Matthews felt strongly that "any move by
U.N. forces north of the Wonsan general area would greatly increase the
risks of Soviet intervention and broadening the conflict," and Harriman
concurred.[123]

In late May and early June, the Truman administration signaled its
desire for an armistice to the Korean conflict and its willingness not to
exploit the disarray of CPVA and KPA forces to seize additional territory
north of the Kansas-Wonsan line. During the May hearings before the
Senate Armed Services and the Foreign Relations Committees, Acheson
testified the administration would accept an armistice at or near the
Thirty-eighth Parallel if there were "reliable assurances" that the fighting "would not be resumed." Marshall and Bradley made similar statements about the desirability of a cease-fire and argued that expanding
the war into China risked precipitating a major war. Bradley famously
observed that the Soviets were the main threat and that attacking China
"would involve us in the wrong war, at the wrong place, at the wrong
time, and with the wrong enemy."[124]

Meanwhile, the Soviet government also signaled its willingness to facilitate a Korean cease-fire based on the status quo antebellum. Chief
among those signals were a series of "off-the-record" contacts in June between Yaacov Malik, the Soviet permanent representative to the United
Nations, with various members of the American UN delegation and private citizens, including George Kennan, former PPS director and State
Department counselor.[125] Kennan conveyed the Truman administration's
interest in an armistice in Korea, with no linkages to various political issues involving the PRC and Taiwan. Malik expressed the Kremlin's interest in a "peaceful solution" without insisting on the withdrawal of
foreign troops from Korea. In letters to Acheson and Matthews, Kennan
urged the administration to move quickly toward a negotiated settlement: the Kremlin wished to avert a military clash with the United
States, but might soon take a more assertive posture if it perceived Soviet
interests as threatened by a continuation of the Korean conflict. In fact,
the Soviet Union sought to halt the war, or at least preclude an escalation
that might bring hostile forces to its borders and increase the unity of the
Western bloc. While the Soviet Union would not directly participate in
negotiations since it was not a belligerent, the Kremlin had and would
continue to bring its pressure "to bear on the North Koreans and the Chinese Communists to show themselves amenable to proposals for a cease
fire."[126] For its part, China found the war to be an economic drain and

the cause of an unwanted dependency on the Soviets for weapons. Even Mao Zedong had abandoned his earlier aim of driving American-led UN forces from Korea. Instead, the Chinese war aims now consisted of a restoration of the Thirty-eighth Parallel, a return to the political status quo antebellum in Korea, and the withdrawal of foreign troops.[127]

On 23 June, Malik delivered an address on the weekly United Nations' radio program, "The Price of Peace." At the close of his remarks, he said, "The Soviet peoples further believe that the most acute problem of the present day—the problem of the armed conflict in Korea—could be settled. This would require the readiness of the parties to enter on the path of a peaceful settlement of the Korean question." As a first step, discussions should start "between the belligerents for a cease-fire and armistice providing for a mutual withdrawal of forces from the Thirty-eighth Parallel."[128] Malik did not mention a foreign troop withdrawal from Korea, PRC membership in the UN, or control of Taiwan.

The *People's Daily*, the official newspaper of the Chinese Communist party, endorsed Malik's proposal for cease-fire talks the following day. Acheson told the House Foreign Affairs Committee on 26 June that the United States would settle for the withdrawal of Chinese and North Korean forces at the Thirty-eighth Parallel and security guarantees for South Korea. The following day, Truman concluded a speech at Tullahoma, Tennessee, with the following statement: "We are ready to join in a peaceful settlement in Korea now, just as we have always been. But it must be a real settlement which fully ends the aggression and restores peace and security to the area and to the gallant people of Korea."[129] During the May hearings on MacArthur's dismissal, Marshall, Bradley, and Collins each testified that the United States would agree to a cease-fire line at the Thirty-eighth Parallel. On 30 June, Truman permitted Ridgeway to accept a proposal from the North Koreans and the Chinese to send negotiators to Kaesong, the ancient Korean capital in the "no man's land" just south of the Thirty-eighth Parallel, but with the stipulation that every major decision would be made in Washington.[130]

The Politics of Peace Talks (July–November 1951)

Truce talks began at Kaesong on 10 July. The UN negotiators, led by Vice Admiral C. Turner Joy, the commander of U.S. Naval Forces—Far East (COMNAVFE), stipulated that they only had authority to discuss cease-fire matters. The opposing delegation, nominally led by Lieutenant General Nam Il, KPA chief of staff, but actually controlled by General Xie Fang, the CPVA chief of staff, proposed an immediate cease-fire; the mutual withdrawal of troops from the Thirty-eighth Parallel followed by the withdrawal of all foreign troops from Korea; the repatriation of all POWs;

and then final status negotiations on the future of Korea. Joy and his team rejected the Thirty-eighth Parallel as the military demarcation line in favor of a more northern position and dismissed the proposal to withdraw all foreign troops as a political ploy. They also rejected the postarmistice repatriation of all POWs (a so-called "all for all" exchange), although this was a long-standing military custom and a requirement of the 1949 Geneva Convention, which the United States had signed but the Senate had not yet ratified. It is worth noting that by July 1951, UN forces held approximately 150,000 Chinese and North Korean POWs, while the Chinese and the North Koreans only held 16,000 American and allied prisoners.[131] Sensing that many enemy POWs did not wish to return to the PRC or the DPRK and conscious of the postarmistice balance-of-forces on the Korean Peninsula, the Truman administration and UN negotiators hoped to extract concessions from the enemy at the negotiating table.[132]

Chinese and North Korean officials conceded the issue of foreign troop withdrawals early in the negotiations. From July until November, however, the MDL emerged as the principal obstacle to a cease-fire. Joy argued that since a cease-fire would include a cessation of military operations in the air and on the sea around the Korean Peninsula—where the United States and its allies had a clear advantage—as well as well as on the ground, the Communists would gain more from an end to the fighting than would the UN command—unless, of course, the latter received compensation for ending its air and sea action against North Korea. That compensation could only come in the form of territory. Chinese and North Korean negotiators initially balked at this demand, citing Acheson's June testimony about the Thirty-eighth Parallel. General Nam derided Joy's argument in favor of the Kansas Line as "naïve and illogical" and claimed that his side's stand on the Thirty-eighth Parallel was "righteous and immovable."[133]

Despite Acheson, Marshall, Bradley, and Collins's testimony in June, by midsummer most senior officials came to favor a more northward demarcation line. In part, a concern for the United States' global position and reputation as the leader of the Western bloc accounts for this shift in the administration's stand. In early August, Nitze wrote that a cease-fire at the Thirty-eighth Parallel "would give the impression that the Chinese and North Korean Communists had been able to achieve somewhat more than an even military result against sixteen nations, including the U.S., U.K., Canada, and France."[134] In part also, the administration pressed for acceptance of the Kansas Line in deference to the South Korean government. President Syngman Rhee of the Republic of Korea was a vocal advocate of rollback in 1950 and continued to press for the military reunification of the peninsula even during the seesaw battles of late

1950 and early 1951. Throughout June and July 1951, Rhee and other South Korean officials stated their opposition to any cease-fire line at the Thirty-eighth Parallel and their desire for a postwar military guarantee.[135] Nonetheless, the primary rationale for the Truman administration's insistence on a more northward MDL was military. Based on the battlefield experience of the past nine months, the JCS and Ridgeway concluded that the Thirty-eighth Parallel was simply indefensible. There was no way that the administration could meet its expectation level—a restoration of the political status quo antebellum in Korea—without establishing a stable border and providing a postwar military guarantee.

The failure of the April and May offensives made it extremely unlikely that the CPVA and the KPA could improve on the line of contact, let alone push UN forces back to the Thirty-eighth Parallel. Nonetheless, North Korean and Chinese negotiators did not immediately concede the demarcation line issue, possibly because Mao still entertained some hope of regaining territory in a renewed offensive. They eventually dropped their insistence on the Thirty-eighth Parallel and proposed instead the battle line at the time the armistice came into effect. The Chinese-North Korean proposal, would, in effect give both sides an incentive to battle for new territory.[136] During the Kaesong phase of the negotiations (10 July to 22 August) and later when truce talks resumed at Panmunjom on 25 October, Joy and his team insisted on the current battle line—Line Kansas—as well as the creation of a demilitarized zone (DMZ) extending for two kilometers on either side of MDL. Ridgeway, however, proposed reverting to the battle line at the time of the armistice so that the UNC could continue to fight for territory. Nonetheless, the JCS deemed the Chinese/North Korean position reasonable and advised Truman to order Ridgeway to agree to the current battle line provided that all other issues were settled within thirty days. Generals Xie and Nam agreed to the current battle line as the demarcation on 26 November.[137]

During the February-June and July-December 1951 periods, the Truman administration rejected calls for an expansion of the war into Chinese territory. Of the five options identified in February, the expansion of the war was clearly the riskiest and perceived as such by civilian and military leaders at the time. Air and ground operations against Manchuria or other parts of the PRC would increase the likelihood of Soviet intervention on behalf of its Chinese Communists and North Korean allies. Even if the expansion of operations beyond the Korean Peninsula did not precipitate a major war the pursuit of this option would likely prolong the United States' involvement in a war in what officials deemed to be a secondary theater in the cold war. The defense of the major centers of industrial power, namely Western Europe, the Middle

East, and Japan, remained the overriding priorities for the Truman administration.

At the same time, Truman and his advisors rejected the option of seizing additional territory above the Kansas-Wyoming lines in North Korea. The general advance option had high potential payoffs, namely the potential to eliminate CPVA and KPA forces, which after the failure of the fifth and sixth offensives appeared close to collapse. A limited offensive might also have provided South Korea with additional territory and perhaps more defensible borders than those afforded by the Kansas Line. Nonetheless, this option entailed high risks. By allowing Van Fleet to pursue a general offensive above the Kansas-Wyoming lines, the Eighth Army, the X Corps, and allied forces would likely overextend their supply lines, while the supply lines of the CPVA and the KPA would become shorter. Although the U.S. Far Eastern Air Forces enjoyed superiority in the air, there was a good chance that Peng and his North Korean counterparts would draw UN forces further north before launching a counteroffensive; a tactic that the CPVA commander had used in November 1950 with devastating effect. There was also the possibility that PRC leader Mao Zedong would redeploy several hundred thousand Chinese troops from Manchuria to North Korea in order to hold the line. Furthermore, although Van Fleet requested authority to conduct such an offensive in May and early June 1951, he never defined the objective. Would the Eighth Army drive all the way to the Yalu or advance to the narrow waist of the peninsula (the Pyongyang-Wonsan line), with the idea of staying there until the conclusion of an armistice?

The third option, and one ultimately chosen, involved a stabilization of the battle line above the Thirty-eighth Parallel and moves toward cease-fire negotiations with the Chinese and the North Koreans. Arguably, this was the more risk averse of the options actively under consideration. By mid May 1951, the UN forces had achieved the administration's short-term objective: the restoration of the Thirty-eighth Parallel and the removal of Chinese and North Korean forces from South Korean territory. Ridgeway and Van Fleet's forces had not only halted the fifth and the sixth CPVA offensives, but they had also taken territory north of the parallel.

Offensive realism and logrolling theory predict that the Truman administration would pursue the risky choice of allowing Van Fleet to conduct a general advance beyond the Kansas Line, but for different reasons. Offensive realism would expect the Truman administration to exploit battlefield and systemic opportunities, as well as the dramatic increase in American military capabilities, and adopt a riskier strategy. A limited offensive in North Korean territory, perhaps to the Pyongyang-Wonsan line, had the potential to eliminate remnants of the defeated

Chinese and North Korean armies. Approving such an advance may not only have given South Korea more defensible borders, but it would have also degraded the enemy's military capabilities, thus improving the United States' bargaining position during the Kaesong and later the Panmunjom negotiations.

Logrolling theory attributes the administration's choice of strategies to coalition formation and logrolling between the Asia-first nationalists in Congress and the Europe-first internationalists in the State and the Defense departments. The price of congressional support for containment in Europe was the pursuit of hard-line strategies toward China and communism in general in East Asia. In the months following China's entry into the Korean War and as the fighting between Chinese Communist and U.S.-led UN forces became a stalemate, Truman's public approval ratings plunged. The members of the China lobby and other congressional Republicans of the administration's foreign policy went on the offensive, accusing Truman and his advisors of not only placing unreasonable restrictions on MacArthur's (and later Ridgeway's) conduct of the war, but also of selling out noncommunist states in East Asia. In light of such criticism, the theory would expect the administration to have seized any opportunity to break the Korean stalemate and demonstrate its willingness to oppose Communist expansion, even at a substantial level of risk. Instead, as balance-of-risk theory expects, Truman, Acheson, Marshall, Lovett, the JCS, and others adopted the less risky strategy of stabilizing the front at the Kansas Line and seeking truce talks with the Chinese and the North Koreans.

Epilogue: The Prisoner of War Issue (1952–53)

The Korean War obviously did not end in 1951. Despite a military stalemate and Chinese and North Korean concessions on territorial issues, the United States demanded that prisoners of war (POWs) only return to their home countries on a voluntary basis. As a result, the truce talks and the fighting dragged on for almost two years, until the China and North Korea conceded the POW issue on 4 June 1953. I do not address the Truman administration's insistence on the "voluntary" repatriation of POWs and the ensuing controversy over the screening (and rescreening) of enemy combatants in UN custody in 1952–53.

This omission does not diminish the importance of the POW issue. American negotiators indicated that China and North Korea could expect the return of approximately 116,000 POWs in April 1952. During the screening of prisoners, only 70,000 expressed a desire to return home, a figure unacceptable to Beijing and Pyongyang. American officials knew that pro-KMT interpreters and guards at the Koje-do Island POW camp brutally intimidated prisoners to refuse repatriation. The insistence on "voluntary" repatriation cost the United States alone 63,200 causalities, including 12,300 deaths (approximately 45 percent of the total American casualties), while other UN forces, mainly the South Korean army, lost more than 50,000. The Chinese and the North Korean armies sustained more than 250,000 casualties from January 1952 to July 1953.[138] The historical literature and published government documents stress the importance of domestic political calculations, the perceived need to score a "psychological victory" over the Communist bloc, and perhaps regret on the part of Truman, Acheson, and other officials about the fate of many Soviet POWs repatriated after World War II in the adoption of the "voluntary" repatriation stand during the Korean War.[139]

Despite the United States' inflexibility on POW repatriation, the crucial decisions to end the Korean War occurred in 1951, not in 1952 or 1953. Truman and his advisors adopted the relatively risk-averse strategy of seeking a truce after UN forces met the expectation level established in June 1950: a restoration of the prewar border and the preservation of an independent, noncommunist South Korea. They rejected the riskier options of allowing the Eighth Army to pursue a "general advance" in North Korea to the Pyongyang-Wonsan line or expanding military operations to China.

Conclusions

This chapter demonstrates the applicability of balance-of-risk theory to other cases of great power intervention in the periphery. Germany's initiation of the 1911 Agadir crisis was another "least likely" case for my theory and "most likely" case for logrolling theory and offensive realism. Kiderlen and Bethmann adopted a risky diplomatic strategy to avert losses to German prestige and economic interests in Morocco created by the impending French annexation of the sultanate. They did not seek to acquire territory or compensation over and above what Germany would have lost once the French consolidated their control over the country. Offensive realism, on the other hand, would expect German leaders to have exploited a favorable balance-of-power in the pursuit of even greater territorial compensation. Logrolling theory attributes the crisis to logrolling among various imperialist groups within German society and the domestic political vulnerability of Kiderlen and Bethmann. However, there is little evidence to suggest that the German foreign minister or chancellor sent the *Panther* to the port of Agadir at the behest of such a logrolled coalition.

The bulk of the chapter addressed two questions: Does balance-of-

TABLE 6.2 *Summary of risk behavior in the control cases*

Case	Expectation level (against which leaders evaluate outcomes)	Perceived position relative to expectation level	Overall risk propensity of leaders	Policy options selected
1911 Agadir crisis (German govt., principally Kiderlen, Bethmann, Wilhelm II, and Moltke)	Status quo (as defined in the 1906 Act of Algeciras)	Loss	Risk acceptance	• Crisis initiation (deployment of the cruiser *Panther* to Agadir); • Demands for territorial compensation from the French govt.
1938 Changkufeng incident (The first Konoe government and the IGHQ)	Expectation of creating a New Order in East Asia	Gain	Risk aversion	• Denial of authorization for the Nineteenth Division to evict Soviet troops from the Changkufeng/Lake Khasan region; • The use of diplomacy to convince Soviet troops to voluntarily leave the area; • Efforts to deescalate the situation once fighting broke out
1939 Nomonhan incident (The Hiranuma cabinet and the IGHQ)	Expectation of creating a New Order in East Asia	Gain	Risk aversion	• Denial of authorization for the Kwantung Army's planned air and ground offensive in the Nomonhan/Khalkhin-gol region; • Efforts to deescalate the situation once the fighting broke out

(continued)

TABLE 6.2 (*continued*)

Case	Expectation level (against which leaders evaluate outcomes)	Perceived position relative to expectation level	Overall risk propensity of leaders	Policy options selected
The United States' efforts to end the Korean War (Feb.–June 1951) (Truman and the principal members of his national security team, along with the JCS)	Status quo ante-bellum in Korea	Gain	Risk aversion	• Rejection of MacArthur's call for expanded ground and air operations in Chinese territory • Rejection of Van Fleet's proposal for a general advance (possibly to the Pyongyang-Wonsan line) • Proposal for truce talks
The United States' efforts to end the Korean War (July–Nov. 1951) (Truman and the principal members of his national security team, along with the JCS)	Status quo ante-bellum in Korea	Gain	Risk aversion	• Initiation of truce talks • Continued rejection of calls to seize additional territory above the current battle line • Insistence that current battle line (not Thirty-eighth Parallel) serve as MDL

risk theory explain attempts by great powers to deescalate or terminate risky intervention strategies? Does the theory account for instances where great powers do not initiate risky interventions or decline to pursue risky strategies vis-à-vis other great powers to perpetuate failing peripheral interventions? Toward the end, I examine four other cases—the Konoe and Hiranuma cabinets and the IGHQ's handling of the 1938 Changkufeng and the 1939 Nomonhan incidents and the Truman administration's decisions to negotiate an end to the Korean War in February–June and July–November 1951. In all four cases, senior officials were reluctant to adopt or to continue arguably risk-acceptant strategies to secure territorial gains over their initial expectation level, despite domestic coalition logrolling, favorable power balances, systemic and/or battlefield opportunities. Instead, as theory expects, officials gravitated toward less risky diplomatic and military strategies.

The cases examined in this chapter should enhance one's confidence in the hypotheses developed elsewhere in the book. In the next and final chapter, I discuss the theoretical implications of my argument and the policy implications for great power intervention today.

[7]

Implications of the Argument

I began this book by posing two questions: First, why do great powers initiate risky diplomatic or military commitments in the periphery, that is, in geographic areas where actual or likely conflict cannot directly threaten the security of a great power's homeland? Second, why do great powers persist in peripheral conflicts despite the diminishing prospects of victory and increasing political, military, and economic costs? I argued that leaders' aversion to perceived losses—in terms of their state's relative power, international status, or prestige—drives great power intervention in peripheral regions.

Drawing on the defensive realist literature in international relations and the prospect theory literature in psychology, I constructed a theory of foreign policy called balance-of-risk theory. Chapters 3 through 5 tested rival hypotheses derived from balance-of-risk theory and its most likely theoretical competitors—offensive realism and the logrolling theory of imperialism—to explain three cases where great powers initiated high-risk interventions in arguably peripheral regions: the German government's initiation of the 1905 Morocco crisis; the Konoe and Tōjō cabinets and Imperial General Headquarters' (IGHQ) 1940–41 war decisions; and the Truman administration's intervention in the Korean War in 1950–51. Chapter 6 examined Germany's initiation of the 1911 Agadir crisis and four additional cases: the Japanese cabinet and IGHQ's handling of the 1938 Changkufeng and the 1939 Nomonhan incidents; the Truman administration's decision to seek an armistice in Korea during winter and spring 1951; and the administration's handling of the opening months of truce talks with China and North Korea in summer and autumn 1951. In each of the four last cases, great powers attempted to withdraw or deescalate risky interventions in the periphery.

Three tasks remain. The first is to summarize and compare the results of the case studies in order to highlight the main theoretical conclusions one might draw from them. The second is to discuss the implications of my argument for the debate between offensive realism and defensive realism and for future applications of prospect theory and other branches of behavior decision theory to the study of foreign policy and international politics. The third and final task is to sketch the policy implications of my argument for great power intervention in the periphery in the twenty-first century.

POWER POLITICS, LOSS AVERSION, AND GREAT POWER INTERVENTION IN THE PERIPHERY

The cases examined in this book generally support the argument that great powers are more likely to undertake risky diplomatic and military interventions in peripheral regions to avoid perceived losses and that great powers are less likely to do so in the pursuit of perceived gains. Below I discuss several phenomena identified by balance-of-risk theory that recur in the three major cases and the five secondary cases. Chief among them are elite perceptions of relative power loss as a catalyst for peripheral intervention; the problem of entrapment and escalating commitment in diplomatic crisis, as well as in actual military interventions; and leaders' preoccupation with their state's prestige and international standing.

Anticipated Power Shifts and Expectation Levels

In two of the three major cases, the leaders of the preponderant state in the international system initiated risky interventions in the periphery as a means to stem perceived losses in their state's relative power and international status. For example, German leaders' fear of encirclement and relative decline in the core led them to initiate a crisis over French colonial policy in Morocco in the spring of 1905. At the time, Germany had few strategic or economic interests in North Africa and its leaders cared little for the preservation of the sultan of Morocco as a sovereign ruler. However, Chancellor Bernhard von Bülow and Foreign Office Counselor Friedrich von Holstein feared that in the absence of some dramatic action, the 1904 Anglo-French *Entente Cordiale* would evolve into a military alliance. This nascent alliance, combined with the existing Russo-French alliance, would leave Germany encircled and completely dependent on its one ally, Austria-Hungary, the weakest of the great powers. Moreover, German leaders feared the growth of Russian eco-

nomic capabilities and estimated that by the middle of the next decade
Russia would overtake Germany as the continent's leading industrial
and military power. In short, by failing to break up the Anglo-French entente in 1904–05, German leaders would soon find themselves faced with
a hostile and potentially more powerful great power coalition, two of
whose members shared a common border with Germany.

Wilhelmine Germany thus initiated a challenge over French colonial
policy in Morocco in the hope that a demonstration of resolve would isolate France, intimidate Great Britain, and destroy the entente. Officials in
Berlin adopted a more favorable international environment, namely the
status quo before the Anglo-French entente, as the expectation level for
diplomatic and military strategies. Since the actual status quo was below
that expectation level, German officials were willing to adopt risk-acceptant strategies to avert perceived relative power and status loss. German
leaders used the threat of war to extract major concessions, including the
dismissal of the French foreign minister and an international conference
designed to humiliate France for violating the 1880 Madrid Convention.
At the same time, Bülow, Holstein, Wilhelm II, Alfred von Schlieffen,
and Helmuth von Moltke had no intention of going to war with France
at that time. Nonetheless, throughout 1905 and early 1906 German leaders ran the risk that their belligerent strategy would draw Britain and
France closer together or even escalate into a military confrontation.

In June 1950, the Truman administration reversed its four-year-old defensive perimeter strategy in East Asia and the Pacific by sending American troops to defend South Korea from a North Korean invasion. Although the United States was preponderant, particularly in economic
capabilities, the Korean War erupted during what officials in Washington perceived as a window of vulnerability. The detonation of a Soviet
atomic bomb several years ahead of CIA estimates, the Communist victory in the Chinese civil war, and the subsequent Sino-Soviet alliance
convinced the Truman administration that the global balance-of-power
would shift against the United States in the absence of corrective action.
Several years of higher defense spending, the development of stronger
military ties with the states of Western Europe and Japan, and the immediate development of the hydrogen bomb would reverse this adverse
trend. In the meantime, however, the United States would avoid any
confrontation that might precipitate a major war, while reaffirming the
priority of Western European defense and the defensive perimeter strategy in Pacific, which limited American military commitments to Japan,
the Ryukus, and the Philippines.

The North Korean invasion represented a dramatic challenge to the
status quo. Since 1948, the Truman administration drew a distinction between the strategic value of the divided Korean Peninsula, which it con-

sidered negligible, and the symbolic importance of preserving South Korea.[1] Convinced that North Korean premier Kim Il Sung would not have undertaken the invasion without Stalin's permission, Harry Truman and his senior advisors deployed four understrength army divisions with the stated aim of restoring the prewar border at the Thirty-eighth Parallel and preserving an independent, noncommunist South Korea. Not intervening in Korea would have meant a sure loss for the Truman administration, but one whose magnitude was difficult to gauge in June 1950. However, military intervention was a risky move given the relative weakness of American conventional forces at the time and the distinct possibility that the North Korean invasion was a diversion for a Soviet-backed probe in Western Europe.

In the third major case, the leaders of a second-tier great power displayed this same preoccupation with avoiding perceived losses in relative power. Drawing on the lessons of Germany's defeat in World War I, military and civilian leaders in Tokyo concluded that expansion on the East Asian mainland and autarky were the only way to reduce Japan's economic vulnerability vis-à-vis the West and the Soviet Union. In the early 1930s, the Kwantung Army embarked on a limited campaign of expansion in Manchuria and later in the northern provinces of China proper. Following the outbreak of a full-scale war with Nationalist China in July 1937, the first Konoe cabinet and the military chiefs of staffs proclaimed the establishment of a New Order in East Asia—a political, economic, and military bloc consisting of the Japanese home islands, Manchuria, northern and central China, and the existing colonies of Korea, Taiwan, and southern Sakhalin—as the expectation level for Japanese grand strategy. In 1940–41, the second and third Konoe cabinets and later the Tōjō cabinet, along with the IGHQ, pursued a series of risky diplomatic and military strategies to perpetuate the war effort against the KMT, including the expansion of the Japanese empire into Southeast Asia, the conclusion of an alliance with Germany and Italy, and finally a decision for war with the United States.

Conversely, in most instances in the major cases, as well as in the four secondary cases, balance-of-risk theory correctly predicted that leaders would gravitate toward less risky options if given the opportunity to secure gains over and above their expectation level. In the Nomonhan and the Changkufeng incidents, insubordinate Korea Army and Kwantung Army commanders took it on themselves to punish border incursions by Soviet troops near the juncture of the contested borders of Japanese-ruled Korea and Manchukuo with the Soviet Union and Outer Mongolia. The reduction of the Soviet military presence in East Asia and the seizure of additional territory beyond Soviet-Manchukuoan and the Manchukuoan-Mongolian border were outcomes beyond the stated expected level of Japanese grand strategy. In both cases, the cabinet of the day (first under Konoe Fumimaro and later under Hiranuma Kiichiro) and the IGHQ in Tokyo acted to avoid further escalation. Similarly, in the spring and summer of 1951, the Truman administration declined an opportunity to destroy the retreating Chinese and North Korean armies and to seize additional territory above the battle line, preferring instead to initiate truce talks.

Admittedly, in one period in the Korean War case, the direction of national leaders' risk taking behavior did not conform to the predictions of balance-of-risk theory. Offensive realism provides the better explanation for the Truman administration's decision to escalate its aims in the Korean conflict from containment to rollback in August and September 1950. Systemic and battlefield opportunities combined to make rollback an increasing attractive option for the administration. These included the success of General Douglas MacArthur's Inchon landing and the subsequent counteroffensive by American-led UN forces; the decreased likelihood of Soviet intervention in Korea or a Soviet move elsewhere in 1950; and the PRC's perceived military weakness. In policy debates during the summer of 1950, proponents of rollback, including George Marshall, Robert Lovett, Omar Bradley and the other members of the Joint Chiefs of Staff (JCS), and Dean Rusk, prevailed over the more cautious officials, such as Dean Acheson, Philip Jessup, and Paul Nitze, in part by pointing to the low-cost opportunity to eliminate the North Korean threat to the South.

In two other observation periods in the major cases, the Japanese leadership's decision to seek a nonaggression pact with the Soviet Union in the spring of 1941 and the German government's decision to have Wilhelm II make a provocative speech at Tangiers expressing German support of Moroccan sovereignty and the 1880 Madrid Convention in spring 1905, are equally consistent with offensive realism. Given the decisive defeat of the Kwantung Army at the hand of the Soviet Far Eastern Army during the 1939 Nomonhan incident and the escalating costs of the war against the KMT, it is not surprising that Konoe, Tōjō Hideki, Prince Kan'in, Sugiyama Gen, and other officials would prefer to stabilize the northern frontier of Manchukuo. The regional balance-of-power simply did not favor Japan. When Matsouka Yosuke proposed joining Nazi Germany in invading the Soviet Union in May 1941, he encountered vehement opposition from Tōjō and Sugiyama. Likewise, in the first Morocco crisis, one cannot rule out a strong element of opportunism in Bülow and Holstein's plan to send the German emperor to Tangiers. The French government's efforts to establish a protectorate in Morocco were a flagrant violation of the 1880 Madrid Convention. The anticipated costs of signaling German displeasure, albeit in a melodramatic fashion, appeared low.

Entrapment and Escalating Commitment to Recover Sunk Costs

Across all three major cases, senior officials in Germany, Japan, and the United States fell victim to entrapment in the periphery. They escalated their commitment to previously chosen, though failing, courses of action in order to justify or "make good on" prior investments. In cases of foreign military intervention, sunk costs often included both the material costs of military operations—such as, casualties, money, lost equipment, or opportunity costs—and whatever political capital or reputation costs that decision makers expended to mount such operations. In the case of diplomatic disputes involving peripheral regions, sunk costs again included reputation and material considerations. The extent and the magnitude of entrapment and escalating commitment varied among the cases.

The most dramatic example of entrapment and escalating commitment was Japan's elusive quest for victory in the so-called China incident. By December 1937, the war against the KMT and the Chinese Communists required the deployment of sixteen divisions and roughly 700,000 troops—virtually the entire peacetime strength of the Imperial Japanese Army—to northern and central China. These deployments left other strategic interests critically exposed, including the ill-defined borders of Japanese-controlled Korea and Manchukuo with Outer Mongolia and the Soviet Union. Moreover, the war created enormous economic dislocations, which had the perverse effect of increasing Japan's dependence on the United States, Great Britain, and the Netherlands for critical war materials and natural resources. At the same time, Tokyo's prosecution of the China incident alienated officials in Washington, London, and The Hague. Yet, at no time during the 1937–41 period, did successive Japanese cabinets and the IGHQ consider a deescalation of the Sino-Japanese War or abandoning the goal of creating a New Order in East Asia. Instead, these officials not only devoted additional troops and resources to a failing war on the mainland, but then undertook a host of risky diplomatic and military strategies vis-à-vis other great powers in an effort to sustain that war effort.

Although less dramatic that the Japanese case, the leaders of Wilhelmine Germany and the Truman administration also fell victim to forms of entrapment. In the 1905 Morocco crisis, once having embarked on an effort to divide the entente by challenging French *pénétration pacifique*, Bülow and Holstein found it very difficult to moderate their belli-

cose diplomacy, even after receiving numerous and substantial concessions from the French government, including the ouster of Théophile
Delcassé, the foreign minister. Despite this, German leaders never abandoned their initial expectation of destroying the Anglo-French entente
and were willing to take additional risks to bring about that outcome.

Similarly, in the 1911 Agadir crisis, the German state secretary for foreign affairs Alfred von Kiderlen-Wächter embarked on a campaign to
preserve Germany's prestige among the great powers, as well as its economic interests in North Africa, by forcing France to make territorial
compensation in the Congo in exchange for the absorption of Morocco.
For Kiderlen and Chancellor Theobold von Bethmann-Hollweg, the status quo as defined in the 1906 Act of Algeciras functioned as the expectation level. Yet, once having provoked an international crisis by sending
the cruiser *Panther* to the waters off Agadir and after the British government signaled its support for France, Kiderlen and Bethmann persisted
in saber rattling rather than suffer a perceived loss to German reputation
by backing down.

Finally, from 7 October to 27 November 1950, the Truman administration escalated its commitment to the achievement of a new war aim codified in NSC81/1—the destruction of the North Korean army and the
military reunification of Korea—by allowing MacArthur to proceed with
an offensive to the Yalu River despite the growing likelihood that doing
so would lead China to enter the war. Marshall, Lovett, and the JCS rejected a British proposal to establish a buffer zone between advancing
U.S. forces and the Sino-Korean border, against the advice of Acheson,
Rusk, and Jessup, among others.

Loss Aversion in Material Capabilities, Reputation, and Prestige

The empirical chapters of the book show that relative material capabilities and anticipated power trends are not the only international factors that shape states' foreign policy. Prestige, that is, a state's reputation
for having power (particularly military power), also plays an important
role in the foreign policies of the great powers. Although subjective and
entirely dependent on other state's assessments, prestige serves an instrumental function as a proxy for the use of military force. Hans J. Morgenthau writes that "in the struggle for existence and power [among
states, as well as among individuals]—which is, as it were, the raw material of the social world—what others think about us is as important as
what we actually are. The image in the mirror of our fellow's mind (that
is, our prestige), rather than the original, of which the image in the mirror may be but the distorted reflection, determines what we are as members of society."[2]

Robert Gilpin takes the concept a step further by explicitly linking the relative distribution of prestige among states with the likelihood of major or hegemonic war. He writes, "An inconsistency may, and in time does, arise between the established hierarchy of prestige and the existing distribution of power among states. As a consequence, the governance of the system begins to break down as perceptions catch up with the realities of power."[3] However, whereas Morgenthau and Gilpin see states' desire to *gain* prestige as motivation for international conflict, balance-of-risk theory and the case studies in this book suggest that the *prospective loss* of relative prestige weigh more heavily in leaders' calculations.

In addition to the instrumental nature of prestige, leaders worry about their state's relative "prestige," "glory," or "national honor" as an end-in-itself.[4] The fear of losing prestige among the great powers, in part, drove German diplomacy in the two Morocco crises. In 1904 and 1905, Holstein argued that a failure to challenge the Anglo-French entente would harm German prestige. The other great powers would infer that they could exclude Germany from future colonial and security agreements with relative impunity. If Germany were so irresolute in opposing a bilateral colonial pact between Britain and France, others would conclude that Germany would back down in other disputes, regardless of the values at stake. Nor did Holstein make these statements as a public rationalization of his preferred strategy. Instead, the private correspondence of Bülow, Holstein, Wilhelm II, and others both before and during the first Morocco crisis contain repeated references to the need to preserve Germany's prestige and the willingness of officials to take great risks to do so.

Similarly, in 1911, Kiderlen feared the long-term consequences of the French occupation of Fez and Rabat for Germany's prestige among the great powers. The anticipated French annexation of Morocco would not only harm the interests of private German firms in that country but would also demonstrate to the world that the German government lacked the resolve to protect its interests. If Germany did not protect its interests in North Africa, the members of the Triple Entente—Britain, France, and Russia—might conclude that they could pursue assertive policies in the core with relative impunity. Only by demanding territorial compensation by France and supporting those demands with a show of German naval prowess, could officials in Berlin demonstrate resolve and thus avert a diminution of Germany's prestige. As with Bülow and Holstein in 1905, Kiderlen made these arguments most forcefully in his private correspondence before and during the crisis, thus minimizing the chances that they were post hoc rationalizations or "strategic myths" designed to mobilize domestic support for the government's foreign policy.

This concern for avoiding losses to American prestige and reputation for resolve pervaded the Blair House meetings between Truman and his senior advisors in the five days following the North Korean invasion in June 1950. From the outset, Acheson and Truman dealt with Korea in a wider cold war context; they wanted to avoid an expanded conflict on the East Asian mainland but feared that the absence of an American military response to naked Soviet-backed aggression in the periphery would reverberate in the core. Truman confided to his aide George Elsey that Korea in 1950 was the Far East equivalent of Greece in 1947 and that a failure to oppose Soviet-backed aggression against South Korea would have adverse consequences for the credibility of American economic and military commitments in Western Europe. "The Korean situation," argued Bradley, "offered as good an occasion for action in drawing the line [against Soviet-backed aggression] as anywhere else."[5]

In addition to material power considerations, prestige and reputation concerns were quite evident in the liaison conferences between the Konoe and Tōjō cabinets and the IGHQ. In September 1940, Foreign Minister Matsouka Yosuke and War Minister Tōjō told the Privy Council that the Tripartite Pact with Germany and Italy would preserve and even enhance Japan's prestige, while an improvement in relations with the United States and Great Britain would do the opposite. To reach a rapprochement with the Americans and the British, Japan would have to terminate the China incident and possibly abandon the goal of creating a New Order in East Asia altogether. Even during the earlier Changkufeng and the Nomonhan incident, the most forceful arguments in favor of escalation presented by the general staff of the Kwantung Army stressed the certain damage to Japan's prestige if its army did not respond forcefully to Soviet border incursions.

To the extent that one can generalize from the cases presented herein, it would appear this concern for international prestige, reputation for resolve, and status are not particular to certain types of international systems or certain types of great powers. The leaders of highly cartelized and (arguably authoritarian) states, such as Wilhelmine Germany (1898–1918) and Japan during the early Shōwa period (1926–45), as well as a liberal democracy, the United States during the early cold war years, displayed a remarkable preoccupation with preserving their states' reputation and prestige. Similarly, the polarity of the international system does not appear to influence leaders' concern for reputation and prestige. Again, the leaders of Wilhelmine Germany and Japan, the preponderant state and a second-tier great power under multipolarity, respectively, as well as the United States, the preponderant state under bipolarity, concluded that a failure to demonstrate resolve in the periphery would likely result in further opportunistic expansion by other great powers, possibly in regions of greater importance.

Recent debates between proponents of rational deterrence theory and social psychological approaches to international relations have focused on the extent to which national leaders draw inferences about one another's future behavior based on their past behavior.[6] Regardless of whether "reputations matter" in deterrence or compliance situations, the evidence presented herein suggests that the leaders of the great powers do worry about their own state's prestige, reputation for resolve, and national honor and that such concerns influence their foreign policy choices. The incorporation of prospect theory into defensive realism appears to provide an internally consistent and generalizable foreign policy theory that explains when leaders will likely worry about reputation and prestige and when such concerns will likely shape great powers' foreign policy.

THEORETICAL IMPLICATIONS

Balance-of-risk theory and the case studies have sought to put defensive realist theories of foreign policy on a stronger theoretical foundation. By incorporating the insights of prospect theory and related psychological research on group risk-taking and goal-setting behavior, I sought to account for the so-called status quo bias displayed by states without resorting to ad hoc explanations or rigid (and untestable) assumptions about the specific types of behavior encouraged by the international system. Instead, I have argued that the tendency of states to value what they already posses over what they seek to acquire and to undertake great risks to maintain their current power positions, may have less to do with anarchy per se than with the way in which leaders (indeed human beings in general) process information under conditions of risk and uncertainty. Systemic variables ultimately drive the foreign policy behavior of the great powers though the medium of their leaders' perceptions, estimates, and calculations. Balance-of-risk theory portrays a decision-making process within the state where losses loom larger than gains, risk propensity varies with the situation, existing possessions have a higher value than those not yet acquired, certain outcomes loom larger than probable ones, and sunk costs receive priority over marginal costs.

Political Psychology and Political Realism

The cases examined both confirm the basic explanatory power of defensive realism and suggests that realist foreign policy theories are most useful when they examine the complex and sometimes indirect linkage between systemic imperatives and the foreign policy choices of national leaders. I noted at the outset that like all variants of structural realism, balance-of-risk theory begins with the assumption that the international system—that is, the ordering principle of the system (anarchy), as well as the relative distribution of material power among states and power trends—set the broad parameters of international outcomes and states' foreign policy. However, systemic imperatives can only influence a state's behavior in the international arena through the calculations and perceptions of the "flesh and blood" officials who act on the state's behalf. A good realist theory of foreign policy, therefore, should be able to specify how those systemic imperatives will likely translate into observable external behavior under a wide range of circumstances.[7]

Some critics of realism contend that any consideration of elite calculations and perceptions of material power automatically removes a theory from the realist research program (or paradigm). Some would even claim that the theory I developed is not an example of realism but instead falls under the rubric of constructivism.[8] For example, Jeffrey Legro and Andrew Moravcsik argue,

> If perceptions and beliefs about effective means-ends calculations, given adequate information, consistently fail to correspond to material power relationships, then power is at best one of a number of important factors and perhaps a secondary one. The parsimony and coherence of realist theory is eroded. When recent realists theorize this relationship more explicitly, they are forced to borrow propositions more fully elaborated in existing epistemic theories, which theorize the influence of societal beliefs that structure means-ends calculations and affect perceptions of the environment.[9]

This is flawed criticism in many respects, but three responses to Legro and Moravcsik's argument are relevant here.[10]

First, no realist of whatever stripe has ever claimed that a state's foreign policies and international political outcomes consistently fail to correspond to material power relationships. On the contrary, the relative distribution of material capabilities ultimately drives the various phenomena that scholars working within the realist research program seek to explain: whether that be trade policies of advanced industrial states, or the likelihood of major war across different types of international systems, or crisis bargaining, or alliance formation. International political outcomes correspond to the relative distribution of material power. In this respect, structural realism provides a set of baseline expectations against which analysts can examine unexpected international outcomes.

In order to explain the likely external behavior of particular states at particular points in time, however, it is useful (indeed necessary) to specify the mechanisms through which policy inputs—the relative distribution of power and power trends—translate into policy outputs—the actual diplomatic, military, and foreign economic strategies that states pursue. As Aaron Friedberg notes: "Structural considerations provide a useful point from which to begin the analysis of international politics rather than a place at which to end it. Even if one acknowledges that structures exist and are important, there is still the question of how statesmen grasp their counters from the inside, so to speak."[11]

Second, defensive realism, in general, and the theory presented this book, in particular, do not posit an autonomous causal role for beliefs, norms, and shared ideas on individual states' foreign policies, let alone on international outcomes. Unlike constructivist theories of international politics, which hold the ideational structures and agents (actors) co-constitute and co-determine each other and that an actor's reality at any point in time is historically constructed and contingent, balance-of-risk theory, like other variants of structural realism, assumes that there is an objective and universal international structure within which sovereign states must operate. At the same time, however, the theory recognizes that leaders' cost-benefit calculations will never be objectively efficient or predictable based on systemic incentives alone, since the decision-making process within the state will skew toward loss avoidance. As Gideon Rose observes, "There is indeed something like an objective reality of relative power, which will, for example, have dramatic effects on the outcomes of state interactions," but central decision makers do not "necessarily apprehend that reality accurately on a day-to-day basis."[12]

Third, there is a common misperception that psychological theories and realism (particularly structural realism and its subvariants) are inevitably in tension with each other. This stems in part from a misreading of Waltz's juxtaposition of the first and the third images of international relations and his subsequent distinction between systemic and reductionist theories. We should challenge this misreading.[13] Ironically, among the "mainstream" schools of international relations theory—realism, liberalism, Marxism, constructivism, and their respective neo-variants—the incorporation of psychological assumptions and concepts is more fully developed within realism.[14] At the same time, I sought to improve on existing defensive realist theories that often posit an intervening role for elite perceptions of systemic variables or that build on Robert Jervis's work on the sources of misperception, but then leave the psychological processes supposedly at work with the "state" underdeveloped or unspecified.[15] By explicitly incorporating a decision model drawn from prospect theory into defensive realism, this book has (at least in part) an-swered critics who claim that contemporary realists invoke perceptions, misperceptions, and psychological variables as a deus ex machina when-ever observed international outcomes or foreign policy behavior appear to embarrass their theories.[16]

Offensive Realism and Defensive Realism as Contingent Models

Offensive realists assume that the international system provides strong incentives for expansion. All states, therefore, constantly strive to maximize their power relative to other states because only the most powerful states can guarantee their survival. They pursue expansionist policies when and where the benefits of doing so outweigh the costs. De-fensive realists assume that the international system provides incentives for expansion only under certain conditions. States often, although not always, pursue expansionist policies because their leaders mistakenly believe that aggression is the only way to make their state secure. Defen-sive realism predicts greater variation in internationally driven expan-sion and suggests that states ought to generally pursue moderate strate-gies as the best route to security. Both schools correctly identify recurrent patterns in world politics and systemic pressures on the foreign policies of individual states. Neither school, however, provides a completely ac-curate picture of international politics or foreign policy at all times and under all circumstances.

It is best to conceive of defensive realism and offensive realism as con-tingent models of international politics and foreign policy: neither is completely accurate all the time but both are likely to yield important in-sights much of the time. Yet to date, there has been little research on the conditions under which the observable behaviors associated with the two camps are most likely to obtain. One avenue for future research would be to specify a priori, the conditions under which states are more likely to maximize relative power as a means to maximize long-term se-curity or instead strive to maximize long-term security through the pur-suit of more moderate strategies.

For example, future research might involve a fusion of offensive real-ist and defensive realist insights with the certainty and pseudo-certainty effects and the probability weighting function identified by prospect the-ory. The experimental literature suggests that most people do not re-spond to probabilities in a linear fashion, but instead tend to overweigh outcomes considered certain compared with those that are merely prob-able. They also tend to overweigh small probabilities (below .10 or .15) and to underweigh moderate and high probabilities. In other words, most experimental subjects tend to give more weight to the utility of a possible outcome than to the probability of its occurrence as long as those probabilities are not small. If the probabilities are extremely small, however, the predicted direction of risk-taking reverses: here most people tend to be risk acceptant for gains and risk averse for losses.[17] To the extent that one can extrapolate to the real world, this would suggest that under most circumstances leaders are more likely to display the behavioral patterns associated with prospect theory and defensive realism, except in situations where the subjective probabilities of adverse outcomes are extremely small.

Prospect Theory and International Relations

Beyond advancing the debate between offensive realism and defensive realism, this book has sought to advance the application of prospect theory in the study of international politics and foreign policy. Prospect theory itself is not a theory of foreign policy or of international political outcomes. Rather, it is an abstract and probabilistic model of decision-making. Like utility-based rational choice theories, one must embed a prospect theory-based decision model into specific political theories by adding substantive assumptions. This book sought to address the following limitations with prospect theory and its extant applications in political science: (1) the aggregation of prospect theory's predictions from individual decision makers to groups; (2) the definition of risk and the relative riskiness of alternatives in foreign policy decision making; and (3) the absence of a theory or mechanism for reference point (or expectation level) selection, maintenance, and change.

One frequent criticism of prospect theory's application to the study of international relations focuses on the limitation of Amos Tversky and Daniel Kahneman's original experiments to individual decision-making. The growing experimental literature on escalating commitment and investment behavior shows that prospect theory provides a descriptive model for organizational and group decision-making. While the present study has not solved prospect theory's aggregation problem—a problem that many utility-based rational choice theories share—it has improved on extant applications of the theory in international relations and foreign policy, which tend to skirt the aggregation issue or limit their analysis to cases with a single foreign policy decision maker.

A related criticism concerns the definition of risk and the determination of what constitutes risk-acceptant and risk-averse behavior outside controlled settings. Critics are correct in observing that states or national leaders do not typically face a discrete choice between a risky gamble and a more certain outcome, unlike Tversky and Kahneman's experiments. Instead, they often must choose among several risky strategies—

that is, among strategies where there is a potentially big downside associated with each option.[18] However, the related literature on goal setting and escalating commitment in groups suggests that prospect theory provides a probabilistic model of decision-making beyond discrete choices between binary options. Moreover, by redefining risk acceptance and risk aversion as a continuum and then attempting to identify the risk assessments or perceptions of decision makers at the time independent of policy outcomes, the present study addressed this criticism.

Finally, proponents and critics of prospect theory recognize that the absence of a model or mechanism for the selection, maintenance, and change of a reference point or expectation level is perhaps the major barrier in the theory's application outside experimental settings. As Jack Levy, one of the foremost proponents of prospect theory in the international relations subfield, observes: "Reference dependence is the key assumption of prospect theory, but we have few hypotheses on how actors actually identify their reference points and no accepted methodology for empirically measuring where those reference points are and when and how they change."[19] Similarly, Dale Copeland, a realist who is critical of prospect theory, writes that previous applications of the theory to the study of international relations "tend to determine the reference point in an ad-hoc manner—that is, to establish it only after the case is analyzed in detail. This creates the risk that an analyst will choose evidence that seems to support prospect theory's prediction when in fact, with a different reference point, the theory would have been disconfirmed."[20]

The present book responded to these challenges in several ways. In ill-structured and complex settings, such as foreign policy, decision makers are more likely to assess outcomes and contingencies in terms of deviations from an *expectation level*, not a neutral reference point that represents the status quo. The experimental literature on goal-setting behavior among managerial groups supports this finding. The behaviors exhibited by decision makers in these settings are consistent with the predictions of prospect theory. More important, from the goal-setting literature and the existing defensive realist literature on relative power shifts I derived and tested hypotheses on how elites select, maintain, and change expectation levels. Senior officials' perception of relative power trends influences the choice of a common expectation level. If decision makers anticipate a diminution of relative power or status over time, they are more likely to adopt a more favorable international environment as their expectation level. Conversely, if officials anticipate a relative increase in power and status over time, they are more likely to adopt the status quo as the expectation level. Furthermore, the ability of senior officials to revise their expectation level in response to adverse outcomes will be directly proportional to the length of time they adhere to a particular expectation level. The longer officials adhere to a common expectation level, the less likely they will be to revise that expectation level downward in response to adverse policy outcomes. The case studies found considerable support for these hypotheses. Again, these hypotheses and the research design employed in the previous chapters are not the definitive resolution to the problem of expectation level (or reference point) selection and change in the prospect theory literature.

For the sake of theory construction and testing, I assumed that leaders evaluate outcomes relative to a single expectation level, defined for a particular realm of policy, that is, the international arena. This assumption is consistent with an underlying theme of defensive realism: in foreign policy making, international factors weigh much more heavily in leaders' calculations than do domestic politics. However, various defensive realist and offensive realist theories acknowledge that domestic politics can limit the efficiency of a state's response to the external environment.[21] Future research might analyze the extent to which domestic political constraints combine with leaders' aversion to losses in relative power and international prestige in shaping foreign policy.

Similarly, like most other applications of prospect theory in the international relations subfield, the present book focused on explaining variation in the foreign policy behavior of individual states.[22] Therefore, it treated the behavior of other states as exogenous. An avenue for future research might involve incorporating insights from prospect theory, other branches of behavioral decision theory, and from behavioral game theory to the study of strategic interactions. Critics of rational deterrence theory, as well as defensive realists, have long recognized that psychological processes contribute strongly to the presence or absence of crisis stability and to the success or failure of deterrence.[23] Jervis speculates that because most people in experimental studies are willing to take unusual risks to recoup recent losses, even if these setbacks are minor, compared to their total assets, "a decision-maker might risk costly escalation or even world war if such a move held out the possibility of reversing a defeat." While a standard expected utility model would predict the decision-maker to cut her losses, prospect theory would predict that she would up the ante. "The danger would be especially great if both sides were to feel that they were losing, something that could easily happen because antagonists often have different perspectives and use different baselines."[24] Recent advances in behavioral game theory—a growing body of experimental literature that predicts how people actually behave by incorporating psychological elements (including loss aversion, reference dependence, and the endowment effect) and learning into game theory—might illuminate various bargaining situations wherein one or both parties perceives itself as facing loss.[25]

POLICY IMPLICATIONS

If the balance-of-risk theory presented above illuminates past episodes of great power intervention in the periphery, then what are the implications of my argument for contemporary international politics and United States foreign policy in the twenty-first century?

Unlike the three great powers examined in this book, Wilhelmine Germany, prewar Japan, and the United States during the first years of the cold war, since 1989–91, the United States has been preponderant in all the underlying components of relative power: military capabilities, economic capabilities, and potential capabilities (such as, population size, access to natural resources, technology, and geography). Realists disagree about the durability of the present unipolar international system and the possibility that the United States will have to confront a peer competitor or a countervailing balancing coalition over the next ten to twenty-five years.[26] A recent RAND Corporation study defines a peer competitor as "a state or collection of challengers with the *power* and the *motivation* to confront the United States *on a global scale* in a sustained way and to a sufficient level where *the ultimate outcome of a conflict is in doubt* even if the United States marshals its resources in a timely and effective manner."[27]

Using this definition as a guideline, it is a safe bet to say that no single state or collection of states is likely to emerge as a peer competitor in the next several decades. Nuclear weapons render the American homeland unconquerable. Despite the obsession of some officials within the George W. Bush administration with national missile defense (NMD), the fact remains that launching a nuclear-armed ballistic or cruise missile against the United States would be to commit suicide. Annual defense expenditures exceed those of the next eight major states combined, five of whom (Great Britain, France, Germany, Italy, and Japan) are close American allies. In short, relative to every other great power in history, the United States currently enjoys both a preponderance of power and a remarkable degree of physical security.

Is American preponderance resulting in the formation of a counterbalancing alliance? By pursuing an assertive strategy in the core and in the periphery will the United States face encirclement in the opening decades of the twenty-first century in much the same manner as Wilhelmine Germany faced encirclement in the first decade of the twentieth century? The evidence of the formation of such a coalition is weak.

There are signs of tension between the United States and its Western European allies. The former French foreign minister, Hubert Védrine, repeatedly complained about America's position as a "hyper power" and once declared that the "entire foreign policy of France is aimed at making the world of tomorrow composed of several poles, not just one." German Chancellor Gerhard Schröder warned against the danger of American unilateralism during the Kosovo war.[28] More recently, during a speech launching his reelection campaign in August 2002, Schröder criticized the George W. Bush administration's repeated threats to use military force to topple Iraqi President Saddam Hussein and said that Germany "would not make itself available for an adventure" in Iraq. The chancellor's remark, intended largely for domestic consumption, prompted a swift reprimand from Washington.[29] In the months following the United Nations Security Council's passage of Resolution 1441, demanding that Iraq "provide immediate, unconditional, and unrestricted access to the UN Monitoring, Verification and Inspection Commission (UNMOVIC)" and the International Atomic Energy Agency (IAEA), several allies openly criticized the administration's push toward war.[30] On 4 March 2003, the Russian, French, and German foreign ministers said that they would not allow a new resolution endorsing military action against Iraq sought by the administration and the government of British prime minister Tony Blair to pass the Security Council. In a televised interview on the eve of an American and British invasion of Iraq, French president Jacques Chirac strongly criticized Washington: "Whether it [the war] involves the necessary disarmament of Iraq or the desirable change of the regime in this country, there is no justification for a unilateral resort to force . . . Iraq today does not represent an immediate threat that justifies an immediate war."[31]

The growing Western European resentment of the unilateral exercise of American military power and wariness about the Bush administration's foreign policy is troublesome.[32] Nonetheless, this resentment does not yet constitute full-scale balancing against the United States. Despite concern on both sides of the Atlantic about the growing disparity in military capabilities and technology between the United States and its NATO allies, illustrated most dramatically during the 1999 Kosovo war (Operation Allied Force) and the fact the Bush administration declined offers for allied military assistance in the 2001 Afghanistan war (Operation Enduring Freedom), few of the Western European states have moved to dramatically increase defense spending or research and development.[33]

If the European Union (EU) were to coalesce into a federal state, it might become a peer competitor of the United States, at least in terms of relative economic power and potential power. Yet, despite the adoption of a common currency—the euro—by nine of the EU members, proposals for a sixty-thousand-man rapid reaction force to deal with regional contingencies, and the creation of the office of high representative for se-

curity and foreign policy (a position held by former Spanish foreign minister and former NATO secretary-general Javier Solana), the union remains devoid of real integration in foreign, and especially military, policy. The EU has a bewildering array of governing bodies and all major
decisions require a consensus among the governments of the twelve
member states. It is highly unlikely that the EU will ever evolve from an
international institution into an actual European federation capable of
projecting military force beyond its borders.[34]

Japan remains in recession after a decade of half-hearted economic reform and its Self-Defense Forces (SDF) lack true power projection capabilities. Despite tension over the behavior of American military personnel stationed on Okinawa, there no evidence to suggest the government
of Prime Minister Koizumi Junichiro or any other likely governing coalition favors a revision of the U.S.-Japan Security Treaty or unilateral rearmament. On the contrary, Japanese leaders favor a strong American military commitment because they as see their neighbors as potential
threats and because the presence of U.S. troops minimizes the security
dilemma in East Asia. Okamato Yukio, the chair of the Japanese prime
minister's task force on foreign relations, observes: "Since abandoning
its sovereign right to use force other than purely defensive purposes,
Japan considers the alliance the sine qua non of the country's security.
The Japan-U.S. alliance is not just Japan's primary security relationship,
it is its only one."[35]

Russia and the People's Republic of China, the two most likely challengers to American preponderance, have resolved many of their outstanding bilateral disputes and concluded a vaguely worded treaty of
friendship and cooperation in July 2001.[36] Occasionally, Russia and
China loudly protest specific aspects of U.S. foreign policy. For example,
in 1994–95, Russian president Boris Yeltsin denounced the Clinton administration's drive to expand NATO eastward. Chinese president Jiang
Zimen and foreign minister Tang Jiaxuan protested the accidental bombing of the PRC embassy in Belgrade during the Kosovo war or the emergency landing of an American EP-3 surveillance plane in Chinese territory. Similarly, in 2003, Russian president Vladimir Putin and his foreign
minister, Igor Ivanov, have joined Jiang and his successor as China's
president, Hun Jintao, in openly challenging the Bush administration's
march toward war in Iraq. Nonetheless, periodic diplomatic protests
and the limited level of cooperation on strategic issues between Beijing
and Moscow pale in comparison to the 1950 Sino-Soviet treaty of alliance
and friendship, let alone the balancing coalitions formed against Habsburg Spain, Napoleonic France, Wilhelmine Germany, Nazi Germany, or
the former Soviet Union.[37]

China is at best a rising regional power. Although it has nuclear missiles capable of reaching North America, Beijing lacks a true blue water navy. The People's Liberation Army has a growing ballistic missile capability, but in the near term, its conventional forces are far from adequate to pursue a decisive range of offensive operations against Taiwan. The Chinese economy has grown at a rate of 7 or 8 percent a year for the past decade. Yet, despite twenty years of economic reforms, begun under the leadership of Deng Xiaoping and continuing under Jiang, China is still a developing economy.[38]

Russia's conventional and nuclear military power has greatly diminished since 1989–90. While the Russian army is still large and heavily armed, the Russian navy is very limited. The Russian nuclear arsenal is aging. The army is still a conscript force. While the economy has certainly recovered since 1998, Russia is still only the twentieth largest industrialized economy. Instead of attempting to balance against the United States, Russian president Vladimir Putin appears to be trying to bandwagon with Washington, particularly since the 11 September terrorist attacks. Russia, for example, has facilitated American access to bases in the former Soviet republics in Central Asia, shared intelligence about the Taliban and Al Qaeda, and issued only mild protests in response to the Bush administration's unilateral withdrawal from the 1972 Anti-Ballistic Missile Treaty.[39]

From the perspective of balance-of-risk theory, it is highly unlikely that American leaders would feel compelled to intervene in peripheral regions as a means to redress objective power shifts in the core, at least anytime in the near future. Instead, the United States is more likely to find itself involved in imperial police actions around the globe. Since 1990, the targets of American military power and economic sanctions have been among the weakest, most impoverished, and politically isolated regimes in the world: Iraq, Haiti, Libya, North Korea, Cuba, Yugoslavia (Serbia and Montenegro), and Afghanistan. Even though Osama bin Laden and his Al Qaeda network masterminded the terrorist attacks on New York and Washington, his organization could only operate from within Taliban-controlled Afghanistan, a textbook example of a "failed state."[40] Stephen Walt, among others, poses the question: "With enemies like these, who needs friends?"[41]

Given American preponderance and the absence of a peer competitor (or even a proto-peer competitor), balance-of-risk theory would expect an aversion to perceived losses in prestige to weigh even more heavily in the calculations of the present administration and its successors. When faced with perceived losses to their state's prestige, leaders are more likely to adhere to the so-called domino theory, a set of interconnected beliefs and assertions regarding the interdependence of strategic commitments, the relative prevalence of bandwagoning over balancing in alliance formation, the opportunistic nature of an adversary's actions, and the cumulative effect of conquests.[42]

Consider, for example, the 1999 Kosovo war. The Clinton administration initiated and then continued the air war against Serbia because senior officials feared a loss of prestige within NATO. Throughout the 1990s, the United States suffered from a credibility dilemma. This dilemma resulted from a contradiction between the Clinton administration's neo-Wilsonian foreign policy rhetoric, on the one hand, and its perceived unwillingness to use force or sustain military casualties, on the other. The failure of the Rambouillet and Paris negotiations in February and March 1999 left the administration little choice but to initiate military action against Serbia and Serb forces in Kosovo rather than suffer a further erosion of American credibility within NATO. When limited bombing not only failed to coerce Milosovic, but also created an opportunity for Serbian forces to kill, brutalize, or displace 800,000 Kosovars, the administration escalated the air campaign. Furthermore, officials dropped hints that a NATO invasion of Kosovo and Serbia itself was likely—an option that President Bill Clinton and others had publicly ruled out in March and April.[43]

Finally, in the aftermath of the 11 September terrorist attacks, the fear of future catastrophic terrorist attacks by transnational groups or rogue states armed with chemical, nuclear, or biological weapons has led to fundamental reorientation of U.S. grand strategy. Since 1945, successive administrations, both Democratic and Republican, contemplated preventive war against rising great powers, as well as preemptive military strikes in the face of imminent threats to the United States and its allies. However, only rarely in its 227–year history has the United States actually resorted to preventive war or preemption. Furthermore, previous administrations never publicly articulated a doctrine of preventive war.[44] In response to the 11 September attacks, however, the George W. Bush administration's *National Security Strategy* openly embraces preventive war. It reads, in part: "Given the goals of rogue states and terrorists, the United States can no longer rely on a reactive posture as we have in the past. The inability to deter a potential attacker, the immediacy of today's threats, and the magnitude of potential harm that could be caused by our adversaries' choice of weapons, do not permit that option. . . . To forestall or prevent such hostile act by our adversaries, the United States will, if necessary, act preemptively."[45] The Bush administration finds itself drawn into expanding the war on terrorism to Iraq and elsewhere, not because of any objective or immediate threat to American security, but rather to avert the possibility that rogue states and terrorist organizations might acquire or use weapons of mass destruction in the future. The potential dangers for Washington are twofold. The first danger is entrapment in the periphery. Preventive war to remove rogue regimes may entail the prolonged occupation and reconstruction of those countries. The presence of large numbers of American troops in Iraq or other Arab countries exacerbates popular anger toward the United States and provides a potential target for terrorists. The second danger of a preventive war strategy involves the United States' relations with second-tier great powers and regional states. While full-scale great power balancing against Washington is unlikely in the near future, other states can and will withhold cooperation in a number of areas. As seen in the months preceding the second Persian Gulf War, so-called soft balancing against the United States involves the use of international institutions, particularly the UN Security Council, economic statecraft, and diplomatic arrangements to limit the use of American power to wage preventive war. As Robert Pape recently observes, "Without broad international support, the strategy of preventive war does not serve U.S. national security interests. Keeping nuclear weapons out of the hands of hostile dictators is important, but even a global superpower cannot afford to provoke—and more importantly, to frighten—virtually the entire world at once."[46]

NOTES

CHAPTER 1. POWER POLITICS AND THE BALANCE OF RISK

1. See Robert McNamara, "Notes from McNamara Memo on the Course of the War in 1966," and John McNaughton, "Further McNaughton Memo on Factors in the Bombing Decision" in *Pentagon Papers* (New York: Bantam Books, 1971), 489–93.

2. Andrew Bennett, *Condemned to Repetition: The Rise, Fall, and Reprise of Soviet-Russian Military Intervention, 1973–1996* (Cambridge: MIT Press, 1999), 215–47; and William Curti Wohlforth, *The Elusive Balance: Power and Perceptions during the Cold War* (Ithaca: Cornell University Press, 1993), 223–51.

3. See Geoffrey Blainey, *Causes of War* (New York: Free Press, 1973), 46–47; Keith Surridge, "Lansdowne at the War Office," in *The Boer War: Direction, Experience, and Image*, ed. John Gooch (London: Frank Cass, 2000), esp. 28–30; and John Gooch, *The Plans of War: The General Staff and British Military Strategy, ca. 1900–1916* (London: Routledge, 1974), 198.

4. For the distinction between theories of foreign policy and theories of international politics see, Kenneth N. Waltz, *Theory of International Politics* (Reading, Mass.: Addison-Wesley, 1979), 71–72; Colin Elman, "Horses for Courses: Why Not Neorealist Theories of Foreign Policy?" *Security Studies* 6, no. 1 (autumn 1996): 7–54; Fareed Zakaria, *From Wealth to Power: The Unusual Origins of America's World Role* (Princeton: Princeton University Press, 1998), 14–18; and Gideon Rose, "Neoclassical Realism and Theories of Foreign Policy," *World Politics* 51, no. 1 (October 1998): 144–72.

5. Robert Jervis, "The Political Implications of Loss Aversion," *Political Psychology* 13, no. 1 (spring 1992): 187–204.

6. Paul M. Kennedy, *The Rise and the Fall of the Great Powers* (New York: Random House, 1987); Robert Gilpin, *War and Change in World Politics* (Cambridge: University Press, 1981), 168–75; Geoffrey Parker, "The Making of Strategy in Habsburg Spain: Philip II's Bid for Mastery," and John Gooch, "The Weary Titan: The Making of Strategy and Policy in Great Britain, 1890–1918," in *The Making of Strategy: Rulers, States, and War*, ed. Williamson Murray, MacGregor Knox, and Alvin Bernstein (Cambridge: Cambridge University Press, 1994), 115–51 and 278–307.

7. Barry R. Posen, *Sources of Military Doctrine: France, Britain, and Germany between the World Wars* (Ithaca: Cornell University Press, 1984), 13.

8. William C. Wohlforth, "The Stability of a Unipolar World," *International Security* 24, no. 1 (summer 1999): 5–41; and Michael Mastanduno, "Preserving the Unipolar Moment: Realist Theories and U.S. Grand Strategy after the Cold War," *International Security* 21, no. 4 (spring 1997): 44–98.

9. On the costs (or lack thereof) the United States incurred during the Bosnia and Kosovo wars, see Daniel A. Byman and Matthew C. Waxman, "Kosovo and the Great Air Power Debate," *International Security* 24, no. 4 (spring 2000): 5–38; and Barry R. Posen, "The War for Kosovo: Serbia's Political-Military Strategy," *International Security* 24, no. 4 (spring 2000): 39–84.

10. "President Bush's Address on Terrorism to a Joint Session of Congress," *New York Times*, 21 September 2001.

11. For a discussion of the implications of the war on terrorism for U.S. grand strategy see, Barry R. Posen, "The Struggle against Terrorism: Grand Strategy, Strategy, and Tactics," *International Security* 26, no. 3 (winter 2001/02): 39–55; and Stephen M. Walt, "Beyond bin Laden: Reshaping U.S. Foreign Policy," *International Security* 26, no. 3 (winter 2001/02): 56–78.

12. For a typology of realist theories, see Jeffrey W. Taliaferro, "Security Seeking under Anarchy: Defensive Realism Reconsidered," *International Security* 25, no. 3 (winter 2000/01): 128–61, esp. 132–35, Table 1. Strictly speaking, balance-of-risk theory falls into the category of "defensive neoclassical realism," according to the typology I develop in that article. While I adopt defensive realist auxiliary assumptions, the dependent variable—the direction of elite risk-taking behavior—pertains to a states' foreign policy, not international outcomes. However, for ease of exposition, I refer to my theory as an example of "defensive realism." For a discussion of neoclassical realism, see Gideon Rose, "Neoclassical Realism and Theories of Foreign Policy," *World Politics* 51, no. 1 (October 1998): 144–72.

13. Overviews of the debate between offensive realism and defensive realism include Sean M. Lynn-Jones and Steven E. Miller, "Preface," in *The Perils of Anarchy: Contemporary Realism and International Security*, ed. Michael E. Brown, Sean M. Lynn-Jones, and Steven E. Miller (Cambridge: MIT Press, 1995), ix–xii; Benjamin Frankel, "Restating the Realist Case: An Introduction," *Security Studies* 5, no. 3 (spring 1996): xiv–xx; and Robert Jervis, "Realism, Neoliberalism, and Cooperation: Understanding the Debate," *International Security* 24, no. 1 (summer 1999): 42–64, esp. 48–50.

14. On the need for head-to-head tests of offensive realist and defensive realist hypotheses, see Sean M. Lynn-Jones, "Realism and America's Rise: A Review Essay," *International Security* 23, no. 2 (fall 1998): 157–83.

15. For a discussion of each, see Barry R. Posen, *Sources of Military Doctrine*, esp. 67–71; Jack S. Levy, "Declining Power and the Preventive Motivation for War," *World Politics* 40, no. 1 (October 1987): 82–107; Stephen M. Walt, *Origins of Alliances* (Ithaca: Cornell University Press, 1987), 21–35; Peter Liberman, *Does Conquest Pay? The Exploitation of Occupied Industrial Societies* (Princeton: Princeton University Press, 1996), 10–14; Stephen Van Evera, *Causes of War: Power and the Roots of Conflict* (Ithaca: Cornell University Press, 1999), 73–104 and 173–92; Waltz, *Theory of International Politics*, 169, 178, 199, 206–7; and Benjamin Miller, *When Opponents Cooperate: Great Power Conflict and Collaboration in World Politics* (Ann Arbor: University of Michigan Press, 1995), 57–88.

16. See Waltz, *Theory of International Politics*, 126.

17. Joseph M. Grieco, *Cooperation among Nations: Europe, America, and Non-Tariff Barriers to Trade* (Ithaca: Cornell University Press, 1990), 39.

18. For various criticisms of defensive realism's so-called status quo bias, see Randall L. Schweller, "Neorealism's Status Quo Bias: What Security Dilemma?" *Security Studies* 5, no. 3 (spring 1996): 90–121, esp. 109–18; Zakaria, *From Wealth to Power*, 25–31; and Richard K. Betts, "Must War Find a Way? A Review Essay," *International Security* 24, no. 2 (fall 1999), 169–70.

19. For a discussion of how the incorporation of prospect theory and other psychological models can enhance the descriptive and predictive accuracy of structural realist theories, see James M. Goldgeier and Philip E. Tetlock, "Psychology and International Relations," *Annual Review of Political Science* 4 (2001): 67–92.

20. For a critique of the bipolar stability argument, see Dale C. Copeland, "Neorealism and the Myth of Bipolar Stability: Toward a Dynamic Realist Theory of

Major War," in *Realism: Restatements and Renewal,* ed. Benjamin Frankel (London: Frank Cass, 1996), 29–89, esp. 38–47. Like Copeland, I use the term *major war* to denote a conflict involving all the great powers in the international system, fought at the highest level of intensity, and were there is the distinct possibility that one or more great powers may cease to exist as an independent entity.

21. See Waltz, *Theory of International Politics,* 171. For an earlier statement of the bipolar stability argument, see Waltz, "The Stability of a Bipolar World," *Daedalus* 93 (summer 1964): 881–909.

22. Robert Jervis, *System Effects: Complexity in Political and Social Life* (Princeton: Princeton University Press, 1997), 118.

23. Ibid., 121 and 165–76.

24. See Waltz, *Theory of International Politics,* 172–73. See also Jervis, *System Effects,* 119, n. 95. Jervis suggests that the contradiction between the prescriptive and descriptive elements of balance-of-power theory might stem from Waltz's growing opposition to the Vietnam War in the late 1960s. See Waltz, "The Price of Peace," *International Studies Quarterly* 11, no. 3 (September 1967): 199–211, esp. 204–7.

25. Examples of defensive realism that focus on the prescriptive aspects of great power intervention in the periphery include Stephen M. Walt, "The Case for Finite Containment: Analyzing U.S. Grand Strategy," *International Security* 14, no. 1 (summer 1989): 5–49; Stephen Van Evera, "Why Europe Matters, Why the Third World Doesn't: Identifying U.S. Strategic Interests in the Periphery," *Journal of Strategic Studies* 13, no. 2 (June 1990): 1–51; Eugene Gholtz, Daryl G. Press, and Harvey M. Sapolsky, "Come Home America: The Strategy of Restraint in the Face of Temptation," *International Security* 21, no. 4 (spring 1997): 5–48; Jerome Slater, "The Domino Theory and International Politics: The Case of Vietnam," and Douglas J. Macdonald, "Falling Dominos and System Dynamics: A Risk Aversion Perspective," *Security Studies* 3, no. 2 (winter 1993/94): 186–224 and 225–58. One book that does begin to address the empirical aspect of this topic from a defensive realist perspective is Robert Jervis and Jack Snyder, eds., *Dominoes and Bandwagons: Strategic Beliefs and Great Power Competition in the Eurasian Rimland* (New York: Oxford University Press, 1991).

26. J. A. Hobson, *Imperialism: A Study* (1902; reprint, Ann Arbor: University of Michigan Press, 1965); and V. I. Lenin, *Imperialism: The Highest Stage of Capitalism* (1917; reprint, New York: International Press, 1939).

27. Joseph Schumpeter, *Imperialism and Social Classes: Two Essays,* trans. Heinz Norden (Cleveland: World Press, 1968).

28. Jack Snyder, *Myths of Empire: Domestic Politics and International Ambition* (Ithaca: Cornell University Press, 1991), 1–2. Snyder originated the distinction between offensive (or aggressive) realism and defensive realism (11–12). He cites his logrolling theory as an example of the latter (64). However, logrolling theory focuses on the domestic determinants of foreign policy to the exclusion of international considerations. Both realists and critics of realism disagree over whether Snyder's theory falls within the boundaries of structural realism. See Elman, "Horses for Courses," 32–41; Fareed Zakaria, "Realism and Domestic Politics: A Review Essay," *International Security* 17, no. 1 (spring 1992): 178–98; Andrew Moravcsik, "Taking Preferences Seriously: A Liberal Theory of International Relations," *International Organization* 51, no. 4 (autumn 1997): 513–53, at 533; and Jeffrey W. Legro and Andrew Moravcsik, "Is Anybody Still a Realist?" *International Security* 24, no. 2 (fall 1999): 5–55.

29. Snyder, *Myths of Empire,* 1.

30. In addition to the collective action literature, Snyder's theory draws heavily

on classical liberalism, Marxist theories of late-nineteenth-century imperialism, and the Fritz Fischer school. See Karl Marx, *The German Ideology*, in Robert C. Tucker, ed., *The Mark-Engels Reader* (New York: W. W. Norton, 1972); Fritz Fischer, *The War of Illusions* (New York: W. W. Norton, 1975); idem, *Germany's Aims in the First World War* (New York: W. W. Norton, 1967).

31. Snyder, *Myths of Empire*, 30.

32. Ibid., 42.

33. Ibid., 41–42. Thomas J. Christensen's domestic mobilization model posits a similar dynamic, which he terms "overactive policies." See Christensen, *Useful Adversaries: Grand Strategy, Domestic Mobilization, and Sino-American Conflict, 1947–1958* (Princeton: Princeton University Press, 1996), 11–14.

34. Snyder, *Myths of Empire*, 44

35. Ibid., 49

36. Eric J. Labs, "Beyond Victory: Offensive Realism and the Expansion of War Aims," *Security Studies* 6, no. 4 (summer 1997): 1–49; idem, "Fighting for More: The Sources of Expanding War Aims," Ph.D. diss., Massachusetts Institute of Technology, 1994; John J. Mearsheimer, "The False Promise of International Institutions," *International Security* 19, no. 3 (winter 1994/95): 5–49; and idem, *The Tragedy of Great Power Politics* (New York: W. W. Norton, 2001), 32–40.

37. On this point, see Stephen G. Brooks, "Dueling Realisms," *International Organization* 51, no. 3 (summer 1997): 177–98; and Mearsheimer, "False Promise of International Institutions," 11–12.

38. John J. Mearsheimer, "Back to the Future: Instability in Europe after the Cold War," in *Theories of War and Peace*, 10. Also see Zakaria, "Realism and Domestic Politics," 470, n. 43.

39. See Labs, "Beyond Victory," 13.

40. Zakaria, *From Wealth to Power*, 20

41. Mearsheimer, *Tragedy of Great Power Politics*, 140–41.

42. Christopher Layne, "The Poster Child for Offensive Realism: America as Global Hegemon," *Security Studies* 12, no. 2 (winter 2002/2003): 119–63, at 125.

43. Mearsheimer, *Tragedy of Great Power Politics*, 142.

44. Layne, "Poster Child for Offensive Realism," 127. Elsewhere, Layne makes a distinction between type I and type II offensive realism. Type I offensive realism explains why great powers engage in expansionist behavior. Type II offensive realism explains why great powers are impelled to seek hegemony. See Layne, "U.S. Hegemony and the Perpetuation of NATO," *Journal of Strategic Studies* 23, no. 3 (September 2000): 59–91, esp. 64–66.

45. Labs, "Offensive Realism and the Expansion of War Aims," 12. See also Elman, "Horses for Courses," 28–29.

46. Zakaria, *From Wealth to Power*, 185. Robert Gilpin observes that "as the power of a state increases, it seeks to extend its territorial control, its political influence, and/or its domination of the international economy." See Gilpin, *War and Change in World Politics*, 106. Likewise, A. F. K. Organski states that rising great powers seek to "impose their rule and their way of life on other nations." See Organski, *World Politics*, 2d ed. (New York: Knopf, 1968), 97.

47. Labs, "Offensive Realism and the Expansion of War Aims," 17, fn. 56.

48. John Gooch, "Soldiers, Strategy, and War Aims in Britain, 1914–1918," in *War Aims and Strategic Policy in the Great War 1914–1918*, ed. Barry Hunt and Adrian Preston (Totowa, N.J.: Rowman and Littlefield, 1977), 21, 29–32; David French, *British Strategy and War Aims, 1914–1916* (Boston: Allen and Unwin, 1986), 15 and 26.

49. For competing explanations of Egyptian calculations between the 1967 and 1973 wars, see Eli Lieberman, "What Makes Deterrence Work? Lessons from the Egyptian-Israeli Rivalry?" *Security Studies* 4, no. 4 (summer 1995): 851–910; and Janice Gross Stein, "Deterrence and Learning in Enduring Rivalry: Egypt and Israel, 1948–73," *Security Studies* 6, no. 1 (autumn 1996): 104–52.

50. For a compilation of experimental studies from which prospect theory derives see, Daniel Kahneman and Amos Tversky, ed., *Choice, Values, and Frames* (Cambridge: Cambridge University Press, 2001). For prospect theory experiments involving group decision making, see Glen Whyte, "Escalating Commitment in Individual and Group Decision-making: A Prospect Theory Approach," *Organizational Behavior and Human Decision Processes* 54, no. 3 (April 1993): 430–55; Robert W. Rutledge, "Escalation of Commitment in Groups and the Effects of Information Framing," *Journal of Applied Business* 11, no. 2 (spring 1995): 17–23.

51. See, for example, Rose McDermott, *Risk-Taking in International Politics: Prospect Theory in American Foreign Policy* (Ann Arbor: University of Michigan Press, 1997); Barbara Farnham, ed., *Avoiding Losses/Taking Risks: Prospect Theory and International Conflict* (Ann Arbor: University of Michigan Press, 1994); Janice Gross Stein and Louis W. Pauly, eds., *Choosing to Cooperate: How States Avoid Losses* (Baltimore: Johns Hopkins University Press, 1992), and Mark L. Haas, "Prospect Theory and the Cuban Missile Crisis," *International Studies Quarterly* 45, no. 2 (June 2001): 241–70. For a review of this literature, see Jack S. Levy, "Loss Aversion, Framing Effects, and International Conflict: Perspectives from Prospect Theory," in *Handbook of War Studies II*, ed. Manus I. Midlarsky (Ann Arbor: University of Michigan Press, 2000), 193–221.

52. Two exceptions are Victor D. Cha, "Hawk Engagement and Preventive Defense," *International Security* 27, no. 1 (summer 2002): 40–78; and James W. Davis, Jr., *Threats and Promises: The Pursuit of International Influence* (Baltimore: Johns Hopkins University Press, 2000), 26–43. Davis examines the efficacy of threats and promises in deterring or compelling adversaries. Drawing on prospect theory, elements of deterrence theory, the security dilemma, and the spiral model, he develops a theory of influence that suggests that promises and assurances are most effective as deterrent or compellent strategies when potential aggressors seek to avert losses. Although Davis does identify himself as a realist, elements of his theory are broadly consistent with defensive realism.

53. On this point see, Robert Jervis, "Cooperation under the Security Dilemma," *World Politics* 30 (January 1978): 167–214; idem., "Realism, Neoliberalism, and Cooperation," esp. 48–50; and Charles L. Glaser, "Realists and Optimists: Cooperation as Self-Help," *International Security* 19, no. 3 (winter 1994/95): 50–90.

54. Zakaria erroneously claims that defensive realism assumes states only pursue minimal security. See Zakaria, *From Wealth to Power*, 23. Instead, defensive realism assumes (as do offensive realists) that at minimum all states seek to survive. For a discussion of the variation in state strategies in defensive realism, see Glaser, "Realists as Optimists," 130–32; and Sean M. Lynn-Jones, "Offense-Defense Theory and its Critics," *Security Studies* 4, no. 4 (summer 1995): 660–91.

55. Waltz, *Theory of International Politics*, 175; and idem, "Reflections on *Theory of International Politics*: A Response to My Critics," in *Neorealism and its Critics*, ed. Robert O. Keohane (New York: Columbia University Press, 1986).

56. See Ashley Tellis, "Political Realism: The Long March to Scientific Theory," *Security Studies* 5, no. 2 (winter 1995/96): 3–105, esp. 44–48; Miles Kahler, "Rationality in International Relations," *International Organization* 52, no. 4 (autumn 1998): 919–41, esp. 924–25; and Randall L. Schweller and William C. Wohlforth, "Power

Test: Evaluating Realism in Response to the End of the Cold War," *Security Studies* 9, no. 3 (spring 2000): 60–108.

57. Aaron L. Friedberg, *The Weary Titan: Britain and the Experience of Relative Decline, 1895–1905* (Princeton: Princeton University Press, 1988), 11.

58. Arguably, this book is an example of neoclassical realism because balance-of-risk theory posits a complex and indirect link between systemic variables and the foreign policies that states actually pursue. See Gideon Rose, "Neoclassical Realism and Theories of Foreign Policy," *World Politics* 51, no. 1 (October 1998): 144–72.

59. Andrew Bennett and Alexander L. George, "Research Design Tasks in Case Study Research," (paper presented at the MacArthur Foundation Workshop on Case Study Methods, Harvard University, 17–19 October, 1997).

60. On this point, see Labs, "Beyond Victory," 6, n. 17; and Stephen Van Evera, *Guide to Methods for Students of Political Science* (Ithaca: Cornell University Press, 1998), 86–87.

61. See Alexander L. George, "Case Studies and Theory Development: The Method of Structured Focused Comparison," in *Diplomacy: New Approaches in History, Theory and Policy*, ed. Paul Gordon Lauren (New York: Free Press, 1979), 44–68; Alexander L. George and Timothy J. McKeown, "Case Studies and Theories of Organizational Decision Making," in *Advances in Information Processing in Organizations* 2 (Greenwich, Conn.: JAI Press, 1985), 21–58, at 34–41; and Van Evera, *Guide to Methods*, 64–66.

62. Van Evera refers to this as strategy as "congruence procedure type II." See Van Evera, *Guide to Method*, 61–64. For a similar discussion on increasing the number of observations, see Gary King, Robert O. Keohane, and Sidney Verba, *Designing Social Inquiry: Scientific Inference in Qualitative Research* (Princeton: Princeton University Press, 1994), 219–22.

63. Such critics will no doubt cite, King, Keohane, and Verba, *Designing Social Inquiry*, 108–9, 129–32, 137–38, and 140–49; and Barbara Geddes, "How the Cases You Choose Affect the Answers You Get: Selection Bias in Comparative Cases," *Political Analysis* 2 (1990): 131–50. One should note, however, that Geddes criticizes comparative politics scholars who misconstrued the normal background levels of the main independent variable they studied—the intensity of labor repression.

64. On this point, see Ronald Rogowski, "The Role of Scientific Theory and Anomaly in Social-Scientific Inference," *American Political Science Review* 89, no. 2 (June 1995): 467–70; and David Collier and James Mahoney, "Insights and Pitfalls: Selection Bias in Qualitative Research," *World Politics* 49, no. 1 (October 1996): 56–91.

65. For a discussion of "most likely" and "least likely" observations see Harry Eckstein, "Case Study and Theory in Political Science," in *Handbook of Political Science*, vol. 7, *Strategies of Inquiry*, ed. Fred I. Greenstein and Nelson W. Polsby (Reading, Mass.: Addison-Wesley, 1975), 79–137.

66. For a discussion of how to test psychological hypotheses in foreign policy decisions see Chaim D. Kaufmann, "Out of the Lab and into the Archives: A Method for Testing Psychological Explanations of Political Decision-making," *International Studies Quarterly* 38, no. 4 (December 1994): 557–86.

67. My definition of risk builds on William E. Boettcher, "Context, Methods, Numbers, and Words: Prospect Theory in International Relations," *Journal of Conflict Resolution* 39, no. 3 (September 1995): 561–83.

68. The study of risk in organizational behavior, sociology, and international relations has evolved way from the economic focus on probability and utility and toward a focus on loss and uncertainty. See Mary Douglas, "Risk as a Forensic Re-

source," *Dædalus* 118, no. 4 (fall 1990): 1–16; J. Frank Yates and Edward Stone, ed. *Risk Taking Behavior* (New York: Wiley, 1992); Zur Shapira, *Risk Taking: A Managerial Perspective* (New York: Russell Sage, 1995); James G. March and Zur Shapira, "Behavioral Decision Theory and Organizational Decision Theory," in *Decision Making: Alternatives to Rational Choice Models,* ed. Mary Zey (Newbury Park, Calif.: Sage Publications, 1992), 273–303.

69. See James D. Morrow, *Game Theory for Political Scientists* (Princeton: Princeton University Press, 1995), 28–33.

70. Yaacov Y. Vertzberger, *Risk Taking and Decisionmaking: Foreign Military Intervention Decisions* (Stanford: Stanford University Press, 1998), 20.

71. Alan C. Lamborn makes a further distinction between "policy risk" and "political risk." Policy risk is the probability that the substantive goals of established policy will not occur. Political risk is the probability that policy choices will have adverse effects on the political fortunes of decision-making factions. See Lamborn, *Price of Power: Risk and Foreign Policy in Britain, France, and Germany* (London: Unwin Hyman, 1990), 57–59. For a recent application of the distinction, see Joseph Lepgold and Brent L. Sterling, "When Do States Fight Limited Wars? Political Risk, Policy Risk, and Policy Choice," *Security Studies* 9, no. 4 (summer 2000): 127–66.

72. Vertzberger draws a distinction between real risk and perceived risk. In his "socio-cognitive" framework, risk-acceptance occurs when perceived risk is acceptable risk, while risk aversion occurs when perceived risk > acceptable risk. See Vertzberger, "Reconceptualizing Risk," 355–56, fn. 6.

73. On the dangers of contamination by "outcome knowledge," see Philip E. Tetlock and Aaron Belkin, "Counterfactual Thought Experiments in World Politics," in *Counterfactual Thought Experiments in World Politics: Logical, Methodological, and Psychological Perspectives* (Princeton: Princeton University, 1996), 33–34.

74. See Van Evera, *Guide to Methods,* 30–34; and King, Keohane, and Verba, *Designing Social Inquiry,* 209–12.

75. Joel Brockner and Jeffrey Z. Rubin, *Entrapment in Escalating Conflicts: A Social Psychological Analysis* (New York: Springer-Verlag, 1985), 3–4.

76. Max H. Bazerman, "Escalation of Commitment in Individual and Group Decision-making," *Organizational Behavior and Human Performance* 33, no. 2 (April 1984): 141–52. Also see John Shaubroeck and Elaine Davis, "Prospect Theory Predictions when Escalation is Not the Only Chance to Recover Sunk Costs," *Organizational Behavior & Human Decision Processes* 57, no. 1 (January 1994): 59–82.

77. Some might argue that the terrorist attacks of 11 September 2001 effectively invalidate this conception of the periphery. However, I would remind the reader that Al Qaeda—a transnational network of Islamic extremists whose leadership received safe haven in Afghanistan—organized and carried out the attacks on the World Trade Center and the Pentagon, not the Taliban government in Kabul. Furthermore, the attack did not involve the use of conventional military force, but rather an elaborate plan to exploit vulnerabilities in airport security and in the air-traffic control system. The Bush administration moved to oust the Taliban because of its tacit and active support of Al Qaeda and Osama bin Laden and to prevent Afghanistan from again becoming a haven for international terrorists. See, Posen, "Struggle against Terrorism," 44–45; and Ray Takeyh and Nikolas Gvosdev, "Do Terrorist Networks Need a Home?" *Washington Quarterly* 25, no. 3 (summer 2002): 97–108.

78. Michael C. Desch, *When the Third World Matters: Latin America and United States Grand Strategy* (Baltimore: Johns Hopkins University Press, 1993), 9–17. Desch draws a distinction among intrinsically valuable areas, extrinsically valuable areas,

and residual areas (those without any intrinsic or extrinsic value). My conception of the periphery merges extrinsically valuable and residual areas into a single category.

CHAPTER 2. EXPLAINING GREAT POWER INVOLVEMENT IN THE PERIPHERY

1. Robert Gilpin, "No One Loves a Political Realist," *Security Studies* 5, no. 3 (spring 1996), 6.

2. For lists of realism's core assumptions see, Benjamin Frankel, "Restating the Realist Case," *Security Studies* 5, no. 3 (spring 1996): ix–xx; Randall L. Schweller and William C. Wohlforth, "Power Test: Evaluating Realism in Response to the End of the Cold War," *Security Studies* 9, no. 3 (spring 200): 60–108; and Colin Elman, "Horses for Courses: Why Not Neorealist Theories of Foreign Policy?" *Security Studies* 6, no. 1 (autumn 1996): 7–53. For a discussion of the auxiliary assumptions that underlie defensive realism, see Jeffrey W. Taliaferro, "Security Seeking under Anarchy: Defensive Realism Revisited," *International Security* 25, no. 3 (winter 2000/01): 128–61.

3. See Daniel Kahneman and Amos Tversky, "Prospect Theory: An Analysis of Decision under Risk," *Econometrica* 47, no. 1 (March 1979): 263–91; and George Quattrone and Amos Tversky, "Contrasting Rational and Psychological Analysis of Political Choice," *American Political Science Review* 82, no. 3 (September 1988): 719–36.

4. For a detailed discussion of the editing operations (coding, framing, simplification, detection of dominance, segregation, and cancellation), see Kahneman and Tversky, "Prospect Theory," 284–85.

5. Kahneman and Tversky's development of prospect theory builds on their earlier work on judgmental heuristics—availability, representativeness, and anchoring. See Daniel Kahneman, Paul Slovic, and Amos Tversky, eds. *Judgment under Uncertainty: Heuristics and Biases* (New York: Cambridge University Press, 1982); Eldar Shafir, "Belief and Decision: The Continuing Legacy of Amos Tversky," *Cognitive Psychology* 38, no. 1 (February 1999): 1–15; and Rose McDermott, "The Psychological Ideas of Amos Tversky and the Their Relevance for Political Science," *Journal of Theoretical Politics* 13, no. 1 (January 2001): 5–33.

6. Tversky and Kahneman argued that scholars ought to abandon normative theories altogether in the study of judgment and choice, because such theories fail to offer an accurate model of actual decision behavior. See Amos Tversky and Daniel Kahneman, "Rational Choice and the Framing of Decisions," *Journal of Business* 59, no. 2 (1986): 251–78. I do not share this view. Descriptive models based on rational choice (or more specifically, expected utility) and prospect theory are not, necessarily, mutually incompatible. See Rose McDermott and Jacek Kugler, "Comparing Rational Choice and Prospect Theory Analyses: The U.S. Decision to Launch Operation 'Desert Storm,' January 1991," *Journal of Strategic Studies* 24, no. 3 (September 2001): 49–85.

7. Jack S. Levy, "Daniel Kahneman: Judgment, Decision, and Rationality," *PS: Political Science and Politics* 35, no. 2 (June 2002): 271–73. A frequent criticism of prospect theory is that leaders do not reflect the propensities of the average subject in controlled experiments. I would remind such critics that the experimental literature in support of prospect theory is quite robust. Furthermore, experimentation is now quite common in economics. Experimental economists, who were determined to (and indeed, expected to) demonstrate that the findings were the artifacts of

flawed experimental designs, confirmed these findings. For a discussion, see Colin F. Camerer, *Behavioral Game Theory* (Princeton: Princeton University Press, forthcoming), chap. 1; and Camerer, "Prospect Theory in the Wild: Evidence from the Field," (Social Science Working Paper 1037, Division of the Humanities and the Social Sciences, California Institute of Technology, May 1998).

8. For summaries of these experimental studies see Paul Slovic, Baruch Fischhoff, and Sarah Lichtenstein, "Response Mode, Framing, and Information Processing Effects in Risk Assessment," in *Decision-Making: Descriptive, Normative and Prescriptive Interactions*, ed. David E. Bell, Howard Raiffa, and Amos Tversky (New York: Cambridge University Press, 1988), 152–66; Amos Tversky, Paul Slovic, and Daniel Kahneman, "The Causes of Preference Reversal," *American Economic Review* 80, no. 1 (March 1990): 204–17; and Amos Tversky and Daniel Kahneman, "Advances in Prospect Theory: Cumulative Representation of Uncertainty," *Journal of Risk and Uncertainty* 5, no. 4 (October 1992): 297–323.

9. See Sandra L. Schneider, "Framing and Conflict: Expectation Level Contingency, the Status Quo, and Current Theories of Risky Choice," *Journal of Experimental Psychology: Learning, Memory and Cognition* 18, no. 5 (September 1992): 1040–57; and Robin Gregory, Sarah Lichtenstein, and Donald McGregor, "The Role of Past States in Determining Reference Points," *Organizational Behavior and Human Decision Processes* 55, no. 3 (June 1993): 195–206.

10. Specifically, prospect theory posits that once the decision maker edits the available options, she then evaluates the edited prospects and selects the one with the highest values, as determined by the product of a value of an outcome and a decision weight. For a discussion of prospect theory's value function, see Tversky and Kahneman, "Prospect Theory," 277; idem, "The Framing of Decisions and the Psychology of Choice," 456.

11. Thomas E. Nygren, "Reacting to Perceived High- and Low-Risk Win-Lose Opportunities in a Risky Decision-Making Task: Is It Framing or Affect or Both?" *Motivation and Emotion* 22, no. 1 (March 1998): 73–98.

12. More formally, prospect theory posits diminished sensitivity: the marginal utility of gains decreases faster than the marginal disutility of losses. Hence, prospect theory posits an S-shaped value function, which is concave for gains (outcomes above the reference point) and convex for losses (outcomes below the reference point). See Jack S. Levy, "Introduction to Prospect Theory," in *Avoiding Losses/Taking Risks*, 11 and 16–17.

13. See Amos Tversky and Daniel Kahneman, "Loss Aversion in Riskless Choice: A Reference Dependent Model," *Quarterly Journal of Economics* 41, no. 4 (November 1991): 1039–69.

14. The endowment effect, however, does not apply to normal commercial transactions. Consumers do not treat money expended on a product as a loss. A good purchased for eventual sale or barter does not generate an endowment effect. See Daniel Kahneman, Jack L. Knetsch, and Richard H. Thayer, "Experimental Tests of the Endowment Effect and the Coase Theorem," *Journal of Political Economy* 98, no. 6 (December 1990): 1325–48.

15. See Tversky and Kahneman, "Loss Aversion in Riskless Choice," esp. 1041–43; Jack L. Knetsch, "The Endowment Effect and Evidence of Nonreversible Indifference Curves," *American Economic Review* 79, 5 (December 1989): 1277–84; Jack L. Knetsch and J. A. Sinden, "Willingness to Pay and Compensation Demanded: Experimental Evidence of an Unexpected Disparity in Measures of Value," *Quarterly Journal of Economics* 99, no. 3 (August 1984): 507–22; idem, "The Persistence of Evaluation Disparities," *Quarterly Journal of Economics* 102, no. 3 (August 1987): 691–96;

and Sankar Sen and Eric J. Johnson, "Mere-Possession Effects without Possession in Consumer Choice," *Journal of Consumer Research* 24, no. 1 (June 1997): 105–17.

16. Quattrone and Tversky, "Contrasting Rational and Psychological Analysis," 722. Prospect theory posits a probability-weighting function, which measures the impact of the probability of an event on the desirability of a prospect. For details see, Paul Slovic, Baruch Fischhoff, and Sara Litchenstein, "Response Mode, Framing, and Information-Processing Effects in Risk Assessment," in *Question Framing and Response Consistency*, no. 11, *New Directions for the Methodology of the Social and Behavioral Sciences*, ed. Robin M. Hogarth (San Francisco: Jossey-Bass, 1982), 24–25.

17. Amos Tversky and Daniel Kahneman, "The Framing of Decisions and the Psychology of Choice," in *Question Framing and Response Consistency*, 8.

18. Eldar Shafir, "Prospect Theory and Political Analysis: A Psychological Perspective," in *Avoiding Losses/Taking Risks*, 147–58, at 149. Also see William Boettcher, "Context, Methods, Numbers, and Words: Prospect Theory in International Relations," *Journal of Conflict Resolution* 39, no. 3 (September 1995): 561–83; and Louise M. Steen-Sprang, "Prospect Theory, Uncertainty, and Decision Making Setting: How Individuals and Groups Make Decisions under Uncertainty" (paper presented at the annual meeting of the American Political Science Association, Atlanta, Ga., 2–5 September 1999).

19. Jack S. Levy, "Prospect Theory, Rational Choice, and International Relations," *International Studies Quarterly* 41, no. 1 (March 1997): 87–112 at 102–3.

20. Recent examples of this maximalist approach include Yaacov Vertzberger, *Risk Taking and Decisionmaking: Foreign Military Intervention Decisions* (Stanford, Calif.: Stanford University Press, 1998); Charles A. Kupchan, *Vulnerability of Empire* (Ithaca: Cornell University Press, 1995); and Andrew Bennett, *Condemned to Repetition? The Rise, Fall, and Reprise of Soviet-Russian Military Interventionism, 1973–1996* (Cambridge: MIT Press, 1999).

21. Jack S. Levy makes this observation about expected utility theory and prospect theory, respectively. See Levy, "The Causes of War: A Review of Theories and Evidence," in *Behavior Society and Nuclear War*, vol. 1, ed. Philip E. Tetlock, Jo L. Husbands, Robert Jervis, Paul C. Stern, and Charles Tilly (New York: Oxford University Press, 1989), 249; and idem, "Prospect Theory, Rational Choice, and International Relations," 106–7.

22. See Stephen Van Evera, *Guide to Methods for Students of Political Science* (Ithaca: Cornell University Press, 1998), 20; and Gary King, Robert O. Keohane, and Sidney Verba, *Designing Social Inquiry: Scientific Inference in Qualitative Research* (Princeton: Princeton University Press, 1994), 100–105.

23. See for example William J. Qualls, "Organizational Climate and Decision Framing: An Integrated Approach to Analyzing Industrial Buying Decisions," *Journal of Marketing Research* 26, no. 2 (May 1989): 179–92; and Howard Garland, "Throwing Good Money After Bad: The Effect of Sunk Costs on the Decision to Escalate Commitment to an Ongoing Project," *Journal of Applied Psychology* 75, no. 6 (December 1990): 728–31.

24. Sunk costs are any costs that decision makers have incurred in the past, which decision makers cannot change by any current or future action. See Robert Jervis, "The Political Implications of Loss Aversion," in *Avoiding Losses/Taking Risks*, 26–27.

25. On expectancy value antecedents for entrapment, see Joel Brockner and Jeffrey Z. Rubin, *Entrapment in Escalating Conflicts: A Social Psychological Analysis* (New York: Springer-Verlag, 1985), 33–39.

26. See David V. Budescu and Wendy Weiss, "The Reflection of Transitive and

Intransitive Preferences: A Test of Prospect Theory," *Organizational Behavior & Human Decision Processes* 39, no. 2 (April 1987): 184–202; and Glen Whyte, "Escalating Commitment in Individual and Group Decision Making: A Prospect Theory Approach," *Organizational Behavior and Human Decision Processes* 54, no. 3 (April 1993): 430–55.

27. Tatsuya Kameda and James H. Davis, "The Function of the Reference Point in Individual and Group Risk Taking," *Organizational Behavior and Human Decision Processes* 46, no. 1 (June 1990): 55–76; and Sandra J. Hartman and Beverly H. Nelson, "Group Decision-making in the Negative Domain," *Group and Organization Management* 21, no. 2 (June 1996): 146–62.

28. Max H. Bazerman, "Escalation of Commitment in Individual and Group Decision-making," *Organizational Behavior and Human Performance* 33, no. 2 (April 1984): 141–52. Also see John Shaubroeck and Elaine Davis, "Prospect Theory Predictions when Escalation is Not the Only Chance to Recover Sunk Costs," *Organizational Behavior & Human Decision Processes* 57, no. 1 (January 1994): 59–82.

29. Whyte, "Escalating Commitment," and Hal R. Arkes and Catherine Blumer, "The Psychology of Sunk Costs," *Organizational Behavior and Human Decision Processes* 35, no. 1 (February 1985): 124–40.

30. Rutledge, "Escalation of Commitment in Groups," 17–23; Kevin Devine and Priscilla O'clock, "The Effects of Sunk Costs and Opportunity Costs on a Subjective Capital Allocation Decision," *Mid-Atlantic Journal of Business* 31, no. 1 (March 1995): 25–39.; D. E. Caldwell and C. A. O'Really, "Responses to Failure: The Effects of Choice and Responsibility on Impression Management," *Academy of Management Review* 25, no. 1 (March 1982): 121–36

31. See Graham Searjeant, "How the Bank Tumbled," *Times* (London), 31 October 1995; Frank Kane and Mark Franchetti, "Leeson Money Making Legend Exposed as Sham," *Sunday Times* (London), 9 July 1995; and "The Crucial Question is Who Knew What and When—Baring's Collapse," *Financial Times* (London), 7 July 1995.

32. See Daniel Kahneman and Amos Tversky, "Choices, Values and Frames," *American Psychologist* 39, no. 2 (April 1984): 341–50.

33. David G. Myers and Helmut Lamm, "The Group Polarization Phenomena," *Psychological Bulletin* 83, no. 4 (July 1976): 602–27; David G. Myers and Paul J. Bach, "Discussion Effects on Militarism-Pacifism: A Test of the Group Polarization Hypothesis," *Journal of Personality and Social Psychology* 30, no. 6 (December 1974): 741–47; Marilynn B. Brewer and Roderick M. Kramer, "Choice Behavior in Social Dilemmas: Effects of Social Identity, Group Size, and Decision Framing," *Journal of Personality and Social Psychology* 50, no. 3 (March 1986): 543–49.

34. One should note, however, that the magnitude of subjects' risk propensity and preference reversals depended, in part, on the design of the experiment. The oft-cited "Asian disease" and "gambling decision" experiments illustrate this. See Anton Kühberger, "The Influence of Framing on Risky Decisions: A Meta-Analysis," *Organizational Behavior and Human Decision Processes* 75, no. 1 (July 1988): 23–56.

35. Kahneman and Tversky, "Prospect Theory: An Analysis of Decision under Risk," 275.

36. See, for example, McDermott, *Risk-Taking in International Politics*, 37–38; Paul D. Huth, D. Scott Bennett, and Christopher Gelpi, "System Uncertainty, Risk Propensity, and International Conflict among the Great Powers," *Journal of Conflict Resolution* 36, no. 3 (September 1992): 478–517; and K. R. De Rouen, Jr., "The Indirect Link: Politics, the Economy and the Use of Force," *Journal of Conflict Resolution* 39, no. 4 (December 1995): 571–83.

37. William A. Boettcher, III, "Smoke or Mirrors? Designing Experiments to Test Framing Effects in the Domain of Foreign Policy," (paper presented at the annual meeting of the International Studies Association, Los Angeles, 14–18 March 2000), 12.

38. This observation, of course, raises the danger that the correction between decision makers' subjective measures of gains and losses and their risk propensity in choosing particular options will be spurious, rather than the product of loss aversion. To minimize this danger, I rely on primary and secondary sources to determine leaders' level of expectation and their perceptions of what would constitute a gain or a loss relative to the level independently of the policies eventually chosen.

39. On German perceptions of relative decline and encirclement after 1903, see Davis, *Threats and Promises*, 94–135; Robert Jervis, *System Effects: Complexity in Political and Social Life* (Princeton: Princeton University Press, 1997), 245–58; Dale C. Copeland, *Origins of Major War* (Ithaca: Cornell University Press, 2000), 56–78; and Kwang-Ching Liu, "German Fear of a Quadruple Alliance, 1904–1905," *Journal of Modern History* 18, no. 3 (September 1946): 222–40.

40. On the German preventive war motivation in 1914, see Copeland, *Origins of Major War*, 79–117; Stephen Van Evera, "The Cult of the Offensive and the Origins of the First World War," *International Security* 9, no. 1 (summer 1984): 58–107; and Jack Snyder, "Perceptions of the Security Dilemma in 1914," in *Psychology and Deterrence*, ed. in Robert Jervis, Richard Ned Lebow, and Janice Gross Stein (Baltimore: John Hopkins University, 1985), 153–79. For a more general analysis of preventive war, see Jack S. Levy, "Declining Power and the Preventive Motivation for War," *World Politics* 40, no. 1 (October 1987): 82–107.

41. See Boettcher, "Smoke or Mirrors?" at 10–11. In fairness to McDermott, she acknowledges this limitation. McDermott, *Risk-Taking in International Politics*, 37–38.

42. Again, the logrolling theory of imperialism holds that domestic considerations weigh more heavily in leaders' calculations than international considerations. This theory would expect that in highly cartelized regimes, leaders' overriding objective is maintain the support of the logrolled coalition of imperialist groups that sustain them in power. See Jack Snyder, *Myths of Empire: Domestic Politics and International Ambition* (Ithaca: Cornell University Press, 1991), 48–49.

43. Boettcher, "Smoke or Mirrors?" 12. Boettcher further notes that most if not all applications of prospect theory in international relations (conscious or unconsciously) focus on leaders' expectation levels rather than reference points. See, for example, Barbara Farnham, "Roosevelt and the Munich Crisis: Insights from Prospect Theory," in *Avoiding Losses/Taking Risks*, 41–72; Audrey McInerney, "Prospect Theory and Soviet Policy Toward Syria, 1966–1967," in ibid., 101–18; and Deborah Spar, "Co-developing the FSX Fighter: The Domestic Calculus of International Cooperation," in *Choosing to Cooperate*, 65–92.

44. Kahneman and Tversky, "Prospect Theory," 274.

45. Ibid., 286.

46. For an overview of the goal-setting and performance see, Norman T. Feather, "Introduction and Overview," in *Expectations and Actions: Expectancy Value Models in Psychology* (Hillsdale, N.J.: Erlbaum, 1982), 1–16; and Edward A. Locke and Gary P. Latham, *A Theory of Goal Setting and Task Performance* (Englewood Cliffs, N.J.: Prentice-Hall, 1990).

47. Chip Heath, Richard P. Larrick, and George Wu, "Goals as Reference Points," *Cognitive Psychology* 38, no. 1 (February 1999): 79–109. Also see Irvin P. Levin, Sandra L. Schneider, and Gary J. Gaeth, "All Frames are Not Created Equal: A Typology and Critical Analysis of Framing Effects," *Organizational Behavior and*

Human Decision Processes 76, no. 2 (1998): 149–88; and Chaim Fershtman, "On the Value of Incumbency: Managerial Reference Points and Loss Aversion," *Journal of Economic Psychology* 17, no. 2 (April 1996): 245–57.

48. Richard P. Larrick, Chip Heath, and George Wu, "Goal-Induced Risk Taking in Strategy Choice" working paper, Graduate School of Business, University of Chicago, 1999.

49. See Levy, "Prospect Theory, Rational Choice, and International Relations," 100–105; idem, "Prospect Theory and International Relations," in *Avoiding Losses/Taking Risks*, 130–32; McDermott, "Psychological Ideas of Amos Tversky," at 18; Davis, *Threats and Promises*, 41–42; Morrow, *Game Theory for Political Scientists*, 29–33; George W. Downs and David M. Rocke, *Optimal Imperfection: Domestic Uncertainty and Institutions in International Relations* (Princeton: Princeton University Press, 1995), 18–19; and Dale C. Copeland, "Theory and History in the Study of Major War," *Security Studies* 10, no. 4 (summer 2001): 212–39, at 218, fn. 14.

50. See, for example, Farnham, "Roosevelt and the Munich Crisis," 63–68; McInerney, "Prospect Theory and Soviet Policy," 112–13; and McDermott, "Prospect Theory in International Relations," 81–88.

51. I am indebted to Jennifer Sterling-Folker for suggesting this point.

52. Robert Gilpin, *War and Change in World Politics* (New York: Cambridge: University Press, 1981), 30–31.

53. Examples of offensive and defensive realist theories that focus on power shifts include Gilpin, *War and Change;* A. F. K. Organski, *World Politics,* 2d ed. (New York: Knopf, 1968); Van Evera, *Causes of War,* 73–116; and Dale C. Copeland, "Neorealism and the Myth of Bipolar Stability: Toward a New Dynamic Realist Theory of Major War," *Security Studies* 5, no. 3 (spring 1996): 29–90.

54. Thomas J. Christensen, "Perceptions and Alliances in Europe, 1860–1940," *International Organization* 51, no. 1 (winter 1997): 65–97.

55. Aaron L. Friedberg, *Weary Titan: Britain and the Experience of Relative Decline, 1895–1905* (Princeton: Princeton University Press, 1988), 279–82.

56. Gregory, Litchenstein, and McGregor, "The Role of Past States in Determining Reference Points."

57. For details of the Kennedy defense buildup see, Aaron L. Friedberg, *In the Shadow of the Garrison State: American Anti-Statism and its Cold War Grand Strategy* (Princeton: Princeton University Press, 2000), 139–48; and Deborah Welch Larson, *Anatomy of Mistrust: U.S.-Soviet Relations during the Cold War* (Ithaca: Cornell University Press, 1997), 115–22. On the nuclear balance between the superpowers in 1960–63, see "Estimated U.S. and Soviet/Russian Nuclear Stockpiles, 1945–94," *Bulletin of the Atomic Scientists* (November/December 1994), 59.

58. See Mark L. Haas, "Prospect Theory and the Cuban Missile Crisis," *International Studies Quarterly* 45, no. 2 (June 2001): 241–60, at 253–57. For a discussion of why Khrushchev viewed numerical parity in nuclear warheads and ICBMs as vital to Soviet security and prestige, see William Curti Wohlforth, *The Elusive Balance: Power and Perceptions during the Cold War* (Ithaca: Cornell University Press, 1993), 157–66 and 179–83; and Vladislav Zubok and Constantine Pleshakov, *Inside the Kremlin's Cold War: From Stalin to Khrushchev* (Cambridge: Harvard University Press, 1996), 188–94.

59. On the Kennedy administration's precrisis warnings against Soviet missile deployments in Cuba and Soviet intelligence estimates on the likelihood of discovery, see, "New Evidence on the Cuban Missile Crisis," *Cold War International History Project Bulletin* no. 5 (spring 1995): 58–59; Aleksandr Furensko and Timothy J. Naftali, *One Hell of a Gamble: Khrushchev, Castro, Kennedy, 1958–1964* (New York: W. W.

Norton, 1997), 191–93; and Ernest R. May and Philip Zelikow, eds. *The Kennedy Tapes: Inside the White House during the Cuban Missile Crisis* (Cambridge: Harvard University Press, 1997), 674–76.

60. Glen Whyte and Ariel S. Levi, "The Origins and Function of the Reference Point in Risky Group Decision Making: The Case of the Cuban Missile Crisis," *Journal of Behavioral Decision Making* 7 (1994): 243–60; and David A. Welch and James G. Blight, "An Introduction to the ExComm Transcripts," *International Security* 12, no. 3 (winter 1987/88): 5–29.

61. John Lewis Gaddis, *Strategies of Containment: A Critical Appraisal of Postwar American National Security Policy* (New York: Oxford University Press, 1982), 359.

62. See Marc Trachtenberg, *History and Strategy* (Princeton: Princeton University Press, 1991), 103–7; Daniel Calingaert, "Nuclear Weapons and the Korean War," *Journal of Strategic Studies* 11, no. 2 (June 1988): 177–202; and Rosemary J. Foot, "Nuclear Coercion and the Ending of the Korean Conflict," *International Security* 13, no. 2 (winter 1988/89): 92–112.

63. Amos Tversky and Daniel Kahneman, "Judgment under Uncertainty: Heuristics and Biases," in *Judgment under Uncertainty*, 14–15. Also, see Richard Nisbett and Lee Ross, *Human Inference: Strategies and Shortcomings of Social Judgment* (Englewood Cliffs, N.J.: Prentice-Hall, 1980), 41–42.

64. Paul Slovic, Baruch Fischhoff, and Sarah Lichtenstein, "Facts versus Fears: Understanding Perceived Risk," in *Judgment under Uncertainty*, 481.

65. Jervis, "Political Implications of Loss Aversion," in *Avoiding Losses/Taking Risks*, 36. He goes on to write that, "For the Soviet Union the status quo may have been the world as it was before the [American] blockade [of Cuba]."

66. Ibid., 36.

67. On each of these factors, see Gaddis, *Strategies of Containment*, 274–308; Dale C. Copeland, "Trade Expectations and the Outbreak of Peace: Détente 1970–74 and the End of the Cold War 1985–91," *Security Studies* 9, no. 1 and 2 (autumn 1999–winter 2000): 15–59; and Bennett, *Condemned to Repetition?* 169–74.

68. Transcript of CPSU CC Politburo Discussions on Afghanistan, 17–19 March 1979, in *Cold War International History Project Bulletin*, nos. 8–9 (winter 1996/1997): 136–45 (hereafter cited as *CWIHP Bulletin*).

69. See Robert Jervis, "Domino Beliefs and Strategic Behavior," in *Dominoes and Bandwagons: Strategic Beliefs and Great Power Competition in the Eurasian Rimland*, ed. Robert Jervis and Jack Snyder (New York: Oxford University Press, 1991), 20–50.

70. See Jerome Slater, "The Domino Theory and International Politics: The Case of Vietnam," *Security Studies* 3, no. 2 (winter 1993/94): 186–224.

71. For a different perspective see Douglas J. Macdonald, "Falling Dominoes and Systemic Dynamics: A Risk Aversion Perspective," *Security Studies* 3, no. 2 (winter 1993/94): 225–58. Macdonald argues, "Under conditions of extreme uncertainty, it is rational for the decision maker to hedge his strategic bets and assume that a lack of short term action will likely lead to long term disaster *even if the probabilities are low.*" (233) I contend, on the other hand, that the prospect of relative power or reputation loss systemically biases decision makers toward the adoption risk-acceptant strategies, in an effort to hedge strategic bets.

72. See "Transcript of Brezhnev-Honecker Summit in East Berlin," 4 October 1979; and "Gromyko-Andropov-Ustinov-Ponomarev Report to CPSU CC," 22 October 1979 in *CWIHP Bulletin*, no. 8–9 (winter 1996/1997), 156–58. Also, see Bennett, *Condemned to Repetition*, 197–200; and Raymond L. Garthoff, *From Détente to Confrontation: American-Soviet Relations from Nixon to Reagan*, rev. ed. (Washington, D.C.: Brookings, 1994), 1046–48.

73. Garthoff, *Détente to Confrontation*, 1037. See also Robert S. Litwak, "The Soviet Union in Afghanistan," in *Foreign Military Intervention: The Dynamics of Protracted Conflict*, ed. Ariel E. Levite, Bruce W. Jentleson, and Larry Berman (New York: Columbia University Press, 1992), 76–78.

74. See Jervis, "Political Implications of Loss Aversion," in *Avoiding Losses/Taking Risks*, 27.

75. It is important to draw a distinction between the balance-of-risk hypothesis on escalating commitment and the rational choice notion of "gambling for resurrection" as a motive for escalatory behavior. See Downs and Rocke, *Optimal Imperfection*, 56–78; George W. Downs and David M. Rocke, "Conflict, Agency, and Gambling for Resurrection: The Principal-Agent Problem Goes to War," *American Journal of Political Science* 38, no. 2 (May 1994): 362–80. Drawing on the principal-agent literature, Downs and Rocke develop a model to explain how information asymmetries and limited liability between the executive (the agent) and the constituency (the principal) give the former an incentive to escalate ongoing, but failing, foreign military interventions. In brief, when faced with adverse military outcomes, the executive will likely escalate the conflict in the hope that the situation will improve, thus avoiding removal from office at the next election (in the case of a democracy) or through popular rebellion (in the case of an autocracy). The "gambling for resurrection" proposition is a subset of the diversionary motive for war literature: leaders' desire to remain in office drives their foreign policy behavior. The balance-of-risk hypothesis, on the other hand, suggests that leaders persist and escalate their commitment to failing intervention strategies in an effort to recoup losses in their state's material power or international reputation.

CHAPTER 3. GERMANY AND THE 1905 MOROCCO CRISIS

1. On Germany's preponderance of military power, see Dale C. Copeland, *Origins of Major War* (Ithaca: Cornell University Press, 2000), 56–78; David G. Herrmann, *The Arming of Europe and the Making of the First World War* (Princeton: Princeton University, 1996), esp. appendices A and B, 233–37; and Paul M. Kennedy, *The Rise and Fall of the Great Powers: Economic Change and Military Conflict from 1500 to 2000* (New York: Random House, 1987), 198–203 and 209–15.

2. For an overview of how bilateral relations among the European great powers in the 1894–1914 period reduced their freedom of maneuver, altered their interests, and generated unexpected outcomes (often despite leaders' expectations and desires), see Robert Jervis, *System Effects: Complexity in Political and Social Life* (Princeton: Princeton University Press, 1996), 243–52.

3. On Bismarck's alliance network see, A. J. P. Taylor, *The Struggle for Mastery in Europe, 1848–1918* (Oxford: Oxford University Press, 1954), chap. 7; and Gordon A. Craig and Alexander L. George, *Foreign and Statecraft: Diplomatic Problems of Our Time*, 2d ed. (New York: Oxford University Press, 1990), 35–48.

4. Paul M. Kennedy, *Rise of Anglo-German Antagonism, 1860–1914*, 4th ed. (London: Ashfield Press, 1989), 205–6; and C. J. Lower and M. L. Dockrill, *The Mirage of Power*, vol. 1, *British Foreign Policy, 1902–1914* (Boston: Routledge and Kegan Paul, 1972).

5. See Kennedy, *Rise of Anglo-German Antagonism*, 410–32; and Gordon A. Craig, *Germany, 1866–1945* (New York: Oxford University Press, 1978), 309–10. Others argue that the primary purpose of the naval building program was to undermine support for the Social Democratic party and prevent the Reichstag from as-

serting a larger role in military affairs. See Volker R. Berghahn, *Germany and the Approach of War in 1914* (New York: St. Martin's, 1973); and Geoff Eley, *Reshaping the German Right: Radical Nationalism and Political Change after Bismarck* (Ann Arbor: University of Michigan Press, 1990).

6. Tirpitz to Wilhelm II quoted in Berghahn, *Germany and the Approach of War in 1914*, 40.

7. See Jonathan Steinberg, *Yesterday's Deterrent: Tirpitz and the Birth of the German Battlefleet* (London: Macdonald, 1965); and Paul M. Kennedy, *The Rise and Fall of British Naval Mastery* (New York: Macmillan, 1983), chap. 8.

8. See Mary Evelyn Townsend, *The Rise and Fall of Germany's Colonial Empire* (New York: Howard Fertig, 1966), 183–86; and Jeffrey Butler, "The German Factor in Anglo-Transvaal Relations," in *Britain and Germany in Africa: Imperial Rivalry and Colonial Rule*, ed. Prosser Gifford and W. M. Roger Lewis (New Haven: Yale University Press, 1967), 202–3.

9. Luigi Albertini, *The Origins of the War of 1914*, vol. 1, *European Relations from the Congress of Berlin to the Eve of the Sarajevo Murder*, trans. and ed. Isabella M. Massey (New York: Oxford University Press, 1952), 144–45.

10. Kennedy, *Rise and Fall of the Great Powers*, 215–19.

11. Figures on relative army expenditures quoted from Herrmann, *Arming of Europe*, 236–37, appendix B1.

12. See Kennedy, *Rise and Fall of the Great Powers*, 203–6.

13. See Brian R. Sullivan, "The Strategy of Decisive Weight: Italy, 1882–1922," in *Making of Strategy: Rulers, States and War*, ed. Williamson Murray, MacGregor Knox, and Alvin Bernstein (Cambridge: Cambridge University Press, 1994), 307–51, esp. 312–20; and Robert L. Hess, "Germany and the Anglo-Italian Colonial Entente," in *Britain and Germany in Africa*, 153–78, esp. 166.

14. John F. V. Keiger, *France and the Origins of the First World War* (London: Macmillan, 1983), 18; and Bertha R. Leaman, "The Influence of Domestic Policy on Foreign Affairs in France, 1889–1905," *Journal of Modern History* 14, no. 4 (December 1942): 449–79.

15. The other signatories were Russia, Austria-Hungary, the United States, Belgium, the Netherlands, Portugal, Spain, and Sweden. See, F. V. Parsons, *The Origins of the Morocco Question, 1880–1900* (London: Duckworth, 1976), 27–86; and Earl Free Cruickshank, *Morocco at the Parting of the Ways* (Philadelphia: University of Pennsylvania Press, 1935).

16. See Eugene N. Anderson, *The First Morocco Crisis, 1904–1906* (Chicago: University of Chicago Press, 1930), 29–32.

17. Memo by Bülow, 12 January 1902, XVII, no. 523, in *German Diplomatic Documents, 1871–1914*, vol. 3, *The Growing Antagonism, 1898–1910*, ed. and trans. E. T. S. Dugdale (New York and London: Harper, 1930), 166–67. Hereafter cited as *GDD*.

18. See Memo by Klehment, 7 September 1902, XVII, no. 702, *GDD*, vol. 3, 167–68.

19. Schlieffen to Richtofen, 14 December 1903, XVII, no. 708, ibid., 169.

20. G. P. Gooch, *Before the War: Studies in Diplomacy*, vol. 1, *The Grouping of the Powers* (New York: Longman, Green, 1936), 127; Anderson, *First Moroccan Crisis*, 26; and Kennedy, *Rise of Anglo-German Antagonism*, 269.

21. For a discussion of the Fashoda crisis see, William L. Langer, *The Diplomacy of Imperialism, 1890–1902*, 2d ed. (New York: Knopf, 1965), 101–44 and 259–302; G. N. Sanderson, *England, Europe, and the Upper Nile, 1882–1899* (Edinburgh: University of Edinburgh Press, 1965), chaps. 12–15; and Darrel Bates, *The Fashoda Incident of 1898: Encounter on the Nile* (New York: Oxford University Press, 1984).

22. See Paul M. Kennedy, *The Rise and Fall of British Naval Mastery* (London: Macmillan, 1976), 205–37; and Aaron L. Friedberg, *The Weary Titan: Britain and the Experience of Relative Decline, 1895–1905* (Princeton: Princeton University Press, 1988), 152–203 and 224–72.

23. Declaration between the United Kingdom and France respecting Egypt and Morocco, signed at London, 8 April 1904 in *British Documents on the Origins of the War, 1898–1914*, vol. 2, *Anglo-Japanese Alliance and the Franco-British Entente*, ed. G. P. Gooch and Harold Temperly (London: His Majesty's Foreign Office, 1926), 385–95. Hereafter cited as *BD*.

24. See Anderson, *First Morocco Crisis*, 118–25.

25. Paul Révoil to Able Comabarieu, secretary to President Emile Loubet, March 1902, quoted in Christopher Andrew, *Théophile Delcassé and the Making of the Entente Cordiale: A Reappraisal of French Foreign Policy* (New York: St. Martin's, 1968), 270.

26. See Radolin to Bülow, 23 March 1904, 20, no. 4, *GDD*, vol. 3, 188–89.

27. Wilhelm II to Bülow, 19 April 1904 in Bernhard von Bülow, *Letters of Bernhard, Fürst von Bülow*, trans. Frederic Whyte (London: Hutchinson, 1930), 54.

28. Baron Friedrich von Mentizen, German minister in Tangier, to Bülow, 5 April 1904, 20, no. 202; Hans von Flotow, chargé d' affaires in Paris, to Bülow, 24 September 1904, 20, no. 189; and Richtofen to Radowitz, in Madrid, 7 October 1904, 20, no. 191, *GDD*, vol. 3, 220–23.

29. For an argument that the adverse economic consequences of French expansion in North Africa prompted Bülow and Holstein to initiate the first Morocco crisis, see James W. Davis, Jr., *Threats and Promises: The Pursuit of International Influence* (Baltimore: Johns Hopkins University Press, 2000), 106–23. While I agree with Davis that economic motivations were present in the documentary record, I contend that German leaders' were *primarily* concerned with preventing the Anglo-French entente from evolving into an alliance (and humiliating Delcassé in the process). The disposition of Morocco and German economic rights there, per se, was not the main motivation for the German challenge. The vast majority of recent scholarly works in diplomatic history and international relations share this second view of German motives, most notably: Kennedy, *Rise of Anglo-German Antagonism*, 275–77; Jervis, *Systems Effects*, 248–49; Chaim D. Kaufmann, "Out of the Lab and into the Archives: A Method for Testing Psychological Explanations for Political Decisionmaking," *International Studies Quarterly* 38, no. 4 December 1994): 557–86; Herrmann, *Arming of Europe*, 37–47; Jonathan Mercer, *Reputation and International Politics* (Ithaca: Cornell University Press, 1996), 76–77; and John J. Mearsheimer, *Tragedy of Great Power Politics* (New York: W. W. Norton, 2001), 152, 188, and 263.

30. Memo by Holstein, 5 June 1904, no. 6516, *Die Grosse Politik der Europäschen Kabinett, 1871–1914*, ed. Johannes Lepsius, Albrecht Mendelssohn Bartholdy, and Friedrich Thimme (Berlin: Deutsche Verlags gesselshaft für Politik und Geschichte, 1922–27), vol. 20, no. 1, 144–45. Hereafter cited as *GP*. See, also Norman Rich, *Friedrich von Holstein: Politics and Diplomacy in the Era of Bismarck and Wilhelm II*, vol. 2 (Cambridge: University of Cambridge Press, 1965), 683. All translations from *Die Grosse Politik* are by Chaim D. Kaufmann, unless noted otherwise. Kaufmann, "Appendix to the Morocco Crisis," (unpublished mimeo, Columbia University, 1994).

31. Bülow to Radolin, 21 July 1904, no. 6523, *GP*, vol. 20, no.1, 214.

32. Wilhelm II to Bülow, 19 August 1904, cited in Albertini, *Origins of the War*, vol. 1, 149.

33. Bülow to Wilhelm II, 20 August 1904, ibid., 149–50. Also, see Memo by Holstein, 8 March 1904, no. 824, in Friedrich von Holstein, *The Holstein Papers*, ed. and

trans. Norman R. Rich and M. H. Fischer (London, Cambridge University Press, 1963), vol. 4, 284.

34. See Metternich to the Reich Foreign Office, 4 June 1904, no. 29, *GDD*, vol. 3, 194–95.

35. Metzingen to Bülow, 5 April 1905, no. 6515; Memo by Prince Karl Max von Lichnowsky, 13 April 1904, no. 6515; and Memo by Brüning, 23 April 1904, no. 6517, *GP*, vol. 20, no. 1, 203–5.

36. Bülow to Wilhelm II, 30 March 1904, no. 6512, *GP*, vol. 20, no. 1, 197–99.

37. See Memo by Holstein, 19 April 1904, no. 6443, ibid., 123–24.

38. Bülow to Count Christian von Tattenbach, no. 6643, 30 April 1905, *GP*, vol. 20, no. 2, 352; and Memo by Bülow, 26 and 29 June 1904, nos. 6038 and 6040, *GP*, vol. 19, no. 1, 186. See, Anderson, *First Moroccan Crisis*, 151.

39. Richtofen to Radowitz, 24 September 1903, no. 5200, *GP*, vol. 19, no. 1, 355.

40. Tschirschky to Bülow, 3 April 1904, no. 6513, *GP*, vol. 20, no. 1, 199–200.

41. See Bülow to Richtofen, 19 April 1904, 20, no. 124, *GDD*, vol. 3, 192.

42. For the text of the private 8 March 1904 Anglo-French agreement concerning New Foundland, West, and Central Africa (including Egypt and the Khedivial Decree), see *BD*, vol. 2, 402–4. Delcassé informed Radolin of the agreement on 23 March. See Radolin to Bülow, 23 March 1904, *GDD*, vol. 3, 190.

43. Rücker-Jenisch to the Foreign Office, 31 May 1904, XX, no. 34, *GDD*, vol. 3, 192.

44. See Lord Lansdowne to Sir Frank Lascelles, 6 May 1904, quoted in Lord Nelson, *Lord Lansdowne: A Biography* (London: Macmillan, 1929), 329.

45. Bülow to Alvensleben, 13 May 1903, XVII, no. 570, *GDD*, vol. 3, 194–95.

46. Bülow to Holstein, 16 January 1904, *Holstein Papers*, vol. 4, 277.

47. Memo to Bülow, 14 February 1904, XIX, no. 62, *GDD*, vol. 3, 180–81.

48. Holstein to Radolin, 19 February 1904, *Holstein Papers*, vol. 4, 279.

49. Memo to Bülow, 22 February 1904, no. 823, ibid., 282.

50. Jonathan Steinberg, "Germany and the Russo-Japanese War," *Journal of Modern History* 75, no. 7 (December 1970): 1965–86, esp. 1970 and 1973–75.

51. See Metternich to the Reich Foreign Office, 18 August 1904, XIX, no. 240, *GDD*, vol. 3, 181–82.

52. Public Records Office, Cabinet Papers, 37/69/32. "Naval Estimates, 1904–5: Possible Reductions," 26 February 1904, quoted in Friedberg, *Weary Titan*, 191.

53. Kennedy, *Rise of Anglo-German Antagonism*, 272.

54. Ibid., 272. See also Memo by Metternich for Bülow, 25 December 1904, XIX, no. 367, *GDD*, vol. 3, 208–12.

55. Clarke to Balfour, 24 September 1904, quoted in George W. Monger, *The End of Isolation: British Foreign Policy, 1900–1907* (London: Thomas Nelson and Sons, 1963), 165.

56. Memo by Metternich for Bülow, 25 December 1904, XIX, no. 367, *GDD*, vol. 3, 208–10.

57. See Memo by Holstein, 22 October 1904, no. 862, in *Holstein Papers*, vol. 4, 311–12. Also, see Townsend, *Rise and Fall of Germany's Colonial Empire*, 316–21; and Kennedy, *Rise of Anglo-German Antagonism*, 271–72.

58. Wilhelm II to Nicholas II, 27 October 1904, *GP*, vol. 19, 303–4 (In English in the original).

59. See Steinberg, "Germany and the Russo-Japanese War," 1978.

60. See Wilhelm to Bülow, 24 November 1904, *GP*, vol. 19, 316.

61. Memo by Holstein, 5 December 1904, no. 6153, ibid., 358–59.

62. Bülow to Holstein, no. 867, 13 December 1904, *Holstein Papers*, vol. 4, 316.

63. See Anderson, *First Morocco Crisis*, 170–72.

64. See Memo by Metternich, 18 December 1904, XIX, no. 332, *GDD*, vol. 3, 184.

65. Wilhelm II to Nicholas II, 21 December 1905, no. 6141, *GP*, vol. 20, no. 1, 340; Nicholas to Wilhelm, 25 December 1904, no. 6145, ibid., 346; and Bülow to Wilhelm, 26 December 1904, no. 6176, ibid., 395.

66. See Rich, *Friedrich von Holstein*, vol. 2, 681.

67. See Memo by Lichnowsky, 13 April 1904, *GP*, vol. 20, no. 6516.

68. Holstein to Bülow and Bülow to Otto Hammann, 11 and 14 July 1904, translated and quoted in Anderson, *First Morocco Crisis*, 159. These letters originally appeared in Otto Hammann, *Bilder aus der lezten Kaiserzeit* (Reimar Hobbing: Berlin, 1922), 33.

69. At the same time, Bülow warned Kühlmann that Berlin could not promise diplomatic or military assistance to Morocco should the French carry out their plans to establish a protectorate over the country. See, Bülow to Kühlmann, 2 January 1905, no. 6544, *GP*, vol. 20, no.1, 242–43.

70. Kühlmann to Bülow, 29 January 1905, no. 6552, *GP*, vol. 20, no.1, 248–49; also see Anderson, *First Morocco Crisis*, 186.

71. See, Bülow to Wilhelm II, 20 March 1905, no. 262, *GDD*, vol. 3, 223.

72. Bülow to Wilhelm II, 26 March 1905, no. 6576, *GP*, vol. 20, no. 1, 273–74.

73. Bülow to Wilhelm II, ibid., 272 (emphasis added); also quoted in Anderson, *First Morocco Crisis*, 190–91.

74. Quoted in Dwight E. Lee, *Europe's Crucial Years: The Diplomatic Background to World War I, 1902–1914* (Hanover, N.H.: Clark University Press, 1974), 114–15. See also Schoen to the Reich Foreign Office, 31 March 1905, no. 6588, *GP*, vol. 20, no.1, 658; and Anderson, *First Morocco Crisis*, 193–94. There are various versions of the speech, since Wilhelm II spoke extemporaneously. The official version appeared in *Allgemeine Zeitung* (Munich), 4 April 1905.

75. See Baron Wilhelm von Schön to the Reich Foreign Office, 31 March 1905, no. 6589, *GP*, vol. 20, no. 1, 658–59. Also see Anderson, *First Morocco Crisis*, 192–94.

76. See Memo by Admiral Prince Louis of Battenberg, 1 April 1905 in Nelson, *Lord Lansdowne*, 333.

77. Quoted in Samuel R. Williamson, Jr., *The Politics of Grand Strategy: Britain and France Prepare for War, 1904–1914* (Cambridge: Harvard University Press, 1969), 31.

78. David E. Kaiser, "Germany and the Origins of the First World War," *Journal of Modern History* 55, no. 3 (September 1983): 442–74, at 472.

79. See Anderson, *First Morocco Crisis*, 192.

80. See Raymond J. Sontag, "German Foreign Policy, 1904–1906," *American Historical Review* 33, no. 2 (June 1928): 278–301, esp. 283, 284–86.

81. See Holstein to Bülow, 4 September 1905, no. 913, *Holstein Papers*, vol. 4, 373.

82. Holstein to Radolin, 11 April 1905, no. 883, ibid., 229–31.

83. Quoted in Kennedy, *Rise of Anglo-German Antagonism*, 276.

84. See Katharine Anne Lerman, *Chancellor as Courtier: Bernhard von Bülow and the Governance of Germany, 1900–1909* (Cambridge: Cambridge University Press, 1990), 74–115.

85. Schlieffen to Bülow, 10 June 1905, *Politisches Archiv des Auswärtiges Amtes*, Bonn, R10449 no. 471, cited in Herrmann, *Arming of Europe*, 41. See also, Arden Bucholz, *Moltke, Schlieffen, and Prussian War Planning* (Oxford: Berg, 1991), 198–99.

86. Rich, *Friedrich von Holstein*, vol. 2, 697–98; Kennedy, *Rise of Anglo-German Antagonism*, 276; Herrmann, *Arming of Europe*, 41–42; and Gordon A. Craig, *Politics of the Prussian Army, 1640–1945* (London: Oxford University Press, 1955), 283.

87. See Holstein to Bülow, 5 April 1905, no. 882, *Holstein Papers*, vol. 4, 328–29.

See, also, Kühlmann to the Reich Foreign Office, 3 April 1905, no. 296, XX, *GDD*, vol. 3, 224.

88. Radolin to Bülow, 30 April 1905, no. 361, XX, *GDD*, vol. 3, 226–27.

89. Bülow to Wilhelm II, 4 April 1905, no. 301, XX, ibid., 225.

90. Quoted in Andrew, *Théophile Delcassé*, 297.

91. Bülow to Wilhelm II, 4 April 1905, no. 301, XX, *GDD*, vol. 3, 224.

92. See Sternburg to the Reich Foreign Office, 25 April 1905, no. 6633, *GP*, vol. 20, 341–42.

93. See Bülow to Sternburg, 27 April 1905, no. 6634, *GP*, vol. 20, no. 2, 342–44.

94. Bülow to the Wilhelm II, 4 April 1905, no. 301, XX, *GDD*, vol. 3, 225.

95. See Tattenbach to the Reich Foreign Office, 27 April 1905, no. 348, XX, ibid., 226.

96. Kennedy, *Rise of Anglo-German Antagonism*, 277.

97. Radolin to the Reich Foreign Office, 9 April 1905, no. 6612, *GP*, vol. 20, no. 2, 316–17.

98. See, Memo by Hammann, 7 April 1905, no. 6607, *GP*, vol. 20, no. 2, 309.

99. Quoted in Anderson, *First Morocco Crisis*, 209.

100. Memo by Mühlberg, 19 April 1905, no. 6623, *GP*, vol. 20, no. 2, 332–33; and Holstein to Josef Neven-Dumont, 20 April 1905, no. 885, *Holstein Papers*, vol. 4, 333–34.

101. Rich, *Friedrich von Holstein*, vol. 2, 795.

102. Quoted in Anderson, *First Morocco Crisis*, 199. See also Lee, *Europe's Crucial Years*, 155.

103. Radolin to the Reich Foreign Office, 14 April 1905, no. 6621, *GP*, vol. 20, no. 2, 328–30.

104. Lord Lansdowne to Sir Francis Bertie, 22 April 1905, no. 90, *BD*, vol. 3, *Testing of the Entente, 1904–1906*, 72.

105. Quoted in Andrew, *Théophile Delcassé*, 279; see also Williamson, *Politics of Grand Strategy*, 32–33.

106. Quoted in G. P. Gooch, *Before the War: Studies in Diplomacy*, vol. 1, *The Grouping of the Powers* (New York: Longman, Green and Co., 1936), 179.

107. Radolin to Bülow, April 30 1905, XX, no. 361, *GDD*, vol. 3, 226–27. Also, see Radolin to the Reich Foreign Office, 25 April 1905, no. 6635, *GP*, vol. XX, no. 2, 344–45.

108. Bülow to the Reich Foreign Office, XX, no. 368, *GDD*, vol. 3, 227–28.

109. Holstein to Radolin, 1 May 1905, no. 866, *Holstein Papers*, vol. 4, 338–39.

110. For accounts of the 6 June cabinet meeting and the debate in the Chamber of Deputies the day before, see Anderson, *First Morocco Crisis*, 229–31; and Flotow to Bülow, 7 June 1905, XX, no. 406, *GDD*, vol. 3, 228–29.

111. Bülow to Radolin, 4 May 1905, *GP*, vol. 20, no. 2, 365–66.

112. Herrmann, *Arming of Europe*, 44–45.

113. See Rich, *Friedrich von Holstein*, vol. 2, 699–700.

114. Quoted in Herrmann, *Arming of Europe*, 52.

115. See Gerhard Ritter, *The Sword and the Scepter: The Problem of Militarism in Germany*, vol. 2, *The European Powers and the Wilheminian Empire, 1890–1914*, trans. Heinz Norden (Coral Gables, Fla.: University of Miami Press, 1970), 194; L. F. C. Turner, "The Schlieffen Plan," in *The War Plans of the Great Powers, 1880–1914*, ed. Paul M. Kennedy (London: Macmillan, 1979), 207–10. Craig, on the other hand, contends that Schlieffen advocated preventive war against France in spring 1905. See Craig, *Politics of the Prussian Army*, 283–85; and idem, *Germany, 1866–1945*, 320, fn. 58.

116. Rich, *Friedrich von Holstein*, vol. 2, 707.

117. Radolin to the Reich Foreign Office, 27 April 1905, no. 6635, *GP*, vol. 20, no. 2, 344–45.

118. Flotow to the Reich Foreign Office, 7 June 1905, no. 6694; Flotow to the Reich Foreign Office, 9 June 1905, no. 6700, *GP*, vol. 20, no. 1, 420 and 425.

119. Holstein to Radolin, no. 891, 14 June 1905, *Holstein Papers*, vol. 4, 342–43.

120. Holstein to Radolin, no. 890, 7 June 1905, ibid., 342.

121. Bülow to Tattenbach, 7 June 1905, XX, no. 418, *GDD*, vol. 3, 230.

122. See Memo by Bülow (an undated, unnumbered and unsigned copy in French), 1 July 1905 (circa), *GP*, vol. 20, no. 2, 497–98.

123. Holstein to Radolin, no. 891, 14 June 1905, ibid., 343.

124. Radolin to Holstein, 22 June 1905, no. 824, ibid., 345.

125. Radolin to the Reich Foreign Office, 21 June 1905, no. 6720, ibid., 452–53.

126. Bülow to Wilhelm II, 22 June 1905, no. 6723, ibid., 455–57.

127. Holstein to Radolin, 23 June 1905, no. 896, *Holstein Papers*, vol. 4, 346.

128. Holstein to Radolin, 23 June 1905, ibid., 346.

129. Radolin to the Reich Foreign Office, 8 July 1905, no. 6767, *GP*, vol. 20, no. 2, 514.

130. Lord Lansdowne to Bertie, 11 July 1905, no. 152, *BD*, vol. 3, 118.

131. Flotow to Bülow, 7 June 1905, XX, no. 625, *GDD*, vol. 3, 229.

132. Quoted in E. Malcolm Carroll, *Germany and the Great Powers, 1866–1914: A Study of Public Opinion and Foreign Policy* (Harden, Conn.: Archon Books, 1966), 529.

133. Metternich to the Reich Foreign Office, 28 June 1905, no. 6860, *GP*, vol. XX, no. 2, 635–36.

134. Metternich to Bülow, 19 July 1905, no. 6864, ibid., 639–40.

135. Metternich to Bülow, 22 July 1905, XX, no. 647, *GDD*, vol. 3, 232–33.

136. Snyder, *Myths of Empire*, 85–89.

137. Snyder does acknowledge a difference between how Bülow and Holstein may have used strategic myths in their public pronouncements. Bülow, in his estimate, was a "politician who basically understood the balancing character of the [international] system and the limits it placed on big stick diplomacy, yet who engaged in the pretense of *Weltpolitik* for purposes of domestic political prestige and minimal payoffs to constituencies who sought a strong, 'national' foreign policy." Holstein also showed a certain duality, although his strategic arguments "slanted more toward genuine faith in waving the big stick." See Snyder, *Myths of Empire*, 87. Nonetheless, the private correspondence and internal memoranda of Bülow and Holstein throughout the crisis contain references to the efficacy of "big stick" diplomacy and paper tiger images of the French.

138. The forgoing discussion of German leaders' continued belligerence in summer 1905 despite growing British opposition raises the question of motivated bias—individuals' needs to maintain their own emotional well-being and to avoid feelings of guilt, fear, and psychological stress. No doubt, Bülow, Holstein, and others felt great psychological pressure to believe that their risky Morocco strategy would succeed in summer 1905, so they systematically downplayed the adverse consequences of continued confrontation. While motivated biases play no role in balance-of-risk theory (and the extant prospect theory literature from which it derives), per se, a consideration of such factors would supplement my analysis. For examinations of the role of motivated bias attribution errors in the 1905 Morocco crisis see, Chaim D. Kauffman, "Out of the Lab and into the Archives: A Method for Testing Psychological Explanation of Political Decision-making," *International Studies Quarterly* 38, no. 4 (December 1994): 79–137; and Mercer, *Reputation and International Pol-*

itics, 74–109. For general discussions of the role of motivated biases in foreign policy decision making, see Richard Ned Lebow, *Between Peace and War: The Nature of International Crises* (Baltimore: Johns Hopkins University Press, 1981), 101–19; Irving L. Janis and Leon Mann, *Decision Making: An Psychological Analysis of Conflict, Commitment, and Choice* (New York: Free Press, 1977); and Robert Jervis, *Perception and Misperception in International Politics* (Princeton: Princeton University Press, 1976). For a recent overview of this literature, see Jack S. Levy, "Political Psychology and Foreign Policy," in David O. Sears, Leonie Huddy, and Robert Jervis, eds., *Handbook of Political Psychology* (New York: Oxford University Press, forthcoming).

139. See Holstein to Radolin, 20 July 1905, no. 903, *Holstein Papers*, vol. 4, 354–56.

140. Holstein to Bülow, 21 July 1905, *GP*, vol. 19, no. 2, 436–39; and Rich, *Friedrich von Holstein*, vol. 2, 714.

141. Bülow to Holstein, 20 July 1905, *GP*, vol. 19, no. 2, 435–36; and Rich, *Friedrich von Holstein*, vol. 2, 714–15.

142. See Holstein to Bülow, 21–24 July 1905, no. 6203–14, *GP*, vol. 19, no. 2, 436–39.

143. Rich, *Friedrich von Holstein*, vol. 2, 715.

144. Tschirschky and the Grand Duke Michael (Mikhail Alexandrovich), the tsar's brother, were also present at the Björkö meeting and countersigned the draft treaty. See Bülow to the Reich Foreign Office, no. 6217, *GP*, vol. 19, no. 1, 453.

145. Accounts of the Björkö meeting include, Wilhelm II to Bülow, 25 July 1905, no. 6220, *GP*, vol. 19, no. 1, 458–59; and Tschirschky to Bülow, 24 July 1905, no. 6218, ibid., 454.

146. See Lerman, *Chancellor as Courtier*, 128–29; and Rich, *Friedrich von Holstein*, vol. 2, 716–17.

147. Memo by Holstein, 31 July 1905, no. 904, *Holstein Papers*, vol. 4, 356–58.

148. Anderson, *First Morocco Crisis*, 294–95.

149. See ibid., 300–304 and Kennedy, *Rise of Anglo-German Antagonism*, 281.

150. Nicholas II to Wilhelm II, 7 October 1905, *GP*, vol. 19, no. 2, 512–13; Witte to Eulenburg, 8 October 1905, ibid., 514.

151. Nicholas II to Wilhelm II, 26 November 1905, no. 6254, *GP*, vol. 19, 522.

152. Interview of Bülow by M. Tardieu, published in *Le Temps*, 3 October 1905, quoted in Anderson, *First Morocco Crisis*, 275.

153. Lascelles to Lansdowne, 15, 16, and 20 October 1905, nos. 102–4, *BD*, vol. 3, 102–5; Metternich to the Reich Foreign Office, 9 October 1905, no. 6873, *GP*, vol. 20, no. 1, 663–64; Bülow to the Reich Foreign Office, 10 and 12 October, nos. 6874 and 6875, ibid., 664–65.

154. Bülow to the Reich Foreign Office, 14 October 1905, no. 6876, *GP*, vol. 20, no. 1, 666.

155. Bülow to the Reich Foreign Office, 15 October 1905, no. 6877, ibid., 667.

156. Holstein to Maximilian von Brandt, 14 November 1905, no. 915, *Holstein Papers*, vol. 4, 375.

157. See Memo by Mühlberg, 30 November 1905, no. 6906, *GP*, vol. 21, 20. Also, see S. L. Meyer, "Anglo-German Rivalry at the Algeciras Conference," in *Britain and Germany in Africa*, 215–44, at 221; and Anderson, *First Morocco Crisis*, 311–12. The intermediaries were M. Vaffier-Pollet, a representative of the Committee on Morocco in Tangiers, and the Comte de Chérisey, former secretary of the French legation in Tangiers.

158. Memo by Bülow, 23 November, no. 6900, *GP*, vol. 21, 14.

159. Holstein to Radowitz and Tattenbach, 1 December 1905, cited in Meyer, "Anglo-German Rivalry," 222.

160. Metternich to Bülow, 2 November 1905, no. 6881, *GP*, vol. 20, no. 2, 625–26; Bülow to Wilhelm II, 3 December 1905, no. 6882, ibid., 679–81; Metternich to the Reich Foreign Office, 4 December 1905, no. 6883, ibid., 681–82; and Bülow to Metternich, 5 December 1905, no. 6885, ibid., 683–84.

161. Holstein to Bülow, January 1906 (no day given), no. 919, ibid., 379.

162. Holstein to Radowitz (and also Tattenbach), 16 January 1906, no. 926, ibid., 387–88 and Holstein to Sternberg, 14 January 1906, no. 925, ibid., 386–87. In the 1906 general election, Campbell-Bannerman's Liberal Party won 399 of the 666 seats in the House of Commons.

163. Radolin to Holstein, 28 January, no. 928 and enclosure: Tschirschky to Radolin, 26 January 1906, *Holstein Papers*, vol. 4, 390–91.

164. See Kennedy, *Rise of Anglo-German Antagonism*, 283.

165. Metternich to Bülow, 3 January 1906, XXI, no. 45, *GDD*, vol. 3, 326.

166. See Williamson, *Politics of Grand Strategy*, 72–77; and Kennedy, *Rise of Anglo-German Antagonism*, 283.

167. Williamson, *Politics of Grand Strategy*, 72–77; and Monger, *End of Isolation*, 96–197, 206, 267, and 276–77.

168. Report by Schulenburg, 31 January 1906, XXI, no. 83, *GDD*, vol. 3, 241–42.

169. Metternich to the Reich Foreign Office, 20 February 1906, XXI, no. 187, ibid., 243–45.

170. Moltke to Bülow, 23 January 1906, XXI, no. 74, ibid., 238–39.

171. Moltke to Bülow, 23 February 1906, XXI, no. 525, ibid., 239–40.

172. Bülow to Monts, 13 February 1906, no. 7000, *GP*, vol. 21, 159–60; and Bülow to Sternburg, 14 February 1906, no. 7005, ibid., 164–65.

173. Rich, *Friedrich von Holstein*, 736. The Rouvier government fell on 7 March 1906, after a contentious debate in the National Assembly over church-state relations. Jean Marie Ferdinand Sarrien formed a government on 14 March and served as premier until 20 October 1906.

174. Wilhelm II to Bülow, 11 February 1906, no. 933, *Holstein Papers*, vol. 4, 395.

175. Memo by Holstein, 22 February 1906, ibid., 396.

176. Holstein to Radolin, 7 February 1906, no. 931, *Holstein Papers*, vol. 4, 392–93.

177. Sternburg to the Reich Foreign Office, 7 March 1906, XXI, no. 259, *GDD*, vol. 3, 244–45.

178. See Sternburg to the Reich Foreign Office, 18 March 1906, XXI, no. 302, ibid., 246–47.

179. Schön to Reich Foreign Office, 20 February 1906, no. 7025, *GP*, vol. 21, 192; and Count Philip zu Eulenberg to Wilhelm II, 22 February 1906, no. 7027, ibid., 194. See also, Rich, *Friedrich von Holstein*, 736; and Sergei Witte, *The Memoirs of Count Witte*, trans. and ed. Abraham Yarmolinsky (Garden City, N.J.: Doubleday, Page, 1921), 414.

180. See Schön to the Reich Foreign Office, 23 February 1906, no. 7037, *GP*, vol. 21, 211–12; and Cecil Spring-Rice, second secretary of the British embassy in Berlin, to Sir Edward Grey, 24 February 1906, no. 308, *BD*, vol. 3, 271–72. See also Anderson, *First Morocco Crisis*, 368–69; Witte, *Memoirs*, 301; and Rich, *Friedrich von Holstein*, 736.

181. Quoted in, Richard Bosworth, *Italy and the Approach of the First World War* (London: Macmillan, 1983), 65.

182. Wedel to the Reich Foreign Office, 5 February 1906, XXI, no. 140, *GDD*, vol. 3, 243.

183. See Wedel to Bülow, 12 February 1906, cited in Oswald Henry Wedel, *Austro-German Diplomatic Relations, 1908–1914* (Stanford, Calif.: Stanford University Press, 1932), 37.

184. Rich, *Friedrich von Holstein*, 738–39.

185. See Memo by Holstein, 29 March 1906, no. 948, *Holstein Papers*, vol. 4, 404.

186. See Memo by Holstein (undated), no. 7059, *GP*, vol. 21, no. 1, 240–41; *Holstein Papers*, 405, fn. 1; and Rich, *Friedrich von Holstein*, 740–41. See, also Wilhelm II to Roosevelt, 12 March 1906, *GP*, vol. 21, no. 2, 276–78; Sternburg to the Reich Foreign Office, 18 March 1906, XXI, no. 302, *GDD*, vol. 3, 246–47 and Bülow to Sternburg, 19 March 1906, XXI, no. 309, ibid., 247–48.

CHAPTER 4. JAPAN AND THE 1940–41 WAR DECISIONS

1. See John J. Mearsheimer, *Tragedy of Great Power Politics* (New York: W. W. Norton, 2001), 180–81 and 219–20.

2. Ibid., 221.

3. Ibid., 219.

4. See Scott D. Sagan, "The Origins of the Pacific War," in *Origins and Prevention of Major Wars*, ed. Robert I. Rotberg and Theodore K. Rabb (New York: Cambridge University Press, 1989), 323–52; idem, "Deterrence and Decision: A Historical Critique of Modern Deterrence Theory," Ph.D. diss., Harvard University, 1983; and Mearsheimer, *Tragedy of Great Power Politics*, 223–24.

5. See Jack Snyder, *Myths of Empire: Domestic Politics and International Ambition* (Ithaca: Cornell University Press, 1991), 150. For similar arguments see, Michael A. Barnhart, *Japan Prepares for Total War: The Search for Economic Security, 1919–1941* (Ithaca: Cornell University Press, 1987); and Herbert Feis, *Road to Pearl Harbor* (Princeton: Princeton University Press, 1950).

6. Charles A. Kupchan originally raised these points about logrolling theory and Japan's 1940–41 war decisions. See, Kupchan, *Vulnerability of Empire* (Ithaca: Cornell University Press, 1995), 354–57.

7. For a discussion of the army factions in the 1930s, see James B. Crowley, "Japanese Army Factionalism in the Early 1930s," *Journal of Asian Studies* 21, no. 3 (May 1962): 309–26; Mark R. Peattie, *Ishiwara Kanji and Japan's Confrontation with the West* (Princeton: Princeton University Press, 1975), 223–65; and Shin'inchi Kitaoka, "The Army as Bureaucracy: Japanese Militarism Revisited," *Journal of Military History* 57, no. 5 (October 1993): 67–86.

8. See Kobayashi Tatsuo, "The London Naval Treaty, 1930," in *Japan Erupts: The London Naval Conference and the Manchurian Incident, 1928–1932*, ed. James William Morely, trans. Arthur E. Tiedemann (New York: Columbia University Pres, 1984), 11–118; and Ben-Ami Shillony, *Revolt in Japan: The Young Officers and the February 26, 1936 Incident* (Princeton: Princeton University, 1973), 135–42.

9. See, for example, Yale Maxon, *Control of Japanese Foreign Policy: A Study of Civil-Military Relations, 1930–1950* (Westport, Conn.: Greenwood Press, 1973), 19–21, and 98–112; James Crowley, *Japan's Quest for Autonomy* (Princeton: Princeton University Press, 1966); Saburo Ienaga, *The Pacific War, 1931–1945*, trans. Frank Baldwin (New York: Pantheon Books, 1978); and Kurt Dassel, "Civilians, Soldiers and Strife: Domestic Sources of International Aggression," *International Security* 23, no. 1 (summer 1998): 107–40, esp. 133–36.

10. At the time, Prince Chichibu (Chichibu no miya Yasuhito Shinnō) was third in line to the throne, behind two-year-old Crown Prince Akihito and six-month-old Prince Masahito (now titled Prince Hitachi). Two of the emperor's uncles, Prince Asaka Yasuhiko and his half-brother Prince Higashikuni Naruhiko, both active-duty generals, also had ties to the *Kōdō*. See Shillony, *Revolt in Japan*, 150–60; and

idem, "The February 26 Affairs: Politics of a Military Insurrection," in *Crisis Politics in Prewar Japan: Institutional and Ideological Problems of the 1930s*, ed. George M. Wilson (Tokyo: Sophia University, 1970), 34–36; and Stephen S. Large, *Emperor Hirohito and Shōwa Japan: A Political Biography* (New York: Routledge, 1992), 64–75.

11. See Crowley, "Japanese Army Factionalism," 323–25; Crowley, *Japan's Quest for Autonomy*, 273–74; and Large, *Emperor Hirohito and Shōwa Japan*, 78.

12. Manchuria, which comprises the northeastern provinces of China—Liaoning, Kirin, and Heilungkiang, is the homeland of the Manchu people and the Qing (or Ch'ing) dynasty that ruled China from 1643 to 1912.

13. On the origins of "total war" planning in the Japanese military, see Barnhart, *Japan Prepares for Total War*, 22–49; and Peattie, *Ishiwara Kanji*, 223–65.

14. For an overview of the field organization of the Imperial Japanese Army, see U.S. War Department, *Handbook on Japanese Military Forces* (Baton Rouge: University of Louisiana Press, 1995), 16–52. The Kwantung Army was an army group or theater command created in 1919 out of soldiers already stationed in southern Manchuria. See Alvin D. Coox, *Nomonhan: Japan Against Russia, 1939*, vol. 1 (Stanford: Stanford University Press, 1985), 1–17.

15. See Maxon, *Control of Japanese Foreign Policy*, 61–62; Large, *Emperor Hirohito and Shōwa Japan*, 8–9; and Tomoko Masuda, "The Emperor's Right of Supreme Command as Exercised up to 1930: A Study Based Especially on the Takarabe and Kuratomi Diaries," *Acta Asiatica* 59 (1990): 77–100.

16. On the economic development of Manchukuo see, Peter Liberman, *Does Conquest Pay? The Exploitation of Occupied Industrialized Societies* (Princeton: Princeton University Press, 1996), 103–11; Katsuji Nakagone, "Manchukuo and Economic Development," in *Japanese Informal Empire in China, 1895–1937*, ed. Peter Duus, Ramon H. Myers, and Mark R. Peattie (Princeton: Princeton University Press, 1989), 133–57; and Ramon H. Myers, *Japanese Economic Development of Manchuria, 1932–1945* (1959; New York: Garland, 1982).

17. For an analysis of the "north China autonomy" movement see Shimada Toshihiko, "Designs on North China," in *The China Quagmire: Japan's Expansion on the Asian Continent, 1933–1941*, ed. James William Morely (New York: Columbia University Press, 1983), 135–56.

18. See Hata Ikuhiko, "The Marco Polo Bridge Incident, 1937," in *China Quagmire*, 245–46, fn. 2; and James B. Crowley, "A Reconsideration of the Marco Polo Bridge Incident," *Journal of Asian Studies* 22, no. 3 (May 1963): 277–91.

19. See Crowley, *Japan's Quest for Autonomy*, 353. Konoe Fumimaro served three terms as prime minister: 4 June 1937 to 5 January 1939, 22 July 1940 to 18 July 1941 and 18 July to 18 October 1941. Konoe, who held the rank of a nonimperial prince or duke (*koshaku*) in the Japanese peerage, was heir to one of five branches of the Fujiwara clan (Konoe, Kujō, Takatsukasa, Ichijō, and Nijō) that held the offices of chancellor (*kwampuko*) and regent (*sesshō*) in the imperial court and that provided the principal consorts of emperors from the tenth century until the Shōwa period. See Gordon M. Berger, "Japan's Young Prince: Konoe Fumimaro's Early Political Career, 1918–1931," *Monumenta Nipponica* 29, no. 4 (winter 1974): 451–75.

20. See Hata, "Marco Polo Bridge Incident," 248–52. Sugiyama Gen (or Hajime) served as war minister from 4 June 1937 to 4 June 1938 and again from 30 June 1944 to 14 August 1945. He served as the chief of the Army General Staff from 3 October 1940 to 21 February 1944. Prince Kan'in Kotohito (Kan'in no miya Kotohito Shinnō), the great uncle to both Emperor Shōwa and his consort, Empress Kojun (Nagako) and head of one of four senior cadet branch of the imperial family (Fushimi no miya, Arisugawa no miya, Katsura no miya, and Kan'in no miya), served as the

chief of the Army General Staff from 5 November 1931 to 3 October 1940. See Foreign Affairs Association of Japan, *Japan Year Book: 1940–41* (Tokyo: Japan Times Press, 1940), 1–14; and Ben-Ami Shillony, *Politics and Culture in Wartime Japan* (Oxford: Clarendon Press, 1981), 38–40 and 187, fn. 88.

21. See Barnhart, *Japan Prepares for Total War*, 84–87. In August 1937, Ishiwara estimated that the army needed to mobilize thirty divisions: six divisions for deployment to China, nineteen divisions for defense against the Soviets, and five reserve divisions stationed in Japan. On the Ishiwara report, see Hata, "The Marco Polo Bridge Incident," in *China Quagmire*, 454–55.

22. See Barnhart, *Japan Prepares for Total War*, 95; and Gordon M. Burger, *Parties out of Power in Japan, 1931–1941* (Princeton: Princeton University Press, 1977), 140–41.

23. Imperial General Headquarters (*Daihon'ei*), consisting of the chiefs and vice-chiefs of the two services, the war and navy ministers, and the inspector-general of military training, had overall responsibility for military planning and command of the armed forces in wartime. Theoretically, IGHQ centralized the emperor's supreme command authority. In reality, it consisted of two independent command authorities—the army section and the navy section—under the control of the two chiefs of staff. See Takushiro Hattori and Katsuhei Nakamura, "The Organization of the Army and Navy High Command at the Time the Pacific War Began," 3 December 1947, doc. No. 50724, Military Intelligence Section, General Headquarters, U.S. Far East Command, *War in Asia and the Pacific*, vol. 3, Center for Military History, Department of the Army and the National Archives, ed. Donald S. Detwiller and Charles B. Burdick (New York and London: Garland Press, 1980), 56–59 [hereafter cited as *WIAP*]; and Hata, "Marco Polo Bridge Incident," 269–72.

24. See David J. Lu, *From the Marco Polo Bridge to Pearl Harbor: Japan's Entry into World War II* (Washington, D.C.: Public Affairs Press, 1961), 8–12; and Large, *Emperor Hirohito and Shōwa Japan*, 78.

25. Coox, *Nomonhan*, vol. 1, 84, table 7.1.

26. Alvin D. Coox, "Effects of Attrition on National War Effort: The Japanese Army Experience in China, 1937–38," *Military Affairs* 32, no. 2 (October 1968): 57–62, at 58–60.

27. Ibid., 57.

28. Hugh Patrick, "The Economic Muddle of the 1920s," in *Dilemmas of Growth in Prewar Japan*, ed. James William Morely (Princeton: Princeton University Press, 1971), 251.

29. For an analysis of the Japanese government's financing of the China incident (1937–41) and later the Second World War (1941–45), see Shinju Fujihira, "Conscripting Money: War Finance and Fiscal Revolution in the Twentieth Century," Ph.D., diss., Princeton University, 2000, chap. 5.

30. See Barnhart, "Japan Prepares for Total War," 109–10.

31. Katsumi Usui, "The Politics of War, 1937–1941," in *China Quagmire*, 364.

32. See Memo by Secretary of State Cordell Hull, 13 July 1937; Japanese foreign minister Hirota Koki to the U.S. ambassador in Tokyo, Joseph Grew, 31 August 1937 in U.S. Department of State, *Foreign Relations of the United States: Japan, 1931–1941*, vol. 1 (Washington, D.C.: GPO, 1943), 318–21, and 358 [Hereafter, cited as *FRUS, Japan*].

33. These figures come from Usui, "Politics of War," 338.

34. Grew to Hull, 2 December 1937; Press Release by the Department of State, 28 January 1937; Grew to Hirota, February 4, 1938; and Hirota to Grew, 12 February 1938, *FRUS, Japan*, vol. 1, 570–73, 578–82.

35. See Hull to Horinouchi Kensuke, 26 July 1939 in Department of State, *Foreign of the United States, 1939,* vol. 3 (Washington, D.C.: GPO, 1955), 558–59 [Hereafter, cited as *FRUS*]. Mearheimer's account greatly understates the degree of American diplomatic and economic pressure exerted on Japan from June 1938 onward. See, Mearsheimer, *Tragedy of Great Power Politics,* 222–23.

36. Army Military History Group, "China Area Operations Record, July 1937–November 1941," *WIAP,* vol. 8.

37. W. G. Beasley states that the term "Greater East Asia Co-prosperity Sphere" first appeared in a Japanese Foreign Ministry press release dated 1 August 1940. See Beasley, *Japanese Imperialism, 1894–1945* (Cambridge: Harvard University Press, 1991), 227. Since Japanese planning documents (particularly after 1939) used the terms "Greater East Asia Co-prosperity Sphere" and "New Order in East Asia" interchangeably, I have chosen to use the latter term here.

38. For an analysis of Wang Ching-wei's defection from the KMT in December 1938 and the Japanese role in establishing him as the premier of the "Reorganized National Government of China" in April 1940, see Usui, "Politics of War," in *China Quagmire,* 379–406; and John Hunter Boyle, "The Road to Sino-Japanese Collaboration: Background to the Defection of Wang Ching-wei," *Monumenta Nipponica* 25, no. 3/4 (1970): 267–301.

39. See Statement by the Japanese Government, 3 November 1938, U.S. Department of State, *FRUS, Japan,* 11–12.

40. "General Principles to Cope with the Changing World Situation," 27 July 1940, reprinted in Appendix No. 2, "Political Strategy Prior to Outbreak of War," Part 2, *WIAP,* vol. 8, 42–45. Konoe, Tōjō, Matsouka, and Yoshida privately agreed to make the conclusion of an alliance with Germany the top priority of the new cabinet. This meeting, held at Konoe's residence at Ogikubo on 19 July, also agreed to conclude a nonaggression pact with the Soviet Union, thus enabling Japan to expand into Southeast Asia. See Hosoya Chihiro, "The Tripartite Pact, 1939–1940," in *Deterrent Diplomacy: Japan, Germany, and the USSR, 1935–1940,* ed. James William Morely (New York: Columbia University Press, 1976), 216–19.

41. For the text of the army proposed draft of "Principles to Cope with the Changing World Situation," see Army History Group, "Political Situation Prior to War" Part 2, *WIAP,* vol. 2, 14

42. Tsunoda Jun, "The Navy's Role in the Southern Strategy," in *Fateful Choice: Japan's Advance into Southeast Asia, 1939–1941,* ed. James William Morely (New York: Columbia University Press, 1980), 248.

43. Army History Group, "Political Situation Prior to War" Part 2, *WIAP,* vol. 2, 14

44. See, Tsunoda, "The Navy's Role in the Southern Strategy," 246.

45. Ibid., 245.

46. Ibid., 246, emphasis added.

47. Ibid., 245–46. Yoshida was the one hold over from the cabinet of Hiranuma Kiichirō.

48. Ibid., 257. Prince Fushimi Hiroyasu (Fushimi no miya Hiroyasu Shinnō) was a nephew of Prince Kan'in Kotohito, a distant cousin of the emperor, and the head of another senior cadet branch of the imperial family. One of his daughters was married to the eldest brother of Empress Kojun, Prince Kuni Asaakira (Kuni no miya Asaakira ō). For a discussion of the role of imperial princes in the prewar Japanese military, see Stephen S. Large, "Emperor Hirohito and Early Shōwa Japan," *Monumenta Nipponica* 46, no. 3 (autumn 1991): 349–68; idem, "Imperial Princes and Court Politics in Early Shōwa Japan," *Japan Forum* 1, no. 2 (October 1989): 257–64.

49. See the entry for 10 August 1940 in Kōichi Kido, *Diary of Marquis Kido, 1931–45*, vol. 2 (Frederick, Md.: University Publications of America, 1984), 814. Imperial conferences or conferences in the emperor's presence (*Gozen Kaigi*) were largely ceremonial gatherings at the Imperial Palace, convened to legitimate major decisions already reached by the cabinet-IGHQ liaison conferences. See Robert J. C. Butow, *Tōjō and the Coming of War* (Stanford, Calif.: Stanford University Press, 1969), 170–71; Lu, *From the Marco Polo Bridge to Pearl Harbor*, 8–12; and Large, *Emperor Hirohito and Shōwa Japan*, 78.

50. See the minutes of the imperial conference, 19 September 1940, in Nobutaka Ike, trans. and ed. *Japan's Decisions for War: Records of the 1941 Policy Conferences* (Stanford: Stanford University Press, 1967), 6–8.

51. Quoted in Tsunoda Jun, "The Navy's Role in the Southern Strategy," 256.

52. See Nagaoka Shinjioro, "Economic Demands the Dutch East Indies," in *Fateful Choice*, 145.

53. Statement to the press by Secretary of State Hull, 17 April 1940; Diplomatic interviews at the Japanese Foreign Ministry, May 1940, reprinted in *Documents on American Foreign Policy, July 1939–June 1940*, ed. S. Shepard Jones and Denys S. Meyers (Boston: World Peace Foundation, 1948), 305–6.

54. Hull to Grew, 30 May 1940 and Grew to Hull, 3 June 1940 in *FRUS, 1940*, vol. 4, 334–42. Also see Robert J. Quinlin, "The United States Fleet: Diplomacy, Strategy and the Allocation of Ships (1940–1941)," in *American Civil-Military Decisions*, ed. Harold Stein (Birmingham: University of Alabama Press, 1963), 158.

55. "Press Release by the White House," 31 July 1939; "Japanese Embassy to the Department of State," 3 August 1939, *FRUS: Japan*, vol. 2, 218–220. See also Lu, *From the Marco Polo Bridge to Pearl Harbor*, 149.

56. Hosoya, "Tripartite Pact," 208–9.

57. For the details of these negotiations, see Nagaoka Shinjiro, "Economic Demands and the Dutch East Indies," in *Fateful Choice*, trans. Scalapino, 209–40.

58. See "Principles for Negotiations with the Dutch East Indies," approved by the Konoe cabinet on 27 August 1940; Quoted in Nagaoka, "Economic Demands on the Dutch East Indies," 143–44.

59. Quoted in Hosoya "Tripartite Pact," 248.

60. On the planning board outline, see Barnhart, *Japan Prepares for Total War*, 165.

61. Irvine H. Anderson, Jr., *The Standard-Vacuum Oil Company and United States East Asian Policy, 1933–1941* (Princeton: Princeton University, 1975), 150–54; Nagaoka, "Economic Demands on the Dutch East Indies," 144–45; and Barnhart, *Japan Prepares for Total War*, 166–67.

62. Hata Ikuhiko, "The Army's Move into Northern Indochina," in *Fateful Choice*, 155–208.

63. See "Appendix 2: The Matsouka-Henry [sic] Pact, 30 August 1940," ibid., 301–2.

64. Statements by Grew to the Japanese foreign minister, Matsouka, 19 September 1940 and Hull to Grew, 19 September 1940 in *FRUS: Japan*, vol. 2, 295–97.

65. Army History Group, "Political Situation Prior to War" Part 2., *WIAP*, vol. 2, 14; Also see Butow, *Tojo and the Coming of War*, 152–53.

66. Hosoya Chihiro, "The Tripartite Pact, 1939–1940," in *Deterrent Diplomacy: Japan, Germany, and the USSR, 1935–1940*, ed. James William Morely (New York: Columbia University Press, 1976), 191–212. Abe was prime minister from 30 August 1939 to 16 January 1940. Yonai held the post from 16 January to 22 July 1940.

67. Appendix no. 7, Tripartite Alliance of Germany, Italy, and Japan and Accompanying Notes, 27 September 1940, in *Deterrent Diplomacy*, 298–305.

68. Statement by Konoe to the Investigation Committee of the Privy Council, 26 September 1940, in "Political Strategy Prior to the Outbreak of the War," Part 2, *WIAP*, vol. 2, 25.

69. Imperial Conference, 9 September 1940, Japan's Decisions for War, 12–13. Also see Tōjō's affidavit in Supreme Commander for the Allied Powers, *Court Papers, Exhibits, Interrogations, Trial Transcripts and Judgments of the International Military Tribunal for the Far East, 1946–1948* (Washington, D.C.: GPO, 1948), S 342: 15; T 36194–95 (hereafter cited as *IMTFE*)

70. Liaison Conference, 14 September 1940 quoted in Hosoya, "The Tripartite Pact," 239 (emphasis added).

71. See Appendix no. 5, "Notes on Conference with Admiral T. Takata, former chief of the First Section, Naval Affairs Bureau, 17 February 1953" and "Notes on Conference with Admiral Kondo, former deputy chief of the Naval General Staff, 17 February 1953," in "Political Strategy Prior to the Outbreak of War," Part II, *WIAP*, vol. 2.

72. Imperial Conference, 19 September 1940, *Japan's Decisions for War*, 5.

73. Hosoya, "Tripartite Pact," 248.

74. Prince Fushimi's statement to the liaison conference, quoted in "Political Strategy Prior to the Outbreak of War," Part II, *WIAP*, vol. 2.

75. Kondo's remarks quoted in "Political Strategy Prior to Outbreak of War," Part II in *WIAP*, vol. 2.

76. Quoted in Hosoya, "Tripartite Pact," 249 (emphasis in original).

77. On Yoshida's opposition to the Tripartite Pact and his forced resignation as navy minister, see Tsunoda, "The Navy's Role in the Southern Strategy," in *Fateful Choice*, 263–65; and Barnhart, *Japan Prepares for Total War*, 167.

78. Imperial Conference, 19 September 1940, *Japan's Decisions for War*, 6.

79. See Barnhart, *Japan Prepares for Total War*, 195–96.

80. Akira Iriye, *Across the Pacific: An Inner History of American–East Asian Relations* (New York: Harcourt Brace Jovanovich, 1967), 201–10.

81. See Barnhart, *Japan Prepares for Total War*, 168.

82. 'hata Tokushirō, "The Anti-Comintern Pact," in *Deterrent Diplomacy*, ed. Morely, trans. Hans H. Baerwald, 74–75.

83. In addition to General Abe, the military officers in the cabinet were the war minister, General Shunroku Hata; the navy minister, Vice Admiral Yoshida Zengo; and the foreign minister, Admiral Nomura Kichiasburō.

84. See Hosoya, "Tripartite Pact," 237, and 240–41.

85. See "Text of Semi-Official Communication from Foreign Minister Matsouka to Foreign Commissar Molotov," 13 April 1941, in *Fateful Choice*, 299–300.

86. Quoted in Hosoya, "Tripartite Pact," 248.

87. Hosoya Chihiro, "The Japanese-Soviet Neutrality Pact," in *Fateful Choice*, 67–69.

88. On the preventive war motivations for Hitler's invasion of the Soviet Union, see Dale C. Copeland, *Origins of Major War* (Ithaca: Cornell University Press, 2000), 139–43, and Stephen Van Evera, *Causes of War: Power and the Roots of Conflict* (Ithaca: Cornell University Press, 1999), 94–99.

89. See Hosoya, "Japanese-Soviet Neutrality Pact," 69.

90. See Gorodetsky, *Grand Delusion: Stalin and the German Invasion of Russia* (New Haven: Yale University Press, 1999), 196–97.

91. See Matsouka-Ribbentrop conference, 27 March 1941 in *IMTFE* Records, exhibits 578–80; Gabriel Gorodetsky, *Grand Delusion*, 194; and Tsunoda Jun, "Leaning Toward War," in *The Final Confrontation: Japan's Negotiations with the United States,*

1941, ed. James William Morely and trans. David A. Titus (New York: Columbia University Press, 1994), 123–24.

92. See Hosoya, "Japan-Soviet Neutrality Pact," 75–76. See also G. Krebs, "Japan and the German-Soviet War, 1941," in *From Peace to War: Germany, Soviet Russia, and the World, 1939–41*, ed. B. Wegner (Oxford: Oxford University Press, 1997), 554–56.

93. See Hosoya, "Japan-Soviet Neutrality Pact," 68–69.

94. Matsouka to Molotov, 13 April 1941, quoted in Hosoya, "Japan-Soviet Neutrality Pact," 79.

95. Mearsheimer, *Tragedy of Great Power Politics*, 221–22.

96. American Draft Proposal handed to the Japanese ambassador (Nomura), 31 May 1941, *FRUS: Japan*, vol. 2, 446–54.

97. Nagaoka, "Economic Demands and the Dutch East Indies," in *Fateful Choice*, 151–53.

98. Twenty-ninth Liaison Conference, 11 June 1941, *Japan's Decisions for War*, 50–51.

99. Thirty-second Liaison Conference, 25 June 1941, *Japan's Decisions for War*, 58. See, also Matsouka's report to the emperor, 22 June 1941, quoted in Tsunoda, "Leaning toward War," in *Final Confrontation*, 136.

100. Thirty-fourth Liaison Conference, 27 June 1941, *Japan's Decisions for War*, 66.

101. Imperial Conference, 2 July 1941, ibid., 88.

102. Thirty-fourth Liaison Conference, 27 June 1941, ibid., 67.

103. Thirty-third Liaison Conference, 26 June 1941, ibid., 62

104. Imperial Conference, 2 July 1941, ibid., 90. Also, see Coox, *Nomonhan*, vol. 2, 1039–40.

105. Thirty-second Liaison Conference, 25 June 1941, *Japan's Decisions for War*, 59.

106. Ibid., 59.

107. See statement by Navy Chief of Staff Nagano, Imperial Conference, 2 July 1941, ibid., 81.

108. Michael A. Barnhart, "Japanese Intelligence before the Second World War: 'Best Case' Analysis," in *Knowing One's Enemies: Intelligence Assessments before the two World Wars*, ed. Ernest R. May (Princeton: Princeton University Press, 1984), 438–39.

109. See Hata Ikuhiko, "The Japanese-Soviet Confrontation," in *Deterrent Diplomacy*, ed. Morely, trans. Alvin D. Coox, 177–78.

110. See Lu, *From the Marco Polo Bridge to Pearl Harbor*, 106.

111. Cited in Tsunoda, "Leaning Toward War," 159.

112. See Statement by Acting Secretary of State Sumner Welles, 24 July 1941, *Department of State Bulletin*, vol. V (Washington D.C.: GPO, 1941), 71.

113. Quoted in Tsunoda, "Leaning Toward War," 142.

114. Cited in Tsunoda, "Navy's Role in the Southern Strategy," 294.

115. Ibid., 292.

116. Ibid., 254.

117. Thirty-Seventh Liaison Conference, 1 July 1941, *Japan's Decisions for War*, 76–77.

118. Imperial Conference, 2 July 1941, ibid., 94.

119. Ibid., 94.

120. Ibid., 95.

121. See Butow, *Tojo and the Coming of War*, 230–33.

122. Fortieth Liaison Conference, 21 July 1941, *Japan's Decisions for War*, 106.

123. See "Essentials for Carrying Out the Empire's Policies," Imperial Conference, 6 September 1941, *Japan's Decisions for War*, 135.

124. John J. Mearsheimer, *Conventional Deterrence* (Ithaca: Cornell University Press, 1983), 14–15 and 23–24. He writes, "Actually the attacker's aim at the conventional level is not merely success but also rapid achievement of objectives on the battlefield. Short conventional wars are more desirable than lengthy ones because the former generally entail lower costs." Although Mearsheimer claims his theory only applies to conventional battlefield operations, the underlying logic of his argument should apply to conventional naval and air warfare as well.

125. Forty-sixth Liaison Conference, 14 August 1941, *Japan's Decisions for War*, 120, and Forty-Ninth Liaison Conference, 30 August 1941, ibid., 127.

126. Fortieth Liaison Conference, 21 July 1941, ibid., 105.

127. Twenty-second Liaison Conference, 8 May 1941, ibid., 30.

128. Imperial Conference, 6 September 1941, ibid., 153.

129. Ibid., 153.

130. Ibid., 148. For a discussion of the army's purge of the planning board and Hoshino's forced resignation on 4 April 1941, see Barnhart, *Japan Prepares for Total War*, 200–201. The purge also resulted in the resignation of Kobayashi as commerce and industry minister on 4 April and his replacement by Toyoda.

131. Imperial Conference, 6 September 1941, *Japan's Decisions for War*, 139 (emphasis mine).

132. See Grew to Toyoda, 10 October 1941 and Hull to Nomura, 9 October 1941, *FRUS, Japan*, vol. 2, 677 and 270.

133. For the circumstances surrounding Konoe's resignation see IPS Doc. no. 497, "Facts Pertaining to the Resignation of the Third Konoe Cabinet," *IMTFE*, Reel WT9; "Memoirs of Prince Konoe," in U.S. Congress, *Joint Committee on the Pearl Harbor Attack: Hearings*, Pt. 20, Exhibit no. 173 (Washington, D.C.: GPO, 1946), 3985–4029; Butow, *Tojo and the Coming of War*, 285–90; and Kido, *The Diary of Marquis Kido*, 312–13.

134. See "Essentials for Carrying out the Empire's Policies," approved by the Imperial Conference, 6 September 1941, *Japan's Decisions for War*, 135.

135. The list of questions appear in the minutes from the sixtieth and sixty-first Liaison Conferences, 24 and 25 October 1941, *Japan's Decisions for War*, 187–96.

136. Fifty-ninth Liaison Conference, 23 October 1941, ibid., 186.

137. Sixty-second Liaison Conference, 27 October 1941, ibid., 191.

138. Sixty-third Liaison Conference, 28 October 1941, ibid., 192.

139. Ibid., 191.

140. Sixty-sixth Liaison Conference, 1 November 1941, ibid., 201–2. Also, see Tsunoda Jun, "The Decision for War," in *Final Confrontation*, 168.

141. Sixty-sixth Liaison Conference, 1 November 1941, *Japan's Decisions for War*, 202.

142. Quoted in Tsunoda, "The Decision for War," in *Final Confrontation*, 258.

143. Sixty-sixth Liaison Conference, 1 November 1941, *Japan's Decisions for War*, 203.

144. Ibid., 207.

145. Ibid., 204.

146. For the text of proposals A and B see Imperial Conference, 5 November 1941, ibid., 209 and IPS, "Proposals A and B," 7 November 1941, *IMTFE*, Exhibit 770.

147. Sixty-sixth Liaison Conference, 1 November 1941, *Japan's Decisions for War*, 205.

148. Tsunoda, "The Decision for War," in *Japan's Road to Pearl Harbor*, 329–30.

149. Hull to Nomura, 7 November 1941, *FRUS, Japan*, vol. 2, 706–10.

150. Sixty-sixth Liaison Conference, 15 November 1941, 245 and Hull to Nomura, 15 November 1941, *FRUS, Japan*, vol. 2, 731–37.

151. Oral Statement handed by Hull to Nomura, 26 November 1941, *FRUS, Japan*, vol. 2, 766–68; Hull to Nomura, 26 November 1941, ibid., 787–92.

152. Statement by Prime Minister Tōjō, Imperial Conference, 1 December 1941, quoted in Tsunoda, "The Decision for War," 321.

Chapter 5. The United States and the Korean War (1950–51)

1. See John Lewis Gaddis, *Strategies of Containment: A Critical Appraisal of American Postwar National Security Policy* (New York: Oxford University Press, 1981), chap. 3; idem, *The Long Peace: Inquires into the History of the Cold War* (New York: Oxford University Press, 1989), esp. 72–103 and 147–95; Robert Jervis, "The Impact of the Korean War on the Cold War," *Journal of Conflict Resolution* 24, no. 4 (December 1980): 563–92; and Aaron L. Friedberg, *In the Shadow of the Garrison State: America's Anti-Statism and its Cold War Grand Strategy* (Princeton: Princeton University, 2000), 115–24.

2. See Eric J. Labs, "Beyond Victory: Offensive Realism and the Expansion of War Aims," *Security Studies* 6, no. 4 (summer 1997): 1–49, esp. 34–39; and idem, "Fighting for More: The Sources of Expanding War Aims," Ph.D. diss., Massachusetts Institute of Technology, 1994, 205–55.

3. Jack Snyder, *Myths of Empire: Domestic Politics and International Ambition* (Ithaca: Cornell University Press, 1991), 255–304, esp. 289–96.

4. Snyder, *Myths of Empire*, 257. In fairness, Snyder acknowledges the absence of strong empirical support for the contention that domestic politics drove the 1950–51 Korean War decisions, per se (see, esp. 295–96). Other works make stronger claims for the influence of domestic politics. See, for example, Robert J. Donovan, *Tumultuous Years: The Presidency of Harry S. Truman, 1949–53* (New York: Norton, 1982), 206–7; William Whitney Stueck, Jr., *The Road to Confrontation: American Policy toward China and Korea, 1947–1950* (Chapel Hill: University of North Carolina Press, 1981), esp. 185–90; and Bruce Cumings, *Origins of the Korean War*, vol. 2, *The Roaring of the Cataract* (Princeton: Princeton University Press, 1990), esp. 12–32 and 708–15. Rosemary Foot, *The Wrong War: American Policy and the Dimensions of the Korean Conflict, 1950–1953* (Ithaca: Cornell University Press, 1985) is noncommittal on the influence of congressional factions on the administration's war decisions. Foot's second book, however, makes a stronger case for the role of Congress in the escalation of war aims in August-September 1950. See idem, *A Substitute for Victory: The Politics of Peacemaking at the Korean Armistice Talks* (Ithaca: Cornell University Press, 1990), esp. ch. 2.

5. See Dale C. Copeland, *Origins of Major War* (Ithaca: Cornell University Press, 2000), 47–48 and 170–74. Following Copeland, I use the term *adverse power oscillation* to denote a relative power shift caused by the short-term success of another great power's arm racing or alliance building.

6. For the text of the Cairo Declaration, see Department of State, *Foreign Relations of the United States, 1943: Conferences at Cairo and Tehran* (Washington, D.C.: GPO, 1961), 449 and 869. All subsequent citations to any volume in the *Foreign Relations of the United States* series are abbreviated as *FRUS*.

7. See Roy E. Appleman, *United States Army in the Korean War*, vol. 1, *South to the Naktong, North to the Yalu* (Washington, D.C.: Center for Military History, 1961), 2–3 (hereafter cited as *USAKW*); James F. Schnabel, *USAKW*, vol. 3, *Policy and Direction: The First Year* (Washington, D.C.: Center for Military History, 1971), 7–8; and the discussions of 25 and 26 June 1945 in *FRUS, Potsdam*, vol. 2, 345–52 and 408–15.

8. See William Stueck, *The Korean War: An International History* (Princeton: Princeton University Press, 1995), 21–22; and Cumings, *Origins of the Korean War,* vol. 2, 223–34.

9. Stalin gave up an opportunity to seize the entire peninsula in August 1945, before the arrival of American troops. See Kathryn Weathersby, "Soviet Aims in the Korean War, 1945–1950: New Evidence from the Russian Archives," Working Paper no. 8, Cold War International History Project, Washington, D.C. (November 1993), 13–14.

10. On the background and anti-Japanese guerrilla activities of Kim Il Sung (born Kim Song-ju) see, Sergei N. Goncharov, John W. Lewis, and Xue Litai, *Uncertain Partners: Stalin, Mao, and the Korean War* (Stanford: Stanford University Press, 1993), 131–32, n. 9; and Bruce Cummings, *The Origins of the Korean War,* vol. 1, *Liberation and the Emergence of Separate Regimes, 1945–1947* (Princeton: Princeton University Press, 1981), 35–38.

11. Report of the Ad-Hoc Committee on Korea, 4 August 1947, *FRUS, 1947,* vol. 6: *The Far East,* 738–41. Also, see Cumings, *Korean War,* vol. 1, 215–18; and James I. Matray, *Reluctant Crusade: American Foreign Policy in Korea, 1941–1950* (Honolulu: University of Hawaii Press, 1985), 119–24.

12. Goncharov, Lewis, and Litai, *Uncertain Partners,* 133; and Cumings, *Korean War,* vol. 2, 382–83.

13. John C. Muccio to George C. Marshall, 12 November 1948, *FRUS, 1948,* vol. 6: *The Far East,* 1326; and CIA, "Review of the World Situation," 16 December 1948, HST, PSF: CIA file, box 230.

14. See, NSC-8/2, "Position of the United States with Respect to Korea," 22 March 1949, *FRUS, 1949,* vol. 7: *The Far East,* 969–78; and Muccio to Acheson, 23 May 1950, *FRUS, 1950,* vol. 7: *Korea,* 86–88.

15. Department of the Army telegram CX 67198, 19 January 1949, cited in Robert K. Sawyer, *Military Advisors in Korea: KMAG in Peace and War,* ed. Walter G. Hermes, *United States Army Military Historical Series* (Washington, D.C.: GPO, 1962), 37. Also, see Kenneth C. Royall to Dean G. Acheson, 25 January 1949, *FRUS, 1949,* Vol. 7, 945–46.

16. See Schnabel, *USAIKW,* vol. 2, 37; Goncharov, Lewis, and Litai, *Uncertain Partners,* 133; and Army Department to State Department, 27 June 1949, *FRUS, 1949,* vol. 7, 1048–49.

17. See Everett Drumright, chargé in Seoul, to Acheson, 11 May 1950, *FRUS, 1950,* vol. 7, 83–84.

18. See NSC-8, "Position of the United States with Respect to Korea," 2 April 1948, *FRUS, 1947,* vol. 6: *The Far East,* 1167 and NSC 8/2, 22 March 1949, *FRUS, 1949,* vol. 7, 969–78; Cummings, *Origins of the Korean War,* vol. 2, 45–54; and Schnabel, *USAIKW,* vol. 3, 30, 35, and 50–51.

19. Memo by W. Walton Butterworth, 17 August 1948, *FRUS, 1948,* vol. 6: *The Far East and Australia,* 1276–79.

20. See Memo of conversation by John M. Allison, 5 March 1948, *FRUS, 1948,* vol. 6, 1139–41. See, also Marshall to Royall, 23 June 1948; Royal to Marshall, 23 June 1948; Lovett to Royall, 8 July 1948; Jacobs to Marshall, 12 August 1948; Butterworth to Marshall, 17 August 1948; and Muccio to Marshall, 12 November 1948, ibid., vol. 6, 1224–26, 1234–35, 1272, 1276–79, and 1325–27.

21. See Royall to Acheson, 25 January 1949; and Johnson to Acheson, 4 May 1949, *FRUS, 1949,* vol. 7, 945–46 and 1007.

22. CX 67198, CINCFE to DA, 24 January 1949, cited in Schnabel, *USAIKW,* vol. 1, 30. See, also "Implications of a Possible Full Scale Invasion from North Korea

Subsequent to Withdrawal of United States troops from South Korea," 27 June 1949, *FRUS, 1949*, vol. 7, 1045–56, esp. 1055–56

23. The CIA previously estimated that "the earliest possible date by which the USSR might be expected to produce an atomic bomb is mid-1950 and the most probable date is mid-1954." CIA Intelligence Memo, no. 225, "Estimates of Status of Atomic Warfare in USSR," 20 September 1949, in Michael Warner, ed., *CIA under Truman* (Washington, D.C.: Center for the Study of Intelligence, 1994), 319–21.

24. See Study prepared by Nitze, 8 February 1950, *FRUS, 1950*, vol. 1: *National Security Affairs*, 146–67 and a longer version in "Recent Soviet Moves," 8 February 1950, HST, PSF: National Security file, box 187, Harry S. Truman Library (hereafter cited as HSTL). For other assessments see CIA, "Review of the World Situation," 15 March 1950, HST, PSF: NSC file, box 205, HSTL.

25. See, Minutes of the PPS, 16 December 1949, *FRUS, 1949*, vol. 1: *National Security*, 414; Report by the Joint Intelligence Committee (JIS), "Soviet Intentions and Capabilities," 18 April 1950, *FRUS, 1950*, vol. 4: *Central and Eastern Europe and the Soviet Union, 1771*; and CIA, "Estimates of the Effects of Soviet Possession of the Atomic Bomb," 6 April 1950, HST, PSF, Intelligence file, box 257.

26. See Thomas J. Christensen, *Useful Adversaries: Grand Strategy, Domestic Mobilization, and Sino-American Conflict, 1947–1958* (Princeton: Princeton University Press, 1996), 59–69; Leffler, *Preponderance of Power*, 246–51; and John Lewis Gaddis, *The Long Peace*, 75–80.

27. See Department of State, *United States Relations with China, with Special Reference to the Period 1944–1949* (Washington, D.C.: GPO, 1949), xvi; reissued as *The China White Paper: August 1949* (Sanford: Stanford University Press, 1967).

28. CIA, "Review of the World Situation," 20 April 1949, HST, PSF, NSC file, box 206, HSTL. See also, Draft of NSC-41, 28 February 1949, and UK Embassy to State Department, 5 April 1949, *FRUS, 1949*, vol. 9, 826–42.

29. See Rusk to Acheson, 30 May 1949, *FRUS, 1950*, vol. 6, 349. On the JCS view, see NSC 22/1, "Possible Courses of Action with Respect to the Critical Situation in China," 6 August 1948, *FRUS, 1948*, vol. 8, 133–34.

30. Senate, Committee on Foreign Relations, *Historical Series: Review of the World Situation, 1949–50* (Washington, D.C.: GPO, 1976), 145–98.

31. See Robert M. Blum, *Drawing the Line: Origins of the American Containment Policy in East Asia* (New York: W. W. Norton, 1982), 131–44; and W. Walton Butterworth, Oral History Interview, 6 June 1971, HSTL. For the circumstances surrounding Dulles's appointment see, Ronald W. Pruessen, *John Foster Dulles: The Road to Power* (New York: Free Press, 1982), 432–36.

32. See Truman to Acheson, 31 January 1950, *FRUS, 1950*, vol. 1, 141–42.

33. For a discussion of the basic continuity between NSC-68 and NSC-20/4, see Leffler, *Preponderance of Power*, 355–60; and Gregory Mitrovich, *Undermining the Kremlin: America's Strategy to Subvert the Soviet Bloc, 1947–1956* (Ithaca: Cornell University Press, 2000), 47–82.

34. CIA, "Review of the World Situation," 1 April 1950, HST, PSF: Intelligence File, box 206, HSTL.

35. For the differences between minimal deterrence and atomic airpower, on the one hand, and a full war fighting posture, on the other, see Friedberg, *Shadow of the Garrison State*, 66–69; and Leffler, *Preponderance of Power*, 358–59. Although NSC-68 did not mention a specific budget target, officials estimated that the proposed military buildup required an increase in defense expenditures from $13 million in FY1950 to $40 million in FY1951 and 1952.

36. See NSC-7, "Position of the United States with respect to Soviet Directed World Communism," 30 March 1949, *FRUS, 1948*, vol. 1, 546–50.

37. See Marc Trachtenberg, *A Constructed Peace: The Making of the European Settlement, 1945–1963* (Princeton: Princeton University Press, 1999), 96–103; Mark S. Sheetz, "American Grand Designs for Postwar European Security," *Security Studies* 8, no. 4 (summer 1999): 1–43; and James McAllister, *No Exit: America and the German Problem, 1943–1954* (Ithaca: Cornell University Press, 2002), 171–92.

38. See NSC-68, "United States Objectives and Programs for National Security,"14 April 1950, *FRUS, 1950*, vol. 1, 205–11 (emphasis mine). For an analysis of NSC-68's arguments on conventional force structure, see David T. Fautua, "The 'Long Pull' Army: NSC-68, the Korean War and the Creation of the Cold War Army," *Journal of Military History* 61, no. 1 (January 1997): 93–120.

39. See Mitrovich, *Undermining the Kremlin*, 52–53; and Leffler, *Preponderance of Power*, 356–57.

40. See NSC-68, 14 April 1950, *FRUS, 1950*, vol. 1, 205–11.

41. See CIA, ORE 17–49, "The Strategic Importance of the Far East to the U.S. and the USSR," 4 May 1949, HST, PSF: box 256, HSTL; State Department Consultants' Report, "Outline of Far Eastern and Asian Policy for Review with the President," 16 November 1949, and NSC-48/2, "The Position of the United States with Respect to Asia," *FRUS, 1949*, vol. 7, 1211–12 and 1215–16.

42. Bradley to Johnson, 23 December 1949, enclosed in NSC 37/9, "Possible United States Military Action toward Taiwan," 27 December 1949, *FRUS, 1949*, vol. 9, 460–61.

43. Memo for the President, Re: NSC Meeting, 30 December 1949, HST, PSF: National Security file, box 219, HSTL. On Acheson's effort to establish diplomatic ties with Beijing in 1949–50, see Christensen, *Useful Adversaries*, 77–122; Leffler, *Preponderance of Power*, 336–40; and Chen Jian, *China's Road to the Korean War: The Making of the Sino-American Confrontation* (New York: Columbia University Press, 1994), 33–63.

44. See Statement by the President, 5 January 1950, George M. Elsey Papers, box 59, HSTL; and NSC-48/2, "The Position of the United States with Respect to Asia," 30 December 1949, *FRUS, 1949*, vol. 7, 1219–20. The administration did not completely write off Taiwan in the event of a general war. On this point, see Press conference with Dean Acheson, 5 January 1950, *Department of State Bulletin* XXII, no. 555 (16 January 1950), 81

45. See Christensen, *Useful Adversaries*, 130–33; and Cumings, *Origins of the Korean War*, vol. 2, 417–20.

46. See Dean G. Acheson, "Crisis in Asia: An Examination of U.S. Policy," *Department of State Bulletin* XXII, no. 556 (23 January 1950). Also, see Memo of conversation with Senator Arthur Vandenberg, 24 January 1950, Dean G. Acheson Papers, box 65, HSTL.

47. State Department, Chronology of Government Meetings, 25 June 1950 to 21 March 1951; and Muccio to the State Department, 25 June 1950, HST, PSF: Historical File, box 230; Princeton Seminars, transcript for 13–14 February 1954, Acheson Papers, HSTL.

48. Memo of conversation with the President and others, Re: Korean situation, 25 June 1950, Acheson Papers, box 65, HSTL. See also Jessup, Memo of conversation with the President and others, Re: Korean situation, 25 June 1950, *FRUS, 1950*, vol. 7, 159.

49. Documents from the Russian archives show that Stalin approved Kim Il Sung's plan to reunify Korea by force. That said, Pyongyang was not merely a pawn of Moscow: ultimate responsibility for the invasion lay with Kim. See Chen, *China's*

Road to the Korean War, 85–91; Goncharov, Lewis, and Litai, *Uncertain Partners*, 130–54; Kathryn Weathersby, "New Russian Documents on the Korean War: Introduction and Translation," *Cold War International History Project Bulletin* 6–7 (winter 1995–96): 30–84 (cited hereafter as *CWIPB*); and Shen Zihua "Sino-Soviet Relations and the Origins of the Korean War: Stalin's Strategic Goals for the Far East," *Journal of Cold War Studies* 2, no. 2 (spring 2000): 44–68.

50. George M. Elsey, Memo of conversation with the President, 25 June 1950, Elsey Papers, box 71, HSTL

51. Kirk to Acheson, 25 June 1950 and Acheson to Kirk, 25 June 1950, *FRUS, 1950*, vol. 7, 139–40 and 148.

52. CIA, "General Soviet Intentions with Respect to the Far East," HST, PSF: CIA File, box 248, HSTL. Also see State Department, Office of Intelligence Research (OIR), Intelligence Estimate, 25 June 1950, *FRUS, 1950*, vol. 7, 148–54

53. See Muccio to Acheson, 26 June 1950; and Acheson to Muccio, 26 June 1950, *FRUS, 1950*, vol. 7, 170 and 178.

54. See Memo of conversation with the President and others, Re: Korean situation, 26 June 1950, Acheson Papers, box 65, HSTL; and Jessup, Memo of conversation with the President and others, 26 June 1950, *FRUS, 1950*, vol. 7, 180–81.

55. Memo of conversation, Re: meeting of the President and Acheson with the congressional leadership, 27 June 1950, Elsey Papers, box 71, HSTL; and Memo of conversation by Jessup, Re: meeting with congressional leadership in the Cabinet Room of the White House," 27 June 1950, *FRUS, 1950*, vol. 7, 200–202.

56. Acheson, Princeton Seminars, transcript for 13–14 February 1954, Acheson Papers, HSTL.

57. Acheson to Johnson, 28 June 1950, *FRUS, 1950*, vol. 7, 217; and Memo of conversation by Jessup, Re: Meeting of the NSC in the Cabinet Room, 28 June 1950, Acheson Papers, box 65, HSTL.

58. See Leffler, *Preponderance of Power*, 363; and W. Averell Harriman, n/d 1971, Oral History Interview, HSTL.

59. Memo of conversation with Sir Oliver Franks by George Perkins, assistant secretary of state for European Affairs, 28 June 1950; Perkins to Embassy in London, 28 June 1950, *FRUS, 1950*, vol. 7, 214 and 233; Memo of conversation with Norman Makin, Australian ambassador, 29 July 1950; and Memo of conversation with Wilhelm Munthe de Morgentierne, Norwegian ambassador, 30 June 1950, Acheson Papers, box 65, HSTL.

60. Memo of conversation by Jessup, Re: Meeting of the NSC in the Cabinet Room, 28 June 1950, Acheson Papers, box 65, HSTL; and Summary of NSC Discussion, 29 June 1950, HST, PSF: National Security File, box 220, HSTL.

61. See MacArthur to the JCS, 30 June 1950, HST, Naval Aide file, box 13, HSTL; Memo by Elsey, Teletype Conference of MacArthur with Collins, Rusk and others; and Walter Sebald to Acheson, 30 June 1950, Elsey Papers, box 71, HSTL; and MacArthur to Acheson, 30 June 1950, *FRUS, 1950*, vol. 7, 248–50.

62. Summary of meeting with the President, Johnson, service secretaries and JCS, 30 June 1950, Elsey Papers, box 71, HSTL.

63. See JCS to MacArthur, 30 June 1950 and JCS to MacArthur, 1 July 1950; Acheson to William J. Sebald, political advisor to SCAP, Japan, 1 July 1950; Dulles to Nitze, 14 July 1950; and Draft Memo by the PPS, 19 July 1950, *FRUS, 1950*, vol. 7, 263, 271, 279, 386–87, and 451–53.

64. Memo of conversation by Frederick Nolting, special assistant to Freeman Matthews, Re: Meeting of State Department officials on Korea, 30 June 1950, *FRUS, 1950*, vol. 7, 258–59.

65. See CIA, "Current Capabilities of the North Korean Regime," 19 June 1950, *FRUS, 1950*, vol. 7, esp. 118–19.

66. Chiang offered to send 33,000 troops to fight alongside U.S. forces in Korea on 30 June. See Memo of conversation with Tan Shan-hwa, minister in the ROC Embassy in Washington, by Fulton Freeman, acting director, Office of Chinese Affairs, 30 June 1950; Acheson to V. K. Wellington Koo, ROC ambassador to Washington, 1 July 1950, *FRUS, 1950*, vol. 7, 262 and 276–77.

67. See CIA, Intelligence Memo 323–SRC, 25 August 1950, HST, PSF: Intelligence File, box 250; and James S. Lay, Jr., NSC executive secretary, to Gordon E. Dean, chairman, Atomic Energy Commission, 6 December 1950, HST, NSC atomic weapons file, box 202, HSTL. In late July, Truman approved the deployment of ten nuclear-configured B-29s from the Strategic Air Command to forward positions in the Pacific. The B-29s, which did not carry fully armed nuclear devices, took no part in the bombing of North Korea and returned to the United States before Chinese forces began crossing the Yalu. See Roger Dingman, "Atomic Diplomacy during the Korean War," *International Security* 13, no. 3 (winter 1988/89): 50–91, at 60–65.

68. Appleman, *USAIKW*, vol. 1, 54. Also, see James F. Schnabel and Robert J. Watson, *History of the Joint Chiefs of Staff*, vol. 3, *Korean War* (Willington, Del.: Michael Glazer, 1979), 44–48; and Schnabel, *USAKW*, vol. 3, 89–90, 104–5, 118–20, and 123.

69. NSC-73 series, "Position and Actions of the United States with Respect to Possible Future Soviet Moves in Light of the Korean Situation, 1 July and 25 August, 1950, *FRUS, 1950*, vol. 1, 331–38 and 375–89.

70. See Christensen, *Useful Adversaries*, 136.

71. Glenn D. Paige, *1950: Truman's Decision: The United States Enters the Korean War* (New York: Chelsea House, 1970), 73.

72. See "Resolution on the Republic of Korea," adopted at the 476th Meeting of the UN Security Council, 7 July 1950, Eben Ayers Papers, box 9, HSTL; and Freeman Matthews to Burns, 25 July 1950, *FRUS, 1950*, vol. 7, 473–74.

73. See Memo of conversation by Jessup, Re: Meeting of the NSC in the Cabinet Room, 28 June 1950, HSTL, Acheson Papers, box 65, HSTL; and Cabinet meeting notes, 7 July 1950, Matthew J. Connelly papers, box 1, HSTL.

74. See Memo to "Paul" (presumably Nitze), 12 July 1950, and Memo for the Record by Jessup, re: meeting between Acheson and Pace, 3 July 1950, Acheson Papers, box 65, HSTL.

75. Memo by Hillenkoetter to Truman, Re: Psychological use of the atomic bomb in Korea Conflict, 6 July 1950, HST: PSF, Intelligence file, box 249, HSTL.

76. See Memo by Lay to the NSC, 17 July 1950, *FRUS, 1950*, vol. 7, 410.

77. See "Address by the President" 19 July 1950, *Public Papers of the President: Harry S. Truman, 1950* (Washington, D.C.: GPO, 1951), 531–36; Lucius D. Battle, special assistant to Acheson, Memo of telephone conversation between Acheson and Johnson, 7 July 1950, Acheson Papers, box 65, HSTL; Memo from Army Department and the JCS, 7 July 1950, HST, PSF: National Security File, box 220, HSTL.

78. See Allison to Rusk, 1 July 1950; and Allison to Rusk, 13 and 15 July 1950, *FRUS, 1950*, vol. 7, 272, 373, and 394.

79. Draft Memo by Allison, 12 August 1950, ibid., vol. 7, 567–73.

80. Dulles to Nitze, 14 July 1950; and Allison to Rusk, 15 July 1950, ibid., vol. 7, 272, 386, and 393–95.

81. Draft Department of Defense Memo, 31 July 1950, ibid., vol. 7, 502–10. See also, Draft Department of Defense Memo, 7 August 1950, ibid., vol. 7, 533; and

Memo by JCS to Johnson, 10 July 1950, HST, PSF: National Security file, box 220, HSTL; and J. Lawton Collins, *War in Peacetime: The History and Lessons of Korea* (Boston: Houghton Mifflin, 1969), 144.

82. Statement to the VFW by MacArthur, 26 August 1950; and Johnson to MacArthur (as dictated by Truman), 27 August 1950, HST, PSF: National Security File, box 220, HSTL; Memo for the Record by Battle, 26 August 1950 and Memo from Acheson to Webb, 27 August 1950, Acheson Papers, box 65, HSTL; and Memo for File by Elsey, 26 August 1950, Elsey Papers, box 72, HSTL.

83. On the circumstances of Johnson's dismissal and Marshall and Lovett's appointment, see: Harriman to Truman, 1 July 1950; and Diary entry by Ayers, 3 July 1950, Ayers Papers, HSTL; Acheson, Princeton Seminars, transcript for 14 February 1954, Acheson Papers, HSTL; Robert A. Lovett, Oral History Interview, 7 July 1971, HSTL; and Doris M. Conduit, *History of the Office of the Secretary of Defense*, vol. 2, *The Test of War, 1950–1953* (Washington, D.C.: Historical Office, Office of the Security of Defense, 1988), 31–39 and 176–78.

84. Memo of conversation by Nolting, Re: Meeting of State Department officials on Korea, 30 June 1950, *FRUS, 1950*, vol. 7, 258–59.

85. Draft Memo by the PPS, 22 July 1950, *FRUS, 1950*, vol. 7, 451.

86. See Memo by the CIA, 18 August 1950, ibid., vol. 7, 600–603.

87. See Kennan to Acheson, 21 August 1950, ibid., vol. 7, 625 (emphasis in the original). See also, Stueck, *Road to Confrontation*, 204–5; idem, *Korean War*, 134–35; and Gaddis, *Long Peace*, 97–99.

88. See Atlee to Truman, 6 July 1950 and Bevin to Acheson, 11 July 1950, *FRUS*, vol. 7, 314–15 and 396–97.

89. On Nehru's July peace initiative see, Kirk to Acheson, 9 July 1950; Acheson to Douglas, 7 and 10 July 1950; Acheson to Kirk, 11 July 1950; and Nehru to Acheson, 17 July 1950, *FRUS, 1950*, vol. 7, 327–28, 340–42, 347–51, and 408. See also Stueck, *Korean War*, 80–81.

90. MacArthur quoted in Trumbill Higgins, *Korea and the Fall of MacArthur* (New York: Oxford University Press, 1960), 51; and Collins, *War in Peacetime*, 83.

91. Memo of conversation by Harriman, Re: meeting with MacArthur in Tokyo, 6 and 8 August 1950, HST, PSF: box 14, HSTL.

92. NCS-81/1, "U.S. Course of Action with Respect to Korea," 9 September 1950, *FRUS, 1950*, vol. 7, 712–21, at 716–17; and Memo of NSC Meeting, 8 September 1950, HST, PSF: National Security file, box 220, HSTL.

93. See Marshall to MacArthur, 29 September 1950, *FRUS, 1950*, vol. 7, 826. For details of the Inchon landing and the subsequent UNC counteroffensive in mid September, see Schnabel, *USAIKW*, vol. 1, chap. 3.

94. See UN General Assembly Resolution 376, 7 October 1950, *FRUS, 1950*, vol. 7, 904.

95. See Kirk to Acheson, 11 August 1950, *FRUS, 1950*, vol. 4, 1231. For similar assessments, see NSC 73/4, "Further Soviet Moves in Light of the Korean Situation," 25 August 1950, ibid., vol. 1, 378–79; and Testimony by Acheson, 24 July 1950, in *Reviews of the World Situation*, 315.

96. *New York Times*, 22 September 1950, 6–7.

97. Stueck, *Korean War*, chap. 3. See also U.S. Delegation to the UN Minutes, 29 August and 1 September 1950, *FRUS, 1950*, vol. 3, 1135–37 and 1167.

98. Memo by CIA, "Threat of Soviet Intervention in Korea," 12 October 1950, *FRUS, 1950*, vol. 7, 936.

99. See Memo by the CIA, "Chinese Intervention in Korea," 12 October 1950,

FRUS, 1950, vol. 7, 934. Also, see Memo by Walter McConaughy to Jessup, Re: notes on NSC senior staff meeting on Korea, 25 August 1950, ibid., vol. 7, 649–52.

100. Memo for the President, Re: NSC Meeting, 7 July 1950, HST, PSF: National Security file, box 220, HSTL.

101. Acheson quoted in Foot, *Wrong War,* 81.

102. CIA, "Critical Situations in the Far East," 12 October 1950, HST, PSF: CIA file, box 250, HSTL.

103. Memo for the President, Re: NSC Meeting, 7 July 1950, HST, PSF: National Security file, box 220, HSTL.

104. See Loy W. Henderson, ambassador in New Delhi, to Acheson, 20 and 21 September 1950, *FRUS, 1950,* vol. 7, 742–43.

105. See Wilkinson to Acheson, 22 September 1950, ibid., vol. 7, 765.

106. See Memo of conversation by Merchant, 27 September 1950, ibid., vol. 7, 793–94. See, also Webb to Rusk, 28 September 1950, ibid., vol. 7, 797–98.

107. See Merchant to Rusk, 3 October 1950, ibid., vol. 7, 848–49.

108. For an account of the meeting, see K. M. Pannikar, *In Two Chinas: Memoirs of a Diplomat* (London: Allen and Unwin, 1955), 109–11.

109. See Clubb to Merchant, 4 October 1950; U. Alexis Johnson to Rusk, 3 October 1950; Henderson to Acheson, 3 October 1950; Kirk to Acheson, 3 October 1950; Webb to Embassy in New Delhi, 3 October 1950; and Wilkinson to Acheson, 2 October 1950; Chapin to Acheson, 3 October 1950, ibid., vol. 7, and 849–52, 858, 864–65.

110. See Memo by CIA, "Chinese Intervention in Korea," 12 October 1950, ibid., vol. 7, 934. See also, Foot, *Wrong War,* 80; and Cumings, *Origins of the Korean War,* vol. 2, 734–35.

111. CIA Report, 6 October 1950, HST, PSF: CIA file, box 250, HSTL; Alexis Johnson to Rusk, 3 October 1950, *FRUS, 1950,* vol. 7, 849. See also, Allen S. Whiting, *China Crosses the Yalu: The Decision to Enter the Korean War* (New York: Macmillan, 1960), 108–9.

112. Christensen, *Useful Adversaries,* 118–19 and 152–53; and Blum, *Drawing the Line,* 61–63.

113. Dean Acheson, *Present at the Creation: My Years at the State Department* (New York: W. W. Norton, 1969), 450–51.

114. Quoted from NSC 73/4, "Possible Further Soviet Moves in Light of the Korean Situation," 25 August 1950, *FRUS, 1950,* vol. 1, 378.

115. On popular support for rollback, see Department of State, Office of Public Affairs, "Monthly Survey of American Opinion on International Affairs," August, September, and October 1950, Elsey Papers, box 60, HSTL; and Mildred Strunk, "The Quarter's Polls," *Public Opinion Quarterly* 14 (winter 1950–1951): 799–819, at 804.

116. For an analysis of Mao's October 2 decision to enter the war, see Chen, *China's Road to the Korea War,* 171–89; and Christensen, *Useful Adversaries,* 163–66.

117. See JCS to MacArthur, 9 October 1950, *FRUS, 1950,* vol. 7, 915. Also, see, Lovett to Truman, 7 October 1950, HST, PSF: National Security file, box 220.

118. Bradley notes, "Substance of Statements Made at Wake Island Conference," 15 October 1950, *FRUS, 1950,* vol. 7, 948–60. See also Memo by Rusk, "Addendum to Notes on Wake Island Conference," ibid., vol. 7, 961–62.

119. For a detailed account of guerrilla activities by the CPVs in October and early November, see Appleman, *USAIKW,* vol. 1, 721–28.

120. See Walter Bedell Smith to Truman, 1 November 1950, *FRUS, 1950,* vol. 7, 1025–26. Smith succeeded Hillenkoetter as director of central intelligence on 7 October 1950.

121. See CIA, "Review of the World Situation," 20 September 1950; and CIA, "Chinese Communist Potential for Intervention in the Korean War," 1 November 1950, HST, PSF: CIA file, box 250; and CIA, NIE, "Chinese Communist Intentions in Korea," 8 November 1950, *FRUS, 1950*, vol. 7, 1001.

122. See Memo of Conversation by Acheson, Re: Meeting with Lovett and Rusk, 6 November 1950; and Matthews to Burns, 6 November 1950, *FRUS, 1950*, vol. 7, 1055 and 1058–59.

123. Memo by Acheson, Re: Telephone Conversation with Truman at Kansas City; and JCS to MacArthur, 6 November 1950, *FRUS, 1950*, vol. 7, 1055–58.

124. See Rusk to Acheson, 7 November 1950, ibid., vol. 7, 1077.

125. See JCS to MacArthur, 6 November 1950; and MacArthur to JCS, 7 November 1950, ibid., vol. 7, 1075–77.

126. See CIA, NIE, "Chinese Communist Intervention in Korea," 8 November 1950; and Smith to NSC, 9 November 1950, *FRUS, 1950*, vol. 7, 1103 and 1122.

127. Views of the JCS, 9 November 1950, HST, PSF: National Security file, box 220, HSTL; and Memo for the President, Re: NSC Meeting, 9 November 1950, HST, PSF: NSC file, box 5, HSTL.

128. Clubb to Rusk, 10 November 1950; Memo of Conversation by Rusk, Re: meeting with Erik Boheman, Swedish ambassador in Washington, 13 November 1950; and Selden Chapin, ambassador at The Hague, to Acheson, 14 November 1950, *FRUS, 1950*, vol. 7, 1123–24 and 1141–42.

129. See Austin to Acheson, 11 November 1950, ibid., vol. 7, 1133–34.

130. See Acheson to UN Mission, 10 November, 1950, ibid., vol. 7, 1127; *Department of State Bulletin* XXII, no. 653 (27 November 1950), 853 and 889; and Press Conference, 16 November 1950, in *Public Papers of the Presidents of the United States: Harry S. Truman, 1950* (Washington, D.C.: GPO, 1965), 711.

131. See Lewis Douglas, ambassador to London, to Acheson, 13 November 1950, ibid., vol. 7, 1138–39; and Acheson to Bevin, 16 November 1950, PSF: Korean War file, box 3, HSTL.

132. See Henderson to Acheson, 7 November 1950; British Embassy to State Department, 16 and 17 November 1950; Pete Jarman, ambassador to Canberra, to Acheson, 17 November 1950; Stanley Woodward, ambassador in Otowa, to Acheson, 14 and 15 November 1950, *FRUS, 1950*, vol. 7, 1093–94, 1123–24, 1152–53, and 1171–75.

133. See Memo by Battle, 8 November 1950; Marshall to Acheson, 10 November 1950; and Text of UN Security Council Resolution 1894, 10 November 1950, ibid., vol. 7, 1096 and 1126–27.

134. See Clubb to Rusk, 1 November 1950; and Memo by Davies, 17 November 1950, ibid., vol. 7, 1023 and 1180–81.

135. See Jessup to Acheson, 20 November 1950, ibid., vol. 7, 1193–9116.

136. Memo of Conversation by Jessup, Re: State-Defense Meeting at the Pentagon, 21 November 1950, Acheson Papers, box 65, HSTL.

137. Memo of Conversation by Jessup, Re: State-Defense Meeting at the Pentagon, 21 November 1950, Acheson Papers, box 65, HSTL. For the JCS recommendation to hold the high ground south of the Yalu and MacArthur rejection of it see JCS to MacArthur, 24 November 1950; and MacArthur to JCS, 24 November 1950, *FRUS, 1950*, vol. 7, 1223–25.

138. Recent scholarship (based upon Russian and Chinese archival materials) suggests that Mao would not have accepted *any* permanent U.S. troop presence in North Korea. This was unknown to the Truman administration and the JCS at the time, however. See Christensen, *Useful Adversaries*, 166–70; and idem, "Threats, As-

surances, and the Last Chance for Peace: The Lessons of Mao's Korean War Telegrams," *International Security* 17, no. 1 (summer 1992): 122–54; Stueck, *Korean War*, 119–21; and Chen, *China's Road to the Korean War*, 190–223.

139. Figures cited in Congressional Quarterly, *Congress and the Nation, 1945–1964: A Review of Government and Politics in the Postwar Years* (Washington, D.C.: Congressional Quarterly, 1965), 63.

140. See, for example, Labs, "Fighting for More," 232–38; idem, "Beyond Victory," 38–39; Donovan, *Tumultuous Years*, 298–305; David Rees, *Korea: The Limited War* (London: Macmillan, 1965), 151; Harry S. Truman, *Memoirs: Years of Trial and Hope*, vol. 2 (Garden City, N.Y.: Doubleday, 1965); and Acheson, *Present at the Creation*, 463–65.

141. See the testimonies of Acheson, Lovett, Bradley, Harriman, and Collins in U.S. Senate, Committees on Armed Services and Foreign Relations, *Military Situation in the Far East: Hearings . . . to Conduct an Inquiry into the Military Situation in the Far East and the Facts Surrounding the Relief of General of the Army Douglas MacArthur from His Assignments in that Area*, 82nd Cong., 1st session, parts 2 and 3 (Washington, D.C.: U.S. Senate, 1951) (hereafter cited as *MacArthur Hearings*).

142. For a refutation of the various myths about the Wake Island Conference, see James Edward Wiltz, "Truman and MacArthur: The Wake Island Meeting," *Military Affairs* 42, no. 4 (December 1978): 169–76; and D. Clayton James, with Anne Sharp Wells, *Refighting the Last War: Command and Crisis in Korea, 1950–1953* (New York: Free Press, 1993), 48–49 and 179–95.

143. Schnabel and Watson, *History of the JCS*, vol. 3, 356.

144. See MacArthur to JCS, 28 November 1950, *FRUS, 1950*, vol. 7, 1237–38.

145. See MacArthur to JCS, 29 November 1950 and JCS to MacArthur, 30 November 1950, ibid., 1253–54. See also James Edward Wiltz, "The MacArthur Hearings of 1951: The Secret Testimony," *Military Affairs* 39, no. 4 (December 1975): 167–73.

146. *U.S. News and World Report*, 29 (8 December 1950): 16–17; and *New York Times*, 2 December 1950, 1 and 4. For a more detailed secondary account of MacArthur's statements Schnabel and Watson, *History of the JCS*, 333–47; and Bradley and Blair, *A General's Life*, 595–604.

147. For the statement by Lovett, see Memo of conversation by Acheson, 2 December 1950, Acheson Papers, box 65, HSTL. For the text of Truman's press clearance directive, see JCS to MacArthur, 6 December 1950, in *MacArthur Hearings*, part 5, 3536.

148. Acheson and Truman's calls for unity appear in *New York Times*, 30 November 1950, 1 and 14; and 1 December 1950, 1. For Cain's speech see *Congressional Record*, 82nd Cong., 1st session, pt. 96 (28 November 1950): 15939–42. For McCarthy's telegram see, *New York Times*, 3 December 1950, 49.

149. On the British reaction, see Rosemary Foot, "Anglo-American Relations in the Korean Crisis, December 1950–January 1951," *Diplomatic History* 10, no. 1 (winter 1986): 43–57; and Stueck, *Korean War*, 130–32. The minutes of the Truman-Atlee, 4–8 December 1950 are in *FRUS, 1950*, vol. 7, 1361–481.

150. See Austin to Acheson, 1 December 1950, ibid., vol. 7, 1300–1301.

151. The UN General Assembly passed an U.S.-sponsored resolution condemning the PRC as an "aggressor nation" by a vote of 44 to 7, with nine abstentions, on 1 February 1951. On the Truman administration's efforts to secure UN Security Council and later General Assembly approval of the resolution, see Stueck, *Korean War*, 134–35 and 151–57.

152. Notes of Cabinet Meeting, 28 November 1950, Matthew Connelly Papers, box 2, HSTL; Memo of conversation, Re: NSC Meeting, 28 November 1950, Elsey

Papers, box 72, HSTL; and CIA, "Soviet Intentions in the Current Situation," 2 December 1950, *FRUS, 1950*, vol. 7, 1310.

153. Memo of conversation by Battle, Re: Meeting of Acheson, Webb, Jessup, Nitze and Kennan on Korean crisis, 4 December 1950, *FRUS, 1950*, vol. 7, 1345–46.

154. Memo of conversation, Re: NSC Meeting, 28 November 1950, Acheson Papers, box 65, HSTL. See also Memo of conversation by Elsey, Re: NSC meeting, 28 November 1950, Elsey Papers, box 72, HSTL.

155. JCS to MacArthur, 29 December 1950, *FRUS, 1950*, vol. 7, 1625.

156. JCS to MacArthur, 9 January 1951, ibid., 42.

157. Memo of conversation, Re: NSC Meeting, 28 November 1950, Acheson Papers, box 65, HSTL.

158. See Dingman, "Atomic Diplomacy," 66–69; and Daniel Calingaert, "Nuclear Weapons and the Korean War," *Journal of Strategic Studies* 11, no. 2 (June 1988): 177–202, at 181–82.

159. See Memo by John K. Emmerson, planning advisor, Bureau of Far Eastern Affairs, to Rusk, 8 1950, *FRUS, 1950*, vol. 7, 1098–101.

160. Truman-Atlee communiqué, 8 December 1950, ibid., vol. 7, 1479.

161. Memo of conversation, Re: NSC Meeting, 28 November 1950, Acheson Papers, box 65, HSTL

162. See Memo by JCS, 6 December 1950, *FRUS, 1950*, vol. 1, 475–77; and NSC 68/4, "United States Objectives and Programs for National Security," 14 December 1950, ibid., vol. 1, 488–89. See also Leffler, *Preponderance of Power*, 401–2; and Marc Trachtenberg, "A 'Wasting Asset': American Strategy and the Shifting Nuclear Balance," *International Security* 13, no. 3 (winter 1988/89): 5–49, esp. 21–30.

163. See Resolution 498 (v) adopted by the United Nations General Assembly (UNGA), 1 February 1951, *FRUS: 1951*, vol. 7, 150–51. For discussion of the findings of the General Assembly's First Committee and the Truman administration's lobbying on behalf of UNGA resolution 498 see, Stueck, *Korean War*, 155–57; and Foot, *Substitute for Victory*, 28–34.

164. Draft State Department memo for Truman, 23 February 1951, *FRUS, 1951*, vol. 7, 192–93.

165. See MacArthur to Department of the Army, 30 December 1950, *FRUS, 1950*, vol. 7, 1631. On the circumstances surrounding Truman's firing of MacArthur and the Joint Chiefs' concurrence see, testimony by MacArthur, *MacArthur Hearings*, part 1, 3–320; Marshall, Bradley, Collins, Vandenberg, and Sherman, ibid., parts 1 and 2, 1187, 1253–54, 1391, 1419, and 1443; Blair and Bradley, *A General's Life*, 630–31; and Truman, *Memoirs: Years of Trial*, 490–510.

166. See Department of State, Office of Public Affairs, "Monthly Survey of American Opinion on International Affairs," December 1950 and January 1951, Elsey Papers, box 60, HSTL; and Mildred Strunk, "The Quarter's Polls," *Public Opinion Quarterly* 15, no. 2 (summer 1951): 386–97. On Lovett's discussion with members of the Armed Services Committee, see Kennan Notes, 6 December 1950, Acheson Papers, box 65, HSTL.

167. See Meetings with Atlee, 4–7 December 1950, *FRUS, 1950*, vol. 3, 1711–14.

168. See, Labs, "Beyond Victory," 37–39.

CHAPTER 6. THE LIMITS OF GREAT POWER INTERVENTION IN THE PERIPHERY

1. See Ima Christina Barlow, *The Agadir Crisis* (Hamden, Conn.: Archon Books, 1971), 68–84; and Dwight E. Lee, *Europe's Crucial Years: The Diplomatic Back-*

ground to World War I, 1902–1914 (Hanover, N.H.: Clark University Press, 1974), 239–41.

2. Memo by Alfred von Kiderlen-Wächter, 28 April 1911, XXIX, no. 97, *German Diplomatic Documents, 1871–1914*, vol. IV, *The Descent to the Abyss, 1911–1914*, ed. and trans. E. T. S. Dugdale (New York: Harper, 1930), 1–2 [hereafter cited as *GDD*].

3. See Lee, *Europe's Crucial Years*, 249–50; Barlow, *Agadir Crisis*, 179, 184–85, 190–94, and 202–5; and Samuel R. Williamson, Jr., *The Politics of Grand Strategy: Britain and France Prepare for War, 1904–1914* (London: Ashfield Press, 1990), 142. On the secret Franco-Spanish protocol for the partition of Morocco see, Eugene N. Anderson, *The First Morocco Crisis: 1904–1906* (Hamden, Conn.: Archon Books, 1966), 118–25.

4. On Anglo-German relations during this period in general, and the Asquith government's ambiguous signals to France about its willingness to fight a war over Morocco, see Paul M. Kennedy, *The Rise of Anglo-German Antagonism, 1860–1914* (London: Ashfield Press, 1980), 446–50; and David G. Herrmann, *The Arming of Europe and the Making of the First World War* (Princeton: Princeton University Press, 1996), 153–54.

5. See Memo by Kiderlen, 3 May 1911, XXIX, no. 105, *GDD*, vol. IV, 3.

6. See James W. Davis, Jr., *Threats and Promises: The Pursuit of International Influence* (Baltimore: Johns Hopkins University Press, 2000), 132–33.

7. Abdu'l Hafiz had offered Germany a coaling station on Morocco's Atlantic coast in December 1909. The German government declined the offer, concluding that the station would be "against the integrity of Morocco guaranteed by the Algeciras Act" and "against [the 1909] Moroccan Accord with France." See Baron Wilhelm von Schön, in Paris, to Theobold von Bethmann-Hollweg, 14 December 1909, no. 10489, in *Die Grosse Politik der Europäischen Kabinett, 1871–1914*, ed. Johannes Lepsius, Albrecht Mendelssohn Bartholdy and Friedrich Thimme (Berlin: Deutsche Verlags Gesellschaft für Politik und Geschichte, 1922–27), vol. 29 [hereafter cited as *GP*]. All translations from *GP* are by Matthias Maass, unless otherwise noted. See, also the discussions in Barlow, *Agadir Crisis*, 86–87; Davis, *Threats and Promises*, 132; and Jonathan Mercer, *Reputation in International Politics* (Ithaca: Cornell University Press, 1996), 162.

8. See Arden Bucholz, *Moltke, Schlieffen, and Prussian War Planning* (Oxford: Berg, 1991), 260–61.

9. Memo by Wandel, 31 August 1911, quoted in Herrmann, *Arming of Europe*, 159–60.

10. Kiderlen originally planned for four cruisers to weigh anchor off Morocco's Atlantic coast: two at Mogador and the two others at Agadir. However, it would have taken too long for the four cruisers to arrive. Eventually, only one cruiser, the *Panther*, en route to Germany from German Southwest Africa, arrived in the port of Agadir on 1 July. See Luigi Albertini, *Origins of the War of 1914*, vol. 1, *European Relations from the Congress of Berlin to the Eve of the Sarajevo Murder*, trans. and ed. Isabella M. Massey (London: Oxford University Press, 1952), 328–29.

11. See Memo by Kiderlen, 3 May 1911, XXIX, no. 105, *GDD*, vol. 4, 3.

12. Memo by Bethmann-Hollweg, XXIX, no. 120, ibid., 5. Wilhelm, his wife, the empress Augusta Victoria ("Dona"), and his only daughter, Princess Victoria Louise of Prussia, had been in London for the unveiling of a memorial to his grandmother, Queen Victoria, in front of Buckingham Palace on 14 May.

13. Schön, in Paris, to Bethmann, 7 May 1911, XXIX, no. 115, ibid., 4.

14. Geneviève Tabouis, *The Life of Jules Cambon*, trans. C. F. Atkinson (London: Jonathan Cape, 1938), 200.

15. Jules Cambon to Jean Cruppe, 22 June 1911, quoted in Barlow, *Agadir Crisis*, 212.

16. On 21 May 1911, just as French troops arrived at Fez, an airplane crashed at a military air show at Issey-les-Moulineaux, killing War Minister Maurice Berteaux and gravely wounding Premier Ernest Monis. The Monis government continued in office until 23 June. Caillaux was not able to form a new government and win a vote of confidence in the French National Assembly until 27 June. See Herrmann, *Arming of Europe*, 150.

17. Kiderlen, Yacht *Hohenzollern* at Kiel, to the Reich Foreign Office, 26 June 1911, XXIX, no. 152; and Kiderlen to Count von Metternich, in London, 30 June 1911, XXIX, no. 155, *GDD*, vol. 4, 6–7.

18. For a detailed discussion of the Cambon-Kiderlen negotiations see, Barlow, *Agadir Crisis*, 253–65

19. Bethmann to Wilhelm, 20 July 1911, quoted in Barlow, *Agadir Crisis*, 266.

20. See Bethmann to Wilhelm, 15 July 1911, XXIX, no. 184, *GDD*, vol. 4, 11. Throughout the Agadir crisis, Wilhelm remained a voice of caution, which prompted Kiderlen to offer his resignation on 17 and 19 July. See Barlow, *Agadir Crisis*, 262–64; and Mary E. Townsend, *The Rise and Fall of Germany's Colonial Empire, 1884–1914*, 2d ed. (New York: Fertig, 1966), 323–25.

21. Count Paul von Metternich, in London, to the Reich Foreign Office, 4 July 1911, XXIX, no. 167, *GDD*, vol. 4, 8–9.

22. Speech quoted in Barlow, *Agadir Crisis*, 328; and "Extract from Speech of Mr. Lloyd George on 21 July 1911," in *British Documents on the Origins of the War, 1898–1914* (hereafter cited as *BD*), vol. 7, *The Agadir Crisis*, ed. G. P. Gooch and Harold Temperley (London: His Majesty's Stationary Office, 1932), no. 412, 391. Also, see Keith Wilson, "The Agadir Crisis, the Mansion House Speech, and the Double-Edgedness of Agreements," *Historical Journal* 15, no. 3 (September 1972): 513–32.

23. The intended "target" of Lloyd George's remarks at the Mansion House is a subject considerable debate among historians. A. J. P. Taylor introduced the thesis that Lloyd George directed his remarks to France, "a warning that Britain could not be left out of any new partition of Morocco." See Taylor, *Struggle for the Mastery of Europe, 1848–1918* (Oxford: Oxford University Press, 1954), 471. For the debate see, Richard A. Cosgrove, "A Note on Lloyd George's Speech at the Mansion House, 21 June 1911," *Historical Journal* 12, no. 4 (December 1969): 698–701; Wilson, "The Agadir Crisis"; and Timothy Boyle, "New Light on Lloyd George's Mansion House Speech," *Historical Journal* 23, no. 2 (June 1980): 431–33.

24. Quoted in Fritz Fischer, *War of Illusions: German Politics from 1911 to 1914* (New York: W. W. Norton, 1975), 72.

25. Metternich quoted in Lee, *Europe's Crucial Years*, 260. For Bethmann's and Kiderlen's initial reactions to the Lloyd George speech and their instructions to Metternich, see Kiderlen to Metternich, 24 July 1911, XXIX, no. 210; and Metternich to the Foreign Office, 25 July 1911, *GDD*, vol. 4, 14–15; and Kiderlen to Metternich, 25 July 1911, *GP*, vol. 29, no. 10625.

26. Winston S. Churchill, *The World Crisis: An Abridgement of the Classic 4 Volume History of World War I* (New York: Scribner's Sons, 1931), 32.

27. King George V raised Richard Burdon Haldane to the peerage as the Viscount Haldane of Cloan on 27 March 1911. Lord Haldane continued to serve as secretary of state for war.

28. Davis, *Threats and Promises*, 134.

29. See Barlow, *Agadir Crisis*, 313; and Herrmann, *Arming of Europe*, 150–53; and Samuel R. Williamson, "Joffre Reshapes French Strategy, 1911–1913," in *The War*

Plans of the Great Powers, 1880–1914, ed. Paul M. Kennedy (London: Macmillan, 1985), 133–54.

30. See Schön to the Foreign Office, 31 July 1911, *GP*, vol. 29, no. 10681. See also Bucholz, *Moltke, Schlieffen, and Prussian War Planning*, 261–62.

31. See Schön to Reich Foreign Office, 11 August 1911, *GP*, vol. 29, no. 10686.

32. Quoted in Fischer, *War of Illusions*, 84–86.

33. Hermann, *Arming of Europe*, 159.

34. Quoted in ibid., 153–54.

35. Quoted in ibid., 134–35. See also William C. Wohlforth, "The Perception of Power: Russia in the Pre-1914 Balance," *World Politics* 39, no. 3 (April 1987): 353–81, at 365–66; and Dale C. Copeland, *Origins of Major War* (Ithaca: Cornell University Press, 2000), 62–63.

36. On this point, see Davis, *Threats and Promises*, 135–36; and Mercer, *Reputation and International Politics*, 160.

37. On the solidification of German preventive war thinking and the European land armaments race after 1911, see Copeland, *Origins of War*, 63–67; and Herrmann, *Arming of Europe*, 173–98.

38. Herrmann, *Arming of Europe*, 149–50.

39. Wolfgang J. Mommsen, *Imperial Germany, 1867–1918: Politics, Culture, and Society in an Authoritarian State*, trans. Richard Deveson (London and New York: Arnold, 1990), 176. On German commercial interests in Morocco, in general, see Joanne Stafford Mortimer, "Commercial Interests and German Diplomacy in the Agadir Crisis," *Historical Journal*, 10, no. 3 (September 1967): 440–56.

40. See Hata Ikuhiko, "The Japanese-Soviet Confrontation, 1935–1939," in *Deterrent Diplomacy: Japan, Germany, and the USSR, 1935–40*, ed. James William Morely, trans. Alvin D. Coox (New York: Columbia University Press, 1976), 129–31.

41. John J. Mearsheimer, *Tragedy of Great Power Politics* (New York: W. W. Norton, 2001), 219–20.

42. Maj. General Honma Masaharu quoted in Alvin D. Coox, *Nomonhan: Japan Against Russia, 1939* (Stanford, Calif.: Stanford University Press, 1985), vol. 1, 85–86. See Gabriel Gorodetsky, *Grand Delusion: Stalin and the German Invasion of Russia* (New Haven: Yale University Press, 1999), 115, 126, and 209; and John Erickson, *The Soviet High Command: A Military-Political History, 1918–1941* (New York: St. Martin's Press, 1962), 449–509.

43. Coox, *Nomonhan*, vol. 1, 1–11; and Ikuhiko Hata, "Reality and Illusion: The Hidden Crisis between Japan and the USSR, 1932–34," (Occasional paper, East Asian Institute, Columbia University, 1967).

44. For a discussion of tradition and belief in the superior morale of Japanese troops among the Kwantung Army leadership, see Edward J. Drea, *In the Service of the Emperor: Essays on the Imperial Japanese Army* (Lincoln: University of Nebraska Press, 1998), 1–14; and Coox, *Nomonhan*, vol. 2, 1082–83.

45. Sadako Ogata, *Defiance in Manchuria: The Making of Japanese Foreign Policy, 1931–1932* (Berkeley: University of California Press, 1964), 120.

46. On army factionalism, see James B. Crowley, "Japanese Army Factionalism in the Early 1930s," *Journal of Asian Studies* 21, no. 3 (May 1962): 309–26; idem, *Japan's Quest for Autonomy: National Security and Foreign Policy, 1930–1938* (Princeton: Princeton University Press, 1966); and esp. Ben-Ami Shillony, *Revolt in Japan: The Young Officers and February 26, 1936 Incident* (Princeton: Princeton University Press, 1973).

47. See Alvin D. Coox, *Anatomy of a Small War: The Soviet-Japanese Struggle for Changkufeng/Khasan, 1938* (Westport, Conn.: Greenwood Press, 1977), 4–20.

48. For details of the Halhamiao (January 1935), Hailastyn-gol or Inukai (June 1935), Chinch'angkou (January 1936), Olankhudak (February 1936), Tauran (March 1936), Changlingtzu (March 1936), and the Kanch'atzu or Amur (June-July 1937) incidents, see Hata Ikuhiko, "Japanese-Soviet Confrontation, 1935–1939," in *Deterrent Diplomacy: Japan, Germany, and the USSR, 1935–1940*, ed. James William Morely, trans. Alvin D. Coox (New York: Columbia University Press, 1976), 128–78, at 134–40; and Coox, *Nomonhan*, vol. 1, 93–101.

49. See Hata, "Japanese-Soviet Confrontation," 131.

50. Amnon Sella, "Khalkhin-gol: The Forgotten War," *Journal of Contemporary History* 18, no. 4 (October 1983): 651–87, at 669.

51. Coox, *Anatomy of a Small War*, 35–46; idem, "The Lake Khasan Affair of 1938: Lessons and Overview," *Soviet Studies* 25, no. 1 (July 1973): 51–65.

52. Hata, "Japanese-Soviet Confrontation," 144; and Coox, *Anatomy of a Small War*, 54–55.

53. Yamamoto, who served as vice navy minister from December 1936, succeeded Yoshida Zengo as commander-in-chief of the Combined Fleet on 30 August 1939.

54. The Five Ministers Conferences (or inner cabinet) consisted of the prime minister and the ministers of foreign affairs, war, navy, and finance. These officials also participated in the cabinet-IGHQ liaison conferences that met regularly from October 1937.

55. Coox, "Lake Khasan Affair," 57.

56. Ugaki quoted in Hata, "Japanese-Soviet Confrontation," 144. Ugaki previously served as war minister in 1925–27 in the cabinets of Prime Ministers Katō Takaai and Wakatsuki Reijirō and again in 1929–31 under Prime Minister Hamauguchi Oschi. He retired from the active list in 1931 and then served as governor-general of Korea (Chosen) until 1936. See Foreign Affairs Association of Japan, *Japan Year Book, 1938–39* (Tokyo: Kenkyusha Press, 1938), 99.

57. Coox, *Anatomy of a Small War*, 58–59.

58. The emperor quoted in Hata, "Japanese-Soviet Confrontation," 141; See, also Coox, *Nomonhan*, vol. 1, 130–31; and Stephen S. Large, *Emperor Hirohito and Shōwa Japan: A Political Biography* (New York: Routledge, 1992), esp. 71. The most complete English-language account of the 20 July audiences at the palace is Coox, *Anatomy of a Small War*, 61–70.

59. Quoted in Hata, "Japanese-Soviet Confrontation," 145.

60. Ibid., 148. See also, Coox, *Nomonhan*, vol. 1, 133–34.

61. Coox, *Nomonhan*, vol. 1, 134; and Hata, "Japanese-Soviet Confrontation," 149.

62. Quoted in Hata, "Japanese-Soviet Confrontation," 150. See also Katsu H. Young, "The Nomonhan Incident: Imperial Japan and the Soviet Union," *Monumenta Nipponica* 22, nos. 1/2 (1967): 82–102, at 84.

63. Hata, "Japanese-Soviet Confrontation," 150.

64. See Coox, *Anatomy of a Small War*, 184–85.

65. See Coox, *Nomonhan*, vol. 1, 135.

66. See Coox, *Anatomy of a Small War*, 297–317; idem, *Nomonhan*, vol. 1, 139–41; and Hata, "Japanese-Soviet Confrontation," 153–57.

67. Coox, *Anatomy of a Small War*, 285.

68. For a brief discussion of the Tauran incident, see Hata, "Japanese-Soviet Confrontation," 136.

69. There are wide discrepancies on the number of Mongolian horsemen that actually crossed the Halha River (or Khalkhin-gol) on 11–12 May 1939. Initial intelli-

gence reports to Kwantung Army headquarters indicated that there were at least 700 Mongolian cavalry. By 17 May, Komatsubara claimed that the report of 700 Mongolians was excessive; he also questioned Japanese air scouting estimates of 100 to 150 horsemen. He suggested that the figure was closer to 30–50 horsemen. See Coox, *Nomonhan*, vol. 1, 191, fn. 21. Different secondary sources cite different figures. See, for example, Young, "Nomonhan Incident," 89; Drea, *In the Service of the Emperor*, 2; and Saboro Hayashi, in collaboration with Alvin D. Coox, *Kaigun: The Japanese Army in the Pacific War* (Quantico: Marine Corps Association, 1951; 1989), 14.

70. For a detailed discussion of the simmering Mongolian-Manchurian border dispute, see Coox, *Nomonhan*, vol. 1, 160–73.

71. See Hata, "Japanese-Soviet Confrontation," 159–60; and Young, "Nomonhan Incident," 88–89.

72. For details of the May fighting near the Halha, see Coox, *Nomonhan*, vol. 1, 200–250. The Yamagata regiment sustained 63 percent casualties before they could break the Soviet encirclement and retreat. See Drea, *In the Service of the Emperor*, 2–3. On the Soviet bombing of Tsitsihar on 16 July, see Hata, "Japanese-Soviet Confrontation," 169–70.

73. Molotov's 31 May 1939 address to the Supreme Soviet quoted in Coox, *Nomonhan*, vol. 1, 251; and John Erikson, *The Soviet High Command: A Military-Political Military History, 1918–1941* (London: Macmillan, 1962), 517. On Molotov's 16 May warning to Tōgō see Union of Soviet Socialist Republics, Institute of the Far East, *The Far East in the Second World War: An Outline History of International Relations and National Liberation Struggles in East and Southeast Asia*, by A. M. Dubinsky (Moscow: Nauka, 1972), 53, cited in Coox, *Nomonhan*, 629, n. 1. On Stalin's dismissal of Litvinov and appointment of Molotov, previously chairman of the Council of Peoples' Commissars, as his replacement on 3 May 1939 see Albert Reis, "The Call of Litvinov: Harbinger of the German-Soviet Non-Aggression Pact," *Europe-Asia Studies* 52, no. 1 (2000): 33–56.

74. Konoe resigned as prime minister on 3 January 1939 because of his inability to persuade the army to end the China incident, a conflict he previously advocated that it should wage. Baron Hiranuma Kiichiro, the president of the Privy Council, became prime minister, while Konoe, in turn, became president of the Privy Council.

75. See Hosoya Chihiro, "The Japanese-Soviet Neutrality Pact," in *The Fateful Choice: Japan's Advance into Southeast Asia, 1939–1941*, ed. James William Morely (New York: Columbia University Press, 1980), 18.

76. See Hata, "Japanese-Soviet Confrontation," 163–64; and Drea, *In the Service of the Emperor*, 2–3. For a detailed discussion of the development of the proposed ground operation and the Kwantung Army general staff's efforts to conceal the planned air assault on Soviet-Mongol airfields from the IGHQ, see Coox, *Nomonhan*, vol. 1, 253–61.

77. For example, when a team of Army General Staff officers attended map maneuvers and operational conferences at Hsinking in early June, Kwantung Army staff officers, including Tsuji Masanobu, repeatedly assured their visitors that they would not enlarge the Nomonhan incident. The delegation from Tokyo included Operations Bureau chief Hashimoto Gun and Lt. Colonel Prince Chichibu, the emperor's eldest brother. See Coox, *Nomonhan*, vol. 1, 253.

78. Hata, "Japanese-Soviet Confrontation," 165.

79. See Young, "Nomonhan Incident," 89–90.

80. Quoted in Hata, "Japanese-Soviet Confrontation," 165.

81. IGHQ Army Directive No. 491, Field Marshal Prince Kan'in to General Ueda, 29 June 1939, quoted in Coox, *Nomonhan*, vol. 1, 282.

82. Drea, *In the Service of the Emperor*, 3–4; U.S. Department of the Army, Headquarters, Army Forces Far East, Military History Section, Japanese Research Division, *Political Strategy Prior to the Outbreak of the War, Part I*, Japanese monograph 144 (Washington, D.C.: Office of the Chief of Military History, 1945–60), 44–45.

83. See Hata, "Japanese-Soviet Confrontation," 167.

84. See Alvin D. Coox, "High Command and Field Army: The Kwantung Army and the Nomonhan Incident," *Military Affairs* 33, no. 2 (October 1969): 302–12, at 305–6; and Young, "Nomonhan Incident," 92–93.

85. See Hata, "Japanese-Soviet Confrontation," 168–69; Coox, *Nomonhan*, vol. 1, 522–28; and Michael A. Barnhart, "Japanese Intelligence Before the Second World War: 'Best Case' Analysis," in *Knowing One's Enemies: Intelligence Assessment Between the Two World Wars*, ed. Ernest R. May (Princeton: Princeton University Press, 1984), 436–37.

86. See Coox, "High Command and Field Army," 304–5.

87. See Hata, "Japanese-Soviet Confrontation," 168–69; and Young, "Nomonhan Incident," 93.

88. Hata, "Japanese-Soviet Confrontation," 173.

89. See Coox, *Nomonhan*, vol. 1, 566–71. The new Sixth Army comprised the Second Infantry Division, the Fifteenth Infantry Brigade (Katayama Detachment), the Fourth Infantry Division, the Seventh Infantry Brigade (Koga Detachment), the Seventh Infantry Division, the Twenty-Third Infantry Division, and the Third Independent Garrison Unit.

90. For a concise discussion of the reorganization of the Soviet Far Eastern Armies in summer 1939, see Sella, "Khalkhin-gol," 676–78.

91. There are disagreements about the exact number of Japanese casualties at Nomonhan. The Kwantung Army's own figures are confusing. However, in autumn 1939, the War Ministry publicly admitted that at least 18,000 Japanese troops lost their lives during the Nomonhan incident. See Hata, "Japanese-Soviet Confrontation," 175–76; and Coox, *Nomonhan*, vol. 2, 914–19, esp. Table 39.1.

92. It part, this was because of the turmoil in the Japanese Foreign Ministry following the resignation of the Hiranuma cabinet on 28 August and the inauguration of a new cabinet under General Abe Nobuyuki two days later. Arita left office on 30 August and his successor Admiral Nomura Kichiasburo did not assume office until 25 September. See Hosoya Chihiro, "The Tripartite Pact, 1939–1940," in *Deterrent Diplomacy: Japan, Germany, and the USSR, 1935–1940*, ed. and trans. James William Morely (New York: Columbia University Press, 1976), 191–97; and Coox, *Nomonhan*, vol. 2, 898–904.

93. Hata, "Japanese-Soviet Confrontation," 174–78; Young, "Nomonhan Incident," 95–98; and Coox, *Nomonhan*, vol. 2, 904–10.

94. Yamagata committed suicide on 24 September 1939. On the purge following the Nomonhan debacle see, Coox, *Nomonhan*, vol. 2, 952–79.

95. See Melvin P. Leffler, *A Preponderance of Power: National Security, the Truman Administration, and the Cold War* (Stanford: Stanford University Press, 1992), 444; and Marc I. Trachtenberg, "A 'Wasting Asset': American Strategy and the Shifting Nuclear Balance, 1949–1950," in Trachtenberg, *History & Strategy* (Princeton: Princeton University Press, 1991), 124–29. On the Truman administration's plans to achieve its 1954 defense goals by mid-1952, see NSC 68/4, "United States Programs and Objectives for National Security," 14 December 1950, *Foreign Relations of the United States, 1950*, vol. 1: *National Security* (Washington, D.C.: GPO, 1976), 488–89 [this and all other volumes in the series are hereafter cited as *FRUS*].

96. For the U.S. intelligence community's assessment of the Chinese troop

buildup in late 1951, see National Intelligence Estimate (NIE) 55, "Communist Capabilities and Probable Courses of Action in Korea through mid-1952," *FRUS, 1951,* vol. 7, pt. 1, 1263–75.

97. Quoted in Rosemary Foot, *A Substitute for Victory: The Politics of Peacemaking at the Korean Armistice Talks* (Ithaca: Cornell University Press, 1990), 38, and in Burton I. Kaufman, *The Korean War: Challenges in Crisis, Credibility, and Command* (Philadelphia: Temple University Press, 1986), 202.

98. See Secretary of State Dean Acheson to the U.S. Mission to the United Nations, 17 February 1951, *FRUS, 1951,* vol. 7, *Korea and China,* part 1, 178–81.

99. The Chinese conventionally divide the battles during the Korean War into five major campaigns or offensives. The first dated from 25 October to 5 November 1950 (the first appearance of the CPVs' in North Korea and their disengagement); the second from 24 November to 24 December 1950 (the CPVA offensive across the Yalu River); the third from 31 December 1950 to 8 January 1951; the fourth from 25 January to 21 April 1951; and the fifth from 22 April to 10 June 1951. After the failure of the fifth offensive, the war became a stalemate along the Thirty-eighth Parallel. See Sergei N. Goncharov, John W. Lewis, and Xue Litai, *Uncertain Partners: Stalin, Mao, and the Korean War* (Stanford: Stanford University Press, 1993), 199–200.

100. See M. L. Dockrill, "The Foreign Office, Anglo-American Relations, and the Korean War, June 1950–June 1951," *International Affairs* 62, no. 3 (summer 1986): 459–76; and Rosemary Foot, "Anglo-American Relations in the Korean Crisis: The British Effort to Avert an Expanded War," *Diplomatic History* 10, no. 1 (winter 1986): 43–57. For Truman's statement, see Statement by the President, 15 February 1951, in *Public Papers of the Presidents of the United States: Harry S. Truman, 1951* (Washington, D.C.: GPO, 1965), 154–55 [hereafter cited as *PPPUS: Harry S. Truman*]

101. See Acheson to UN Mission, 17 February 1951, *FRUS, 1951* vol. 7, 178–79.

102. Acheson to Marshall, 23 February 1951, ibid., vol. 7, 193.

103. Truman to MacArthur, 13 January 1951 quoted in Harry S. Truman, *Memoirs: Years of Trial and Hope, 1946–1952* (New York: Signet, 1956), 435–36; and in James F. Schnabel and Robert J. Watson, *History of the Joint Chiefs of Staff: The Joint Chiefs of Staff and National Policy 1951–1953, The Korean War,* vol. 3, pt. 2 (Washington, D.C.: Office of the Chairman of the Joint Chiefs of Staff, 1998), 420 [hereafter cited as *History of the JCS*].

104. Collins quoted in Trachtenberg, "A Wasting Asset," in *History and Strategy,* 124.

105. See Roger Dingman, "Atomic Diplomacy during the Korean War," *International Security* 13, no. 1 (winter 1988/89): 50–91, at 69–71. Whether or not Truman and his advisors actually intended to use tactical nuclear weapons in Korea or Manchuria in the spring of 1951 is unclear. On 28 April, four days after the start of the CPVA sixth offensive in Korea, Truman sent a nuclear command-and-control team to Tokyo, approved a second westward movement of nuclear-armed B-29s, and authorized reconnaissance flights over airfields in Manchuria and Shantung. Truman ordered the nuclear-armed bombers home in late June 1951, weeks before truce talks began at Kaesong. See also Daniel Calingaert, "Nuclear Weapons and the Korean War," *Journal of Strategic Studies* 11, no. 2 (June 1988): 177–202.

106. Vandenberg quoted in Rosemary Foot, *The Wrong War: American Strategy and the Dimensions of the Korean Conflict, 1950–1953* (Ithaca: Cornell University Press, 1985), 136–37.

107. For a summary of the diplomatic maneuvering by countries that contributed troops to the UNC and neutral states, including the so-called Good Offices Committee at the UN, see Stueck, *Korean War,* 170–78 and 204–15.

108. For the text of MacArthur's 24 March statement and the diplomatic fallout, see Acheson to Certain Diplomatic Offices, 24 March 1951; and Austin to Acheson, 26 March 1951, *FRUS, 1951*, vol. 7, 264–66.

109. See Truman statement of 29 March 1951, *PPPUS: Harry S. Truman, 1951*, 203–7.

110. See Memo of Conversation by Hickerson, 6 April 1951; and Memo of Conversation by Nitze, 6 April 1951, *FRUS, 1951*, vol. 7, 268–69 and 306–9.

111. For the exchange of letters between Martin and MacArthur on 8 and 20 March, see Editorial note, *FRUS, 1951*, vol. 7, 298–99, and U.S. Senate, Committees on Armed Services and Foreign Relations, *Military Situation in the Far East: Hearings . . . to Conduct an Inquiry into the Military Situation in the Far East and the Facts Surrounding the Relief of General of the Army Douglas MacArthur from His Assignments in that Area*, 82nd Cong., 1st session, parts 2 and 3 (Washington, D.C.: U.S. Senate, 1951), 3182 (hereafter cited as *MacArthur Hearings*).

112. See Memo of telephone conversation with Gen. Omar N. Bradley by Dean Rusk, 1 March 1951; Marshall to Acheson, 1 March 1951; and Memo on the Substance of Discussions at a Department of State-Joint Chiefs of Staff Meeting, 15 March 1951, *FRUS, 1951*, vol. 7, 188–95, 201–2, 202–6, and 232–35.

113. Memo by the JCS to Marshall, 27 February 1951, *FRUS, 1951*, vol. 7, 205.

114. See Memo on the Substance of Discussions at a Department of State-JCS Meeting, 15 March 1951, ibid., vol. 7, 232–34.

115. Quoted in Memo by the JCS to Marshall, 27 March 1951, ibid., vol. 7, pt. 1, 285–88.

116. See also JCS to Marshall, 5 April 1951, ibid., vol. 7, pt. 1, 295–96.

117. Schnabel and Watson, *History of the JCS*, vol. 3, 1–10 and 564–66.

118. See Matthew B. Ridgeway, *The Korean War, 1950–1953* (New York: Da Capo Press, 1967), 175.

119. For details of the April and May 1951 CPVA offensives see Richard Whelan, *Drawing the Line: The Korean War, 1950–1953* (Boston: Little, Brown, 1990), 307–21; and James F. Schnabel, *United States Army in the Korean War*, vol. 1, *Policy and Direction: The First Year* (Washington, D.C.: Center for Military History, Department of the Army, 1972; 1992), 387–90.

120. Whelan, *Drawing the Line*, 307–21; D. Clayton Jones, *Refighting the Last War: Command and Crisis in Korea, 1950–1953* (New York: Free Press, 1993), 222–23; and Ridgeway, *Korean War*, 170–83. For a discussion of the adoption of the air interdiction strategy in spring 1951, see Robert A. Pape, *Bombing to Win: Air Power and Coercion in War* (Ithaca: Cornell University Press, 1996), 146–52.

121. See JCS to Ridgeway, 1 May 1951, *FRUS, 1951*, vol. 7, 394–96.

122. Quoted in Memo Containing the Sections Dealing with Korea from NSC 48/5, 17 May 1951, *FRUS, 1951*, vol. 7, 439–42. The full text of NSC 45/8, "United States Objectives, Policies, and Courses of Action in Asia," appears in *FRUS, 1951*, vol. 6, part 1, 33.

123. Memo of Conversation by Nitze, re: State-JCS Meeting, 29 May 1951, *FRUS, 1951*, vol. 7, pt. 1, 470–72.

124. See Acheson's testimony, 1 to 9 June 1951, esp. his reply to questions from Senator H. Alexander Smith (R-New Jersey) on 2 June, *MacArthur Hearings*, pt. 1, 1782–83. See also John Edward Wiltz, "The MacArthur Hearings of 1951: The Secret Testimony," *Military Affairs* 39, no. 4 (December 1975): 167–73.

125. Stueck, *Korean War*, 204–8.

126. See Kennan to Matthews, 31 May and 5 June 1951; and Kennan to Acheson,

20 June 1951, *FRUS, 1951*, vol. 1, pt. 1, 483–87, 507–11, and 536–38. See also Stueck, *Korean War*, 204–10.

127. For concise discussions of Soviet and Chinese views on the emerging Korean stalemate and desirability of a negotiated settlement, see Vladislav Zubok and Constantine Pleshakov, *Inside the Kremlin's Cold War: From Stalin to Khrushchev* (Cambridge: Harvard University Press, 1996), 70–72; Michael H. Hunt, "Beijing and the Korean Crisis, June 1950–June 1951," *Political Science Quarterly* 107, no. 3 (autumn 1992): 453–78, at 467–469; and Shu Guang Zhang, *Mao's Military Romanticism: China and the Korean War, 1950–1953* (Lawrence: University of Press of Kansas, 1995), 217–22.

128. See, *New York Times*, 24 June 1951, 4; reprinted in Editorial Note, *FRUS, 1951*, vol. 7, pt. 1, 547.

129. On PRC *People's Daily* article, see Walter S. Gifford, ambassador in the United Kingdom, to Acheson, *FRUS, 1951*, vol. 7, 552–53; Remarks by the President, 25 July 1951, *PPPUS: Harry S. Truman, 1951*, 362–63.

130. JCS to Ridgeway, 30 June 1951, *FRUS, 1951*, vol. 7, pt. 1, 598–99; Ridgeway to commander-in-chief, Communist Forces in Korea, 29 June 1951, in Department of State, *Bulletin*, 9 July 1951, 43; Kim Il Sung, supreme commander, KPA, and Peng Teh-Huai (a.k.a., Peng Te-haui or Peng Dehaui), commander, CPVA, to Ridgeway, 6 July 1951; and Ridgeway to Kim and Peng, 6 June 1951, *FRUS, 1951*, vol. 1, pt. 1, 623–25.

131. On the limits of the UNC delegation's mandate and for accounts of the opening discussions at Kaesong, see JCS to Ridgeway, 10 July 1951; Ridgeway to JCS, 10 July 1951; Ridgeway to JCS, 11 July 1951, *FRUS, 1951*, vol. 7, pt. 1, 649–56 and 658–59. On U.S. acceptance of the 1949 Geneva Convention, see Stueck, *Korean War*, 212–13; and Ridgeway, *The Korean War*, 182.

132. For a discussion of the origins of the POW issue, see Bernstein, "Struggle over the Korean Armistice," 261–75, and Foot, *Substitute for Victory*, 108–29.

133. Ridgeway to JCS, re: Armistice conference at Kaesong, 27 July 1951, *FRUS, 1951*, vol. 7, pt. 1, 740–45.

134. Nitze quoted in Foot, *Substitute for Victory*, 45–46.

135. On the opposition of Rhee and other ROK officials to a restoration of the Thirty-eighth Parallel see, John Muccio, ambassador in Seoul, to Acheson, 1 June 1951; Muccio to Acheson, 9 June 1951; Memo of Conversation by Arthur B. Emmons, officer in charge of Korean Affairs, 28 June 1951; Muccio to Acheson, 10 July 1951; Muccio to Acheson, 17 July 1951, 694–96; and Muccio to Acheson, 31 July 1951, *FRUS, 1951*, vol. 7, pt.1, 496–97, 526–27, 574–76, 644–45, and 764–65.

136. See, Pape, *Bombing to Win*, 105; Arnold A. Offner, *Another Such Victory: President Truman and the Cold War, 1945–1953* (Stanford: Stanford University Press, 2002), 407–8; and Walter C. Hermes, *Truce Tent and Fighting Front* (Washington, D.C.: GPO, 1966), 113 and 158.

137. For a detailed account of the breakdown of the talks at Kaesong on 22 August and their resumption on 25 October at Panmunjom, see Stueck, *Korean War*, 221–48; and Foot, *Substitute for Victory*, 42–73.

138. Numerous scholars make this point on the POW issue, including, Rosemary Foot, *Substitute for Victory*, esp. 108–29 and 219–22; Stueck, *Korean War*, 258–65; Barton J. Bernstein, "The Struggle over the Korean Armistice: Prisoners or Repatriation," in *Child of Conflict: The Korean-American Relationship, 1943–1953*, ed. Bruce Cumings (Seattle: University of Washington Press, 1983), 261–308; and Offner, *Another Such Victory*, 409–23.

139. For detailed discussion of the Truman administration's motivations on the POW issue, see Schnabel and Watson, *History of the JCS*, vol. 3, 358–68; Foot, *Substitute for Victory*, 108–58; Offner, *Another Such Victory*, 410–17; and Stueck, *Korean War*, 266–307.

CHAPTER 7. IMPLICATIONS OF THE ARGUMENT

1. See NSC-8, "Position of the United States with Respect to Korea," 2 April 1948, *Foreign Relations of the United States, 1947*, vol. 6: *The Far East* (Washington, D.C.: GPO, 1977), 1167 [hereafter cited as *FRUS*]; and NSC 8/2, 22 March 1949, *FRUS, 1949*, vol. 7, 969–78.

2. Hans J. Morgenthau, *Politics among Nations: The Struggle for Power and Peace*, 3d ed. (New York: Knopf, 1965), 73. For an interesting analysis of the role of prestige in classical realist thought (especially in the writings of Thucydides, Machiavelli, Hobbes, and Rousseau) and a call to explicitly reincorporate the concept in contemporary realism, see Daniel Markey, "Prestige and the Origins of War: Returning to Realism's Roots," *Security Studies* 8, no. 4 (summer 1999): 126–73.

3. Robert Gilpin, *War and Change in World Politics* (New York: Cambridge University Press, 1981), 33. For a similar discussion, see Randall L. Schweller, "Realism and the Present Great Power System: Growth and Positional Conflict over Scarce Resources," in *Unipolar Politics: Realism and State Strategies after the Cold War*, ed. Ethan B. Kapstein and Michael Mastanduno (New York: Columbia University Press, 1999), esp. 28–68.

4. See Markey, "Prestige and the Origins of War," esp. 168–71. Markey suggests that the concrete objects of prestige-motivated competition (e.g., diplomatic precedence, weapons systems, ancestral homelands, etc.) are socially (or linguistically) constructed. While I do not reject the possibility that such prestige objects are social constructions, such considerations are beyond the scope of the theory I developed in this book.

5. Memo of conversation with the President and others, Re: Korean situation, 25 June 1950, Acheson Papers, box 65, Harry S. Truman Library.

6. For the debate see Jonathan Mercer, *Reputation in International Politics* (Ithaca: Cornell University Press, 1996); Dale C. Copeland, "Do Reputations Matter?" *Security Studies* 7, no. 1 (autumn 1997): 33–71; Paul K. Huth, "Reputations and Deterrence: A Theoretical and Empirical Assessment," *Security Studies* 7, no. 1 (autumn 1997): 72–99; and Mercer, "Reputation and Rational Deterrence Theory," *Security Studies* 7, no. 1 (autumn 1997): 100–113.

7. Stephen Van Evera refers to this as "type IV realism." It differs from other strands of structural realism and classical realism in locating the proximate causes of war in national misperceptions of the fine-grained structure of international power. See Van Evera, *The Causes of War: Power and the Roots of Conflict* (Ithaca: Cornell University Press, 1999), 10–11. Similarly, Gideon Rose distinguishes realist theories that explicitly examine how leaders perceive (or misperceive) systemic pressures, although he groups such theories under the label of "neoclassical realism" and tries to separate them from offensive realism and defensive realism. See Rose, "Neoclassical Realism and Theories of Foreign Policy," *World Politics* 51, no. 1 (October 1998): 144–72, esp. 157–61.

8. Space constraints do not allow me to provide an exhaustive bibliography, but a cross section of important constructivist works might include Nicholas G. Onuf, *World of Our Making* (Columbia: University of South Carolina Press, 1989); Alexander

Wendt, "The Agent-Structure Problem in International Relations Theory," *International Organization* 41, no. 3 (summer 1987): 335–70; Wendt, "Anarchy Is What States Make of It: The Social Construction of Power Politics," *International Organization* 46, no. 2 (spring 1992): 391–425; idem, *Social Theory of International Politics* (Cambridge: Cambridge University Press, 1999); Martha Finnemore, *National Interests in International Society* (Ithaca: Cornell University Press, 1996); Peter J. Katzenstein, ed., *The Culture of National Security: Norms and Identity in World Politics* (New York: Columbia University Press, 1996); Ted Hopf, "The Promise of Constructivism in International Relations Theory," *International Security* 23, no. 1 (summer 1998): 171–200; and Glenn Chafetz, Michael Spirtas, and Benjamin Frankel, eds., *Security Studies* 8, no. 2/3 (winter 1998/99–spring 1999), special issue on the origins of national interests.

9. Jeffrey Legro and Andrew Moravcsik, "Is Anybody Still a Realist?" *International Security* 24, no. 2 (fall 1999): 5–55, at 35. For similar criticisms of the incorporation of unit-level variables in structural realist theories, see John A. Vasquez, "The Realist Paradigm and Degenerative versus Progressive Research Programs: An Appraisal of Neotraditional Research on Waltz's Balancing Proposition," *American Political Science Review* 91, no. 4 (December 1997): 899–912; Richard Ned Lebow, "The Long Peace, the End of the Cold War, and the Failure of Realism," *International Organization* 48, no. 2 (spring 1994): 249–78; and Richard Rosecrance and Arthur A. Stein, eds., *The Domestic Bases of Grand Strategy* (Ithaca: Cornell University Press, 1993).

10. This section draws on two lengthier responses to Legro and Moravcsik's article: Jeffrey W. Taliaferro, "Security Seeking under Anarchy: Defensive Realism Revisited," *International Security* 25, no. 3 (winter 2000/01): 128–61, at 154–57; idem, "Correspondence: Brother, Can You Spare a Paradigm? (Or Was Anybody Ever a Realist?), *International Security* 25, no. 1 (summer 2000): 178–82.

11. Aaron L. Friedberg, *The Weary Titan: Britain and the Experience of Relative Decline, 1895–1905* (Princeton: Princeton University Press, 1988), 8, n. 24.

12. Rose, "Neoclassical Realism and Theories of Foreign Policy," 153.

13. James M. Goldgeier and Philip E. Tetlock originally raised these points. See, Goldgeier and Tetlock, "Psychology and International Relations," *Annual Review of Political Science, 2001* 4: 67–92, at 69–70. See Waltz, *Man, the State, and War: A Theoretical Analysis* (New York: Columbia University Press, 1959); Waltz, *Theory of International Politics* (New York: Macmillan, 1979), 48–49, 78, 87, 121–23; Waltz "Reflections on *Theory of International Politics*: A Response to My Critics," in *Neorealism and Its Critics*, ed. Robert O. Keohane (New York: Columbia University Press, 1986), 327–28 and 343; idem, "Structural Realism after the Cold War," *International Security* 25, no. 1 (summer 2000): 5–41.

14. Goldgeier and Tetlock, "Psychology and International Relations," 69–70.

15. Robert Jervis, *Perception and Misperception in International Politics* (Princeton: Princeton University Press, 1976), esp. chapters 3–4. Select examples of defensive realism that posit a role for perceptions of relative power, threat, or other systemic or dyadic variables include Stephen M. Walt, *Origins of Alliances* (Ithaca: Cornell University, 1987); Walt, *Revolution and War* (Ithaca: Cornell University Press, 1996); Van Evera, *Causes of War: Power and the Roots of Conflict*; Thomas J. Christensen and Jack Snyder, "Chain-Gangs and Passed Bucks: Predicting Alliance Patterns under Multipolarity," *International Organization* 44, no. 2 (spring 1990): 137–68; Thomas J. Christensen, "Perceptions and Alliances in Europe," *International Organization* 51, no. 1 (winter 1997): 65–97; and Michael Mastanduno, "Preserving the Unipolar Moment: Realist Theories and U.S. Grand Strategy after the Cold War," *International Security* 21, no. 4 (spring 1997): 49–88.

16. See, for example, the letters by James W. Davis, Jr., and the reply by Stephen Van Evera in "Correspondence: Taking Offense at Offense-Defense Theory," *International Security* 23, no. 3 (winter 1998/99): 179–206, at 179–82 and 195–200; and Legro and Moravcsik, "Is Anybody Still a Realist?" 34–40.

17. Jack S. Levy laments that applications of prospect theory to political science have paid more attention to loss aversion and framing effects than to probability weighting. See Levy, "Loss Aversion, Framing, and International Conflict: Perspectives from Prospect Theory," in *Handbook of War Studies II*, ed. Manus I. Midlarsky (Ann Arbor: University of Michigan Press, 2000), 193–221; idem, "Prospect Theory, Rational Choice, and International Relations," *International Studies Quarterly* 41, no. 1 (March 1997): 87–112.

18. Dale C. Copeland, "Theory and History in the Study of Major War," *Security Studies* 10, no. 4 (summer 2001): 212–39, at 218.

19. Levy, "Loss Aversion, Framing Effects, and International Conflict," 217.

20. Copeland, "Theory and History in the Study of Major War," 218, fn. 14. In fairness to Copeland, he wrote this response to my review essay of his book, *The Origins of Major War* (Ithaca: Cornell University Press, 2000). See Taliaferro, "Realism, Power Shifts, and Major War," *Security Studies* 10, no. 4 (summer 2001): 145–78. Although I commend Copeland's dynamic differentials theory, I argue that it fell short as a theory of foreign policy and suggested the incorporation of prospect theory as a modification.

21. Prominent examples include Thomas J. Christensen, *Useful Adversaries: Grand Strategy, Domestic Mobilization, and Sino-American Conflict, 1947–1958* (Princeton: Princeton University Press, 1996); Fareed Zakaria, *From Wealth to Power: The Unusual Origins of America's World Role* (Princeton: Princeton University Press, 1997); Aaron L. Friedberg, *In the Shadow of the Garrison State: America's Anti-Statism and its Cold War Grand Strategy* (Princeton: Princeton University, 2000); Charles A. Kupchan, "Hollow Hegemony or Stable Multipolarity?" in *America Unrivaled: The Future of the Balance-of-Power*, ed. G. John Ikenberry (Ithaca: Cornell University Press, 2002), 68–97; and, arguably, Kupchan, *The Vulnerability of Empire* (Ithaca: Cornell University Press, 1995).

22. A few works do apply concepts and propositions derived from prospect theory to the study of two or more state's foreign policies. See, for example, James W. Davis, Jr., *Threats and Promises: The Pursuit of International Influence* (Baltimore: Johns Hopkins University Press, 2002); and Mark L. Haas, "Prospect Theory and the Cuban Missile Crisis," *International Studies Quarterly* 45, no. 2 (June 2001): 241–70. Again, in both of these studies, the dependent variable is foreign policy behavior, not an international political outcome.

23. See, for example, Richard Ned Lebow and Janice Cross Stein, "Rational Deterrence Theory: I Think, Therefore I Deter," *World Politics* 41, no. 2 (January 1989): 208–24; Robert Jervis, Richard Ned Lebow, and Janice Gross Stein, *Psychology and Deterrence* (Baltimore: Johns Hopkins University Press, 1985); Richard Ned Lebow, "Deterrence: A Political and Psychological Critique," in *Perspectives on Deterrence*, ed. Paul C. Stern, Robert Axelrod, Robert Jervis, and Roy Radner (New York: Oxford University Press, 1989); Robert Jervis, *The Meaning of the Nuclear Revolution* (Ithaca: Cornell University Press, 1989), chapter 5; and Mercer, *Reputation in International Politics*.

24. Robert Jervis, "The Political Implications of Loss Aversion," in *Avoiding Losses/Taking Risks: Prospect Theory and International Conflict* (Ann Arbor: University of Michigan Press, 1994), 33–34.

25. See Colin F. Camerer, "Progress in Behavioral Game Theory," *Journal of Economic Perspectives* 11, no. 4 (fall 1997): 167–88.

26. A sample of the realist debates about the durability of the current unipolar international system and the possible emergence of a peer competitor to the United States might include William C. Wohlforth, "The Stability of a Unipolar World," *International Security* 24, no. 1 (summer 1999): 5–41; Kenneth N. Waltz, "Structural Realism after the Cold War," *International Security* 23, no. 1 (summer 2000): 5–41; Christopher Layne, "From Preponderance to Offshore Balancing: America's Future Grand Strategy," *International Security* 22, no. 1 (summer 1997): 86–124; Layne, "The Unipolar Illusion: Why New Great Powers Will Arise," *International Security* 17, no. 4 (spring 1993): 5–51; and John J. Mearsheimer, *The Tragedy of Great Power Politics* (New York: W. W. Norton, 2001), 360–402.

27. Thomas S. Szayna, Daniel L. Byman, Steven C. Bankes, Derek Eaton, Seth Jones, Robert Mullins, Ian O. Lesser, and William Rosenau, *The Emergence of Peer Competitors: A Framework for Analysis*, MR-1346–A, 2001 (Santa Monica, Calif.: RAND, 2001), chapter 2 (emphasis in the original).

28. Védrine and Schröder quoted in Craig R. Whitney, "NATO at 50: With Nations at Odds, Is it a Misalliance?" *New York Times*, 15 February 1999, A7.

29. See Steven Erlanger, "U.S. Quietly Chides German for His Dissension on Iraq," *New York Times*, 17 August 2002, A4.

30. See United Nations, Security Council, Resolution 1441, S/Res/1441 (2002), 8 November 2002 <http://www.un.org/Depts/unmovic/documents/1441.pdf>.

31. Chirac quoted in Timothy L. O'Brien, "At U.N., Russian, French, and German Diplomats Urge Peace," *New York Times*, 19 March 2003, A1.

32. For overviews of trans-Atlantic tensions and the need for some type of readjustment, see Ivo H. Daalder, "The United States and Europe: from Primacy to Partnership?" in *Eagle Rules? Foreign Policy and American Primacy in the Twenty-First Century*, ed. Robert J. Lieber (Upper Saddle River, N.J.: Prentice-Hall, 2002), 70–97; Klaus Larres, "Mutual Incomprehension: U.S.-German Value Gaps beyond Iraq," *Washington Quarterly* 26, no. 2 (spring 2003): 23–42.

33. See Guillaume Parmentier, "Redressing NATO's Imbalances," *Survival* 42, no. 2 (summer 2000): 96–112; and François Hesibourg, "Europe's Strategic Ambitions: The Limits of Ambiguity," *Survival* 42, no. 2 (summer 2000): 5–15. See also John E. Peters, Stuart E. Johnson, Nora Bensahel, Timothy Liston, and Traci Williams, *European Contributions to Operation Allied Force: Implications for Transatlantic Cooperation*, MR-1391–AF (Santa Monica, Calif.: RAND, 2001), esp. chapter 2. For a more optimistic assessment of the EU's ability to emerge as great power, see Charles A. Kupchan, "Hollow Hegemony or Stable Multipolarity," 68–97; and idem, *The End of the American Era: U.S. Foreign Policy and the Geopolitics of the Twenty-first Century* (New York: Alfred A. Knopf, 2002).

34. Stephen G. Brooks and William C. Wohlforth, "American Primacy in Perspective," *Foreign Affairs* 81, no. 4 (July/August 2002), 20–33, at 24–26.

35. Okamato Yukio, "Japan and the United States: The Essential Alliance," *Washington Quarterly* 25, no. 2 (spring 2002): 59–72. See also Thomas J. Christensen, "China, the U.S.-Japan Alliance, and the Security Dilemma in East Asia," *International Security* 23, no. 4 (spring 1999): 49–80.

36. See, "Russia and China Sign Friendship Pact," *New York Times*, 17 June 2001, A1 and A8.

37. Stephen M. Walt, "Keeping the World Off Balance: Self Restraint and U.S. Foreign Policy," in *America Unrivaled*, 121–54, at 125–26.

38. For a summary of the issues dividing the Washington and Beijing and the rise of PRC economic and military capabilities see, Aaron L. Friedberg, "11 September and the Future of Sino-American Relations," *Survival* 45, no. 1 (spring 2002): 33–50; Evan A. Feigenbaum, "China's Challenge to Pax Americana," *Washington Quarterly* 24, no. 3 (summer 2001): 31–43; and Christensen, "China, the U.S.-Japan Alliance, and the Security Dilemma in East Asia." On the limitations of the PRC's military capabilities, see Robert S. Ross, "The Geography of Peace: East Asia in the Twenty-First Century," *International Security* 23, no. 4 (spring 1999): 81–118; John Wilson Lewis and Xue Litai, "China's Search for a Modern Air Force," *International Security* 24, no. 1 (summer 1999): 64–95; and Michael O'Hanlon, "Why China Can't Conquer Taiwan," *International Security* 25, no. 2 (fall 2000): 51–86.

39. See Steven E. Miller, "The End of Unilateralism or Unilateralism Redux?" *Washington Quarterly* 25, no. 1 (winter 2002): 15–29; and Michael F. McFaul, "U.S.-Russian Relations after September 11, 2001," Subcommittee on Europe, House Committee on International Relations, *U.S.-Russian Relations: An Assessment*, 107th Cong., 2nd Sess., 27 February 2002 <http://commdocs.house.gov/committees/intlrel/hfa77893.000/hfa77893_of.htm>.

40. Robert I. Rotberg defines a failed state as sovereign political community that has little or no ability to provide basic public goods to its populace. Rotberg, "The New Nature of Nation-State Failure," *Washington Quarterly* 25, no. 3 (spring 2002): 85–96. See also, Ray Takeyh and Nikolas Gvosdev, "Do Terrorist Networks Need a Home?" *Washington Quarterly* 25, no. 3 (summer 2002): 97–108.

41. Walt, "Keeping the World 'Off Balance'" in *America Unrivaled*, 127.

42. See Robert Jervis, "Domino Beliefs and Strategic Behavior," in *Dominoes and Bandwagons: Strategic Beliefs and Great Power Competition in the Eurasian Rimland*, ed. Robert Jervis and Jack Snyder (New York: Oxford University Press, 1991), 20–50.

43. Sean Kay, "After Kosovo: NATO's Credibility Gap," *Security Dialogue* 31, no. 1 (March 2000): 71–84.

44. For example, between 1946 and 1954 the Truman and the Eisenhower administrations repeatedly considered preventive war against the Soviet Union. For a discussion see, Marc Trachtenberg, "A 'Wasting Asset'" American Strategy and the Shifting Nuclear Balance, 1949–1954," in Trachtenberg, *History and Strategy* (Princeton: Princeton University Press, 1991), 100–153; Melvin P. Leffler, *A Preponderance of Power: National Security, the Truman Administration, and the Cold War* (Stanford: Stanford University Press, 1992), 329–33; and Copeland, *Origins of Major War* (Ithaca: Cornell University Press, 2000), 146–75. Likewise, the Kennedy administration contemplated preventive war against China to forestall Beijing's acquisition of nuclear weapons. See William Burr and Jeffrey T. Richelson, "Whether to 'Strangle the Baby in the Cradle": The United States and the Chinese Nuclear Program, 1960–64," *International Security* 25, no. 3 (winter 2000/01): 54–99.

45. George W. Bush, *National Security Strategy of the United States of America, September 2, 2002* (Washington, D.C.: GPO, 2002), 15. Although the Bush administration and the American media refer to this strategy as "preemption," the document actually calls for preventive war. For the distinction between the two, see Van Evera, *Causes of War*, 40–41, n. 18; and Lawrence Freedman, "Prevention, Not Preemption," *Washington Quarterly* 26, no. 2 (spring 2003): 105–14. For a provocative, yet ultimately unpersuasive, argument that preemptive wars are exceedingly rare, see Dan Reiter, "Exploding the Powderkeg Myth: Preemptive Wars Almost Never Happen," *International Security* 20, no. 1 (fall 1995): 5–34.

46. Robert A. Pape, "The World Pushes Back," *Boston Globe*, 23 March 2003, H3.

Index

CORNELL STUDIES IN SECURITY AFFAIRS

A SERIES EDITED BY Robert J. Art, Robert Jervis, AND Stephen M. Walt

Societies and Military Power: India and Its Armies
    by Stephen Peter Rosen

Winning the Next War: Innovation and the Modern Military
    by Stephen Peter Rosen

Vital Crossroads: Mediterranean Origins of the Second World War, 1935–1940
    by Reynolds Salerno

Fighting to a Finish: The Politics of War Termination in the United States and Japan, 1945
    by Leon V. Sigal

Corporate Warriors: The Rise of the Privatized Military Industry
    by P. W. Singer

Alliance Politics
    by Glenn H. Snyder

The Ideology of the Offensive: Military Decision Making and the Disasters of 1914
    by Jack Snyder

Myths of Empire: Domestic Politics and International Ambition
    by Jack Snyder

The Militarization of Space: U.S. Policy, 1945–1984
    by Paul B. Stares

The Nixon Administration and the Making of U.S. Nuclear Strategy
    by Terry Terriff

The Ethics of Destruction: Norms and Force in International Relations
    by Ward Thomas

Causes of War: Power and the Roots of Conflict
    by Stephen Van Evera

Mortal Friends, Best Enemies: German-Russian Cooperation after the Cold War
    by Celeste A. Wallander

The Origins of Alliances
    by Stephen M. Walt

Revolution and War
    by Stephen M. Walt

The Tet Offensive: Intelligence Failure in War
    by James J. Wirtz

The Elusive Balance: Power and Perceptions during the Cold War
    by William Curti Wohlforth

Deterrence and Strategic Culture: Chinese-American Confrontations, 1949–1958
    by Shu Guang Zhang